TELLING TYPES

IN LITERATURE

By

John B. Opdycke

New York · *The* MACMILLAN *Company* · *1939*

To

T. H.

Foreword

THAT magazine editor who was invited to speak at a convention of writers on the subject of rejection slips found himself in a peculiarly unenviable spot—naturally. Yet he made a sensational impression upon them when, instead of enlarging upon the customary reasons for the rejection of manuscripts, he said that much copy was returned with the pink slip because aspiring young writers failed so often to fit thought to form with logical nicety. Many of them, he revealed, attempted to express an emotional impact through a long narrative poem rather than through a short lyric, an introspective analysis through a short story rather than through a reflective or analytical essay, and so on. Here was something that had not been sufficiently enforced, perhaps, in school and college classrooms. As students of writing, many of them had been trying to turn out drama on subjects not dramatic, novels on subjects that lacked all possibility of the scope and fullness of treatment required by the novel. "The orchids for milady's corsage," said the editor, "are not to be delivered in a moving van, nor the draperies for milady's boudoir in a jewel case."

Teachers of literature may commit at least two "virtuous faults." The one would be overanalysis or systematization, with the perfectly good intention, of course, of making the masterpiece more absorbable and palatable. Overemphasis upon form comes easily and naturally and almost unconsciously to the best of instruction, for the good teacher is nothing if not an analyst—must be this if even a moiety of his instruction is to "take." This results too often in the death of the spirit of literature, and the intensified survival of its letter or technique. How a thought is expressed is ever made more important than the thought itself.

> Lord Angelo is precise;
> Stands at a guard with envy; scarce confesses
> That his blood flows, or that his appetite
> Is more to bread than stone. . . .

v

> . . . O form,
> How often dost thou with thy case, thy habit,
> Wrench awe from fools, and tie the wiser souls
> To thy false seeming!
>
> SHAKSPERE *Measure for Measure*

This is a tendency that has been inherited from the classicists who, as a rule, permitted thought to be cribbed, cabined, and confined by form, no matter what expressional impulses had to be throttled, what perversion of phraseology resulted. Alexander Pope, the strictest of them all, could prove briefly in his *Pastorals* that freedom of form is as desirable as freedom of thought. But in the main he, like his contemporaries, allowed the one to restrain and warp the other. All of them took the romantic Edmund Spenser's *An Hymne in Honour of Beautie* too literally, especially such gems as

> For of the soule the bodie forme doth take;
> For soule is forme, and doth the bodie make.

The other fault would be the opposite—that, namely, of leaning backward to avoid this overemphasis upon form. This may easily become an annoying pose to the effect that complete freedom of thought and its expression means utter negation of form, that what is in your mind is all that matters and that how it finds its way out is of no consequence. Thus, the distant call from Pope's pestiferous form

> Unblessed thy hand, if in this low disguise
> Wander, perhaps, some inmate of the skies.

to Gertrude Stein's pestiferous lack of form

> An open object is establishing the loss that there was when the vase was not inside the place. It is not wandering.

These, to be sure, are extreme illustrations of the ebb-and-flood movement, of the recurrent enslavement to and escape from mere form, that has characterized the history of literary expression. The good teacher is also nothing if not an inspirer, and mere form, true enough, has never yet done much by way of inspiration. But the teacher who would disregard form entirely, who would place tabu upon consideration of manner of expression in comparison with content, is inevitably a "blind mouth" and runs risk of turning out not only loose and confused thinkers, but disordered and irresponsible individuals as well.

This book would draw a mean, and a sharper one than is indicated in Samuel Taylor Coleridge's

> What outward form and feature are
> He guesseth but in part;
> But what within is good and fair
> He seeth with the heart.

It would not for the world emphasize form at the expense of content, or vice versa, for the two are "twinned as horse's ear and eye." The good teacher, again, is in the difficult, not to say paradoxical, position of inspiring and at the same time holding in check, of grinding the bit and at the same time encouraging free rein. He knows and teaches that

> The thought decides the form—
> Whatever you may say;
> The form reflects the content—
> To state another way.

The book attempts, in short, to clarify by means of definition and illustration the major forms of literary expression, that is, the principal ways in which man has been able up to date to set down his thought most effectively and conveniently and economically, and thus the principal ways that students will be required to follow whether they express themselves formally in Sunday-go-to-meeting or casually in the everyday dress of life.

There are no new major forms of thought expression. Since literary time began, those forms explained in this book have served all the needs of man's complex expressional apparatus. Two or three revised or modified forms have, however, come into being during the past quarter or half century—the capsule radio play and the captioned moving-picture scenario, both offshoot variations of the drama proper; the free-verse forms or defiance of forms, which like so many other "new" things were used by the Chinese centuries ago; the Omar sonnet consisting of three Omar quatrains and a concluding interlocking couplet; possibly the descriptive vignette. With these partial exceptions, literary forms have remained constant and standard since before the epigrammatic essays of Confucius, the epics of Firdusi, the lyrics of Solomon, the epistles of Saint Paul, the short-stories of *The Arabian Nights,* the dialogues of Plato, the orations of Demosthenes, the odes of Horace, and so forth.

Moving-picture literature is a mongrel form. Early in its history the moving picture was regarded as par excellence a medium for epic representation, as indeed it was and still is by virtue of its breadth of scope and inclusiveness. Covered wagons cannot move around at will in mere conventional drama. But the movies are now the medium of practically every literary form—novel, short-story, sketch, idyl, essay, poem, lyric, biography, intimate drama, and the rest. Adaptation of literature to the screen invariably requires some reconstruction of originals. For one thing frequent change of scene is imperative. Movie audiences become restless unless they are given almost momentary shifting of backgrounds. Prolonged dialogue and action against the same setting, however engaging, cannot hold them very long. This may be a reason why Shaksperean plays cannot be produced on the screen exactly as they are written—rarely are they today on the legitimate stage. It is only one of the requirements of scenario writing that make it special if not unique.

In all consideration of literary forms, students must of course weigh the personal equation of an author if his output is to be understood. There are authors whose vision is narrative, others whose vision is expository, others with lyric vision, still others with dramatic vision. This does not necessarily mean that an author confines his work to a single type, but it does mean that he has greater facility in one type than in another. George Bernard Shaw has always been a philosophic essayist. During his middle period he was also a dramatist. But his later plays are little more than dramatic essays, and he never wrote a play without a prefatory essay and without writing essays into the dialogue. His has always been primarily the gear of the essay. This personal element in the consideration of types goes even further, into characteristics of diction and style. The dean of a great law school once said that no lawyer without expert ability in the use of the historical present, should ever be permitted to plead a case involving capital punishment.

Many years ago schools and colleges introduced a subject correlative to literature which they called "the study of authors." This would have been excellent had it been confined chiefly or even in part to the philosophic and psychologic analysis of authors' bents or dominant expressional tendencies—of Eliot's narrative vision, say; of Milton's epic vision; of Shakspere's dramatic vision. Too, the study of an author's output in relation to contemporary political and economic and social conditions would have added interest and understanding to this innovation. But it floundered on the low levels of Poe's alcoholism, Coleridge's drug addiction, Austen's frustration, D'Avenant's illegitimacy, and the like, and it deservedly died of its own futility.

The student of literature should certainly be taught *Hamlet,* and also why *Hamlet* is inescapably drama. He should be taught *Adam Bede,* and also why *Adam Bede* is inescapably novel. He should be taught *Paradise Lost,* and also why *Paradise Lost* is inescapably epic. He should be taught, that is to say, that the best literary thought inevitably gets itself expressed in that form best suited for its fullest and most potent revelation; that one of the important reasons why the best literature lives is that its content is adapted with nicety to its form—the subjective emotional flight to lyric form, the account of outward event and incident to narrative form, the elucidation of meaning and purpose to essay form, the impressionistic picture to descriptive form, and so forth.

The dramatized novel succeeds but rarely—usually in proportion to its degree of departure from the original. The novelized drama is usually but a popular catchpenny device. The drama *The Only Way* is but pale and puny progeny indeed of *A Tale of Two Cities.* Shaksperean plays remain Shaksperean plays; the Charles and Mary Lamb stories could not convey them to the general field of fiction except for young people—and for reading fakers. A sonnet may not be a narration of incidents any more than a ballad may be the expression of a single emotion, sentiment, or reflection. Charles Lamb's essay *Dream Children* must be an essay, not a short-story. Mary E. Wilkins-Freeman's *A New England Nun* must be a short-story, not an essay. The epics of Homer stubbornly resist genuine translation into other forms, as do the tragedies of Aeschylus and the sonnets of Petrarch, except for unworthy and makeshift purposes.

Also, the student of literature must be taught to understand and to *feel* these differences and differentiations in the spirit as well as in the letter. Whether he reads to feed thought or judgment or imagination, or for knowledge or mere information, he must be trained to read form as well as content, inasmuch as the two are manifesta-

tions of one and the same impulse or urge. If culture means instinc-
tive discernment of the fitness of things, then the ability to recognize
the subtleties involved in the exact adaptation of content to form
constitutes one of the most delicate discernments in the study of literature. This applies to both objective and subjective culture—to
the Thing Beyond and to the Thing Within, to the Foreign Circum-
ference and to the Native Center. And Emerson included it in his
Culture:

> Can rules and tutors educate
> The semigod whom we await?
> He must be musical,
> Tremulous, impressional,
> Alive to gentle influence
> Of landscape and of sky.
> And tender to the spirit-touch
> Of man's or maiden's eye;
> But, to his native centre fast,
> Shall into Future fuse the Past,
> And the world's flowing fates in his
>   own mould recast.

J. B. O.

ACKNOWLEDGMENTS

For permission to use copyrighted materials, the author is indebted to D. Appleton-Century Company; Albert and Charles Boni; Cassell and Company; Dodd, Mead and Company; Farrar and Rinehart; Hale, Cushman and Flint; Harper and Brothers; Houghton Mifflin Company; Henry Holt and Company; Alfred A. Knopf, Inc.; *New York Herald Tribune*; *The New Yorker*; Oxford University Press; *Popular Mechanics Magazine*; G. P. Putnam's Sons; Charles Scribner's Sons; The Derrydale Press; The Macmillan Company; *The New York Times*; *Commonweal*; *The Poetry Journal*; *The Cosmopolitan Magazine*; Twentieth Century-Fox Film Corporation; and to Mr. George S. Brooks, Miss Edna Ferber, Mr. Paul Gallico, Miss Theresa Helburn, the Honorable Cordell Hull, Mr. Alfred Kreymborg, Mr. Stephen Leacock, Mr. Neil Moran, Miss Dorothy Parker, Miss Sonia Raiziss, Mr. Vincent Sheean, and His Royal Highness the Duke of Windsor. For many valuable suggestions and for patient and painstaking assistance with proofs, he acknowledges his indebtedness to Miss Olive I. Carter and to Miss Adna Woodward.

Table of Contents

PROSE AND POETRY

Prose and Poetry

THE two great divisions of expression are *prose* and *poetry*. Prose is the medium through which ideas are expressed and exchanged in general everyday communication of thought. It makes its appeal for the most part strictly to the intelligence and the understanding. It is ordinary speech and writing, without conscious metrical structure and without predominant appeal to the feelings, except in certain special forms. In the literary sense, however, prose is pervaded by the artistic or the esthetic spirit, by beauty of construction, by purity and fitness and grace and vigor, and by catholicity of reason and judgment.

The tone or mood or quality or "feeling" of prose gives to it that subtle characteristic called style. And style is manner or method (or both) of expression as distinguished from content. Lord Chesterfield called style the dress of thought. Style is to literature what personality is to the individual. A piece of prose may impress you as being *flat, loose, trite, weak,* or *wordy,* and as a consequence you will not enjoy reading it, and may not understand it easily. It may, on the other hand, have *charm, ease, grace, flow, melody, rhythm, smoothness, simplicity,* and it may thus carry you along without the slightest effort—almost without your being aware of the act of reading. Again, it may be so *abrupt, aggressive, climactic, didactic, eloquent, emotional, epigrammatic, exclamatory, graphic, impassioned, virile,* or *vivid* that it will pull you out of your chair and make you feel like taking action of some sort. It may be *anecdotal, cautious, intimate, plain, quaint, restrained,* and, as a consequence, make you feel, while you are reading it, that you are having a tête-à-tête with a friend who is letting you into secrets that he would not for all the world divulge to any one else. It may be *humorous* and thus make you laugh aloud; *witty,* and make your eyes sparkle; *droll,* and make you pucker your lips and put your tongue in your cheek. It may be *serious* and *pathetic* and thus make you brush away a tear or turn a thought into a philosophy. It may be allusive, and keep you on the alert looking

3

up people and events that you should well-nigh have forgotten or never have known about, had you not thus been spurred. It may be *ornate* or *florid*, that is, it may "put on airs," and make you wonder and perhaps admire, without envy.

In some of these style moods prose will sometimes seem to come very close to poetry indeed, just as poetry in some of its moods may verge very closely upon prose. Prose may have rhythm; it may be highly figurative; it may be musical; it may be polyphonic, that is, it may have sound values that produce a kind of orchestral effect or a wealth of pipe-organ harmonies. In addition to being rhythmic, polyphonic prose may even become metrical in part, and in part cadenced and stately and oratorical. It may also have random rhyme as well as assonance and alliteration. But polyphonic prose is not yet by any means a frequently used form.

The borderland between prose and poetry may thus never be quite rigidly drawn. Poetry is primarily the expression or language of emotion, of feeling, of fancy, of imagination. But this is not to be taken to mean that poetry does not also appeal to the intelligence, any more than it can be truly said that certain types of prose do not appeal to the emotions. Definitions of either prose or poetry are certain to be unsatisfactory because each evades complete definition and explanation, because they are mutually both inclusive and exclusive. The dictionary says that poetry is the emotional interpretation of nature and life through the fancy and the imagination, in beautiful metrical (or at least consciously rhythmic) language; that it is the type of literature in which the ruling impetus is quickened emotion, the proper language figurative, the natural form verse, and the chief aim to impart imaginative and emotional pleasure. This is an inadequate definition because it leaves the appeal to intelligence almost entirely out of the reckoning, and thus excludes much of William Shakspere and William Wordsworth and Robert Browning, and a host of others.

Edmund Clarence Stedman said that poetry is rhythmical imaginative language expressing the invention, taste, thought, passion, insight of the human soul. Theodore Watts-Dunton defined it as the concrete and artistic expression of the human mind in emotional and rhythmical language. John Ruskin called it the suggestion by the imagination, in musical words, of noble grounds for noble emotions

—love, veneration, admiration, and joy, with their opposites. Matthew Arnold called poetical literature a criticism of life. Thomas Carlyle wrote: "I find considerable meaning in the old vulgar distinction of poetry being *metrical,* having music in it, being a song. Truly, if pressed to give a definition one might say this as soon as anything else: If your delineation be authentically musical not in word only but in heart and substance, in all the thoughts and utterances of it, in the whole conception of it, then it will be poetical; if not, not." Samuel Johnson said that poetry is the art of uniting pleasure with truth by calling imagination to the help of reason.

Nearly all great writers have at some time or other struggled to find an all-inclusive definition of poetry. The definitions above given are but very few of those to be found in the pages of literature. Perhaps the simplest and most satisfactory definition of all is this one by Percy Bysshe Shelley: "Poetry is the record of the best and happiest moments of the happiest and best minds." This is much the same thing as saying that poetry is the beautiful expression of high thought and pure emotion. Every serious and sincere student of literature will want to set up his own definition and explanation of poetry, to devise a statement saying what poetry means to him. This is distinctly as it should be, for it is altogether likely that poetry is one thing to one person and another to another—this to thee and that to me. It is decidedly *not* all things to all men.

Poetry employs a more precious diction than prose, or should do so. The language of the rustic, once so nobly championed by Wordsworth as suitable for poetical expression, is in the main discarded by poets. Poetry may take liberties with diction and sentence that are not permitted to prose. And poetry must needs be more concrete than prose in treatment of subject matter; it expresses general truth by special instance, to a far greater extent than prose does. Again, poetry must be more economical—less voluble—than prose. It is not privileged to "ramble on and on." The poet is held in by prescription of form, no matter how free the verse he turns out. The prose writer, having no such rigidity of form to comply with, is privileged to write *ad lib.,* less economically, less concentratedly, and naturally, therefore, less conscientiously about saying the most possible in the fewest possible words. He may add here and there after his work is supposedly finished; he may re-phrase and re-form altogether. But the poet must gear his expression to the elusive word and phrase and verse, and charge his output with subtle connotation and between-the-line inference. It is for this reason that every prose writer should practice writing verse and stanza forms indefatigably. Such training will school him in the principles of economy and restraint as no other training will do.

Mechanically, prose and poetry are of course easily differentiated. The set-up of prose moves from margin to margin in regular lines, and paragraphs are indented or blocked or extended. Poetry is usually written in shorter lines, those rhyming in one key sometimes starting from a different margin from those rhyming in another. First lines of poetry begin with capital letters, regardless of sentence structure. This latter mechanical characteristic may not be true of free verse (see page 386), but even in this form, it will be noted, the linage of poetry is distinctive and unlike that of prose. Poetry makes use of figures of speech somewhat more consciously than even the most impassioned prose, and, as above pointed out, the rhythm of poetry is always more evident—more apparently devised—than that of the most rhythmic prose. But poetical prose may always be arranged as free verse, and usually with distinct advantages for reading. Prose-poetry may always be set up as straight prose, and usually, again, with distinct advantages for reading. To illustrate: Abraham Lincoln's *Gettysburg Address* has the simplicity, the unpretentiousness, of poetical prose. It has lofty purpose, great dignity, high thought, beauty of sincerity, the inevitable rhythm and figure of the best poetry, and the restraint, charm, ease, flow, virility, and seriousness that mark the poetic flights of real genius. It is, moreover, clearly marked off into stanzas as indicated:

I

YESTERDAY *

Fourscore and seven years ago
Our fathers brought forth upon this continent a new nation,
Conceived in liberty,
And dedicated to the proposition
That all men are created equal.

* Arranged by the author for the Vigilantes during the World War.

II

TODAY

Now we are engaged in a great civil war,
Testing whether that nation, or any nation so conceived and so dedi-
    cated, can long endure.
We are met on a great battlefield of that war.
We have come to dedicate a portion of that field as a final resting place
For those who here gave their lives that that nation might live.
It is altogether fitting and proper that we should do this.
But in a larger sense we cannot dedicate,
We cannot consecrate,
We cannot hallow this ground.
The brave men, living and dead, who struggled here,
Have consecrated it far above our poor power to add or detract.

III

TOMORROW

The world will little note, nor long remember, what we say here,
But it can never forget what they did here.
It is for us, the living, rather to be dedicated here to the unfinished work
Which they who fought here have thus far so nobly advanced.
It is rather for us to be here dedicated to the great task remaining be-
    fore us,
That from these honored dead we take increased devotion to that cause
For which they gave the last full measure of devotion;
That we here highly resolve that these dead shall not have died in vain,
That this nation, under God, shall have a new birth of freedom,
And that government
Of the people,
By the people,
And for the people,
Shall not perish from the earth.

ABRAHAM LINCOLN *Gettysburg Address*
(November 19, 1863)

Whether the following piece of free verse be written in accordance
with the mechanical requirements of poetry or as straightaway prose
matters little. It remains prose-poetry in either form.

As toilsome I wander'd Virginia's woods,
To the music of rustling leaves kick'd by my feet (for 'twas autumn),
I mark'd at the foot of a tree the grave of a soldier;
Mortally wounded he and buried on the retreat (easily all could I understand),
The halt of a midday hour, when up! no time to lose—yet this sign left,
On a tablet scrawl'd and nail'd on the tree by the grave,
Bold, cautious, true, and my loving comrade.

Long, long I muse, then on my way go wandering,
Many a changeful season to follow, and many a scene of life,
Yet at times through changeful season and scene, abrupt, alone, or in the crowded street,
Comes before me the unknown soldier's grave, comes the inscription rude in Virginia's woods,
Bold, cautious, true, and my loving comrade.

WALT WHITMAN *As Toilsome I Wander'd Virginia's Woods*

As toilsome I wandered Virginia's woods, to the music of rustling leaves kicked by my feet (for it was autumn), I marked at the foot of a tree the grave of a soldier; mortally wounded he and buried on the retreat (easily all could I understand), the halt of a midday hour, when up! no time to lose—yet this sign left, on a tablet scrawled and nailed on the tree by the grave, *Bold, cautious, true, and my loving comrade.* Long, long I muse, then on my way go wandering, many a changeful season to follow, and many a scene of life, yet at times through changeful season and scene, abrupt, alone, or in the crowded street, comes before me the unknown soldier's grave, comes the inscription rude in Virginia's woods, *Bold, cautious, true, and my loving comrade.*

In rhymed poetry both the rhyme and the rhythm help to indicate the linage. But in unrhymed poetry the rhythm alone must be depended upon to do so. Rhythm is swing or lilt or singsong or cadence or undulation or regularity of movement, and this is sufficient for the proper partitioning of the waves of thought and emotion in both prose and poetry. Indeed, the rhythm in poetical composition unconsciously forces upon the reader's mind units of grasp or understanding that are themselves equivalent to the melodic units in a piece of music; in other words, it phrases just as the bar or two of a "hummable" tune do.

The word *verse* is used to indicate general poetical composition that is referred to in contradistinction to prose. It is used also to indicate a *line* of poetry. It is sometimes used, again, to denote any ordinary advertising or household rhymes, such as

> Thirty days hath September,
> April, June, and November.

or

> If you'll call upon Old Dutch
> Cleaning will not trouble much.

Such rhyming is also called *jingle* or *doggerel,* and does not in any sense belong in the category of poetry. Prose that likewise descends to the commonplace and down-at-heel is sometimes called *prosaic* or *pedestrian,* and is of course also excluded from our discussion here. The story of the editor of a college publication who "edited down" Lincoln's *Gettysburg Address* is now a classic among editorial jokes. The speech was sent to him anonymously, and he mistook it for an original contribution. He went to the trouble to revise it elaborately —to "boil it down"—with this very prosaic result : *

87 years ago our forefathers set up a new nation, based upon liberty and announcing that all men are equal. Now we are at war to find out whether such a nation can live. We are met on a battlefield of that war. We come to dedicate a part of that field, as the cemetery for the men who died upon it. But we cannot dedicate, consecrate, or hallow this spot. The men who fought here did these things better than we could ever do them. The world will not notice what we say here, but it will never forget their great fighting. The living should be dedicated to carry on the work which they who battled here have so nobly begun. We should ourselves be dedicated to the great task that remains in order that we may become the more devoted to the cause for which they died. Let us here resolve that these dead shall give this nation a new birth of freedom in order that this government may be continued.

The marginal editorial notes that accompanied the manuscript as it was returned to the supposed author, revealed the fact that the young editor had taken the principles of economy and condensation too seriously as they were given him in his classroom studies, and that he had not thought sufficiently about tone and rhythm and simple beauty in the quality of expression.

* From the *Columbia Jester.* Used by permission of Miss Margaret Noonan, secretary to the director of King's Crown Activities.

WORK

I. The first two excerpts below have been called "prose rhapsodies"; the last, a "prose sermon in verse" (it is frequently quoted by funeral orators, especially the second stanza). Discuss them with your fellow students.

To what extent are the four types of composition—exposition, narration, description, argument—mixed in them? What poetical qualities and what prose qualities are there in all three excerpts? Try writing the first two as verse and the last as prose, and tell what is lost or gained (if anything) by the rearrangement:

I saw—I now see—a woman-Titan: her robe of blue air spreads to the outskirts of the heath, where yonder flock is grazing; a veil white as an avalanche sweeps from her head to her feet, and arabesques of lightning flame on its borders. Under her breast I see her zone, purple like that horizon: through its blush shines the star of evening. Her steady eyes I cannot picture; they are clear—they are deep as lakes—they are lifted and full of worship—they tremble with the softness of love and the lustre of prayer. Her forehead has the expanse of a cloud, and is paler than the early moon, risen long before dark gathers: she reclines her bosom on the ridge of Stilbro' Moor; her mighty hands are joined beneath it. So kneeling, face to face she speaks with God. That is Jehovah's daughter, as Adam was his son.

CHARLOTTE BRONTË *Shirley*

Of scenes like these, I say, who writes—whoe'er can write the story? Of many a score—aye, thousands, north and south, of unwrit heroes, unknown heroisms, incredible, impromptu, first-class desperations—who tells? No history ever—no poem sings, no music sounds, those bravest men of all—those deeds. No formal general's report, nor book in the library, nor column in the paper, embalms the bravest, north or south, east or west. Unnamed, unknown, remain, and still remain, the bravest soldiers. Our manliest—our boys—our hardy darlings; no picture gives them. Likely, the typic one of them (standing, no doubt, for hundreds, thousands,) crawls aside to some bush-clump, or ferny tuft, on receiving his death-shot—there sheltering a little while, soaking roots, grass and soil, with red blood—the battle advances, retreats, flits from the scene, sweeps by—and there, haply with pain and suffering (yet less, far less, than is supposed,) the last lethargy winds like a serpent round him—the eyes glaze in death—none recks—perhaps the burial-squads, in truce, a week afterwards, search not the secluded spot—and there, at last, the Bravest Soldier crumbles in mother earth, unburied and unknown.

WALT WHITMAN *Specimen Days and Collect*

We count the broken lyres that rest
　Where the sweet wailing singers slumber,
But o'er their silent sister's breast
　The wildflowers who will stoop to number?

A few can touch the magic string,
　And noisy Fame is proud to win them:
Alas for those that never sing,
　But die with all their music in them!

Nay, grieve not for the dead alone
　Whose song has told their heart's sad story—
Weep for the voiceless who have known
　The cross without the crown of glory!

Not where Leucadian* breezes sweep
　O'er Sappho's memory-haunted billow,
But where the glistening night-dews weep
　On nameless sorrow's churchyard pillow.

O hearts that break and give no sign
　Save whitening lip and fading tresses,
Till Death pours out his longed-for wine
　Slow-dropt from Misery's crushing presses—

If singing breath or echoing chord
　To every hidden pang were given,
What endless melodies were poured,
　As sad as earth, as sweet as heaven!

OLIVER WENDELL HOLMES *The Voiceless* †

* The ancient name of Santa Maura Island, Ionia, Greece, was Leucas; hence, the adjective for Leucadian. It was in the Ionian Islands that Sappho lived and sang.

† "Read what the singing-women—one to ten thousand of the suffering women —tell us, and think of the griefs that die unspoken! Nature is in earnest when she makes a woman; and there are women enough lying in the next churchyard with very commonplace blue slate stones at their head and feet, for whom it was just as true that 'all sounds of love assumed one tone of love' as for Letitia Landon, of whom Elizabeth Browning said it; but she could give words to her grief, and they could not. Will you hear a few stanzas of mine?" *The Autocrat of the Breakfast Table.*

II. Write the following in the form dictated by the rhythm and the rhyme:

Young Harry was a lusty drover, and who so stout of limb as he? His cheeks were red as ruddy clover, his voice was like the voice of three. Auld Goody Blake was old and poor, ill fed she was, and thinly clad; and any man who passed her door, might see how poor a hut she had.

All day she spun in her poor dwelling, and then her three hours work at night! alas! 't was hardly worth the telling, it would not pay for candlelight. This woman dwelt in Dorsetshire, her hut was on a cold hillside, and in that country coals are dear, for they come far by wind and tide. . . .

Now when the frost was past enduring, and made her poor old bones to ache, could anything be more alluring, than an old hedge to Goody Blake? And now and then, it must be said, when her old bones were cold and chill, she left her fire, or left her bed, to seek the hedge of Harry Gill.

Now Harry he had long suspected this trespass of old Goody Blake, and vowed that she should be detected, and he on her would vengeance take. And oft from his warm fire he'd go, and to the fields his road would take, and there, at night, in frost and snow, he watched to seize old Goody Blake.

And once behind a rick of barley, thus looking out did Harry stand; the moon was full and shining clearly, and crisp with frost the stubble land. He hears a noise—he's all awake—again!—on tiptoe down the hill he softly creeps. 'T is Goody Blake! she's at the hedge of Harry Gill. Right glad was he when he beheld her: stick after stick did Goody pull: he stood behind a bush of elder, till she had filled her apron full. When with her load she turned about, the by-road back again to take, he started forward with a shout, and sprang upon poor Goody Blake.

And fiercely by the arm he took her, and by the arm he held her fast, and fiercely by the arm he shook her, and cried, "I've caught you then at last!" Then Goody, who had nothing said, her bundle from her lap let fall; and kneeling on the sticks, she prayed to God that is the judge of all. She prayed, her withered hand uprearing, while Harry held her by the arm, "God! who art never out of hearing, O may he never more be warm!" The cold, cold moon above her head, thus on her knees did Goody pray: young Harry heard what she had said, and icy cold he turned away.

No word to any man he utters, abed or up, to young or old; but ever to himself he mutters, "Poor Harry Gill is very cold." Abed or up, by night or day, his teeth they chatter, chatter still: now think, ye farmers all, I pray, of Goody Blake and Harry Gill.

WILLIAM WORDSWORTH *Goody Blake and Harry Gill*

III. Write each of the following in the free verse style of Lincoln's *Gettysburg Address,* on pages 6 and 7, and tell what is lost or gained by way of impressiveness:

And it came to pass, when the Philistine arose and came and drew nigh to meet David, that David hasted and ran toward the army to meet the Philistine. And David put his hand in his bag and took thence a stone, and slang it, and smote the Philistine in his forehead so that the stone sunk into his forehead; and he fell upon his face to the earth. So David prevailed over the Philistine with a sling and with a stone and smote the Philistine and slew him, but there was no sword in the hand of David. Therefore David ran and stood upon the Philistine, and took his sword, and drew it out of the sheath thereof, and slew him, and cut off his head therewith. And, when the Philistines saw their champion was dead, they fled. And the men of Israel and of Judah arose, and shouted, and pursued the Philistines until they came to the valley and to the gate of Ekron. And the wounded of the Philistines fell down by the way to Shaaraim, even unto Gath, and unto Ekron. And the children of Israel returned from chasing after the Philistines, and they spoiled their tents. And David took the head of the Philistine and brought it to Jerusalem; but he put his armour in his tent.

I Samuel XVII:48–54

It is now sixteen or seventeen years since I saw the Queen of France, then the dauphiness, at Versailles; and surely never lighted on this orb, which she hardly seemed to touch, a more delightful vision. I saw her just above the horizon, decorating and cheering the elevated sphere she just began to move in—glittering like the morning-star, full of life, and splendour, and joy. Oh! what a revolution! and what a heart must I have, to contemplate without emotion that elevation and that fall! Little did I dream when she added titles of veneration to those of enthusiastic, distant, respectful love, that she should ever be obliged to carry the sharp antidote against disgrace concealed in that bosom; little did I dream that I should have lived to see such disasters fallen upon her in a nation of gallant men, in a nation of men of honour, and of cavaliers. I thought ten thousand swords must have leaped from their scabbards to avenge even a look that threatened her with insult. But the age of chivalry is gone. That of sophisters, economists, and calculators has succeeded; and the glory of Europe is extinguished for ever. Never, never more shall we behold that generous loyalty to rank and sex, that proud submission, that dignified obedience, that subordination of the heart, which kept alive, even in servitude itself, the spirit of an exalted freedom. The unbought grace of life, the cheap defence of nations, the nurse of manly sentiment and heroic enterprise is gone! It is gone, that sensibility of principle, that chastity of honour, which felt a stain like a wound, which inspired courage whilst it mitigated ferocity, which ennobled whatever it touched, and under which vice itself lost half its evil, by losing all its grossness.

EDMUND BURKE *Reflections on the Revolution in France*

My Lords, this ruinous and ignominious situation, where we cannot act with success, nor suffer with honor, calls upon us to remonstrate in the strongest and loudest language of truth, to rescue the ear of Majesty from the delusions which surround it. The desperate state of our arms abroad is in part known. No man thinks more highly of them than I do. I love and honor the English troops. I know their virtues and their valor. I know they can achieve anything except impossibilities; and I know that the conquest of English America is an impossibility. You cannot, I venture to say it, you cannot conquer America. Your armies' last war effected everything that could be effected; and what was it? It cost a numerous army, under the command of a most able general, now a noble lord in this House, a long and laborious campaign to expel five thousand Frenchmen from French America. My Lords, *you cannot conquer America.*

LORD CHATHAM *On American Affairs*

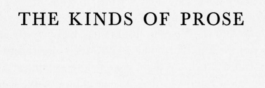

THE KINDS OF PROSE

The Kinds of Prose

ALL oral and written composition, as it is focused upon some objective, takes certain form, adheres to certain style, follows certain channels, in order the better to achieve that objective. The idea or concept that a writer or a speaker has in mind before he begins to give expression to it, decides what form, what style, what channel his expression is to adopt for its greatest effectiveness. By and large, a poetical idea inescapably gets itself expressed in poetical form; a forensic idea in oratorical form; a philosophical idea in essay or treatise form; a fictional idea in story or novel form, and so forth.

No one of these forms or styles or channels is pure, that is, none is isolated or hard and fast. All, or at least more than one, are intermixed and kept interdependent in order that the thought behind them may be truly expressed, for thought is fluid and varied and many hued; and also in order that the type of composition that predominates may be the more completely realized and the more richly enforced. Each channel is, in other words, a composite or conglomerate make-up, tributaries of all kinds and from all sources running into the main channel of expression for the sake of contributing to the rounded and well-blended stream of thought. The channels of poetry are detailed on pages 305 to 346. The channels of prose—conventionally and conveniently classified as exposition or explanation, narration or recounting of incidents and events, description or picturization, persuasion or argument—are discussed and illustrated on pages 69 to 301. The first two are the major types. A very large part of all speaking and writing is exposition and narration. Description is a serving form; it is nearly always subordinate, nearly always dependent upon the call or the need of exposition and narration for clarification and elaboration. Argument is almost entirely a composite form, made up of the others for the special purpose of convincing and persuading. Not only is it true that the type of composition that predominates in a given case classifies the composition, but it is also true that the predominant impression left by a theme upon the mind of a reader or

17

a listener decides what kind of theme it is. If you are given a *sense* of action through description—through a series of pictures (as in *The Mountain Woman* on page 331)—the theme is thus nevertheless narration. If you are given an *understanding* of something primarily through narrative—through the recital of events (as in pages 100 to 105)—the theme is nevertheless exposition.

Read the following excerpt. Here the total impression is undoubtedly the barbaric cruelty of an *action* (narration) but it is built through vivid and essential explanation (exposition) and picturization (description), and the whole constitutes an eloquent argument for the punishment of such cruel and criminal indifference as that evinced by the Nabob.

Then was committed that great crime, memorable for its singular atrocity, memorable for the tremendous retribution by which it was followed. The English captives were left to the mercy of the guards, and the guards determined to secure them for the night in the prison of the garrison, a chamber known by the fearful name of the Black Hole. Even for a single European malefactor, that dungeon would, in such a climate, have been too close and narrow. The space was only twenty feet square. The air holes were small and obstructed. It was the summer solstice,* the season when the fierce heat of Bengal can scarcely be rendered tolerable to natives of England by lofty halls and by the constant waving of fans. The number of the prisoners was one hundred and forty-six. When they were ordered to enter the cell, they imagined that the soldiers were joking; and, being in high spirits on account of the promise of the Nabob † to spare their lives, they laughed and jested at the absurdity of the notion. They soon discovered their mistake. They expostulated; they entreated; but in vain. The guards threatened to cut down all who hesitated. The captives were driven into the cell at the point of the sword, and the door was instantly shut and locked upon them.

Nothing in history or fiction, not even the story which Ugolino ‡ told in the sea of everlasting ice, after he had wiped his bloody lips on the scalp of his murderer, approaches the horrors which were recounted by the few survivors of that night. They cried for mercy. They strove to burst the door. Holwell, who even in that extremity retained some presence of mind, offered large bribes to the jailers. But the answer was

* Summer solstice was June 20, 1756.
† Nabob is Hindoo for viceroy or governor.
‡ An Italian nobleman pictured in Dante's *Inferno* as frozen in a lake of ice.

that nothing could be done without the Nabob's orders, that the Nabob was asleep, and that he would be angry if anybody woke him. Then the prisoners went mad with despair. They trampled each other down, fought for the places at the windows, fought for the pittance of water with which the cruel mercy of the murderers mocked their agonies, raved, prayed, blasphemed, implored the guards to fire among them. The jailers, in the meantime, held lights to the bars and shouted with laughter at the frantic struggles of their victims. At length the tumult died away in low gaspings and moanings. The day broke. The Nabob had slept off his debauch, and permitted the door to be opened. But it was some time before the soldiers could make a lane for the survivors, by piling up on each side the heaps of corpses on which the burning climate had already begun to do its loathsome work. When at length a passage was made, twenty-three ghastly figures, such as their own mothers would not have known, staggered one by one out of the charnel house. A pit was instantly dug. The dead bodies, a hundred and twenty-three in number, were flung into it promiscuously, and covered up.

THOMAS BABINGTON MACAULAY *Lord Clive*

WORK

I. Nathaniel Hawthorne's *The Ambitious Guest* is here set up in four parallel columns. The first column contains the story or the narration proper; the second the expository parts; the third the descriptive parts; the fourth the argumentative part (very slight in this story). Read vertically column by column, and tell what is lost or gained by segregating or setting off the distinct composition types. Then read across to get the story as it is actually written. What proportion of the whole is really narration? What important elements would be lost to the story if the expository and descriptive parts were omitted? Show the interdependence of all four groups, and explain what their blending adds to totality of impression. Discuss the story also in connection with the qualities of style listed on page 3. It must be remembered that it is impossible to make such division of a story into its component composition types a strict and rigid division. Sometimes a single sentence may contain qualities of two or more kinds of composition. The best that can be done is to associate sentences and paragraphs in which one kind or another is dominant. But the following affords a sufficiently close alignment to make such study interesting and informing.

NARRATION

EXPOSITION

One September night, a family had gathered round their hearth, and piled it high with the driftwood of mountain streams, the dry cones of the pine, and the splintered ruins of great trees, that had come crashing down the precipice. Up the chimney roared the fire, and brightened the room with its broad blaze. The faces of the father and mother had a sober gladness; the children laughed; the eldest daughter was the image of happiness at seventeen; and the aged grandmother, who sat knitting in the warmest place, was the image of happiness grown old. They had found the "herb, heart's-ease," in the bleakest spot of all New England. This family were situated in the Notch of the White Hills, where the wind was sharp throughout the year, and pitilessly cold in the winter,—giving their cottage all its fresh inclemency, before it descended on the valley of the Saco. They dwelt in a cold spot and a dangerous one; for a mountain towered above their heads, so steep, that the stones would often rumble down its sides, and startle them at midnight.

The daughter had just uttered some simple jest, that filled them all with mirth, when the wind came through the Notch and seemed to pause before their cottage,—rattling the door, with a sound of wailing and lamentation, before it

DESCRIPTION | ARGUMENT

NARRATION	EXPOSITION
passed into the valley. For a moment, it saddened them, though there was nothing unusual in its tones. But the family were glad again, when they perceived that the latch was lifted by some traveller, whose footsteps had been unheard amid the dreary blast, which heralded his approach, and wailed as he was entering, and went moaning away from the door.	Though they dwelt in such solitude, these people held daily converse with the world. The romantic pass of the Notch is a great artery, through which the life-blood of internal commerce is continually throbbing, between Maine on one side and the Green Mountains and the shores of the St. Lawrence on the other. The stage-coach always drew up before the door of the cottage. The wayfarer, with no companion but his staff, paused here to exchange a word, that the sense of loneliness might not utterly overcome him, ere he could pass through the cleft of the mountain, or reach the first house in the valley. And here the teamster, on his way to Portland market, would put up for the night; and, if a bachelor, might sit an hour beyond the usual bedtime, and steal a kiss from the mountain-maid, at parting. It was one of those primitive taverns, where the traveller pays only for food and

DESCRIPTION | ARGUMENT

NARRATION

EXPOSITION

lodging, but meets with a homely kindness, beyond all price.

When the footsteps were heard, therefore, between the outer door and the inner one, the whole family rose up, grandmother, children, and all, as if about to welcome some one who belonged to them, and whose fate was linked to theirs.

The door was opened by a young man.

He felt his heart spring forward to meet them all, from the old woman who wiped a chair with her apron, to the little child that held out its arms to him. One glance and smile placed the stranger on a footing of innocent familiarity with the eldest daughter.

"Ah, this fire is the right thing!" cried he; "especially when there is such a pleasant circle round it. I am quite benumbed; for the Notch is just like the pipe of a great pair of bellows, it has blown a terrible blast in my face, all the way from Bartlett."

"Then you are going toward Vermont?" said the master of the house, as he helped to take a light knapsack off the young man's shoulders.

DESCRIPTION | ARGUMENT

His face at first wore the melancholy expression, almost despondency, of one who travels a wild and bleak road, at nightfall and alone, but soon brightened up, when he saw the kindly warmth of his reception.

"Yes; to Burlington, and far enough beyond," replied he. "I meant to have been at Ethan Crawford's to-night; but a pedestrian lingers along such a road as this. It is no matter; for, when I saw this good fire, and all your cheerful faces, I felt as if you had kindled it on purpose for me, and were waiting my arrival. So I shall sit down among you, and make myself at home."

The frank-hearted stranger had just drawn his chair to the fire, when something like a heavy footstep was heard without, rushing down the steep side of the mountain, as with long and rapid strides, and taking such a leap, in passing the cottage, as to strike the opposite precipice. The family held their breath, because they knew the sound, and their guest held his by instinct.

"The old mountain has thrown a stone at us, for fear we should forget him," said the landlord, recovering himself. "He sometimes nods his head, and threatens to come down; but we are old neighbors, and agree together pretty well, upon the whole. Besides we have a sure place of refuge, hard by, if he should be coming in good earnest."

Let us now suppose the stranger to have finished his supper of bear's meat; and by his natural felicity of manner, to have placed

DESCRIPTION | ARGUMENT

himself on a footing of kindness with the whole family, so that they talked as freely together, as if he belonged to their mountain brood. He was of a proud, yet gentle spirit,—haughty and reserved among the rich and great; but ever ready to stoop his head to the lowly cottage door, and be like a brother or a son at the poor man's fireside. In the household of the Notch, he found warmth and simplicity of feeling, the pervading intelligence of New England, and a poetry of native growth, which they had gathered, when they little thought of it, from the mountain peaks and chasms, and at the very threshold of their romantic and dangerous abode. He had travelled far and alone; his whole life, indeed, had been a solitary path: for, with the lofty caution of his nature, he had kept himself apart from those who might otherwise have been his companions. The family, too, though so kind and hospitable, had that consciousness of unity among themselves, and separation from the world at large, which, in every domestic circle, should still keep a holy place, where no stranger may intrude. But, this evening, a prophetic sympathy impelled the refined and educated youth to pour out his heart before the simple mountaineers, and constrained them to answer him with the same free con-

DESCRIPTION | ARGUMENT

fidence. And thus it should have been. Is not the kindred of a common fate a closer tie than that of birth?

The secret of the young man's character was a high and abstracted ambition. He could have borne to live an undistinguished life, but not to be forgotten in the grave. Yearning desire had been transformed to hope; and hope, long cherished, had become like certainty, that, obscurely as he journeyed now, a glory was to beam on all his pathway,—though not, perhaps, while he was treading on it. But, when posterity should gaze back into the gloom of what was now the present, they would trace the brightness of his footsteps, brightening as meaner glories faded, and confess, that a gifted one had passed from his cradle to his tomb, with none to recognize him.

"As yet," cried the stranger,

"as yet, I have done nothing. Were I to vanish from the earth tomorrow, none would know so much of me as you; that a nameless youth came up, at nightfall, from the valley of the Saco, and opened his heart to you in the evening, and passed through the Notch, by sunrise, and was seen no more. Not a soul would ask, 'Who was he? Whither did the wanderer go?'

DESCRIPTION	ARGUMENT

his cheek glowing and his eye flashing with enthusiasm—

NARRATION

EXPOSITION

But, I cannot die till I have achieved my destiny. Then, let Death come! I shall have built my monument!"

There was a continual flow of natural emotion, gushing forth amid abstracted revery, which enabled the family to understand this young man's sentiments, though so foreign from their own. With quick sensibility of the ludicrous, he blushed at the ardor into which he had been betrayed.

"You laugh at me," said he, taking the eldest daughter's hand, and laughing himself. "You think my ambition as nonsensical as if I were to freeze myself to death on the top of Mount Washington, only that people might spy at me from the country round about. And truly, that would be a noble pedestal for a man's statue!"

"It is better to sit here by this fire," answered the girl, blushing, "and be comfortable and contented, though nobody thinks about us."

"I suppose," said her father, after a bit of musing, "there is something natural in what the young man says; and if my mind had been turned that way, I might have felt just the same. It is strange, wife, how this talk has set my head running on things that are pretty certain never to come to pass."

"Perhaps they may," observed the wife. "Is the man thinking

DESCRIPTION

ARGUMENT

NARRATION

EXPOSITION

what he will do when he is a widower?"

"No, no!" cried he, repelling the idea with reproachful kindness. "When I think of your death, Esther, I think of mine too.

But I was wishing we had a good farm, in Bartlett, or Bethlehem, or Littleton, or some other township round the White Mountains; but not where they could tumble on our heads. I should want to stand well with my neighbors, and be called Squire, and sent to General Court for a term or two; for a plain, honest man may do as much good there as a lawyer. And when I should be grown quite an old man, and you an old woman, so as not to be long apart, I might die happy enough in my bed, and leave you all crying around me. A slate gravestone would suit me as well as a marble one,—with just my name and age, and a verse of a hymn, and something to let people know that I lived an honest man and died a Christian."

"There now!" exclaimed the stranger; "it is our nature to desire a monument, be it slate, or marble, or a pillar of granite, or a glorious memory in the universal heart of man."

"We're in a strange way, tonight," said the wife, with tears in her eyes. "They say it's a sign of

DESCRIPTION | ARGUMENT

NARRATION	EXPOSITION

something, when folks go a wandering so. Hark to the children!"

They listened accordingly. The younger children had been put to bed in another room, but with an open door between, so that they could be heard talking busily among themselves. One and all seemed to have caught the infection from the fireside circle, and were outvying each other in wild wishes and childish projects of what they would do when they came to be men and women.

At length, a little boy, instead of addressing his brothers and sisters, called out to his mother.

"I'll tell you what I wish, mother," cried he. "I want you and father and grandma'm, and all of us, and the stranger, too, to start right away, and go and take a drink out of the basin of the Flume!"

Nobody could help laughing at the child's notion of leaving a warm bed, and dragging them from a cheerful fire, to visit the basin of the Flume,—a brook which tumbles over the precipice, deep within the Notch. The boy had hardly spoken, when a wagon rattled along the road, and stopped a moment before the door. It appeared to contain two or three men, who were cheering their hearts with the rough chorus of a song, which resounded, in broken notes, between the cliffs, while the

DESCRIPTION | ARGUMENT

NARRATION	EXPOSITION

singers hesitated whether to continue their journey, or put up here for the night.

"Father," cried the girl, "they are calling you by name."

But the good man doubted whether they had really called him, and was unwilling to show himself too solicitous of gain, by inviting people to patronize his house.

He therefore did not hurry to the door; and the lash being soon applied, the travellers plunged into the Notch, still singing and laughing, though their music and mirth came back drearily from the heart of the mountain.

"There, mother!" cried the boy again. "They'd have given us a ride to the Flume."

Again they laughed at the child's pertinacious fancy for a night ramble.

But it happened, that a light cloud passed over the daughter's spirit; she looked gravely into the fire, and drew a breath that was almost a sigh. It forced its way, in spite of a little struggle to repress it. Then starting and blushing, she looked quickly round the circle, as if they had caught a glimpse into her bosom.

The stranger asked what she had been thinking of.

"Nothing," answered she with a downcast smile. "Only I felt lonesome just then."

"O, I have always had a gift of

DESCRIPTION | ARGUMENT

feeling what is in other people's hearts!" said he, half seriously. "Shall I tell the secrets of yours? For I know what to think, when a young girl shivers by a warm hearth, and complains of lonesomeness at her mother's side. Shall I put these feelings into words?"

"They would not be a girl's feelings any longer, if they could be put into words," replied the mountain nymph, laughing, but avoiding his eye.

And this was said apart. Perhaps a germ of love was springing in their hearts, so pure that it might blossom in Paradise, since it could not be matured on earth; for women worship such gentle dignity as his; and the proud, contemplative, yet kindly soul is oftenest captivated by simplicity like hers.

DESCRIPTION	ARGUMENT
But, while they spoke softly, and he was watching the happy sadness, the lightsome shadows, the shy yearnings of a maiden's nature, the wind, through the Notch, took a deeper and drearier sound. It seemed, as the fanciful stranger said, like the choral strain of the spirits of the blast, who, in old Indian times, had their dwelling among these mountains, and made their heights and recesses a sacred region. There was a wail, along the road, as if a funeral were passing. To chase away the gloom, the family threw pine branches on	

NARRATION | EXPOSITION

"Old folks have their notions," said she, "as well as young ones. You've been wishing and planning; and letting your heads run on one thing and another, till you've set my mind a-wandering too. Now what should an old woman wish for, when she can go but a step or two before she comes to her grave? Children, it will haunt me night and day till I tell you."

"What is it, mother?" cried the husband and wife, at once.

Then the old woman, with an air of mystery, which drew the circle closer round the fire, informed them that she had provided her graveclothes some years before,—a nice linen shroud, a cap with a muslin ruff, and everything of a finer sort than she had worn

DESCRIPTION	ARGUMENT
their fire, till the dry leaves crackled and the flame arose, discovering once again a scene of peace and humble happiness. The light hovered about them fondly, and caressed them all. There were the little faces of the children, peeping from their bed apart, and here the father's frame of strength, the mother's subdued and careful mien, the high-browed youth, the budding girl, and the good old grandam, still knitting in the warmest place. The aged woman looked up from her task, and, with fingers ever busy, was the next to speak.	

NARRATION | EXPOSITION

since her wedding day. But, this evening, an old superstition had strangely recurred to her. It used to be said, in her younger days, that, if anything were amiss with a corpse, if only the ruff were not smooth, or the cap did not set right, the corpse, in the coffin and beneath the clods, would strive to put up its cold hands and arrange it. The bare thought made her nervous.

"Don't talk so, grandmother!" said the girl, shuddering.

"Now," continued the old woman, with singular earnestness, yet smiling strangely at her own folly, "I want one of you, my children,—when your mother is dressed and in her coffin,—I want one of you to hold a looking-glass over my face. Who knows but I may take a glimpse at myself, and see whether all's right?"

"Old and young, we dream of graves and monuments," murmured the stranger youth, "I wonder how mariners feel, when the ship is sinking, and they, unknown and undistinguished, are to be buried together in the ocean,—that wide and nameless sepulchre?"

For a moment, the old woman's ghastly conception so engrossed the minds of her hearers, that a sound abroad in the night, rising like the roar of a blast, had grown broad, deep, and terrible, before the fated group were conscious of

DESCRIPTION	ARGUMENT

NARRATION	EXPOSITION

it. The house, and all within it, trembled; the foundations of the earth seemed to be shaken, as if this awful sound were the peal of the last trump. Young and old exchanged one wild glance, and remained an instant, pale, affrighted, without utterance, or power to move. Then the same shriek burst simultaneously from all their lips:

"The Slide! The Slide!"

The simplest words must intimate, but not portray, the unutterable horror of the catastrophe. The victims rushed from their cottage, and sought refuge in what they deemed a safer spot,—where, in contemplation of such an emergency, a sort of barrier had been reared. Alas! they had quitted their security, and fled right in the pathway of destruction. Down came the whole side of the mountain, in a cataract of ruin. Just before it reached the house, the stream broke into two branches,— shivered not a window there, but overwhelmed the whole vicinity, blocked up the road, and annihilated everything in its dreadful course. Long ere the thunder of that great Slide had ceased to roar among the mountains, the mortal agony had been endured, and the victims were at peace. Their bodies were never found.

DESCRIPTION	ARGUMENT

The next morning, the light smoke was seen stealing from the cottage chimney, up the mountain

|

All had left separate tokens, by which those who had known the family were made to shed a tear for each.

Who has not heard their name? The story has been told far and wide, and will forever be a legend of these mountains. Poets have sung their fate.

DESCRIPTION

ARGUMENT

side. Within, the fire was yet smouldering on the hearth, and the chairs in a circle round it, as if the inhabitants had but gone forth to view the devastation of the Slide, and would shortly return, to thank Heaven for their miraculous escape.

There were circumstances which led some to suppose that a stranger had been received into the cottage on this awful night, and had shared the catastrophe of all its inmates. Others denied that there were sufficient grounds for such a conjecture. Woe, for the high-souled youth, with his dream of earthly immortality! His name and person utterly unknown; his history, his way of life, his plans, a mystery never to be solved; his death and his existence equally a doubt! Whose was the agony of that death moment?

NATHANIEL HAWTHORNE *The Ambitious Guest*

II. Now read the following story,* keeping in mind the foregoing paralleling of types in *The Ambitious Guest*. While here again you will find them often so closely interrelated as to be almost if not quite inseparable, you can nevertheless set apart large sections from beginning to end as narration proper, exposition, description, and argument. Here, too, the last will yield least, and this is as it should be, for "the story's the thing." But may this story as a whole be considered an argument? In addition to writing a "corking" story, did the author also give us an impressive and irrefutable argument? (The stories on pages 130 to 173 may be similarly treated.

I was all set to enjoy myself at the annual women's national golf championship to be held that year at the Beech Hollow Country Club in Dallas, one of my favorite clubs, when the chief sent for me.

Business hadn't been any too good, I knew, what with the recession and conditions. And the new fourteen-club limit wasn't the best thing in the world for us, because we used to sell a lot of extra gadgets like chippers and heavy wedges, heavy putters, special mashie niblicks, jiggers, and the like, and now, of course, the tournament players were limited to four woods, eight irons, a wedge and a putter, or whatever combination they liked, as long as it wasn't more than fourteen. And already the dubs were beginning to follow suit.

You could tell how tough times were by the long waits you'd have when playing a round of golf—guys up ahead looking for a lost ball. In the old days, if a chump dumped one out of bounds or into a thicket, he'd say, "Never mind, son, drop another," and off they'd go. Now they'd hold you up until they found it. Which meant we weren't selling as many golf balls.

So I had some slight misgivings when I bounced into A. R.'s office— A. R. Mallow, president of A. R. Mallow & Co., makers of Tru-Distance Irons, Far-Fli Woods, the Thunderbolt and Tuff-Hide ball, and the famous Scraggins Sighter. My misgiver was hitting on all six.

"H'm," said A. R. "Oh, yes, Fowler. You—ah—were going to the Women's National at Dallas, weren't you?"

I didn't know what was coming, except that I wasn't going to like it, so just to play safe I gave it the casual approach.

"Why, yes," I said, "I was going to take a run down, A. R., just to be there, you know, look around and maybe pick up a little business. It doesn't do any harm."

* Copyright 1938 by Paul Gallico. Used by permission.

"I see," said A. R., looking at me over his glasses. "Well, while you're down there you might see what you can do about this. Wilcoxen sent it in this morning at my request. I am frank to confess that I am more than a little upset about it."

He tossed a memo over to me. C. A. Wilcoxen was advertising manager of A. R. Mallow & Co., and I was his assistant.

It read like this:

Memo: C. A. to A. R.: Here is the list you requested:

Myra Wrenn	Accu-Flite
Edith Adams	Accu-Flite
Tomboy Torrance	Accu-Flite
Marjorie Siller	Putt-Rite
Joan Sawyer	Midwest Dormy
Helen Ames	Midwest Dormy
Francine Delafield	Accu-Flite
Seena Godette	Putt-Rite
Peggy Lord	Accu-Flite
Jane Twedell	Thunderbolt

A. R. pointed a long finger at the sheet in my hands and said, "Do you realize that those are the ten best women golfers in the United States, and only one of them plays our Thunderbolt golf ball? And three, the first three, including Myra Wrenn, the present champion, play Fairgreen's Accu-Flite. (The Fairgreen Company, makers of the Accu-Flite ball, were our biggest rivals.) Well, sir?"

I didn't know what to say, so I said, "It's that diamond chip they claim they put in the center of their golf ball. Gals go for boloney like that."

A. R. ignored that one and kind of closed the interview by saying, "Fowler, this company advertises its Thunderbolt as 'The Champion Ball, the Golf Ball of Champions.' When you return from Dallas, I trust that list will be considerably revised."

So I beat it. What was the use of my trying to tell A. R. that dames were like nothing else on two legs, none of the rules went for them? They'd play any golf ball they felt like, and not for any reason anybody else would. Or maybe it was that they thought that one seventy-five-cent golf ball was just like another six-bit pill, and bought them for the color, or the feel, or the paint job.

And so, "bang" went the nice time I was going to have in Dallas, shooting a little golf, going to parties and watching the gals claw one another. And there wasn't any use trying to tell A. R., or Wilcoxen either, that an amateur tournament, particularly the Women's, isn't like a professional show, where you can throw your weight around, and bargain and dicker and offer dough, and maybe swindle and cross and chisel a little. They don't give a hoot about big business, those gals don't, or any business. They come on to that tournament to do a little gossiping and a little scratching, besides playing a lot of golf, and they don't like to be bullied or pestered. The Federal Trade Commission put a stop to our giving golf balls and clubs away, so we couldn't bribe 'em any more. And anyway, they're ladies, those gals, leastways all except Tomboy Torrance, and you can't shove a lady around, and if you tried it on the Tomboy, she'd like as not swing on your chin, and anything she connected with she generally flattened.

No, what you did at a women's amateur was show up and dress nice, and behave yourself, give a few good parties, make yourself useful at the dances as an extra man, pay some attention to the poor old hen golfers who'd be wallflowers otherwise, and generally make yourself agreeable. If the gals got to like you and trust you and found out you were pushing a certain line of goods, maybe they'd switch to your clubs or golf ball just because you were a nice guy, or just because. But you couldn't hire 'em, or pay 'em, or threaten 'em, or strong-arm 'em. And that's just what A. R. was expecting me to do. I thought I was in pretty solid with my company because of a couple of deals I had put over at the Men's Open in the past two years that got us a lot of business, but I guess those big corporations have hair-trigger forgetters. You have to keep on pitching to stick.

So I tossed my dinner clothes into a bag and hoisted myself and my mallets aboard the rattler for Dallas in what may be described as a state of mind. I knew I wasn't expected to deliver that whole list. But I'd better have the champion and the runner-up playing our ball when that tournament was over.

The first person I ran into in the lobby of the Adolphus Hotel, when I got there, was Tomboy Torrance. She said, "Hi, kid!" and hit me a clout on the back that sent me spinning into the cigar stand. When I recovered and staggered back, she nearly yanked my arm out of its socket and shouted, "Glad to see you, boy! You're talking to the next women's champion. Ah'm jes' naturally gonna knot these dames so they'll never come untied. The championship's in mah bag. These golfers here are just a lot of sissies."

I got my arm back into my shoulder and said, "Okay, Butch. I believe you. What ball you playing?" You could use an approach like that with Tomboy. Subtlety was not her number.

She backed off a little and said, "What's it to you? Ah'm playin' the good old Accu-Flite and Ah'm a-knockin' it outa sight. What cheap truck you peddlin'?"

That was Tomboy for you. Her name was Eula Torrance, and she came from some little place in Oklahoma in the oil country. But nobody ever called her Eula. She was known as Tomboy Torrance all over the country. And was she known! She was a great athlete, that kid, tough and hard as nails. She could run, jump, throw the javelin, swim, play basketball, peg a baseball or a football like a man, and too handy with her mitts besides.

She stood five foot five, weighed a hundred and thirty-eight pounds, and it was all sinew. And she wasn't kidding about knocking a golf ball out of sight. She could. She'd only been playing golf two years, and there she was in her first national championship.

She had a thin, pert, leathery face, a hoyden's face, with bright blue eyes and a mess of sand-colored hair that was never combed. She never wore a hat. She never wore anything but an old skirt and a brown sweater and a brown oil-country leather jacket that still had a lot of Oklahoma oil on it. Her old man was a driller from around Ardmore, and she was Oklahoma's pride and joy. She was a ferocious competitor. I guess she never had anything else in her life. It seemed to gripe her that she had to compete against women instead of men, and she had a supreme contempt for them all, or appeared to. She sure was going to smear some color over that National; though, of course, at the time, I never dreamed that it would end in a near riot, plus the goofy scene at the prize-giving at the clubhouse when it was all over. You read about it in the papers, but a lot of it didn't get printed. That was because your Uncle William Fowler was on the inside of it. Everything seems to happen to me.

So, just for contrast, the next person I bumped into on my way to the elevators was Edith Adams. That Edie was a darling. Boy, she was a lady. If some day I've got to give in and spend the rest of my life with one dame, I hope it'll be someone like Edie Adams. She had everything. She was handsome, in a fine, clear, honest way, with rich chestnut hair and very light blue eyes. She loved life and parties and people, but you'd never see her raucous. She was folks, too; came from one of the oldest families in San Antonio. She played in tournaments because she enjoyed it and had a good time. But she never got too serious about it, which may have been why she hadn't won the National yet, though she had been trying for four years. She would never admit it, but I think her heart was pretty well set on taking that title. And do you know who pulled for her most to win, besides the whole state of Texas? The gals she played against. They all loved her. And listen, when a girl is liked by other women, she's got something, hasn't she?

She threw her arms around my neck—I'd known her for three years —and said, "Bill, I'm so glad to see you. They didn't tell me you were coming down. We're all going to be in the Mirror Room tonight. Come along with us. There'll be ever so many pretty girls." She didn't think she was pretty, see?

I said, "I'll be there, Edie. Save me a place next to you. How are you hitting 'em?"

"Sh-h-h-h," said Edie, "I'm afraid to say anything. It's too good to last. I had a seventy-five yesterday from the back tees. I've finally found a ball I can putt. I had six one-putt greens."

My heart came right up and kicked me under the chin. Maybe I was getting a break. "Good old Thunderbolt, eh?" I suggested. "You can't keep it out of the cup."

Edie looked severe. "It isn't the Thunderbolt at all. It's the Accu-Flite. And don't you try to get me to switch. I wouldn't change for anything in the world now. If that's what you came down here for, you can go home. But come to the party first."

So that was that.

Boy, that was some week! And at the end of it I had got nowhere. I don't have to tell you how the tournament went. Edie and Tomboy were in separate brackets, and Tomboy had the easier half. When it came down to the semifinal round on Friday, Edie played Myra Wrenn, the defending champion in the upper half. Tomboy Torrance and Seena Godette were the other semifinalists. Tomboy mopped up the course with Seena, 7 and 6, but Edie and Myra had a thriller, and Edie won the match one up when she chipped into the cup from off the twentieth green. Myra, who is a sweet person, dropped a few tears when it was over and the tension released, and threw her arms around Edie and said, "Oh, darling! I'm so glad it was you. You'll win tomorrow, and we'll all be so proud of you."

That brought Edie and Tomboy into the thirty-six-hole finals, match play, for the championship the next day.

I'd been following Edie, so I didn't see anything of the unruly gallery that got to following Tomboy. But I heard about it when we got back to the clubhouse.

Seena Godette, a big, tall, blond girl from Michigan, was holding forth outside the caddie house where she was changing her shoes. "Excuse me!" she said. "I don't want any more of that young lady.

You can have her and her gallery. They nearly tore my clothes off. Edie, you'd better wear some old things tomorrow, and I wish you joy of that mob."

Edie just smiled and said nothing, because Seena was inclined to squawk a little anyway when she was beaten.

But that night when we got back to town and I went out to get some air after dinner, I noticed that the city was filling up with a horde of tough-looking monkeys, in high-laced boots and oil-stained hats and leather jackets.

There was a gang of 'em in the lobby of the Adolphus later, big, loud, hard-looking guys, offering as much as 4 and 5 to 1 on Tomboy against that "stuck-up gal from San Antone." Me, I am not the betting type, but I just took myself a hundred dollars' worth of that 5-to-1, because I thought maybe if I was to be looking for a job when the tournament was over, it might be smart to have a little nest egg. We put the dough up with the hotel manager, who stuck it in his safe. I thought it would be nicer that way. Those were very ominous-looking parties.

By 9:30 the next morning the course was jammed with them. There must have been three or four thousand, and plenty of women amongst 'em too. There were about a thousand or so people there from around Dallas and Fort Worth, which was about normal for what the women's national will draw, but they sure were lost in that wild-eyed mob from Oklahoma. And they'd all paid their $2.20 admission fee and wore their tags. They were gathered around the porticoed front of the Beech Hollow clubhouse, and they let out a yell to split the sky when Tomboy came out and started over for the caddie house.

"Whee-e! At-ta-gal, Tomboy! You're a-goin' out there and win!"

"Give it to her, Tomboy! We're all with you!"

So that's the way it was going to be. Oh, but that was nothing.

Edie and Tomboy met outside the caddie master's shop. There was a mob of Tomboy's gallery surging behind the ropes that ran along the path. Edie smiled, and was going to say something, when Tomboy stopped in the middle of the path, blocking her way, put her hands on her hips and said flatly, "Ah'm gonna whop you today!"

There was a roar of delight from the Oklahomans.

Edie stopped in her tracks. She was looking cute as the dickens in a white serge skirt and a pink brushed-wool sweater, and pink bandeau around her hair. She simply stared at Tomboy as though she hadn't heard correctly.

"Ah am jes' goin' to unravel you," said Tomboy, succinctly, "and Ah can do it. That's all."

"Oh, Tomboy! Tell her some more!"

"She won't talk to you, Tomboy! She's too stuck up!"

"Make her squeal, Tomboy! She won't be so tony when you get done with her!"

"See if she'll take a little bet, Tomboy! I got the money right here!" One of them hauled a big roll of bills from his pocket.

I began to see some dark red. I said, "Why don't you mugs keep quiet? This isn't a prize fight. This is a golf tournament."

"Oh, a fresh guy, eh? Look out you don't get them nice ice-cream pants spoiled, son!"

I started to crack back, when Edie suddenly said, "Sh-h-h, Bill. Don't, please," and ran into the golf shop.

I went in after her. She donned her spikes coolly. I said, "Edie, if those—"

She said, "Oh, Bill, they're all right. They don't understand. Most of them have never even seen a golf match before. Of course, they want Tomboy to win. She belongs to them. Walk with me a little when we get out on the course."

She was a honey all right. Her caddie reported at the door and she went off with him. I went back behind where the golf bags were racked and pulled my big, heavy No. 3 iron out of the bag. I like to have a golf club in my hand when I am following a match. They're handy as canes, or to use as a brace to lean against when you're standing around a green. It was one of our Scraggins Sighters, with a little hump on the back of the blade. And anyway, I had a funny hunch that I'd find some use for that iron before the day was over. I figured I'd wrap it around somebody's neck maybe.

When I got to the first tee, Tomboy had won the toss and was just hitting as I came up. She knocked one straight down the middle for two-five-oh. There was a roar from the gallery that was cut by the fairway, and off they went in a rush and a whoop and a holler to cluster around Tomboy's ball. Edie hadn't even hit yet. Well, there was no place to hit to. The whole fairway was covered with people. She sat down quite calmly on the tee and waited. A lot of marshals ran down and sweated with the crowd and finally got them parted and standing still. Edie laid one down ten yards back of Tomboy. They both got home with mashies and halved the hole.

The crowd was humming and buzzing. Edie had been right. Most of that wild gang from the oil fields didn't have the faintest notion what golf was about. I heard one of them say, "What's that about them splittin' the hole? Don't Tomboy get nothin' for hittin' further? She was ten yards out in front of that other gal."

They halved the second and Edie won the third when she sank a thirty-footer, a sweet putt.

There was grumbling when she teed up on the fourth. Someone shouted, "Pretty lucky for you there, sister! Bet you don't do that again!"

Another voice said, "Here, here, what you getting up there fust for? Tomboy, she won that toss!"

Greg Halliday, the U. S. G. A. official and referee, came forward on the tee and asked for quiet while the contestants were playing their shots.

Someone cried, "What for? We paid our money, didn't we?"

The fourth was a dog-leg. Edie set her drive nicely at the turn, so that she had an open shot for the green. Tomboy passed her by fifteen yards, and the crowd raised another great shout and immediately closed in on the two balls. We trudged down to them and they opened up a lane for us to get through. When Edie got to her ball, I noticed that she knelt down to examine it, so I pushed out and went to see what was the matter. It was only half showing in the fairway. Somebody had done a nice job of stepping on it. Tomboy was standing near by with her hands on her hips, grinning from ear to ear.

As Edie got up, someone said, "Let's see her hit that one."

I said, "Just a minute. What the hell is this?"

Greg called up the fore caddie, but he said the gallery had run right over him. Then he gave the marshals hell, but it was no use. It was a rub of the green and had to be played. Edie cut it out with her niblick and took a five on the hole to Tomboy's four.

I walked down the fifty fairway with Edie and said, "That was done deliberately. They're out to give you the works, Edie."

"It might have been an accident," Edie said, and clipped at some clover with her brassie. "I prefer to think it was. Isn't Tomboy playing well?"

At the eighth, Tomboy smothered her drive and was left with a long shot to a small green. The girl had plenty of guts all right. The green, two hundred and thirty yards away, was already banked around with people. Tomboy took out her brassie and hit a magnificent shot, a screamer. But it was just a little too strong. It hit the green and rolled over. I liked that just fine, because the eighth was well bunkered, especially on the far side, where there was a mean lip. Tomboy's ball just trickled in. When we got there, the crowd had opened a lane from the bunker to the pin. The ball wasn't in the sand pit. It was sitting up nicely in the grass on the far edge. I'd like to know how it got there. Bunkers aren't built to do that to a ball. Edie came over and had a look, and then smiled a little smile to herself. Tomboy just grinned.

A voice from the crowd called, "Take a good look! It ain't where you thought it was!"

Another said, "Thought you had her there, didn't you?"

The works were in, all right. It happened again on the eleventh; only this time they did it to Edie's ball. Oh, it was slick, all right. The Oklahomans had begun to get an inkling of the rules of the game, and knew they mustn't get caught at it. As soon as Edie's ball lit, there'd be a rush to screen it. Edie's No. 4 iron on eleven had a little fade, but luckily it was short too. It rolled to within three feet of the edge of the bunker and stopped. But when we got there, Edie's ball was in the sand. It wasn't on top of the sand either. It was lying in a heel print that looked like a shell hole, the kind of heel print you might make with one of those big high-laced boots. It took Edie two to get out, and she lost the hole with a seven to Tomboy's weak six. She would have had a good chance for a four, and a sure five.

Greg Halliday was boiling mad. After they had holed out, he stopped them on the green and said, "Miss Adams, do you wish to protest this match? I will entertain a protest if you wish to make one."

There was a groan and a "Boo-o-o-o-o!" from the gallery that drowned out the applause. That Oklahoma crowd was about four to one.

"She'll protest all right!"

"Stick to it, Tomboy! Yuh got 'em squealin'!"

"Go on, play the game!"

There were two little pink spots in Edie's cheeks, but that was all. She smiled at Greg. "Thank you, no, Mr. Halliday. I think it's a most exciting match. I have no protest to make."

Greg announced, "At the next evidence I have of anyone tampering with or changing the lie of either ball to the advantage of Miss Torrance, I will declare this match and championship forfeited to Miss Adams."

There was another groan and someone said, "That's the only way she will win it."

Walking off the green, I heard Edie saying earnestly to Greg, "But you don't understand, Mr. Halliday. They don't mean any harm. They don't know any better. They're just crazy to see her win. I don't mind, really."

But I went up with the fore-caddies, where I thought I could do some good. On seventeen, Edie hooked into the woods, and I was right in there after her ball. It wasn't a bad lie, and there was a fair enough opening for a low shot to the green.

A guy started to edge over to the ball, and when he bent down, I said, "Brother, I wouldn't do that, if I were you."

He was going to get tough until he saw that I was swinging that three iron like a baseball bat. Then he mumbled something about just wanting to have a look at it and went off. I knew that three iron was going to come in handy. But it wasn't until the luncheon period that I thought of another use for it.

Edie came in five down after the first eighteen holes.

I talked to Edie after lunch, before they went back onto the tee for the final round, and put up an awful beef about what was going on.

She said, "Oh, Bill, what's the use? I don't like it any better than you do. But it's gone beyond just a golf match now. It's become a question of—oh, I don't know how to put it. But they want to see me lose my temper. Well, I won't. I'm just mean enough not to give them that much satisfaction."

The officials had been busy during the intermission, and they had matters much better in hand for the afternoon round. They had a lot more fore-caddies out ahead of each shot, and marshals with rope barriers, and a lot of the members who had volunteered as watchers. So there was no more monkey business with the ball.

But they couldn't control the talk, and the whooping, and the baiting. After all, they had taken admission money from the people, and there was nothing in the contract or the rules that called for them to keep quiet. Edie's serene acceptance of it all was making them mad too. They knew by now that she was right and they were wrong. They were just like a lot of big rowdy kids.

Edie started off by winning back the first three holes. And then that wild bunch got on her again. They began to whoop and holler around the tee: "Come on, you, Tomboy! Don't let that stuck-up gal beat you!"

It was worse around the greens. When Edie would be putting, they'd keep quiet all right until just as she was about to hit the ball, and then you'd hear a voice say, "Dollar says she don't make it."

Then there'd be a lot of indignant shushing and "quiet" from the home folk, but they were outnumbered, and there'd be voices speaking in injured tones:

"Why don't you keep quiet?"

"We paid our money. We got a right to talk if we want to."

"Talkin' don't bother Tomboy none."

And in those walks from shot to ball— They ran over her, stepped on her feet, shouted, laughed, jostled, galloped, bumped us—because a half dozen of us had closed around Edie—and had themselves a time. You could see they were enjoying golf. It was a sort of a new kind of baseball to them, where, instead of sitting in the stands to root and heckle, you got right down close to the players and did it.

Well, do you know who was really getting sore?

The Tomboy!

And I couldn't figure at what. She'd been taking all the breaks she had been getting with a big grin. And there she was, all of a sudden walking along mad as a wet cat. Oh, I could tell. Her face was getting redder and redder, and her mouth was closing down in a straight line, and getting thinner and thinner. Edie was swinging along easily, chatting and laughing with Greg and Myra Wrenn and some of the girls.

But it was tough playing golf under those conditions. Edie had a good game, but it couldn't stand up under that. And then, besides, stamping along, her eyes blazing, her mouth buttoned up tight, that Tomboy was playing herself some golf. Edie was three down coming up to the sixteenth. She won that, and Tomboy worried a little. She didn't want to be carried extra holes.

Edie topped her drive, and Tomboy pressed. Her drive was longer but ended up in the short rough—nasty, tough, spinachy stuff—on the left. She had a hundred and ninety yards to get home, and there was no getting at the ball with a spoon or a brassie. Edie had to play the odd, and was on with a fine brassie, eighteen feet from the pin.

You could see Tomboy doing some thinking. Edie was certain to get a four. If Tomboy failed to get home, she would have to sink a putt for her half and the match. And if she missed and lost the hole, Edie might catch fire. A hundred and ninety yards with an iron out of rough is a long sock for a girl. It's a good belt for a pro.

Tomboy called for her bag, and the eightball brought it over. Tomboy fingered a couple of clubs, and I saw her frown suddenly and look puzzled, and then pull out a heavy iron. She hefted it and then swung it once or twice, stepped up to the ball and let fly.

Yes, sir, it was a great shot. Boy, what a yell went up when that ball sailed up and on, dropped and rolled and stopped six feet from the cup.

Edie, her eyes shining, cried, "Bravo! Bravo! Oh, fine shot!"

Tomboy never even looked at her. The gallery around the green was jumping up and down and whooping and thumping backs.

The two girls came onto the carpet. Edie had a long putt for her three now. If she made it, Tomboy still could drop hers, halve the hole and win the match. If Edie missed, it was all over, because Tomboy was certain to get down in two from six feet, and the half was all she needed.

There was only one crack made while Edie was lining up her putt and studying the ground. Someone said, "Ah'll bet she don't go over and shake hands if she misses it."

Edie stepped up to putt, and there wasn't a sound.

She hit the ball a nice, smooth, firm tap. But it broke away at the end of the roll and stopped a foot from the cup.

That gang, unfamiliar with golf, was not yet quite sure what had happened, so there still wasn't a sound when Edie, not even making Tomboy putt, walked across the green, knocked both balls away, held out her hand and said clearly, "Well done, Tomboy. You deserved to win. You played beautifully."

I just heard the same guy who had made the crack, say, "Well, I'll be damned!" when the roar went up. I couldn't hear what Tomboy said to Edie, but I saw what she did. Her eyes were still blazing. Her hard little mouth opened. She snapped something, ignored Edie's hand, turned her back and walked away and into a crowd of her friends, and that was the last I saw of her.

Then a big voice made itself heard above the racket. It said, "Hey, boys! What do you say we give a cheer for the Adams gal? I say she's a good sport! Hip-hip!"

That was a cheer too. It outdid the victory yell, and all of a sudden all those big monkeys were crowding around Edie and patting her on the back and telling her how swell she was, and how sorry they were for some of the things they had said. They marched all the way back to the clubhouse with her. You'd have thought she was the winner.

Me, I was feeling pretty lousy for Edie's sake, even though she had put on such a wonderful show and won that hostile crowd, because I knew she wanted that title and might never again have such a good chance for it. I hadn't even got around to thinking about that hundred I'd blown, or what I would tell A. R. when I got back to New York.

I went up to the clubhouse for a while, and then out on the lawn to watch the cups being awarded—a big one for Tomboy, and a little one for Edie. I was curious how it would go, after that scene on the green.

The mob banked around was something to see. Edie was there, and the two cups, and the movie men and the photographers and officials. But nothing was happening. They were just standing around waiting. And then I saw why. Tomboy wasn't there.

Greg called out, "Is Miss Torrance here? Will she please come forward to receive her cup?"

Nothing happened. One of the girls went to look in the locker room. But she wasn't there, nor was she in the golf shop or the clubhouse. They all just stood around and waited.

That was when your Uncle William had his hunch. I don't get 'em often, but when I do, I've learned to play 'em. I hollered out to Greg over the heads of the crowd, to wait a minute, that maybe I could find her, and then turned and ran. I ran straight down the eighteenth fairway and then cut over into the woods that bordered the seventeenth.

That's where she was, all right.

She was lying on the ground on her stomach, screaming and kicking, and every once in a while clawing at the earth and the weeds. The eightball was standing near by, still with her bag of clubs, looking scared to death. I watched her for a minute, and then said, "They're waiting for you up at the clubhouse to give you your cup, Tomboy."

She spun around as though a snake had bit her, and glared at me from the ground for a moment. Then she whipped to her feet.

"Ah don't want their damned cup!" she shouted. "Or you, or any of them! Ah don't want to see any of 'em! Ah don't ever want to see that gal again! She didn't care! Ah whopped her and she didn't care! She and her nicey-nice 'Well done, Tomboy! You deserved to win!' She didn't care a damn!"

So that, I thought, was why she was so sore on the back nine. Which will show you that I'm not the smartest guy in the world when it comes to dames.

She was standing in front of me, looking as though she were going to claw my eyes out.

I said, "That's where you're wrong, kid. She did care. She cared a lot. The only difference is, she can take it. Can you?"

She just stood there, staring at me for a moment. A lot of the wildness went out of her eyes.

I said, "There's a lot more to this game than winning or getting putts down. Edie has been trying for that championship for five years. She'll probably never have another chance like this to win it. But, you see, she's a—"

Something stopped me. I guess the look on her face. She put her hands out in front of her as though she were going to block a blow. "Don't say it!" she wailed. "Don't say it!"

And then she fell right forward on her knees and put her hands to her face and began to sob. She sobbed so I got cold all over. I'd never heard anyone cry like that, and every once in a while I could make out a little of what she was saying: "Ah don't want any cups or championships. Ah want to be a lady. Ah want to be like her. Ah just cain't ever face her again. Ah didn't win that championship. Mah friends cheated for me and Ah let 'em. Ah'm no lady. Ah'm a dirty little cheat. They did terrible things to her and she came over and gave me her hand. Ah couldn't take it, because Ah couldn't look her in the face. Ah cain't ever look no one in the face." And then that awful hurt crying.

After a while she said, "Ah cain't go back. It isn't my championship. It's hers. And Ah cain't give it to her. It's too late now. It's all over. There's nothing Ah can do. Why can't Ah die? Ah'd give anything in the world for her to win that championship. Anything!"

The eightball holding her bag gave a big sniff and rolled his eyes. He sure was one unhappy-looking African. But he put the idea into my head again. But only because I knew deep down that the Tomboy was on the level.

I said, "What would you do for me if I found a way out for you?"

She broke away and looked at me with her eyes like dinner plates.

"Bill—Bill, Ah'd do anything!"

I grinned for a moment. "Even to playing the Thunderbolt?"

I got my face straight just in time.

"Bill," she wailed, "Ah'd—Ah'd eat 'em!"

I said, "Go look at your clubs."

She didn't seem to understand, so I nodded my head in the direction of her bag and repeated, "Go look at your clubs.'

She went over slowly, a little bewildered, and did what I told her. She was so miserable and desperate that she just looked at them literally. Then she fell to fingering them, and suddenly she let out a yell and began to scrabble amongst 'em so that they clinked and clattered, and finally she hollered, "Chickey! Come on!" grabbed the eightball by the hand and moved him so fast that he darn near was parallel with the ground.

So that was how we came back to the clubhouse, all out of breath and messy, Tomboy, her face tear-streaked, her hair looking like a mop, still lugging that Ethiopian.

The crowd opened up when they saw us coming, and we burst right into the middle.

I could hear those newsreel cameras begin to grind while Tomboy stood there fighting for her breath. When she got it, she began to talk, and you could hear every word, because there wasn't a sound.

She spoke to Greg. She said, "Mr. Halliday, Ah came to tell you Ah didn't win that championship. Miss Adams did. Ah got to be disqualified."

Nobody was even breathing now. There was just the whir of those cameras.

"Ah played with fifteen clubs in mah bag."

Greg said, "You what, Miss Torrance?"

"Played with fifteen clubs in mah bag. Look. Ah got to be disqualified. Ah got to be."

How that hum raced through the crowd. The officials went over and looked at Tomboy's bag. There were fifteen clubs in it all right. Then Edie went over and looked, too, and I started to shake. She laid her hand on the bag, fingered a club, looked at me, then looked at Tomboy.

Then she said, "Did you know you were playing fifteen clubs?"

The hum of talk died down and it was dead quiet again.

"Yes," said Tomboy, "Ah knowed it all along." And then, looking directly at Edie, she added so desperately that it was fit to break your heart, "Please! Oh, please!"

Edie seemed to have made up her mind suddenly, because she let the club slip back into the bag, walked over quickly to Tomboy and put her arms about her. And then they were both crying.

I didn't even wait to hear Greg's announcement with regret that he was forced to disqualify Miss Torrance and that Miss Edith Adams was the new champion. I blew.

But Edie caught me later, trying to sneak into a taxi from the back door of the clubhouse. She said, "Bill! Come here."

I went over, but kind of slow. Boy, I knew I was in for it.

She said, "Bill, how did your Number Three iron get into Tomboy's bag?"

"I put it there."

"When? It wasn't there when we teed off. I counted her clubs when I counted mine. I do it automatically since they put that new rule in."

"I sneaked it in after lunch."

"Why did you do it, Bill?"

I said, "I'm sorry, Edie. I was sore at the rotten deal you were getting. You were being robbed. I thought I'd give 'em a little dose of their own stuff and see how they liked it. I was going to turn her in on the last green, when the match was over, if she won."

I couldn't get away from Edie's level eyes. She had me pinned just the way you stick a butterfly to a box. "And why didn't you go through with it?"

I dug one toe into the gravel and felt like a caught kid. "I—I couldn't do it, I guess, Edie. Watching you and seeing how—well, what a great person you are, made me realize, I guess, that a dirty trick doesn't make up for another dirty trick. Funny thing. She used my three iron to make that great shot to the seventeenth. She never would have got home with one of her light clubs. She didn't even know she was using it."

Edie's tone never changed, or her gaze.

"And what made you change your mind?"

"I didn't, Edie. Honestly, I didn't. It was the kid. She was so desperate. I found her down the woods, bawling. She'd had a chance to look at herself. She knew that you really won that match, that they had cheated for her. It was killing her. Do you know what she said down there? She said, 'I don't want any cups or championships. I just want to be a lady like her.' I never want to have another moment like that one in front of the clubhouse when you spotted my club in her bag. I didn't know what you were going to do. If—if you hadn't accepted her sacrifice, Edie, it would have destroyed her."

For the first time she dropped her eyes, and I could breathe again. Her voice was different too. She said, gravely and thoughtfully, "Y-yes. I felt something like that. I didn't know, but I could feel it—so terribly, poor child. Else I should never have done it."

Suddenly she reached up, took my face in her hands and kissed me.

"Bill," she said, "you're a louse and a no-good. But maybe you saved a girl's soul. And I'll play your Thunderbolt ball."

PAUL GALLICO *The Tomboy and the Lady*

III. The two episodes related below are stenographic, that is, the bald facts are reported with a minimum of descriptive and expository and argumentative detail. The first is a brief news story; the second, a fifteenth-century tale. Write into these narratives here and there phrases or sentences or paragraphs that describe and explain and argue. Tell what is lost or gained by the process.

Two fifteen-year-old boys abandoned plans for an expensive vacation in Canada today because one of them never could spell "sencible," "bussiness" and "gaurd."

Katherine Geoghan, seventh grade teacher, received a note commanding her to place $500 and a gun at a certain spot. She called police, who could find no one at the appointed spot.

So Miss Geoghan reread the note. She was to be "sencible" about the "bussiness" because the extortionists would be on "gaurd."

Then she remembered those were the very words she had struggled in vain to get Ken Thompson to spell.

District Attorney F. C. Clowdsley said Ken confessed he wrote the note, dictated by Raymond Hattler. He hasn't decided what to do with the boys.

Jacobus de Vetriaco tells how that there was once a very religious man that trowed he was a passing good singer, notwithstanding he was not so. So on a day there was a gentlewoman that sat behind and heard him sing, and she began to weep; and he, trowing that she wept for sweetness of his voice, began to sing louder than he did tofore; and aye the higher she heard him sing, the faster wept she.

Then the man asked her why she wept so as she did, and she answered him again and said: "Sir, I am a poor gentlewoman, and the last day I had no calf but one; and the wolf came and had it away from me; and ever when that I hear you sing, anon I remember me how that my calf and ye cried alike."

And when the man heard this, anon he thought shame, and remembered him that thing that he thought was great loving unto God, was unto Him great shame and villainy; and from thenceforth he sang never so loud.

ESSAY

Essay

THE book of any kind of directions, the treatise, the thesis, the classroom text, the essay are all expository types. They are exposition "grown up." Of these the essay is the most widely used literary form of exposition—the one that we shall most frequently read and most frequently use as we grow older. Newspaper columns and editorials and general articles all belong to the essay type. Your diary is made up of a series of thumbnail essays. Even the letters you write and receive are, as a rule, little essays. You find essays imbedded in every novel you read and in many of the daily news accounts as well. The essay is the best field for practice in writing. Your daily or weekly themes are really short essays. Your brief talks before your classmates on subjects of general school interest are oral essays. The word *paper* is sometimes loosely used to mean essay. When you say "Here is my paper" you usually mean "Here is my essay."

The essay is so fluid and so comprehensive a form that it defies any but the most general definition and classification. It is a kind of improvisation or soliloquy in writing. It is thinking aloud, or, at least, thinking spontaneously and extemporaneously on paper. Samuel Johnson called it "a loose sally of the mind; an irregular, undigested piece; not a regular and orderly performance." The dictionary calls it "a composition of moderate length on any particular subject or branch of a subject . . . limited in range . . . sometimes elaborate in style . . . an irregular and undigested piece." The *Encyclopedia Britannica* defines the essay as "a composition of moderate length, usually in prose, which deals in an easy, cursory way with the external conditions of a subject, and, in strictness, with that subject only as it affects the writer." The essay is subjective, that is, it is unfolded through the writer's own mind and thought and feeling; you see his subject through him. It is to prose what the lyric is to poetry (see page 305). In style it is tentative, natural, conversational, easy, serious or whimsical, formal or informal, intimate or impersonal. It makes no attempt to place event and character in plotted relationship to each other. It assumes no obligation to treat a subject systematically or even logically, and in this respect it differs radically from the other forms of exposition. It is very likely to be little more than an arbitrary arrangement of casual notes made as result of observation and interest and reflection.

But withal, the essay form is expository principally. It shows relationships, expounds reactions, informs regarding events and conditions, and analyzes results of discovery and invention and speculation. And these terms, like those applied in the paragraph above, indicate to some extent the different kinds or classifications of essays. There are not only many different kinds—all loosely interrelated—but a single essay may of itself reveal many different methods of treatment, and thus be a composite type. The class name as a rule explains the essay type, but in a few instances a brief definition in addition may be necessary for complete classification. An argumentative essay, for instance, is naturally one that argues or discusses some question; a biographical essay is one that sketches a life; an informative essay is one that gives instruction and clarifies, and so on, with essays called autobiographical, character, controversial or polemic (see page 237), conversational, critical, descriptive, didactic, editorial, epigrammatic or aphoristic, familiar, historical, periodical, personal, philosophic, reflective, social, speculative. There may be almost as many classifications as there are titles or authors in this field of subjective expression.

The classification may be made, quite as loosely of course, in this way:

As to method the essay may be

> argumentative
> conversational
> critical
> descriptive
> epigrammatic (aphoristic)
> expository
> impressionistic
> narrative
> stenographic

As to aim the essay may be

> autobiographical
> biographical
> character
> didactic
> editorial
> entertaining
> informative

As to mood the essay may be

> controversial or polemic
> familiar
> humorous
> intimate
> personal
> philosophic
> quaint
> reflective
> serious
> speculative

As to medium the essay may be

> book or booklet
> column
> letter
> newspaper
> periodical
> poem

As to subject the essay may be

> academic
> classic
> educational
> historical
> political
> psychological
> scholastic
> scientific
> socialistic
> *etc.*

The informative essay is sometimes called the intellectual essay, and sometimes, again, the analytical essay. An essay that makes broad use of classical allusion is sometimes called the classic essay. The reflective essay may be a philosophic essay, but it may report merely the meditations of the writer and thus be more properly called a meditative essay. The familiar essay yields entertainment through appeals to emotion and imagination. It is usually more subjective and personal than the general essay—subject and author and style being inextricably linked in it—and, as such, it may very often quite properly be designated as the personal or the intimate essay. The editorial essay is not the average newspaper editorial, but the special one written as a rule for an occasion and having more literary quality than the regular daily editorial. The epigrammatic or aphoristic essay is written in short staccato sentences, almost every one of which has motto quality, that is, it holds easily in the mind as a saying. This type has been called the notebook essay and also the stenographic essay. The didactic essay may be devoted to the enforcement of a moral lesson (in which aim the essay really originated) and thus be called the moral essay. If it aims at teaching or instruction for general community uplift and enlightenment, it may be called a lay sermon or a social or a pedagogic essay. The speculative essay may "get nowhere," that is, it may do nothing more than speculate or pose questions about an interesting subject; thus it may be called the problem essay. The narrative essay makes use of incident or event for the sake of developing the theme of the writer, rather than for the sake of the story itself. It is sometimes called the story-essay, and it may be little more than a simple short-story. But it enforces aim entertainingly; it does not make "the story the thing." The character essay may analyze character or it may be a character sketch (see page 100). The periodical essay, appearing now and again in periodical publications, may be called the occasional essay. And so forth. Enough has been said to show that the essay is not merely a highly fluid type of expression, but a well-nigh vagabond type as well.

Reviewing—book reviewing, play reviewing, art reviewing in any field—is a form of reporting. The reviewer is concerned chiefly with exposition, not with argument. The critic, on the other hand, is primarily an arguer, that is, he is concerned chiefly with pointing out merit and demerit (the one or the other, perhaps, by inference or indirection). His criticism—his critical essay—may be entirely constructive, that is, he may dwell upon merit only, even though it be slight, and concentrate upon this to the exclusion of any mention whatever of faults in a work; or it may be destructive, that is, he may dwell upon demerit to the exclusion of almost everything else, and thus hope to enable an author to better his artistic output. The two attitudes of the critic in a critical essay are sometimes designated as the scientific method and the individualistic method.

The scientific method in literary criticism is sometimes called the greater, in distinction from individualistic criticism, which is termed the less. The former presupposes a sympathetic understanding of a piece of literature and an attitude of justice toward it, as the result of comprehensive literary background on the part of the critic. It analyzes and judges, and attempts to arrive at just interpretations and accurate evaluations of a piece of literature *per se,* without extended (if any) comparative estimates, and certainly without prejudice or predilection or "snap finality." The author's style, the author's method, the author's aim, the author's claim upon the serious attention of his constituency, the author's place in the literary firmament, and the author's gift for awakening and, perhaps, rendering permanent the interests that his work hinges upon—these are the peaks of the scientific method in literary criticism.

In other words, the scientific critic goes about his work microscopically in order that he may arrive at a telescopic conclusion; he presents a close-up view of a work itself in order that, later, he may the more intelligibly and the more accurately place it in proper perspective. He assorts and classifies and makes or implies general comparisons, but always objectively; never subjectively, as the individualistic critic does. He differentiates *and* discriminates. While he does not attack eccentricity or idiosyncrasy, he does not mistake the one for genius or the other for originality, and he is not much concerned with either as such. He arrives at his final compilation of merits (with his final elimination of demerits) in a work chiefly as the result of considerations from within the work itself. Doing this, he is confronted with two external influences upon those considerations that may or may not be inescapable: first, his own literary tradition and philosophy; second, the primary cause and the ultimate effect of the work criticized. He may try, as the individualistic critic never does, to detach himself from his literary heritage in order thus to liberate his point of view. He cannot succeed wholly in this, and it does not matter, for his wide and varied and critical reading will have equipped him to bring a wealth of discerning experience to bear. And while he may often prefer to omit or to keep at a minimum any exposition of an author and his audience, he cannot ignore either entirely, any more than a naturalist can ignore the soil and the atmosphere in his analysis of a plant. On the other hand, he may not give major considerations to the author and the audience, no matter how stubbornly they insinuate themselves.

The individualistic critic, however, does just this. For the scientific critic the work's the thing; for the individualistic critic, the author or the fashion or the mere critical opinion (rather than judgment) is the thing.

The poet Byron once capped the climax of succinct individualistic reviewing and criticism combined. His erstwhile sweetheart, Caroline Lamb, wrote a novel entitled *Glenarvon,* and made him the hero of it. She confessed that she was "on fire" to know what he thought of it. He "told the world"—and her—as follows:

> I read the *Christabel;*
>   Very well:
> I read the *Missionary;*
>   Pretty—very:
> I tried at *Ilderim;*
>   Ahem!
> I read a sheet of *Marg'ret of Anjou;*
>   Can you?
> I turned a page of Webster's *Waterloo*—
>   Pooh! Pooh!
> I looked at Wordsworth's milk-white *Rylstone Doe;*
>   Hillo!
> I read *Glenarvon,* too, by Caro Lamb—
>   God Damn!

The treatise, the thesis, and the textbook are expository types of prose. The first two are ambitious and exhaustive presentations of a subject, and are generally to be considered a contribution to the field of learning. They are adult forms, for adult consumption. The textbook, on the other hand, is a treatment of some unit or phase of learning, simple in exposition and pedagogic in presentation, calculated to standardize some branch of knowledge for the easy but permanent grasp of those who are being educated in that branch. It is, in other words, focused toward the learning mind. The treatise and the thesis are focused toward the learned mind. The greatest men and women of all civilized times have regarded the textbooks that were most valuable to them in procuring education as the most precious and most sacred of their possessions.

It is obviously impossible to include in this section illustrations of all kinds of exposition, or even of all kinds of essays. But a few of the leading types of essays are here included for your study. You should add to these from your general reading in books, periodicals, and newspapers. You should use them as models for your own practice in essay writing.

The following is an epigrammatic or aphoristic essay. There is not much plan in it. Rather, it is a collection of more or less sharp epigrams, once jotted down in a notebook, or so it would seem, and then run together in a rambling but nevertheless interesting style.

It had been hard for him that spake it to have put more truth and untruth together in a few words, than in that speech, *Whosoever is delighted in solitude is either a wild beast or a god.* For it is most true that a natural and secret hatred and aversation towards society in any man, hath somewhat of the savage beast; but it is most untrue that it should have any character at all of the divine nature; except it proceed, not out of a pleasure in solitude, but out of a love and desire to sequester a man's self for a higher conversation: such as is found to have been falsely and feignedly in some of the heathen; as Epimenides the Candian, Numa the Roman, Empedocles the Sicilian, and Apollonius of Tyana; and truly and really in divers of the ancient hermits and holy fathers of the church. But little do men perceive what solitude is, and how far it extendeth. For a crowd is not company, and faces are but a gallery of pictures, and talk but a tinkling cymbal, where there is no love. The Latin adage meeteth with it a little, *Magna civitas, magna solitudo;** because in a great town friends are scattered; so that there is not that fellowship, for the most part, which is in less neighborhoods. But we may go further, and affirm most truly that it is a mere and miserable

* "Great citizenship, great solitude."

solitude to want true friends, without which the world is but a wilderness; and even in this sense also of solitude, whosoever in the frame of his nature and affections is unfit for friendship, he taketh it of the beast, and not from humanity.

A principal fruit of friendship is the ease and discharge of the fulness and swellings of the heart, which passions of all kinds do cause and induce. We know diseases of stoppings and suffocations are the most dangerous in the body; and it is not much otherwise in the mind: you may take sarza to open the liver, steel to open the spleen, flower of sulphur for the lungs, castoreum for the brain; but no receipt openeth the heart, but a true friend, to whom you may impart griefs, joys, fears, hopes, suspicions, counsels, and whatsoever lieth upon the heart to oppress it, in a kind of civil shrift or confession.

It is a strange thing to observe how high a rate great kings and monarchs do set upon this fruit of friendship whereof we speak: so great, as they purchase it many times at the hazard of their own safety and greatness. For princes, in regard of the distance of their fortune from that of their subjects and servants, cannot gather this fruit, except (to make themselves capable thereof) they raise some persons to be as it were companions and almost equals to themselves, which many times sorteth to inconvenience. The modern languages give unto such persons the name of favourites, or privadoes; as if it were matter of grace, or conversation. But the Roman name attaineth the true use and cause thereof, naming them *participes curarum*;* for it is that which tieth the knot. And we see plainly that this hath been done, not by weak and passionate princes only, but the wisest and most politic that ever reigned; who have oftentimes joined to themselves some of their servants, whom both themselves have called friends, and allowed others likewise to call them in the same manner, using the word which is received between private men.

L. Sylla, when he commanded Rome, raised Pompey (after surnamed the Great) to that height, that Pompey vaunted himself for Sylla's overmatch. For when he had carried the consulship for a friend of his, against the pursuit of Sylla, and that Sylla did a little resent thereat, and began to speak great, Pompey turned upon him again, and in effect bade him be quiet; *for that more men adored the sun rising than the sun setting.* With Julius Cæsar, Decimus Brutus had obtained that interest, as he set him down in his testament for heir in remainder after his nephew. And this was the man that had power with him to draw him forth to his death. For when Cæsar would have discharged the senate,

* "participants of cares."

in regard of some ill presages, and specially a dream of Calpurnia, this man lifted him gently by the arm out of his chair, telling him he hoped he would not dismiss the senate till his wife had dreamt a better dream. And it seemeth his favour was so great, as Antonius, in a letter which is recited *verbatim* in one of Cicero's Philippics, calleth him *venefica,* "witch"; as if he had enchanted Cæsar. Augustus raised Agrippa (though of mean birth) to that height, as, when he consulted with Mæcenas about the marriage of his daughter Julia, Mæcenas took the liberty to tell him, *that he must either marry his daughter to Agrippa, or take away his life; there was no third way, he had made him so great.* With Tiberius Cæsar, Sejanus had ascended to that height, as they two were termed and reckoned as a pair of friends. Tiberius in a letter to him saith, *Hæc pro amicitiâ nostrâ non occultavi*;* and the whole senate dedicated an altar of Friendship, as to a goddess, in respect of the great dearness of friendship between them two. The like or more was between Septimus Severus and Plautianus. For he forced his eldest son to marry the daughter of Plautianus; and would often maintain Plautianus in doing affronts to his son; and did write also in a letter to the senate by these words: *I love the man so well, as I wish he may over-live me.* Now if these princes had been as a Trajan, or a Marcus Aurelius a man might have thought that this had proceeded of an abundant goodness of nature; but being men so wise, for such strength and severity of mind, and so extreme lovers of themselves, as all these were, it proveth most plainly that they found their own felicity (though as great as ever happened to mortal men) but as an half piece, except they might have a friend to make it entire: and yet, which is more, they were princes that had wives, sons, nephews; and yet all these could not supply the comfort of friendship.

It is not to be forgotten, what Comineus observeth of his first master, Duke Charles the Hardy; namely, that he would communicate his secrets with none, and least of all, those secrets which troubled him most. Whereupon he goeth on and saith that towards his latter time *that closeness did impair and a little perish his understanding.* Surely Comineus might have made the same judgment also, if it had pleased him, of his second master, Lewis the Eleventh, whose closeness was indeed his tormentor. The parable of Pythagoras is dark, but true; *Cor ne edito,* "Eat not the heart." Certainly, if a man would give it a hard phrase, those that want friends to open themselves unto are cannibals of their own hearts. But one thing is most admirable (wherewith I will con-

* "Because of our friendship I have not hidden these things," or freely translated, "no secrets among friends."

clude this first fruit of friendship), which is, that this communicating of a man's self to his friend works two contrary effects; for it redoubleth joys, and cutteth griefs in halfs. For there is no man that imparteth his joys to his friend, but he joyeth the more; and no man that imparteth his griefs to his friend, but he grieveth the less. So that it is in truth of operation upon a man's mind, of like virtue as the alchymists use to attribute to their stone for man's body, that it worketh all contrary effects, but still to the good and benefit of nature. But yet, without praying in aid of alchymists, there is a manifest image of this in the ordinary course of nature. For in bodies, union strengtheneth and cherisheth any natural action; and on the other side weakeneth and dulleth any violent impression: and even so is it of minds.

The second fruit of friendship is healthful and sovereign for the understanding, as the first is for the affections. For friendship maketh indeed a fair day in the affections, from storm and tempests; but it maketh daylight in the understanding, out of darkness and confusion of thoughts. Neither is this to be understood only of faithful counsel, which a man receiveth from his friend; but before you come to that, certain it is that whosoever hath his mind fraught with many thoughts, his wits and understanding do clarify and break up, in the communicating and discoursing with another; he tosseth his thoughts more easily; he marshalleth them more orderly; he seeth how they look when they are turned into words; finally, he waxeth wiser than himself; and that more by an hour's discourse than by a day's meditation. It was well said by Themistocles to the king of Persia, *that speech was like cloth of Arras, opened and put abroad, whereby the imagery doth appear in figure; whereas in thoughts they lie but as in packs.* Neither is this second fruit of friendship, in opening the understanding, restrained only to such friends as are able to give a man counsel (they indeed are best); but even without that, a man learneth of himself, and bringeth his own thoughts to light, and whetteth his wits as against a stone, which itself cuts not. In a word, a man were better relate himself to a statua or picture, than to suffer his thoughts to pass in smother.

Add now, to make this second fruit of friendship complete, that other point, which lieth more open and falleth within vulgar observation; which is faithful counsel from a friend. Heraclitus saith well in one of his enigmas, *Dry light is ever the best.* And certain it is that the light that a man receiveth by counsel from another is drier and purer than that which cometh from his own understanding and judgment; which is ever infused and drenched in his affections and customs. So as there is as much difference between the counsel that a friend giveth, and that a man giveth himself, as there is between the counsel of a friend and of a flatterer. For there is no such flatterer as is a man's self; and there is no such remedy against flattery of a man's self as the liberty of a friend. Counsel is of two sorts; the one concerning manners, the other concerning business. For the first, the best preservative to keep the mind in health is the faithful admonition of a friend. The calling of a man's self to a strict account is a medicine, sometime, too piercing and corrosive. Reading good books of morality is a little flat and dead. Observing our faults in others is sometimes improper for our case. But the best receipt (best, I say, to work, and best to take) is the admonition of a friend. It is a strange thing to behold what gross errors and extreme absurdities many (especially of the greater sort) do commit, for want of a friend to tell them of them, to the great damage both of their fame and fortune. For, as St. James saith, they are as men *that look sometimes into a glass, and presently forget their own shape and favour.* As for business, a man may think, if he will, that two eyes see no more than one; or that a gamester seeth always more than a looker-on; or that a man in anger is as wise as he that hath said over the four and twenty letters; or that a musket may be shot off as well upon the arm as upon a rest; and such other fond and high imaginations, to think himself all in all. But when all is done, the help of good counsel is that which setteth business straight. And if any man think that he will take counsel, but it shall be by pieces—asking counsel in one business of one man, and in another business of another man— it is well (that is to say, better perhaps than if he asked none at all); but he runneth two dangers; one, that he shall not be faithfully counselled; for it is a rare thing, except it be from a perfect and entire friend, to have counsel given, but such as shall be bowed and crooked to some ends which he hath that giveth it. The other, that he shall have counsel given, hurtful and unsafe (though with good meaning), and mixed partly of mischief and partly of remedy; even as if you would call a physician that is thought good for the cure of the disease you complain of, but is unacquainted with your body; and therefore may put you in way for a present cure, but overthroweth your health in some other kind; and so cure the disease and kill the patient. But a friend that is wholly acquainted with a man's estate will beware, by furthering any present business, how he dasheth upon other inconvenience. And therefore rest not upon scattered counsels; they will rather distract and mislead than settle and direct.

After these two noble fruits of friendship (peace in the affections, and support of the judgment) followeth the last fruit, which is like the pomegranate, full of many kernels; I mean aid and bearing a part in all actions and occasions. Here the best way to represent to life the manifold use of friendship is to cast and see how many things there are which a man cannot do himself; and then it will appear that it was a sparing speech of the ancients, to say, *that a friend is another himself;* for that a friend is far more than himself. Men have their time, and die many times in desire of some things which they principally take to heart; the bestowing of a child, the finishing of a work, or the like. If a man have a true friend, he may rest almost secure that the care of those things will continue after him. So that a man hath as it were two lives in his desires. A man hath a body, and that body is confined to a place; but where friendship is, all offices of life are as it were granted to him and his deputy. For he may exercise them by his friend. How many things are there which a man cannot, with any face or comeliness, say or do himself! A man can scarce allege his own merits with modesty, much less extol them; a man cannot sometimes brook to supplicate or beg; and a number of the like. But all these things are graceful in a friend's mouth, which are blushing in a man's own. So again, a man's person hath many proper relations which he cannot put off. A man cannot speak to his son but as a father; to his wife but as a husband; to his enemy but upon terms: whereas a friend may speak as the case requires, and not as it sorteth with the person. But to enumerate these things were endless; I have given the rule, where a man cannot fitly play his own part; if he have not a friend, he may quit the stage.

FRANCIS BACON Of Friendship

The critical essay below is one of the great imbedded essays in English. It is taken from Thomas De Quincey's *Alexander Pope.* For those interested in business composition this essay has special value, for it divides all literature into human-interest copy and reason-why copy.

What is it that we mean by *literature?* Probably, and amongst the thoughtless, it is held to include everything that is printed in a book. Little logic is required to disturb *that* definition. The most thoughtless person is easily made aware that in the idea of *literature* one essential element is some relation to the general and common interest of man—so that which applies to a local, or professional, or merely personal interest, even though presenting itself in the shape of a book, will not belong to literature. So far the definition is easily narrowed; and it is as easily expanded. For not only is much that takes a station in books not literature, but, inversely, much that really *is* literature never reaches a station in books. The weekly sermons of Christendom, that vast pulpit literature which acts so extensively upon the popular mind,—to warn, to uphold, to renew, to comfort, to alarm,—does not attain the sanctuary of libraries in the ten-thousandth part of its extent. The drama, again—as, for instance, the finest part of Shakespeare's plays in England, and all leading Athenian plays in the noontide of the Attic stage,—operated as a literature on the public mind, and were (according to the strictest letter of that term), *published* through the audiences that witnessed their representation some time before they were published as things to be read; and they were published in this scenical mode of publication with much more effect than they could have had as books during ages of costly copying or of costly printing.

Books, therefore, do not suggest an idea coextensive and interchangeable with the idea of literature; since much literature, scenic, forensic, or didactic (as from lecturers and public orators), may never come into books, and much that does come into books may connect itself with no literary interest. But a far more important correction, applicable to the common vague idea of literature, is to be sought not so much in a better definition of literature as in a sharper distinction of the two functions which it fulfills. In that great social organ which, collectively, we call literature, there may be distinguished two separate offices that may blend, and often *do* so, but capable, severally, of a severe insulation, and naturally fitted for reciprocal repulsion. There is, first, the literature of *knowledge,* and, secondly, the literature of *power.* The function of the first is—to *teach*; the function of the second is—to *move*: the first is a rudder, the second an oar or a sail. The first speaks to the *mere* discursive understanding; the second speaks ultimately, it may happen, to the higher understanding or reason, but always *through* affections of pleasure and sympathy. Remotely, it may travel toward an object seated in what Lord Bacon calls "dry light"; but proximately it does and must operate—else it ceases to be a literature of *power*—on and through that *humid* light which clothes itself in the mists and glittering *iris* of human passions, desires, and genial emotions. Men have so little reflected on the higher functions of literature as to find it a paradox if one should describe it as a mean or subordinate purpose of books to give information. But this is a paradox only in the sense which makes it honorable to be paradoxical. Whenever we talk in ordinary language of seeking information or gaining knowledge, we understand the words as connected with something of absolute novelty. But it is the grandeur of all truth which *can* occupy a very high place in human interests that it is never absolutely novel to the meanest of minds; it exists eternally by way of germ or latent principle in the lowest as in the highest, needing to be developed, but never to be planted. To be capable of transplantation is the immediate criterion of a truth that ranges on a lower scale.

Besides which, there is a rarer thing than truth; namely, *power*, or deep sympathy with truth. What is the effect, for instance, upon society, of children? By the pity, by the tenderness, and by the peculiar modes of admiration which connect themselves with the helplessness, with the innocence, and with the simplicity of children, not only are the primal affections strengthened and continually renewed, but the qualities which are dearest in the sight of heaven—the frailty, for instance, which appeals to forbearance, the innocence which symbolizes the heavenly, and the simplicity which is most alien from the worldly—are kept up in perpetual remembrance, and their ideals are continually refreshed. A purpose of the same nature is answered by the higher literature; namely, the literature of power. What do you learn from "Paradise Lost"? Nothing at all. What do you learn from a cookery book? Something new, something that you did not know before, in every paragraph. But would you therefore put the wretched cookery book on a higher level of estimation than the divine poem? What you owe to Milton is not any knowledge, of which a million separate items are still but a million of advancing steps on the same earthly level; what you owe is *power*—that is, exercise an expansion to your own latent capacity of sympathy with the infinite, where every pulse and each separate influx is a step upward, a step ascending as upon a Jacob's ladder from earth to mysterious altitudes above the earth. All the steps of knowledge, from first to last, carry you further on the same plane, but could never raise you one foot above your ancient level of earth; whereas the very *first* step in power is a flight—is an ascending movement into another element where earth is forgotten.

Were it not that human sensibilities are ventilated and continually called out into exercise by the great phenomena of infancy, or of real life as it moves through chance and change, or of literature as it recombines these elements in the mimicries of poetry, romance, etc., it is certain that, like any animal power or muscular energy falling into disuse, all such sensibilities would gradually droop and dwindle. It is in relation to these great *moral* capacities of man that the literature of power, as contradistinguished from that of knowledge, lives and has its field of action. It is concerned with what is highest in man; for the Scriptures themselves never condescended to deal by suggestion or coöperation with the mere discursive understanding. When speaking of man in his intellectual capacity, the Scriptures speak not of the understanding, but of "the understanding heart"—making the heart, that is, the great *intuitive* (or nondiscursive) organ, to be the interchangeable formula for man in his highest state of capacity for the infinite. Tragedy, romance, fairy tale, or epopee,* all alike restore to man's mind the ideals of justice, of hope, of truth, of mercy, of retribution, which else (left to the support of daily life in its realities) would languish for want of sufficient illustration.

What is meant, for instance, by "poetic justice"? It does not mean a justice that differs by its object from the ordinary justice of human jurisprudence, for then it must be confessedly a very bad kind of justice; but it means a justice that differs from common forensic justice by the degree in which it attains its object—a justice that is more omnipotent over its own ends, as dealing, not with the refractory elements of earthly life, but with the elements of its own creation and with materials flexible to its own purest preconceptions. It is certain that, were it not for the literature of power, these ideals would often remain amongst us as mere arid notional forms; whereas, by the creative forces of man put forth in literature, they gain a vernal life of restoration and germinate into vital activities. The commonest novel, by moving in alliance with human fears and hopes, with human instincts of wrong and right, sustains and quickens those affections. Calling them into action, it rescues them from torpor. And hence the preëminency over all authors that merely *teach* of the meanest that *moves,* or that teaches, if at all, indirectly *by* moving. The very highest work that has ever existed in the literature of knowledge is but a *provisional* work—a book upon trial and sufferance and *quamdiu bene se gesserit.*† Let its teaching be even partially revised, let it be but expanded,—nay, even let its teaching be but placed in a better order,—and instantly it is superseded. Whereas the feeblest works in the literature of power, surviving at all, survive as finished and unalterable amongst men. For instance, the "Principia" of Sir Isaac Newton was a book *militant* on earth from the first. In all stages of its progress it would have to fight for its existence: first, as regards absolute truth; secondly, when that combat was over, as regards its form or mode of presenting the truth. And as soon as a Laplace,‡ or anybody else, builds higher upon the foundations laid by this book, effectually he throws it out of the sunshine into decay and darkness; by weapons won from this book he superannuates and destroys this book,

---

* Epic poem.
† "during good behavior."
‡ A French mathematician and astronomer (1749–1827).

so that soon the name of Newton remains as a mere *nominis umbra,*[*] but his book, as a living power has transmigrated into other forms. Now, on the contrary, the Iliad, the "Prometheus" of Æschylus, the "Othello" or "King Lear," the "Hamlet" or "Macbeth," and the "Paradise Lost," are not militant, but triumphant forever, as long as the languages exist in which they speak or can be taught to speak. They never *can* transmigrate into new incarnations. To reproduce *these* in new forms or variations, even if in some things they should be improved, would be to plagiarize. A good steam engine is properly superseded by a better. But one lovely pastoral valley is not superseded by another, nor a statue of Praxiteles by a statue of Michael Angelo. These things are separated not by imparity, but by disparity. They are not thought of as unequal under the same standard, but as different in *kind,* and, if otherwise equal, as equal under a different standard. Human works of immortal beauty and works of nature in one respect stand on the same footing; they never absolutely repeat each other, never approach so near as not to differ, and they differ not as better and worse, or simply by more and less: they differ by undecipherable and incommunicable differences, that cannot be caught by mimicries, that cannot be reflected in the mirror of copies, that cannot become ponderable in the scales of vulgar comparison. . . . At this hour, five hundred years since their creation, the tales of Chaucer, never equaled on this earth for their tenderness and for life of picturesqueness, are read familiarly by many in the charming language of their natal day, and by others in the modernizations of Dryden, of Pope, and Wordsworth. At this hour, one thousand eight hundred years since their creation, the pagan tales of Ovid, never equaled on this earth for the gayety of their movement and the capricious graces of their narrative, are read by all Christendom. This man's people and their monuments are dust, but *he* is alive; he has survived them, as he told us that he had it in his commission to do, by a thousand years, "and shall a thousand more."

All the literature of knowledge builds only ground nests, that are swept away by floods or confounded by the plow; but the literature of power builds nests in aërial altitudes of temples sacred from violation, or of forests inaccessible to fraud. *This* is a great prerogative of the *power* literature, and it is a greater which lies in the mode of its influence. The *knowledge* literature, like the fashion of this world, passeth away. An encyclopedia is its abstract, and in this respect it may be taken for its speaking symbol—that before one generation has passed, an encyclopedia is superannuated; for it speaks through the dead memory

* "Shadow of a name."

and unimpassioned understanding, which have not the repose of higher faculties, but are continually enlarging and varying their phylacteries. But all literature properly so called—literature κατ' ἐξοχήν *—for the very reason that it is so much more durable than the literature of knowledge, is (and by the very same proportion it is) more intense and electrically searching in its impressions. The directions in which the tragedy of this planet has trained our human feelings to play, and the combinations into which the poetry of this planet has thrown our human passions of love and hatred, of admiration and contempt, exercise a power for bad or good over human life that cannot be contemplated, when stretching through many generations, without a sentiment allied to awe. And of this let everyone be assured: that he owes to the impassioned books which he has read many a thousand more of emotions than he can consciously trace back to them. Dim by their origination, these emotions yet arise in him and mold him through life like forgotten incidents of his childhood.

Thomas De Quincey Literature of Knowledge and Literature
of Power (from Alexander Pope)

Here is a familiar essay. The author evinces keenness of observation with intimate personal comment. But, again, the essay is not familiar or personal merely. It is, in addition, a kind of lay sermon. Will you, perhaps, shake hands differently hereafter?

Among the first things which we remember noticing in the manners of people were two errors in the custom of shaking hands. Some, we observed, grasped everybody's hand alike,—with an equal fervour of grip. You would have thought that Jenkins was the best friend they had in the world; but on succeeding to the squeeze, though a slight acquaintance, you found it equally flattering to yourself; and on the appearance of somebody else (whose name, it turned out, the operator had forgotten) the crush was no less complimentary:—the face was as earnest and beaming, the "glad to see you" as syllabical and sincere, and the shake as close, as long, and as rejoicing, as if the semi-unknown was a friend come home from the Desarts.

On the other hand, there would be a gentleman now and then as coy of his hand as if he were a prude, or had a whitlow. It was in vain that your pretensions did not go beyond the "civil salute" of the ordinary shake; or that being introduced to him in a friendly manner and expected to shake hands with the rest of the company, you could not in

* "of eminence."

decency omit his. His fingers, half coming out, and half retreating, seemed to think that you were going to do them a mischief; and when you got hold of them, the whole shake was on your side: the other hand did but proudly or pensively acquiesce—there was no knowing which; you had to sustain it, as you might a lady's in handing her to a seat; and it was an equal perplexity to know how to shake or to let it go. The one seemed a violence done to the patient; the other an awkward responsibility brought upon yourself. You did not know, all the evening, whether you were not an object of dislike to the person; till on the party's breaking up, you saw him behave like an equally ill-used gentleman to all who practised the same unthinking civility.

Both these errors, we think, might as well be avoided: but of the two we must say we prefer the former. If it does not look so much like particular sincerity, it looks more like general kindness; and if those two virtues are to be separated (which they assuredly need not be, if considered without spleen) the world can better afford to dispense with an unpleasant truth than a gratuitous humanity. Besides, it is more difficult to make sure of the one, than to practise the other; and kindness itself is the best of all truths. As long as we are sure of that, we are sure of something, and of something pleasant. It is always the best end, if not in every instance the most logical means.

This manual shyness is sometimes attributed to modesty, but never, we suspect, with justice, unless it be that sort of modesty whose fear of committing itself is grounded in pride. Want of address is a better reason, but this particular instance of it would be grounded in the same feeling. It always implies a habit either of pride or mistrust. We have met with two really kind men, who evinced this soreness of hand. Neither of them, perhaps, thought himself inferior to anybody about him, and both had good reason to think highly of themselves; but both had been sanguine men contradicted in their early hopes. There was a plot to meet the hand of one of them with a fish-slice, in order to show him the disadvantage to which he put his friends by that flat mode of salutation; but the conspirator had not the courage to do it. Whether he heard of the intention, we know not; but shortly afterwards he took very kindly to a shake. The other was the only man of a warm set of politicians who remained true to his first love of mankind. He was impatient at the change of his companions and at the folly and inattention of the rest; but though his manner became cold, his consistency still remained warm; and this gave him a right to be as strange as he pleased.

JAMES HENRY LEIGH HUNT *Shaking Hands*
(from *The Indicator*, July 12, 1820)

The abstruse subject of psychology is engagingly presented in the following psychological essay.* This is also a didactic essay, a social essay, an analytical essay, and to a considerable degree an argumentative essay.

"Habit a second nature! Habit is ten times nature," the Duke of Wellington is said to have exclaimed; and the degree to which this is true no one probably can appreciate as well as one who is a veteran soldier himself. The daily drill and the years of discipline end by fashioning a man completely over again, as to most of the possibilities of his conduct.

"There is a story," says Professor Huxley, "which is credible enough, though it may not be true, of a practical joker who, seeing a discharged veteran carrying home his dinner, suddenly called out, 'Attention!' whereupon the man instantly brought his hands down, and lost his mutton and potatoes in the gutter. The drill had been thorough, and its effects had become embodied in the man's nervous structure."

Riderless cavalry horses, at many a battle, have been seen to come together and go through their customary evolutions at the sound of the bugle call. Most domestic beasts seem machines almost pure and simple, undoubtingly, unhesitatingly doing from minute to minute the duties they have been taught, and giving no sign that the possibility of an alternative ever suggests itself to their minds. Men grown old in prison have asked to be readmitted after being once set free. In a railroad accident a menagerie tiger, whose cage had broken open, is said to have emerged, but presently crept back again, as if too much bewildered by his new responsibilities, so that he was without difficulty secured.

Habit is thus the enormous flywheel of society, its most precious conservative agent. It alone is what keeps us all within the bounds of ordinance, and saves the children of fortune from the envious uprisings of the poor. It alone prevents the hardest and most repulsive walks of life from being deserted by those brought up to tread therein. It keeps the fisherman and the deck hand at sea through the winter; it holds the miner in his darkness, and nails the countryman to his log cabin and his lonely farm through all the months of snow; it protects us from invasion by the natives of the desert and the frozen zone. It dooms us all to fight out the battle of life upon the lines of our nurture of our early choice, and to make the best of a pursuit that disagrees, because there

* From William James, *Principles of Psychology*, I. Used by permission of Henry Holt and Company.

is no other for which we are fitted, and it is too late to begin again. It keeps different social strata from mixing. Already at the age of twenty-five you see the professional mannerism settling down on the young commercial traveler, on the young doctor, on the young minister, on the young counselor-at-law. You see the little lines of cleavage running through the character, the tricks of thought, the prejudices, the ways of the "shop" in a word, from which the man can by and by no more escape than his coat-sleeve can suddenly fall into a new set of folds. On the whole, it is best he should not escape. It is well for the world that in most of us, by the age of thirty, the character has set like plaster, and will never soften again.

If the period between twenty and thirty is the critical one in the formation of intellectual and professional habits, the period below twenty is more important still for the fixing of *personal* habits, properly so called, such as vocalization and pronunciation, gesture, motion, and address. Hardly ever is a language learned after twenty spoken without a foreign accent; hardly ever can a youth transferred to the society of his betters unlearn the nasality and other vices of speech bred in him by the associations of his growing years. Hardly ever, indeed, no matter how much money there be in his pocket, can he ever learn to *dress* like a gentleman-born. The merchants offer their wares as eagerly to him as to the veriest "swell," but he simply *cannot* buy the right things. An invisible law, as strong as gravitation, keeps him within his orbit, arrayed this year as he was the last; and how his better-clad acquaintances contrive to get the things they wear will be for him a mystery till his dying day.

The great thing, then, in all education, is to *make our nervous system our ally instead of our enemy.* It is to fund and capitalize our acquisitions, and live at ease upon the interest of the fund. *For this we must make automatic and habitual, as early as possible, as many useful actions as we can,* and guard against the growing into ways that are likely to be disadvantageous to us, as we should guard against the plague. The more of the details of our daily life we can hand over to the effortless custody of automatism, the more our higher powers of mind will be set free for their own proper work. There is no more miserable human being than one in whom nothing is habitual but indecision, and for whom the lighting of every cigar, the drinking of every cup, the time of rising and going to bed every day, and the beginning of every bit of work, are subjects of express volitional deliberation. Full half the time of such a man goes to the deciding, or regretting, of matters which ought to be so ingrained in him as practically not to exist for his consciousness at all. If there be such daily duties not yet ingrained in any one of my readers, let him begin this very hour to set the matter right.

In Professor Bain's chapter on "The Moral Habits," there are some admirable practical remarks laid down. Two great maxims emerge from his treatment. The first is that in the acquisition of a new habit, or the leaving off of an old one, we must take care to *launch ourselves with as strong and decided an initiative as possible.* Accumulate all the possible circumstances which shall reënforce the right motives; put yourself assiduously in conditions that encourage the new way; make engagements incompatible with the old; take a public pledge, if the case allows; in short, envelop your resolution with every aid you know. This will give your new beginning such a momentum that the temptation to break down will not occur as soon as it otherwise might; and every day during which a breakdown is postponed adds to the chances of its not occurring at all.

The second maxim is: *Never suffer an exception to occur till the new habit is securely rooted in your life.* Each lapse is like the letting fall of a ball of string which one is carefully winding up; a single slip undoes more than a great many turns will wind again. *Continuity* of training is the great means of making the nervous system act infallibly right. As Professor Bain says:

> The peculiarity of the moral habits, contradistinguishing them from the intellectual acquisitions, is the presence of two hostile powers, one to be gradually raised into the ascendant over the other. It is necessary, above all things, in such a situation, never to lose a battle. Every gain on the wrong side undoes the effect of many conquests on the right. The essential precaution, therefore, is so to regulate the two opposing powers that the one may have a series of uninterrupted successes, until repetition has fortified it to such a degree as to enable it to cope with the opposition, under any circumstances. This is the theoretically best career of mental progress.

The need of securing success at the *outset* is imperative. Failure at first is apt to damp the energy of all future attempts, whereas past experiences of success nerve one to future vigor. Goethe says to a man who consulted him about an enterprise but mistrusted his own powers: "Ach! you need only blow on your hands!" And the remark illustrates the effect on Goethe's spirits of his own habitually successful career.

The question of "tapering off," in abandoning such habits as drink and opium indulgence, comes in here, and is a question about which experts differ within certain limits, and in regard to what may be best for an individual case. In the main, however, all expert opinion would agree that abrupt acquisition of the new habit is the best way, *if there be a real possibility of carrying it out.* We must be careful not to give the will so stiff a task as to insure its defeat at the very outset; but, *provided one can stand it,* a sharp period of suffering, and then a free time, is the best thing to aim at, whether in giving up a habit like that of opium, or in simply changing one's hours of rising or of work. It is surprising how soon a desire will die of inanition if it be *never* fed.

> One must first learn, unmoved, looking neither to the right nor left, to walk firmly on the strait and narrow path, before one can begin "to make oneself over again." He who every day makes a fresh resolve is like one who, arriving at the edge of the ditch he is to leap, forever stops and returns for a fresh run. Without *unbroken* advance there is no such thing as *accumulation* of the ethical forces possible, and to make this possible, and to exercise us and habituate us in it, is the sovereign blessing of regular work.*

A third maxim may be added to the preceding pair: *Seize the very first possible opportunity to act on every resolution you make, and on every emotional prompting you may experience in the direction of the habits you aspire to gain.* It is not in the moment of their forming, but in the moment of their producing *motor effects,* that resolves and aspirations communicate the new "set" to the brain. As the author last quoted remarks:

> The actual presence of the practical opportunity alone furnishes the fulcrum upon which the lever can rest, by means of which the moral will may multiply its strength, and raise itself aloft. He who has no solid ground to press against will never get beyond the stage of empty gesture-making.

No matter how full a reservoir of *maxims* one may possess, and no matter how good one's *sentiments* may be, if one have not taken advantage of every concrete opportunity to *act,* one's character may remain entirely unaffected for the better. With mere good intentions, hell is proverbially paved. And this is an obvious consequence of the principles we have laid down. A "character," as J. S. Mill says, "is a completely fashioned will"; and a will, in the sense in which he means it, is an aggregate of tendencies to act in a firm and prompt and definite way upon all the principal emergencies of life. A tendency to act only be-

* J. Bahnsen, *Beiträge zur Charakterologie* (1867), I, 209.

comes effectively ingrained in us in proportion to the uninterrupted frequency with which the actions actually occur, and the brain "grows" to their use. When a resolve or a fine glow of feeling is allowed to evaporate without bearing practical fruit it is worse than a chance lost; it works so as positively to hinder future resolutions and emotions from taking the normal path of discharge. There is no more contemptible type of human character than that of the nerveless sentimentalist and dreamer, who spends his life in a weltering sea of sensibility and emotion, but who never does a manly concrete deed. Rousseau, inflaming all the mothers of France, by his eloquence, to follow Nature and nurse their babies themselves, while he sends his own children to the foundling hospital, is the classical example of what I mean. But every one of us in his measure, whenever, after glowing for an abstractly formulated Good, he practically ignores some actual case, among the squalid "other particulars" of which that same Good lurks disguised, treads straight on Rousseau's path. All Goods are disguised by the vulgarity of their concomitants, in this workaday world; but woe to him who can only recognize them when he thinks them in their pure and abstract form! The habit of excessive novel-reading and theater-going will produce true monsters in this line. The weeping of the Russian lady over the fictitious personages in the play, while her coachman is freezing to death on his seat outside, is the sort of thing that everywhere happens on a less glaring scale. Even the habit of excessive indulgence in music, for those who are neither performers themselves nor musically gifted enough to take it in a purely intellectual way, has probably a relaxing effect upon the character. One becomes filled with emotions which habitually pass without prompting to any deed, and so the inertly sentimental condition is kept up. The remedy would be never to suffer oneself to have an emotion at a concert without expressing it afterward in *some* active way. Let the expression be the least thing in the world—speaking genially to one's grandmother, or giving up one's seat in a horse car, if nothing more heroic offers—but let it not fail to take place.

These latter cases make us aware that it is not simply *particular lines* of discharge, but also *general forms* of discharge, that seem to be grooved out by habit in the brain. Just as, if we let our emotions evaporate, they get into a way of evaporating; so there is reason to suppose that if we often flinch from making an effort, before we know it the effort-making capacity will be gone; and that, if we suffer the wandering of our attention, presently it will wander all the time. Attention and effort are, as we shall see later, but two names for the same psychic fact. To what brain-processes they correspond we do not know. The strongest reason for believing that they do depend on brain-processes at all, and are not pure acts of the spirit, is just this fact, that they seem in some degree subject to the law of habit, which is a material law. As a final practical maxim, relative to these habits of the will, we may, then, offer something like this: *Keep the faculty of effort alive in you by a little gratuitous exercise every day.* That is, be systematically ascetic or heroic in little unnecessary points, do every day or two something for no other reason than that you would rather not do it, so that when the hour of dire need draws nigh, it may find you not unnerved and untrained to stand the test. Asceticism of this sort is like the insurance which a man pays on his house and goods. The tax does him no good at the time, and possibly may never bring him a return. But if the fire *does* come, his having paid it will be his salvation from ruin. So with the man who has daily inured himself to habits of concentrated attention, energetic volition, and self-denial in unnecessary things. He will stand like a tower when everything rocks around him, and when his softer fellow-mortals are winnowed like chaff in the blast.

The physiological study of mental conditions is thus the most powerful ally of hortatory ethics. The hell to be endured hereafter, of which theology tells, is no worse than the hell we make for ourselves in this world by habitually fashioning our characters in the wrong way. Could the young but realize how soon they will become mere walking bundles of habits, they would give more heed to their conduct while in the plastic state. We are spinning our own fates, good or evil, and never to be undone. Every smallest stroke of virtue or of vice leaves its never-so-little scar. The drunken Rip Van Winkle, in Jefferson's play, excuses himself for every fresh dereliction by saying, "I won't count this time!" Well, he may not count it, and a kind Heaven may not count it; but it is being counted none the less. Down among his nerve cells and fibers the molecules are counting it, registering and storing it up to be used against him when the next temptation comes. Nothing we ever do is, in strict scientific literalness, wiped out. Of course this has its good side as well as its bad one. As we become permanent drunkards by so many separate drinks, so we become saints in the moral, and authorities and experts in the practical and scientific spheres, by so many separate acts and hours of work. Let no youth have any anxiety about the upshot of his education, whatever the line of it may be. If he keep faithfully busy each hour of the working day, he may safely leave the final result to itself. He can with perfect certainty count on waking up some fine morning, to find himself one of the competent ones of his generation, in whatever pursuit he may have singled out. Silently, between all the details of his business, the *power of judging* in all that class of matter will have built itself up within him as a possession that will never pass away. Young people should know this truth in advance. The ignorance of it has probably engendered more discouragement and faint-heartedness in youths embarking on arduous careers than all other causes put together.

WILLIAM JAMES *The Importance of Habit*

For unusual point of view and elfish quality of fancy, Gilbert K. Chesterton has been excelled by none and equaled by few in essay writing. No better example of the casual and familiar essay than the following * is to be found in English. Its engaging playfulness with an idea and its stimulating inventiveness of presentation make it a reading experience indeed.

The middle classes of modern England are quite fanatically fond of washing; and are often enthusiastic for teetotalism. I cannot therefore comprehend why it is that they exhibit a mysterious dislike of rain. Rain, that inspiring and delightful thing, surely combines the qualities of these two ideals with quite a curious perfection. Our philanthropists are eager to establish public baths everywhere. Rain surely is a public bath; it might almost be called mixed bathing. The appearance of persons coming fresh from this great natural lustration is not perhaps polished or dignified; but for the matter of that, few people are dignified when coming out of a bath. But the scheme of rain in itself is one of an enormous purification. It realizes the dream of some insane hygienist: it scrubs the sky. Its giant brooms and mops seem to reach the starry rafters and starless corners of the cosmos; it is a cosmic spring-cleaning.

If the Englishman is really fond of cold baths, he ought not to grumble at the English climate for being a cold bath. In these days we are constantly told that we should leave our little special possessions and join in the enjoyment of common social institutions and a common social machinery. I offer the rain as a thoroughly Socialistic institution. It disregards that degraded delicacy which has hitherto led each gentleman to take his shower-bath in private. It is a better shower-bath, because it is public and communal; and, best of all, because somebody else pulls the string.

. . . .

As for the fascination of rain for the water drinker, it is a fact the neglect of which I simply cannot comprehend. The enthusiastic water

* From G. K. Chesterton, *A Miscellany of Men.* Used by permission of the publishers, Dodd, Mead, and Company, Inc.

drinker must regard a rainstorm as a sort of universal banquet and debauch of his own favourite beverage. Think of the imaginative intoxication of the wine drinker if the crimson clouds sent down claret or the golden clouds hock. Paint upon primitive darkness some such scenes of apocalypse, towering and gorgeous skyscapes in which champagne falls like fire from heaven or the dark skies grow purple and tawny with the terrible colours of port. All this must the wild abstainer feel, as he rolls in the long soaking grass, kicks his ecstatic heels to heaven, and listens to the roaring rain. It is he, the water drinker, who ought to be the true bacchanal of the forests; for all the forests are drinking water. Moreover, the forests are apparently enjoying it: the trees rave and reel to and fro like drunken giants; they clash boughs as revellers clash cups; they roar undying thirst and howl the health of the world.

All around me as I write is a noise of Nature drinking; and Nature makes a noise when she is drinking, being by no means refined. If I count it Christian mercy to give a cup of cold water to a sufferer, shall I complain of these multitudinous cups of cold water handed round to all living things; a cup of water for every shrub; a cup of water for every weed? I would be ashamed to grumble at it. As Sir Philip Sidney said, their need is greater than mine—especially for water.

.　　　.　　　.　　　.　　　.　　　.　　　.

There is a wild garment that still carries nobly the name of a wild Highland clan: a clan come from those hills where rain is not so much an incident as an atmosphere. Surely every man of imagination must feel a tempestuous flame of Celtic romance spring up within him whenever he puts on a mackintosh. I could never reconcile myself to carrying an umbrella; it is a pompous Eastern business, carried over the heads of despots in the dry, hot lands. Shut up, an umbrella is an unmanageable walking-stick; open, it is an inadequate tent. For my part, I have no taste for pretending to be a walking pavilion; I think nothing of my hat, and precious little of my head. If I am to be protected against wet, it must be by some closer and more careless protection, something that I can forget altogether. It might be a Highland plaid. It might be that yet more Highland thing, a mackintosh.

And there is really something in the mackintosh of the military qualities of the Highlander. The proper cheap mackintosh has a blue and white sheen as of steel or iron; it gleams like armour. I like to think of it as the uniform of that ancient clan in some of its old and misty raids. I like to think of all the Macintoshes, in their mackintoshes, descending on some doomed Lowland village, their wet waterproofs flashing in the sun or moon. For indeed this is one of the real beauties of rainy weather, that while the amount of original and direct light is commonly lessened, the number of things that reflect light is unquestionably increased. There is less sunshine; but there are more shiny things; such beautifully shiny things as pools and puddles and mackintoshes. It is like moving in a world of mirrors.

. . . .

And indeed this is the last and not the least gracious of the casual works of magic wrought by rain: that while it decreases light, yet it doubles it. If it dims the sky, it brightens the earth. It gives the roads (to the sympathetic eye) something of the beauty of Venice. Shallow lakes of water reiterate every detail of earth and sky; we dwell in a double universe. Sometimes walking upon bare and lustrous pavements, wet under numerous lamps, a man seems a black blot on all that golden looking-glass, and could fancy he was flying in a yellow sky. But wherever trees and towns hang head downwards in a pigmy puddle, the sense of Celestial topsy-turvydom is the same. This bright, wet, dazzling confusion of shape and shadow, of reality and reflection, will appeal strongly to any one with the transcendental instinct about this dreamy and dual life of ours. It will always give a man the strange sense of looking down at the skies.
                            GILBERT K. CHESTERTON *The Romantic in the Rain*

The simplest, most obvious subjects are not infrequently the most difficult to write about. Who can explain money, really? The wisest of our economists have about concluded, haven't they, that nobody knows anything about it. The expository periodical essay below * should be read with this comment in mind. Put yourself in the author's place, and say whether you could write on such an elusive yet commonplace subject and make it one-tenth as readable and logical and provocative.

There is sound prejudice among right-minded people against admitting a love of money. It is supposed to be the trait of the wicked miser, the dishonest banker, the grasping landlord and the villain in the detective story. We ought to be above such characteristics (or at least above such admissions!), according to the best opinion now going. We should turn our minds to higher and better things.

Maybe so. But in answer to the question, "What interests you most

* Reprinted by special permission of the *Cosmopolitan Magazine* and of the author.

in the world?" I should say, without a doubt, money. Not, perhaps, money as a theoretical science—although that, too, is fascinating—but the use of money as an instrument of life, money as a practical daily problem. What will you do for money? What will you not do for money? How much money do you think you need? Where is it going to come from, anyhow? In short—in the slang phrase—what are you going to use for money?

Rare persons scattered along the course of history have been able to ignore these questions. Diogenes was one; he lived in a tub. But if you don't happen to like tubs you are obliged to face the questions, whether you are a businessman or a schoolteacher, a politician or a chorus girl. You may be bored by the necessity, but face it you must.

What, exactly, would you do for money? Will you steal? Lie? Cheat at cards? Practically everybody would make an indignant reply to such queries, and yet men of high repute cheat the tax collector, and women of unimpeachable virtue tell lies and defraud the customs inspectors at the port of New York.

Obviously the question is not simple. It involves the drawing of a line—which, as is well known, is the most difficult of all operations to the human intellect.

They say that open confession is good for the soul, and I may therefore make no bones about the surprising fact that this article is written for money. A very large part of any writer's output is written for money, in the sense that he hopes to make some money out of it sometime. He usually has other purposes as well, primarily or in second place: that is, he wants to do a good job, to say something clearly, to convince or move other people, and in rare cases even to create a work of art. But he does all this in print (instead of by conversation or in some simpler way) because print is the way fate and his own nature have pointed out for him to use in making a living.

Once you introduce that purpose—to make a living—you have brought up a host of questions, none of which will be answered in exactly the same way by more than one person.

The professional writer I know best is possibly myself; and it is curious indeed to observe where the money-making line is drawn in my case. I write this article for money because I was asked a question, and if I can get paid for answering a question in my own way (that is, by writing) I am ready and anxious to do so. But observe: a sum of money many times as large would fail (and actually has failed) to make me either deliver lectures or speak over the radio. This is odd, because writers of much greater accomplishment than I constantly do both.

The writer's craft may seem to be too specialized to afford material for generalization, and yet I cannot help thinking that many problems of exactly the same nature arise in the daily life of the butcher, the baker, the candlestick-maker and every other person who earns money. The drawing of that mysterious line is a wondrous moral or psychological spectacle. Criminals are said to be great line-drawers, and a burglar would scorn to pick a pocket, as a confidence trickster would disdain to kidnap a baby.

Money, therefore, exercises its baleful power upon the individual only up to a certain point, after which other considerations (an idea or an ideal, or perhaps simple vanity and pigheadedness) prevail over it. You might say that such ideas or ideals, whatever they may be, are therefore in themselves more interesting than money. True, if you take them one by one. That is, if you are in love, obviously love is more interesting than money; if you really want to paint a beautiful picture you will do it even if it brings no reward. But taken all together, these desires, passions, dreams and delights of the human spirit represent the triumphs of culture and leisure; they are results, not causes. Your course isn't to supplant love, art, life itself, by an interest in money, but to arrange your fundamental interest in money (that is, in the continuance and enjoyment of life, the minimum purposes of all human beings) so that the other things can become possible.

A world without money may some day exist. When you consider how all of us have had to alter our notions about the nature and use of money since 1919, anything seems possible. Obviously, nobody knew exactly what a currency was before about 1920; not many people know even today.

The wise and great in all countries have made fools of themselves whenever they chose to utter on the subject. We have only to remember Lord Snowden's speech on the unshakability of the pound sterling in 1931, or some of the speeches made about the dollar since then, to perceive that even experts in these matters talk straight through their hats when they treat money as a fixed or absolute thing.

It is an instrument; it is a convenience; and it is quite possible that some day the instrument will so change its character as to be unrecognizable. But since this instrument does play such a tremendous part in the world we live in, we do well to think about it sensibly, to treat it as a subject of prime interest instead of as a boring necessity. And if you have ever had to do without this useful instrument for long stretches of time, as I have, I believe you will at least tend to agree with me.

VINCENT SHEEAN *Money*

It would be difficult to conceive of a more excellent journalistic essay than this one on current political and economic conditions.* Timed as it is to a special world situation—journalistic writing must apply primarily to the ever-fleeting present—it nevertheless enunciates a political philosophy that yields an enduring quality. Note, among other elements, the perfect organization of material.

We live in a time when great masses of civilized men have either voluntarily surrendered their personal liberties or at least have submitted without serious protest or resistance to the destruction of their liberties. It is important that we should understand the causes. This is not too difficult. For while a library of books might profitably be written on the subject, one fundamental aspect of the question at least is clear enough to any one who passes back and forth between the totalitarian and the free nations of Europe.

It is that the peoples who have lost their civil rights had previously lost or had never obtained the means of economic independence for individuals, families and local communities. It is very clear, I think, that the masses who have fallen under the spell of demagogic dictators and their terroristic bands were recruited from individuals who had no property, no savings, and either no job at all or a job which they could not feel sure of holding. They were in the exact sense of the term proletarians even if they happened to be earning fairly high salaries at the moment. For they had no reserves to fall back upon. They could not afford to lose their jobs. They could not afford, therefore, to speak their minds or to take any risks, to be in any real sense of the word individual citizens. They had to be servile or they starved. Wherever a dictatorship has been set up in Europe, the mass of individuals had already become so insecure that they no longer dared to exercise the legal liberties that the demagogue was attacking.

. . . .

To have economic independence a man must be in a position to leave one job and go to another; he must have enough savings of some kind to exist for a considerable time without accepting the first job offered. Thus the peasant, for all his poverty and the exploitation which he suffers, is relative to his own needs still the freest man in central Europe. The fact that he can exist by his own labor on his own piece of land gives him an independence which every dictatorial regime, except the Russian perhaps, has been forced to respect.

* Used by permission of the *New York Herald Tribune, Inc.*

But the industrial worker who has a choice between working in one factory and not working at all, the white collar intellectuals who compete savagely for the relatively few private positions and for posts in the bureaucracy—these are the people who live too precariously to exercise their liberties or to defend them. They have no savings. They have only their labor to sell, and there are very few buyers of their labor. Therefore, they have only the choice of truckling to the powerful or of perishing heroically but miserably. Men like these, having none of the substance of liberty themselves, have scant respect for any law or any form of civil rights.

．　　．　　．　　．　　．　　．　　．

The reason why the love of liberty, as we understand it in America, is so strong in France is undoubtedly, it seems to me, that France still is a country where the great mass of the people have their own farms, their own shops, their own little business enterprises and some savings for a rainy day and an emergency. This is the solid foundation of French liberty. The French electorate, except perhaps in a few industrial centers, is not a frightened crowd but a collection of independent families, stubbornly attached to their farms, shops, homes and bank accounts.

They are not easy to terrorize because they have reserves for their independence. They have resistance to mass propaganda because they have so much independence as individuals. And that is why they have such a dread of inflation, which would destroy their individual savings, and such a dislike of monopoly and the concentrating of big business, which would make them the hirelings of a single master.

．　　．　　．　　．　　．　　．　　．

The more I see of Europe the more deeply convinced do I become that the preservation of freedom in America, or anywhere else, depends upon maintaining and restoring for the great majority of individuals the economic means to remain independent individuals. The greatest evil of the modern world is the reduction of the people to a proletarian level by destroying their savings, by depriving them of private property, by making them the helpless employees of a private monopoly or of government monopoly. At that point they are no longer citizens. They are a mob. For when the people lose this sense of their separate and individual security, they cease to be individuals. They are absorbed into a mass. Their liberties are already lost and they are a frightened crowd ready for a master.

Though the actual measures to be taken are debatable, the objective for a free government is, I think, clear. It should use its authority to enable the independent farmer, the small and moderate sized enterprise, the small saver, to survive. It should use its authority to see that large enterprise is no larger than technology requires, depriving big business of corporate privileges and other forms of legal and economic advantage which make it bigger than on economic grounds it needs to be. A resolute democracy should favor the dispersion of industry rather than its concentration, and it should favor the rise in as many communities as possible of different kinds of enterprise rather than a high degree of specialization on some one product.

For unless the means of independence are widely distributed among the people themselves, no real resistance is possible to the advance of tyranny. The experience of Europe shows clearly that when a nation becomes proletarian, the result is not, as the communists taught, a dictatorship by the proletariat but a dictatorship over the proletariat.

WALTER LIPPMANN *How Liberty Is Lost*

The following * is a quaint, humorous, "personal" essay in which the human element and the narrative method are skilfully combined to make a delightful and engaging "character" sketch. The Society for Prevention of Cruelty to Animals might well call it a propaganda essay.

The impressive thing about Banbury—he was seldom called by his full name except in horse-show programmes—was that, like certain well-known baseball pitchers, he was an iron man. Richard Sheahan brought him over from Ireland in '22 or '23, and, at the first sight of him, you knew you had to buy him.

He was an Irish cob, gray, almost white, standing fifteen-two or thereabouts, with a bright brown eye, a wide forehead backed up with brains, and hindquarters to jump over a house. He was close-coupled and strong, a great deal of horse for his cubic content. And there was something endearing about this brave little creature, half pony, half horse, which made everyone on the place regard him with a peculiar affection. Every groom's face would break out in a smile when I asked, "How's Banbury to-day? He hit that wall in Shirley terribly hard." "Oh, sure, he's as fine as can be. It was the stones in the wall that got hurt."

He was ridden, almost exclusively, by my huntsman, Fred Armstrong, and for long years it was a race for Martha Doyle to keep

* From *Martha Doyle and Other Sporting Memories,* by permission of The Derrydale Press, New York.

ahead of the pair of them, Fred pretending to pull and haul and swear at the little horse, and Banbury going all out like a gray locomotive. Sometimes I was annoyed and said, "Fred, I'm hunting the hounds and you're whipping in. I don't want you to get in front of me." He would say, "It's that Banbury; he pulls till it'd break your back." "All right," I would answer, "there's a nice one-eyed mare in the stable, and Gayley, who goes very well except when she goes sideways. You can ride either of them next Wednesday and rest your back." "Oh no, sir. I'll put a curb on Banbury; I'd rather ride him."

Banbury loved hounds and was never really happy unless he was with them. He was an excellent hunter, but the sloppiest jumper, the most incorrigibly knock-'em-down horse at any obstacle, I have ever known. Always he kept his feet and went on happily, no matter what appalling wall or unbreakable post and rail he had demolished. He had iron legs. Sometimes we would go back over the ground and gaze with awe at the great boulders which Banbury had squandered with his knees. And never a mark on them, never a day when he was sick or sorry.

This was an interesting phenomenon, which defied all the maxims in the book, but it was a habit which did not make for a confident ride and it did pile up a lot of damages and complaints from farmers. Whenever—no, that's not fair—but often, when Banbury crossed a pasture, the cattle seemed to know that the way would be cleared to greener meadows, and we would come back to find them standing, like Ruth, "amid the alien corn." I don't want to give the wrong impression—Banbury could and did jump beautifully again and again. It was only when he was bored or when he yielded to a spirit of mischief that he became really destructive. He was essentially a humorist with iron legs, but most of the time he kept his exuberance under control.

Of course we tried all the tricks, collected schooling over low jumps, gradually raised, throwing a rail at his front legs as he rose—everything we knew. Bless you, what did a rail more or less matter to Banbury Cross? He must have chuckled to himself as he watched our absurd efforts to educate him.

So at last the better minds of the household and stable and kennels went into a huddle and evolved a hellish plot which would teach Banbury the salutary lesson that he *must,* he MUST pick up those forelegs. Down below the kennels we constructed an innocent-looking brush jump about four feet four in height. At the very top, cunningly concealed behind sprigs of pine and fir, was a large telegraph pole, securely fastened at both ends, immovable as the Rock of Gibraltar. A suicidal young man in the stable volunteered to ride Banbury for a fall, and on the appointed day we all gathered at some distance from the jump to await developments.

Now Banbury was not afraid of any obstacle in the world; in fact I think it was largely to show his contempt for barriers that he knocked them all down. I would say that he rated a brush jump as beneath his contempt; a sheep hurdle was made of matchsticks for him; a stout post and rails was a challenge; stone walls he simply pushed over with a science all his own. He respected big "chicken coops," though on several occasions he turned them over, thus effectually blocking the way to any followers. So, when he saw himself confronted with one of those really laughable brush jumps, a gleam came in his eye, he pawed the ground, shouted "Ha, ha!" among the captains.

The suicide put him at it, and Banbury, ears forward as if he were the most careful horse in the world, cantered at the jump and as usual tried to brush through the top two feet of it. The suicide shook loose from his stirrups and, with his hands on the horse's neck, flung himself cleverly to one side and landed on his feet, quite unhurt. Not so Banbury. As he breasted the telegraph pole, an expression of astonishment was clearly discernible on his face. Then in a slow, majestic arc, as though tied by the forelegs to the jump, he turned a complete somersault, landing flat on his back.

He lay there for a while, feebly kicking, then scrambled to his feet, shaking his head as though he were saying, "There is something wrong, something very wrong, with this picture." He wandered around, going nowhere, still shaking his head and wondering what had hit him. Suddenly my wife whistled to him and called out, "Come here, Banbury!" He looked up, saw her, trotted over to her, and put his head on her shoulder, seeking comfort in his bewilderment.

We had been laughing uproariously at the whole performance, but when we saw poor Banbury, like a hurt child, go to those understanding arms, and saw my wife pet him and brush the earth and leaves from his face and ears, none of us wanted to laugh any more. I heard a groom behind me say, in a hushed voice, " 'E's like a 'uman being, 'e is!"

For quite a while this lesson tempered the destructive tendencies of the little horse, and, whenever he forgot to remember, he would be taken down and merely shown the brush *cum* telegraph pole jump below the kennels. Then he would wheel and gallop as fast as he could go to the stable and clamor to get into his familiar box with its rustling straw. For the next week or two he would clear everything by a foot or more.

One other incident will illustrate the spirit and—to me—the charm of the horse whom everybody loved. It seemed a waste of energy that so strong and willing an animal should do no useful work during the summer. So he was broken, quite easily, to harness and taught to pull a rake during the haying season. I think he enjoyed it thoroughly. The rattle of the rake behind him was music in his ears. He marched proudly, turning sharply, and stopped short when told to. It was like a little boy playing at being a soldier.

The old country road to Shirley comes past our foxhound kennels and after a while reaches the stable paddock and the stable, then swings to the right past apple orchards, and so on. For some reason, on this summer morning, Banbury's work had been temporarily halted, and, still harnessed to his hayrake, he was tied to an apple tree, behind the stable and away from the paddock. Fred Armstrong, as it happened, was walking the hounds along the Shirley road for morning exercise. In his white kennel coat he strode along, whistling that little birdlike call so characteristic of him and calling from time to time, "Come along, Coop! Come along, Coop! Gently, Challenger! Have a care, there, Chorister." His littlest son, Jackie, no bigger than a pint of milk, whipped in from the rear, rating on the laggards and cracking a portentous whip. It was an idyllic summer scene.

But Banbury heard the whistle and the voice and perhaps the rustle of hounds passing on the soft road. At any rate, he lifted his head and whinnied. Then, deciding that he would do no more servile labor on that day, he broke his halter and, with the rake behind him, took the shortest road to his beloved hounds. This involved jumping into the paddock and out again into the road. At the point which he chose for the "in," the paddock fence was at least six feet high. Nothing daunted, Banbury took off, hayrake and all, crashed the two upper rails, and, as his harness parted with pistol-shot noises and the hayrake subsided with a death rattle, picked himself off the ground, smiling broadly, crossed the paddock, and jumped through a five-foot fence into the Shirley road. In an instant he was with hounds, sniffing at Trinket, snuffling at Warrior, playfully kicking—very slowly—at old Rambler, and ignoring the young entry as beneath his notice. He trotted carefully through the pack till he caught up with Fred, and then walked along beside him in his rightful place, proud as a peacock and snorting with glee.

He could, on occasion, when his virtuosity as a destroyer was not in question, perform extraordinary feats. Once I laid out a horse-show ring surrounded, until the rail could be built, by one strand of stout manila rope about four feet high. The jumps were to be more or less permanent, and I wanted to be sure that they were properly spaced, so I asked one of the grooms, named Malcolm, to bring a horse down and try them out. He arrived, to my astonishment, mounted on Banbury Cross. "Farewell rewards and fences!" I said to myself. I explained to him that he was to take the brush jump first, then the stone wall with the rider, next a post and rails, followed by a white gate. Then he was expected to turn down the middle of the ring for an in-and-out of post and rails and repeat the process.

Malcolm nodded and trotted to the end of the ring. As always, Banbury went at his jump like Heatherbloom or Great Heart, but when he hit the brush jump there was a positive explosion of evergreens. As the cloud of pine, spruce, and fir slowly settled, you expected to see an army of bare-legged Scots appear carrying Birnam Wood to Dunsinane. My heart bled for the stone wall—so carefully and painfully constructed. When Banbury had finished his work, it looked like a village in the war zone after three years' intensive bombardment. The post-and-rails jump was not solid, so it merely disintegrated without great damage, but Banbury smote the gate, hip and thigh, and highly expensive carpenters were later called in to construct a new one.

Having destroyed four jumps, Banbury decided to go home and, taking a firm hold, began to run for the corner of the ring. (If I seem to square a circle too flippantly, it is because I don't know the proper geometrical expression for this contradiction in terms.) As I said above, there was one strand of rope, four feet high, pinch-hitting for the rail around the ring. As they passed me, I murmured, "Good-bye, Malcolm. You were a good boy." Not at all. Banbury cleared that almost invisible death trap with a foot to spare and disappeared into the woods beyond. When Malcolm brought him back some time later, the rider was pale and shaken, but Banbury was quivering with happiness. I doubt if he had ever had more fun in his life.

"That was fine, Malcolm," I said. "You proved to me that the intervals between jumps were exactly right. But I think in the show we ought to have a special event—'Rope Skipping for Hunters'—or something like that. You can ride Banbury Cross and Fred can ride the blind mare and—"

"Excuse me, sir!" said Malcolm. "My grandmother is very ill and I promised I'd go down to Medford to see her the day of the show."

Nowadays our stable is full up with some twenty horses; most of them are good, some of them are better than others, and a few are relics whom we cannot bear to destroy. They whinny when they hear us coming, bearing sugar; they paw in their stalls and glare ferociously. They caper and prance in the paddocks; and they and we know that they are touched in the wind or bowed, in some way incurably afflicted. But among them all there is, to me, not one horse of the color and character and quality of Waynefleet or Martha Doyle or Banbury Cross. "All, all are gone, the old familiar faces"—but I cannot and never could forget them. And of them all no image shines more brightly in my memory than that of the little gray-white horse with the iron legs and the sense of humor.

RICHARD ELY DANIELSON Banbury Cross

Scientific and technical subjects offer an ever-increasing field of opportunity for those writers who can make them interesting to the general reader and at the same time give them value for the specialist. This periodical essay * achieves both ends easily, and at the same time educates by means of lucid exposition that really constitutes argument.

Suppose a 1918 automobile selling for $1,500 had been sealed so tightly in a glass case as to be entirely unaffected by the march of time. The car is still like new. Nothing has deteriorated. There's not a particle of rust on it, not even a speck of dust.

How much would you offer today for that $1,500 car of twenty years ago if it were in the same condition as when it rolled off the assembly line? Would you bid $100? You would probably get it if you did because most people wouldn't accept it as a gift.

And yet, nothing has happened to this theoretical car to alter its value. It's still brand new. The car has been made worthless, not by what has happened to it, but by what has happened to automobiles since it was built. That 1918 car was built of makeshift materials, many of them not adapted to the purposes for which they were used. Today's car is constructed of tailor-made materials, new products and processes developed largely by chemical research.

And as the magic hand of the chemist has touched one part of the car after another, each part in turn has been made not only better but less costly. As a result, better cars are made today for less money—so much better and for so much less that most people wouldn't accept a brand new 1918 model as a gift!

Consider the finish of that 1918 job—some fifteen or twenty coats of paint and varnish laboriously applied and slowly dried over a period of several weeks. When the paint faded and cracked—and it always did—repainting cost from $75 to $100 and your car was in the paint

* Used by permission of *Popular Mechanics Magazine.*

shop two or three weeks. Even as late as 1922, body finishing required
a week and a half. Enamel had to be baked on fenders by a slow, expensive process. And the enamel had to be black. In one factory
$20,000,000 worth of cars were tied up at one time awaiting various
stages of body finishing. That delayed deliveries and cost money. The
automobile industry clamored for a finish which could be applied in
hours instead of days and weeks, one which would not require high
drying temperatures and which would be applicable to all colors and
would last the lifetime of the car.

And chemistry gave the car industry just that. Research men of
E. I. du Pont de Nemours and Company knew toy manufacturers were
using a colorful lacquer but many coats of it would be required to give
a durable film. Then they experimented with cellulose nitrate, used for
making smokeless powder, and found how to reduce its viscosity. Finally
they discovered that butyl alcohol, long a drug on the market, could
be used as a lacquer solvent just as effectively as amyl alcohol or "banana
oil" which had become scarce. They introduced other substances to give
durability and the result was "Duco," a glossy, durable finish to which
pigments and dyes could be added and which dried quickly and could
be sprayed on.

Today nearly all cars have a lacquer finish but the finish on your car
today is far different from the lacquer of five years ago. Some of the
early lacquer finishes had a tendency to "chalk" and some of the colors
did not stand up. Today a good lacquer job will last as long as your car
lasts. Colors do not fade appreciably and the gleaming surface remains
bright and shining if the finish is kept free of dirt and grime. And this
beautiful, durable finish can be applied quicker and costs less than the
old paint and varnish job. Chemistry has given you a better "paint job"
for less money.

Tires on that 1918 car were good for a few thousand miles of very
uncertain service. Only fifteen years ago, hardly anyone dared make a
trip without a tire repair kit tucked under the front seat. Today, riding
on tires that cost less, you expect 15,000 or 20,000 miles of virtually
trouble-free service. The raw rubber used in tires today is about the
same as that used twenty years ago. Tires have been improved in design
and structurally and the carcass has been strengthened by the use of
cord fiber, but the better wearing properties of treads result from
the addition of about a dime's worth of chemicals in each modern
tire.

Ninety-nine years ago Charles Goodyear discovered that heating rubber with sulphur caused the rubber to become tough, very strong and elastic. This process is known as vulcanization. The characteristics of rubber can be further altered by incorporating in it various minerals, carbon black and chemicals. When vulcanization first was discovered, the chemical reaction between the rubber and sulphur required several hours. Today accelerators and vulcanization activators speed up the process and well-cured rubber is obtained in a few minutes instead of several hours.

While these accelerators—products of chemical research—have reduced the time and temperatures required for curing, they have done much more than that. The accelerators are entirely consumed in the curing process and add desirable properties to the rubber. They also make it possible to use a smaller amount of sulphur, and rubber with a small amount of sulphur is better for tires.

Since rubber is a vegetable product, it is perishable. It is subject to oxidation, it hardens and decomposes rapidly when subjected continuously to high temperatures, its useful life is shortened by long exposure to sunlight and it has a tendency to crack when flexed rapidly and continuously. An automobile tire is brought into contact with the worst enemies of rubber—heat, oil, gasoline, sunshine and oxygen. This accounts for the short life of those early rubber compositions.

Today, chemists produce not only accelerators to speed up curing but other chemicals which, incorporated in rubber, slow down oxidation and make the rubber resistant to heat and flexing. Rubber tires contain carbon black to make them tougher. This also makes them harder and reduces their resistance to flexing, and the tread has a greater tendency to crack. So a flex-resisting anti-oxidant is added to make the stiff rubber stand flexing and that—in a tire—means long tread wear.

If it were not for anti-oxidants, the thin side walls of low-pressure tires which are constantly being flexed would soon crack, and bus and truck tires would soon melt or be ruined by the intense heat developed in them. All these improvements in tires—longer wear, greater mileage, lower cost, trouble-free service—have been brought about by using a few cents' worth of chemical per tire, plus a lot of research.

But even the best rubber today has its limitations for some parts of the car. No natural rubber will stand up long against gasoline, oil and grease. For years man tried to produce a synthetic rubber to overcome these limitations. And he failed. Then du Pont chemists attacked the problem from a different angle. Why, they asked themselves, try to imitate rubber? Why not make a product with the good qualities of rubber but without its poor ones? And that is what they did. They built a new material, chemically unlike rubber, from such things as limestone and coal and salt and water. The result has been "Neoprene," a synthetic material which performs virtually all the services of rubber—and also does many things rubber cannot do.

Today you find Neoprene being used in motor cars for such things as gaskets, oil seals, covers on ignition cables, in connecting hose and in other places where a material is needed which will resist oil, heat, ozone and corrosive liquids better than rubber. It carries the usefulness of rubber to new heights because it protects rubber parts themselves from their own weaknesses as evidenced by its use for the inner lining in gasoline hose at service stations.

More than four-fifths of the weight of a car is iron and steel. The average passenger car contains about a ton and one-half of iron parts but in early cars only two types of alloy steel were used. Today there are more than forty, each designed for a particular purpose. The chemist has helped produce each of these forty kinds of metal. Chemicals are required in pickling and cleaning metals in the foundry, in case-hardening iron and in all types of metal plating. Modern cars could not be built out of the metals available ten or fifteen years ago and the new alloys could never have been produced without the aid of industrial chemistry.

The engine of that 1918 car and the engine of a modern car are about the same size and weight. Yet today's engine delivers two or three times as much power. Many improvements contribute to this addition of power without increasing weight but one of importance has been the chemical treatment of oil and gasoline. When people demanded faster cars and more power a few years ago, engine designers were faced with alternate calamities.

They could increase the size of the power plant—which would leave no space for the passengers. Or they could increase the compression in the cylinders—which started the engine knocking. The idea was to get the added compression without the knock. Watching the flame of exploding gas in the engine, they discovered that when the knock occurred, the flame was yellowish or orange instead of blue. Iodine, they found, changed the color of the flame, but iodine cost a lot of money. Another chemical eliminated the knock—and also the spark plugs. A third had an odor—an odor like garlic. Finally they hit on tetraethyl lead. Today it is used in more than eighty per cent of all gasoline sold and without it the modern high compression engine would be impossible.

The chemist has also developed anti-oxidants for gasoline to inhibit the formation of gums which result in clogging the motor and fuel lines. But that is not all. Chemistry has, in effect, doubled our oil reserves as far as gasoline is concerned, because, by the operation known as "cracking," the amount of gasoline obtained from a given crude is double that formerly obtained by straight distillation. Furthermore, cracked gasoline has a higher octane rating, that is, less tendency to "knock," but it is less stable than straight-run gas unless refined by methods which tend to destroy its high octane value. Here the chemist has stepped into the picture again with stabilizing agents which, without influencing the good antiknock properties of cracked gasoline, prevent the formation of gums which clog the fuel lines.

More recently, the chemist has given automobile owners improved lubricants and also what are known as extreme pressure lubricant bases which, when added to an oil or grease, make it possible for bearings and gears to withstand much higher pressure without actually touching and possibly "seizing." Extreme pressure lubricant bases have made possible the use of silent-action hypoid gears because the peculiar frictional forces in such gears would quickly squeeze out the film of any ordinary oil, leaving the metal surfaces in direct contact.

Nor do the contributions of chemistry to your car stop with oils and fuels. Safety glass consists of two layers of glass welded together sandwichlike by an interlayer of cellulose plastic—a product of the chemist. Chemical research has produced the molded plastics for steering wheels, gear shifts and door-handle knobs, ash trays, cigar lighters, window trim and dash panels. Man-made fabrics have been developed by the chemist for the automobile industry—such things as tire covers, curtains, upholstery for open cars and trucks, fender welting, trunk and deck materials, cushions and tool bags. These man-made fabrics have been designed to stand all kinds of weather and wear on the road—demands which leather and ordinary cloths could not meet.

The acid in your battery, the antifreeze solution in your radiator, the polish and cleaner you use on the finish—chemistry has developed them all.

The automobile has been described as a chemical factory on wheels, a factory which takes gasoline, the raw product, and converts it into power to move the rear wheels. But the modern car is more than a chemical factory on wheels. It is an outstanding example of chemical magic, a product of chemical research from bumper to bumper.

H. W. MAGEE *Chemistry and Your Car*

WORK

I. Following are a hundred subjects for essay writing. Use some of them for practice in writing essays of one kind or another. But if these do not appeal to you, then draw upon your daily experiences for essay material. As you grow older you will increasingly find your thoughts accumulating on certain subjects which you are interested in and about which you have strong feelings. These constitute the very best of subject matter for essay treatment.

On making a new friend
On wearing a new suit
On deceiving the enemy
On the joys of exercise
On the thrills of competition
On the correcting of mistakes
On the permanence of last impressions
On taking a stitch in time
On electing electives
On my favorite enemies
On using one's friends
On abusing one's enemies
On needles in haystacks
On you *versus* me
On being a freshman
On being a senior
On the advantages of conceit
On the inferiority complex
On humbugs
On saying too much
On too many cooks
On those lovely bores
On cheating cheaters
On books that I like
On paying the fiddler
On taking things too seriously
On crossing bridges
On letting George do it
On looking alive
A sense of order

The champion loser
Fighting to be an optimist
Too much imagination
Revenge is—sour
Afraid to be alone
Company behavior
Forward, march!
"Had he his wounds before?"
"The quality of mercy"
"All the world's a stage"
Honor in examinations
Dogs, and others
So they say
I'm telling you
It seems to me
Laughter as tonic
Whys and wherefores
What I like
Better late—sometimes
The art of speeding
The tonic of a good fight
Playing your part
"Pleased to meet you"
At your face value
The oldfashioned girl
Safety first, last, and always
Dragon flies
Harmonies
Human pests
In a rut
Television tells all

Salespeople I have known
It's smart to be tardy
It's wise to be punctual
Appearances do not deceive
Classroom etiquette
My destiny—and how!
Esprit de corps
Ambition, and its wear and tear
Students are people
The fun of persuading
The gospel of little things
Never again!
Getting and giving
Make up your mind
Failing to fail
Succeeding to fail
Moving in circles
Character through the voice
"Step on it"
"Never mind the cost"

"Flunked again!"
Popular falsehoods
Be yourself
Getting into high
Human sponges
The uses of a watch
Birds of a feather
The pleasures of high school
Present, past, and future
Dreams—and waking!
Smokestacks
Smells
Movie influences
Twiddling
Grouches
Human taximeters
Sleepiness
Cider
Sneezes
Alarm clocks

II. Using Banbury Cross (page 100) as a model, write engaging character sketches of some of the following:

Of "Sinister"	a donkey
Of "Pecker"	a pet rooster
Of "Cork"	a light-footed terrier
Of "Spinach"	a strong horse
Of "Nervy"	a Persian cat
Of "Do-Do"	a talkative parrot
Of "Skimpy"	a tiny, bedraggled chicken
Of "Smooth"	a dachshund
Of "Patience"	an elephant
Of "Pinky"	a little pig
Of "Steady"	a watch dog
Of "Drowsy"	a cow

III. Using *The Romantic in the Rain* (page 93) as model, write fanciful and playful essays on some of the following:

On trudging through the snow
On a snowfall—from a window

On a pair of new shoes—anticipatingly
On a pair of old shoes—reminiscently
On the sounds in the country
On the sounds in the city
On the motor car—after an accident
On the old lady who crochets—and chatters
On the realistic in regard to marks
On the romantic in regard to study
On the house that somehow resembles its owner
On the person who makes you feel superior—or inferior

IV. Using *Of Friendship* (page 75) as a model, write brief aphoristic essays on some of the following suggestions. These are suggestions only, remember. Use as a title in each instance either a single challenging word or a short quotation from literature:

On an automobile from the point of view of a chauffeur who treats it as if it were human

On a photograph of you taken many years ago, published now in your school or college paper, and embarrassing to you "no end"

On a friend of yours at the time when he was protesting against a traffic officer's reproof for speeding on the parkway

On your feelings when you were deprived of some award, because, in spite of your meriting it, you had been too active in some disapproved organization

On what you wanted to say and do when your long theme was returned to you with this comment in your instructor's familiar hand: "This was an excellent idea when Emerson first expressed it!"

STORY

STORY

HISTORY, biography, autobiography, travel reports, diaries, newspaper write-ups, prose drama, novel, short-story are all types that have to do with incidents and happenings. They are narration "grown up." In novel, drama, and short-story, incidents are deliberately arranged for the purpose of getting definite effects. These are called the *creative* forms of narration. In the other types of narration—called *factual*—the movement or unfoldment is as a rule chronological, that is, in the order of occurrence.

The short-story is or should be the most compactly written form of narration. Its aim is to produce with the greatest possible emphasis and economy of expression a unity and singleness of narrative impression. Long interpolations by way of character exposition and situation analysis are not suitable for the short-story. It may be a long short-story or novelette, running to as many as fifteen or twenty thousand words. It may be a short short-story—little more than an expanded anecdote—of one thousand words, more or less. Compression is in each case imperative; to say as much as possible in as few words as possible is the short-story challenge. Novel, history, biography, and the rest are by no means so rigidly harnessed.

As in the case of the essay, classification of the short-story may be highly extended, and it must needs be loose and fluid, however detailed. There are all kinds of animal stories—dog stories, cat stories, bird stories, and the like. There are again all kinds of adventure stories—hair-raising experiences in the jungle, on the sea, in the air, for instance. There are many different kinds of allegorical stories—narratives conveyed through figurative symbols to teach a lesson. And there are, of course, fables, legends, folklore, chronicles, parables, anecdotes. In addition, the following terms indicate both definition and classification of other types of short-stories: biographical, character, detective, didactic, episodic (the story of incident), fantastic, imbedded (a section or chapter constituting a unified short-story in a longer work), impressionistic, local color, love, mystery, poetic, problem, psychological, realistic, romantic, sketch, supernatural, terror, thesis. The names of the classes overlap here as elsewhere in attempts to pigeonhole types of literature, and a single story, like an essay, may have in it elements of two or more of the kinds listed. But such classification nevertheless has the use of convenience if not of accuracy. Sometimes stories are classified according to the emotion they are most likely to arouse—pity, fear, love, humor; or according to theme or subject matter—heroism, sacrifice, courage, superstition, suspicion; or according to some particular period or place—a World War story, a Kentucky mountain tale; or according to method—conversational, deductive, first personal, report, atmosphere, diary, letter, and so on.

A few of the foregoing classifications may need explanation—but a few only: A sketch is an incomplete but suggestive delineation or presentation of some subject or section thereof, brief in content and usually slight and meandering in construction. It may or may not have plot. As a rule it does not have. It presents merely a phase or a "side" without assuming any responsibility by way of building a conflict, later to be resolved. It may be pure description or exposition, and as such deserves no consideration as narrative. Washington Irving's *Sketch Book,* although badly titled, nevertheless shows to some extent how the short-story evolved from the mere sketch, as *The Spectator* had previously done in England. Some of the sketches in the *Sketch Book* are merely pictures and explanations; some are "tinged" with action; some are loose short-stories; many are story essays. Even *Rip van Winkle* and *The Legend of Sleepy Hollow* are too rambling and inchoate in construction to come strictly under the definition of short-story. They lack, in other words, the singleness of effect and the compression and the condensation that Edgar Allan Poe set down as the elementary essential—the *sine qua non*—of the short-story as a distinct type of literature. For the term *short-story* is to be hyphenated if for no other reason than to assert it as a qualitative type rather than a quantitative type, that is, it is not a story that happens to be short or that may perhaps be made longer. It necessarily differs in kind as well as in degree from the novel and the other narrative forms. It is a cameo, not a grand sculpture carved from the side of a mountain range.

The so-called story of incident is a story wherein the movement of events constitutes the whole or nearly the whole of the story interest. Happenings lead in rapid succession from one to another, and are in themselves self-explanatory not only, but explanatory also of character, situation, plot, and general theme. They are the major issue.

The detective story and the mystery story have much in common but they are nevertheless distinct types. Strictly speaking, a detective story is one in which the detection of crime and the revelation of the criminal are the paramount issues. It is sometimes called a crime story and also a "crook" story. It is less accurately referred to as a mystery story, though this term applies to it (and is generally applied to it by the average person). A mystery story, however, is in no sense necessarily concerned with detectives and crooks and crimes, though it may be. It is more likely, by accurate definition, to be concerned with the running down of treasure by means of a key map, the deciphering of a secret code, the solution of an apparently difficult but really simple disappearance of something or somebody, and the like.

The novel is a type of prose in which a fictitious tale of considerable length is developed. Real life and character are depicted in the novel through the workings of a plotted and episodic action. It is more complex and involved than the short-story, and is therefore representative of a larger canvas of life. Inasmuch as the form is fluid, not confined to the strict give-and-take of dramatic dialogue or to the metrical limitations of the poem, it offers opportunity to the author to "appear and disappear" at will, to interrupt action with the elaboration of analysis and speculation.

Like the short-story before and the drama to follow, the novel may be realistic or romantic, and it may be further classified almost as extensively as the essay and the short-story. The names used in the following classification of novels, like those in the above classifications of essays and stories, sufficiently define and explain types indicated to render further definition unnecessary. Broadly, novels may be grouped under the following heads: novels of *incident,* novels of *purpose,* novels of *character,* and novels of *impressionism.* But these main heads indicate dominant motifs only. They stand as a most general classification of fiction next below the more general one of realistic fiction and romantic fiction. To be sure, a novel of incident may be, frequently is, a novel of purpose, and a novel of purpose or of character may be written impressionistically. By another classification (or by a slightly extended one) novels may be classified exactly as short-stories are on pages 126 to 130.

A novel of incident may be subclassified according as adventure or artifice or detection of crime (the "crook" novel) or history or travel is made the central motivation of the action. The old rogue-hero or picaresque novel, in which the varied exploits of the faithless and shameful ne'er-do-well adventurer were revealed, was an early novel of incident, as well as of character, to a degree.

A novel of character may be subclassified into autobiographical or biographical or psychological or provincial. The last may localize character portrayal and delineation against a special setting of locale, and may thus easily fall into a separate classification sometimes called local-color fiction.

A novel of purpose may be subclassified, again, according to the subject that motivates the action and the characterization. It may deal with some particular class, and become a novel of manners or fashion. It may treat of some particular problem—social, political, economic, humanitarian—and thus become a problem novel. It may aim to teach and uplift or, at least, to change public taste or thought, and be properly called a didactic novel. The method of the novelist may be satirical, and his work thus be classed as satirical fiction.

A novel of impressionism is one such as Horace Walpole's *The Castle of Otranto* or Charles William Beckford's *Vathek*. These are sometimes called terror or Gothic novels. In such fiction grim and supernatural incidents—pictures that come to life, secret passages that open and yield treasure, ominous and inarticulate sounds that haunt old castles—are of paramount importance. In addition, the impressionistic novel may be one in which fantastic and mysterious elements are brought to bear upon everyday problems, or one that creates in the mind and heart of the reader a mood, rather than any definite solution of problem or elaboration of facts. Henry James' novels are good examples of this school of fiction.

The drama and the short-story are very similar in essentials. Both are imperatively compact or compressed, presenting "much in little." Both follow the pyramidal development, adapted from Gustav Freytag's *Technique of the Drama,* illustrated in the diagram.

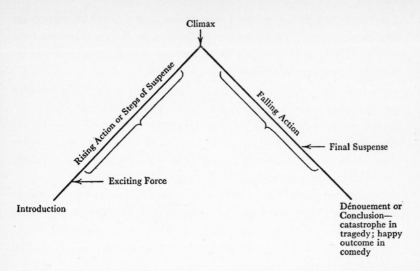

But the method in drama is more sheer, that is, its action and situation and character are revealed entirely by means of dialogue; in the short-story they are dispensed by the author through conversation and through the medium of expository and descriptive, and, it may be, argumentative writing. In the one the characters speak for themselves and convey the story from their own lips; in the other the author takes charge of both, either himself or through interlocutor.

Drama,* like didactic and satirical and philosophic literature in general, may be either prose or poetry. Much drama is a combination of both poetry and prose. This is abundantly illustrated in the Shaksperean drama.

A dramatic composition is usually calculated for presentation in the theater. As such it is called a play, and the two words—*play* and *drama*—are used henceforth interchangeably. Some dramatic composition, however, is for reading chiefly, rather than for direct presentation. Many plays that were once popularly produced in the theater are now produced no longer, and have therefore fallen into the classification of "plays to be read." But after a play has had its "run" in the theater it may disappear altogether, for the drama is the most ephemeral type of literature.

* Though drama may be either prose or poetry, it is treated here because it is fundamentally and first of all a story. This section should be referred to in connection with dramatic poetry (page 332).

The drama differs further in form from other types of literature, in that the characters speak and act through a series of scenes and acts especially constructed for the development of plot and the staging of dramatic situations. The people impersonating characters "play parts," and appear in make-up and costume for the purpose of creating an atmosphere of reality. Scenery is built and painted and set upon the stage for the same purpose. A drama may consist of a single act—the one-act play—or it may be divided into two, three, four, or five acts. The Elizabethan drama is five-act drama, in the main. The present-day drama rarely exceeds four acts, and, as a rule, modern plays are divided into three acts only, though some have only two, and the full-length one-act play can no longer be called unique.

The two principal divisions of dramatic literature are *tragedy* and *comedy*. Tragedy treats of the serious theme of a human will struggling against the dictates of fate. By means of foreshadowing—"coming events cast their shadows before"—it aims to inspire the reader or auditor with awe and terror and pity. Its story is developed through introduction, rising steps of suspense, and tragic moment or impulse (usually acts one, two, and three in a five-act play), to a final suspense, and a consequential catastrophe or dénouement (usually acts three, four, and five in a five-act play). The last step—the catastrophe—must overthrow the evil or mistaken forces that have been at work, and must be felt to be the result of some power beyond human control (see diagram on page 119). Poetry—blank verse—is considered a more suitable medium for tragedy than is prose. It has a more solemn and majestic sweep; it lifts an audience above the colloquial language of everyday life; it more easily and more completely intrigues the imagination.

Comedy has to do with the whims and fancies and humors of life. It aims to amuse and to beget merriment. It ends always happily and satisfactorily, and often surprisingly. Though the construction of comedy must be consistently wrought through steps of suspense and climax and final suspense and pleasing or surprising dénouement, it portrays no solemn and serious struggle with the forces of nature, and it foreshadows nothing. It treats, rather, of the casual ins and outs, and ups and downs, of average life and experience, revealing the "funny side" of things by way of plot and situation and characterization, all three. Because of its "lower levels" of portrayal, comedy uses prose as its vehicle to a far greater degree than tragedy does.

Reconciling or mediated drama or tragi-comedy is drama in which elements of both tragedy and comedy appear. It is usually written in both prose and poetry. The play at first seems to be serious, and tends toward a tragic catastrophe. But at the end disaster is adroitly averted, and all comes out well. Shakspere's *The Merchant of Venice* is an excellent example of mediated drama.

The terms *classic* and *romantic* and *realistic* are important general terms of classification in the discussion of any type of literature. They have been and still are important to the classification of dramatic literature.

The word *classic,* broadly used, has come to mean the best or the choice or the cultural. You read certain *classic* literature for the creation of cultural and elementary backgrounds. The word *classic* is used also to refer to the so-called Augustan period of English literature—the early eighteenth century—when the Augustan period of Roman culture, with its precision and refinement and formalism in style, made its influence felt through the medium of French imitation. The finished closed couplet (see page 366) of Alexander Pope, and the polite, indoor, artificial drama of Dryden and Congreve and Etherege and Wycherly (following the Augustan models of Molière and Racine in France) belong to the classic school of English literature.

Classic is also sometimes used to connote the three unities to which Greek and Latin drama held more or less strictly—the unities of time and place and action. The action of a play was held to one and the same place (Hamlet's "scene individable"—Act II, scene II—refers to unity of place) ; to one unit of time—twenty-four hours or preferably no longer than would be required were the represented action actually to happen—and to one single action without extraneous incident and episode, each minor event having a distinct and essential relationship to the main or central plot. The classic unities have been observed but slightly by English dramatists. Matthew Arnold's dramatic epic *Sohrab and Rustum* perfectly illustrates the classical unities, though the original story upon which it is based does not observe them. Shakspere's *Titus Andronicus* is, with slight modification, a good example of classic tragedy. Shakspere's *A Comedy of Errors* is a good example of classic comedy.

The word *romantic,* as applied to literature, means freedom in the range of imaginative play, and in the treatment brought to bear upon a theme. Victor Hugo called romanticism liberalism in literature (see also pages 311 to 317). Love, passion, emotion, adventure are expansively in evidence in romantic literature, and they expand and loosen, so to say, the vehicle of expression. The run-on couplet (see page 367) reflects romantic thought; the freer choice of subject matter and the consequent liberty of treatment bespeak the unlimited imaginative realms in which thought and expression may roam. The Elizabethan period of English literature was in very large part a romantic period. It followed the broadening of vision and the expansiveness of spirit that were inevitably evinced in the Italian Renaissance. Shakspere's *Romeo and Juliet* and *Much Ado About Nothing* are, respectively, excellent examples of romantic tragedy and romantic comedy. The early nineteenth century was preeminently a period of romanticism in English literature, though it was in no sense a period noted for drama. But Wordsworth and Shelley and Byron and Keats, and others of their school, emphatically broke away from the hard-and-fast formalism of the classic period preceding, and in their revolt, liberalized literature both in form and content until they were falsely accused by classicists of making it "inchoate and promiscuous."

The word *realistic,* as applied to literature, implies that the author of an imaginative work has succeeded in presenting scene and character and situation and action *as they are in life*—has achieved *actuality* in the presentation of his theme. Realism, in other words, means the delineation of character and portraiture of scene without any attempt at idealization, without any of the glamor of romance, without any of the artificiality of classicism. It achieves its ends to a considerable extent through microscopic attention to detail. The perfection of stage mechanical devices has done much toward encouraging the composition of realistic drama. The plays of Henrik Ibsen are probably the best examples of this type.

Historical drama, as its name implies, is drama that deals with some historical event and with historical personages. It may be either tragedy or comedy. Under this general heading belongs that type of drama that faithfully reproduces a picture of a past time. Costume, setting, dialogue, custom, and mannerism are all presented as nearly true to the period represented as study and research can make them. The name *period play* or *costume play* is sometimes given to this type of historical drama when it is produced.

Character drama is, again, clarified by name. It is drama in which all action and movement and plotting, as well as situation and minor characterization, are developed around and about one central character, with the purpose of making that character dramatically impressive. Character drama may be either tragedy or comedy, and it may be historical. The historical plays of Shakspere are built around a central character for whom they are named. They are combination character-historical dramas.

Melodrama formerly meant drama freely interspersed with songs, semiheroic in atmosphere, and highly sensational in its effects. It has now become somewhat modified. Melodrama at present rarely contains music; it is usually somewhat mysterious and romantic in atmosphere; and it is emotional in its appeal. It is sometimes called, more or less accurately, emotional drama. In melodrama the story is preeminently the thing. The characters must be fitted into the story, and the episodes must be closely coherent with it.

Mystery or "crook" drama is a popular form of dramatic composition in which mysteries—usually crimes—are dramatically and as a rule surprisingly solved, and justice is meted out to criminal offenders. It is melodramatic tragi-comedy. It may take the form of *satirical drama*—tragic, comic, or tragic-comic—in which comment upon life and human experience is paramount. Bitter or nonchalant criticism of life may, in satirical drama, leave upon the audience the impression of indifference regarding things as they are, and of utter hopelessness regarding things as they ought to be. As such, satirical drama may stand distinctly apart from the "crook" play, and constitute a type of dramatic literature by itself. It is rarely a popular form—the average audience stubbornly prefers the "full-dress" or "Pollyanna" ending.

Social or polite drawing-room drama—comedy, as a rule—is drama that holds up to ridicule, sharp or restrained, the follies and foibles of social doings and of social personages. It may be merely a humorous picture of a phase of life among the better society classes. But it may, on the other hand, take the form of satirical drama, and attempt to correct and reform by means of ironic situation and characterization and happening. A play defined as "smart" usually belongs in this classification.

Polite drama may become nothing more or less than the comedy of manners, comedy, that is, in which much attention is given to characterization. Conventional character types are featured as they appear in any class of society, and all their whims of mannerism and absurdities of belief and behavior are capitalized for dramatic purposes.

Fantastic drama or comedy is the drama specifically of "Let's pretend!" It may be odd or grotesque or capricious in the claims it makes upon the human fancy. It may be a dramatized fairy tale, or it may be an allegorical deduction or interpretation of contemporary life and events. Shakspere's *A Midsummer Night's Dream* is a fantastic comedy, as are also Sir James Barrie's *Peter Pan, The Lady Leonora,* and *A Kiss for Cinderella.*

Farce is exaggerated comedy. It exaggerates plot, situation, and characterization in order to make them ludicrous. It adds highly laughable incident and episode to ordinary happening, very often as result of making characters humorously the victims of circumstance, and it enriches the humorous atmosphere by apt and brilliant lines. While comedy aims to make the auditor smile or laugh with, perhaps, gentle restraint, farce aims to make him laugh uproariously and hold his sides. Shakspere's *The Merry Wives of Windsor* contains many farcical elements.

Dramatic burlesque portrays personages of high rank and culture in a trivial and ludicrous manner. Dramatic travesty portrays trivial and insignificant characters as enacting the roles of great personages.

The mask or masque was a sort of composite dramatic form, made up of song and dance and pantomime, enacted by *masked* characters for the most part in the roles of shepherds and shepherdesses and allegorical or supernatural beings. It was pastoral in tone and quality, of slight plot, and usually had some marked didactic aim. It was purely poetic, consisting of blank verse in part, and in part of lyrics of varied structure. John Milton's *Comus* is the outstanding masterpiece in this type of composition.

Expressionism is the revolt of modern art from realism. Instead of attempting to imitate life—reproduce life by imitation—it makes use of any means at its disposal to create desired emotions, and in so doing transcends all conventional limitations. It is the free expression by objective means of the subjective emotions of an individual or a group through any artistic medium—music, painting, literature, and so on. It dramatizes state of mind; it uses symbols for ideas and emotions; it stages puppets for characters. And the moment after it does all of these unusual things in art, it may turn again to the most realistic conventions to achieve a certain purpose or effect. It has been called the fourth dimension in art. The foregoing definition applies chiefly to the expressionistic drama, but not alone to this. The general principles here set down apply also to expressionistic poetry and fiction, and to painting and sculpture.

History is a systematic record of past events, and especially of such events a man has taken part in. History is likewise highly classifiable. It may deal with the political affairs of a state or a nation; it may deal with the social affairs of a unit of human society—race, nation, settlement, or community; it may deal with some institution—educational, religious, military, and the like; it may deal with some particular subject, such as the history of art or music or literature or religion. The central aim of historical writing should always be to present records from impartial and detached points of view, and to organize them in such manner as to convey coherent development and proportion in their unfoldment and relationship. Lord Bolingbroke said that history is philosophy teaching by examples.

Narration of fact must not be taken to mean a mere listing or chronicling of dates and happenings. This would be but almanac compilation. It is, rather, a life-giving undertaking based upon the actual facts gathered about its subject. It is sometimes called derivative narrative in contradistinction to creative narrative—novel, drama, and short-story. The author may not create from his imagination in telling the story of real people and real happenings, or he will justifiably be accused of misrepresentation and prejudice. But he may logically derive from his intensive study of a given event or of a person's life such elements as are consistent with the facts that he exhaustively investigates. Many a history text has come in for severe criticism for the very reason that this distinction has not always been observed by its author. The historian could not resist the temptation to be creative, whereas his job was to be logically and consistently derivative after he had studiously exhausted his facts.

For the same reason there are many biographies and autobiographies, and adventure and travel stories that are not trustworthy. Their authors have allowed creative imagination to run away with them, instead of adhering strictly to facts. There are, of course, such things as fictitious biography and autobiography, fictitious adventure story and "travelog," and these are frequently the most interesting reading to be found. But of recent years real biography and autobiography as well as travel and adventure have been treated in original and entertaining and at the same time truthful ways. The methods of fiction and drama have been brought to bear upon them without in any way invalidating truth. Gossip and chattiness and conversational verisimilitude have concretized and vivified lives and events, with the consequence that trustworthiness of account and readableness of copy have been developed in parallel.

There are many terms that belong to the field of creative story writing. A few of them are listed below in lexicon form. They will help a great deal both in your reading of fiction and in your practice writing.

Character and *characterization* refer to the unfoldment of the characters of the people in a story—the changes that the characters undergo as result of action and of interrelationships, and of stress of conflict.

Climax is that part of the story—close to the end in the average short-story—where the plot complication is at its height and the reader's feelings therefore at the highest pitch of interest. It is the topmost rung in the ladder of suspense.

Crisis is a decisive action or event—a turning-point in a chain of events.

Dénouement is the outcome of the sequence of events that constitute the main action or plot of a story.

Direct story is one told directly by a narrator in the third person or in the first.

Episode is a slight or unobtrusive incident. Dropping a handkerchief is an episode or an incident. A detective's picking it up designedly is a major incident or an event. His using it to run down a crime develops a *train of events* or *dramatic sequences*.

Exciting force is a movement or episode or incident or situation that inspires abrupt active consequences, and thus advances toward the climax.

Final suspense is that episodic device of a story (usually a dramatic story) that holds interest after the climax is done with. It hangs upon some plant or foreshadowing earlier in the story, and remains to be cleared up. The ring plot in *The Merchant of Venice* constitutes final suspense.

Human interest is strong appeal to the heart or the emotion of the reader.

Impressionistic stories are stories that aim to place the reader in a certain mood, to create in him a certain feeling. They are sometimes called atmosphere stories. A local-color setting will help to do this, but it is by no means necessary. Atmosphere effects are procurable by choice of diction, by structure of sentences and paragraphs, by the author's writing for weird and bizarre effects.

Indirect story is one told through some kind of report (see below) or in the person of another (interlocutor), the narrator himself taking no responsibility. Conan Doyle relates the Sherlock Holmes stories indirectly through Doctor Watson.

Integration means the weaving together of all the threads of a story to one end—all events as well as all characters and situations naturally "belong" in the setting and the development of the narrative theme.

Local color is setting that pertains intensively to some special locale, such for instance as a southern cabin or a western prairie. Such a setting obligates the author to develop character and action in keeping with it; hence, a local-color story.

Mood or *keynote* is an early indication—very often in the first sentence—of exactly what feeling the story is to be written in, whether tragic or comic. To play up comedy elements unduly or disproportionately in a story that is essentially tragic in its tone and outcome, is to be inartistic as well as confusing and incoherent.

Objective hero is one whose fight is made against odds or obstacles outside himself. Caesar is a signal illustration.

Opposing forces in a story are the two sides of the conflict or plot— the *for* and *against* elements between which the hero or the heroine must make a fight.

Outside material is information that derives from beyond the story —either before it opens or at intervals during its progress—and that the reader must have knowledge of for a complete and sympathetic understanding of the action. In the movies a *flash-back* or a *cut-in* is used for the same purpose. This exposition of event or situation may be made deliberately by the author, or through character action and conversation. Always the author aims to get it done without interrupting the thread of the main story and thus without sacrificing reader interest.

Period stories are stories that are set in definite past periods of history, with customs and costumes and scenery in strict keeping with the time represented.

Person refers to the narrator of a story—first personal if it is told by a participant or participants (*I* or *we*) in the action; third personal if the author writes *about* all the characters as *he, she, they*. Stories may be told in the second person—by use of *you*—but they rarely are, except in letters and diaries and logs and memoranda.

Plant is some apparently negligible episode or object or remark that later looms large in the sequence of events. A lady drops her handkerchief in a car. Nobody notices—but a plain-clothes man. He picks it up unobserved, finds a thumbprint in blood on it, and runs down a murderer. The gift of the rings in *The Merchant of Venice* is a plant upon which the last scene of the play is hung. The term *foreshadowing* is sometimes used to mean much the same thing.

Plot means conflict in the action of a story. It is developed through a series of events or episodes that are connected and that lead one out of the other into a more and more serious complication. Conflict is the germ of plot.

Ratiocination means that the appeal is made to the processes of reasoning, as in mystery and detective stories. A ratiocinative story is a reason-why story (see page 80).

Realism means strict adherence to the fact and truth of life. The realist in fiction aims to tell the whole truth and no more about the actual events of life and those people concerned in them (see page 122).

The *realistic method* in story telling and writing is inductive. It accumulates a number of special cases through which the reader is permitted eventually to apply and understand a certain theme.

Report story is one told by some interpolated paper, such as a diary, a letter, a log, a report, either entirely or in part during the temporary, enforced absence of the narrator.

Resolution is that part of the story following the climax in which justice may be meted out or disposition of characters finally made.

Romanticism means the refashioning and idealizing of life and event and human character in accordance with the writer's wishes or some one else's. The romanticist sees deeper meanings in things and evokes spiritual and emotional aspects from them. To make this possible he makes them strange and unusual and striking, and perhaps grotesque and bizarre. In short-stories both realism and romanticism are frequently employed. The incidental details are kept true to life and character, but the result or outcome is oftentimes romantic in its solution of the enigmatic and its vanquishing of the insurmountable (see page 122).

The *romantic method* in story telling and writing is deductive. It takes a theme at the outset, and then develops it through special application and special cases. This will be recognized as in part the method of mystery and detective stories.

Setting means the place, environment, surroundings of the action. Sometimes it is deliberately built in by the writer, just as a stage set is designed and built and set up physically. Sometimes it is implied by the writer's communicating mood or tone or atmosphere, as in many of Edgar Allan Poe's stories.

Situation is the tableau or the condition of events at given points and at given times in a story. The word is usually used to indicate some crucial circumstance or turning point in the progress of a story.

Subjective hero is one whose fight is made against odds in his own mind. Hamlet is a signal illustration.

Surprise means an outcome of a story as a whole or of some part of it entirely unexpected and entirely unguessable at any point of it. It is sometimes a trick device. Portia makes use of two surprise notes in the famous courtroom scene in *The Merchant of Venice*. One is that just one pound of flesh shall be cut—no more, no less. The other is that no blood may be shed. The bond says explicitly one pound of flesh !

Suspense means the increasing, step-by-step complication in a story, as a result of which the reader's expectation becomes more and more tense and his interest more and more intensified.

Symbolism means the use of a character to indicate a quality or characteristic or an event to denote "more than meets the eye." *Mr. Thornhill* may be a bad man, a troublesome enemy, a "thorn in somebody's flesh." A glittering eye that arrests and holds two wedding guests bent upon a good time may be used to stand for the Evil Eye.

Thesis story is a story that deliberately sets out to teach something or to promulgate some belief or story. Such story is sometimes called a propaganda story. It is also a didactic story. *Uncle Tom's Cabin* was a thesis novel.

Verisimilitude is a term commonly used in connection with realism. It means strict adherence to the facts and truths of life, so that the reader or hearer is made for the time being to live without himself in the environment thus created. A common definition is "Likelihood and appearance made so real as to deceive people into taking them for truth."

A few of the most important types of stories are here included for your reading and study. Read them primarily for enjoyment, of course. But look also into

1. the style (see pages 3 and 4)
2. the aim and the central theme of each
3. the proportions of description, exposition, narration, and argument
4. the mood or tone of the story as a whole
5. the method of workmanship (see page 119)
6. the singleness or totality of effect
7. the rigidity with which extraneous matter has been eliminated
8. the organization or planning of the story progress
9. the logic and naturalness by which the climax is attained
10. the relationships among plot and situation and characterization.

The following is a short short-story. It is likewise atmospheric, indirect, impressionistic, and partly first-personal. The effects of setting and mood should be especially noted.

The chateau into which my valet had ventured to make forcible entrance, rather than permit me, in my desperately wounded condition, to pass a night in the open air, was one of those piles of commingled gloom and grandeur which have so long frowned among the Apennines, not less in fact than in the fancy of Mrs. Radcliffe. To all appearance it had been temporarily and very lately abandoned. We established ourselves in one of the smallest and least sumptuously furnished apartments. It lay in a remote turret of the building. Its decorations were rich, yet tattered and antique. Its walls were hung with tapestry and bedecked with manifold and multiform armorial trophies, together with an unusually great number of very spirited modern paintings in frames of rich golden arabesque. In these paintings, which depended from the walls not only in their main surfaces, but in very many nooks which the bizarre architecture of the chateau rendered necessary—in these paintings my incipient delirium, perhaps, had caused me to take deep interest; so that I bade Pedro to close the heavy shutters of the room—since it was already night—to light the tongues of a tall candelabrum which stood by the head of the bed—and to throw open far and wide the fringed curtain of black velvet which enveloped the bed itself. I wished all this done that I might resign myself, if not to sleep, at least alternately to the contemplation of these pictures, and the perusal of a small volume which had been found upon the pillow, and which purported to criticize and describe them.

Long—long I read and devoutly, devotedly I gazed. Rapidly and gloriously the hours flew by, and the deep midnight came. The position of the candelabrum displeased me, and outreaching my hand with difficulty, rather than disturb my slumbering valet, I placed it so as to throw its rays more fully upon the book.

But the action produced an effect altogether unanticipated. The rays of the numerous candles (for there were many) now fell within a niche of the room which had hitherto been thrown into deep shade by one of the bed-posts. I thus saw in vivid light a picture all unnoticed before. It was the portrait of a young girl just ripening into womanhood. I glanced at the painting hurriedly, and then closed my eyes. Why I did this was not at first apparent even to my own perception. But while my lids remained thus shut, I ran over in mind my reasons for so shutting them. It was an impulsive movement to gain time for thought—to make sure that my vision had not deceived me—to calm and subdue my fancy for a more sober and more certain gaze. In a very few moments I again looked fixedly at the painting.

That I now saw aright I could not and would not doubt; for the first flashing of the candles upon that canvas had seemed to dissipate the dreamy stupor which was stealing over my senses, and to startle me at once into waking life.

The portrait, I have already said, was that of a young girl. It was a mere head and shoulders, done in what is technically termed a *vignette* manner, much in the style of the favorite heads of Sully. The arms, the bosom, and even the ends of the radiant hair, melted imperceptibly into the vague yet deep shadow which formed the background of the whole. The frame was oval, richly gilded and filigreed in Moresque. As a thing of art nothing could be more admirable than the painting itself. But it could have been neither the execution of the work, nor the immortal beauty of the countenance, which had so suddenly and so vehemently moved me. Least of all, could it have been that my fancy, shaken from its half slumber, had mistaken the head for that of a living person. I saw at once that the peculiarities of the design, of the *vignetting,* and of the frame, must have instantly dispelled such idea—must have prevented even its momentary entertainment. Thinking earnestly upon these points, I remained, for an hour, perhaps, half sitting, half reclining, with my vision riveted upon the portrait. At length, satisfied with the true secret of its effect, I fell back within the bed. I had found the spell of the picture in an absolute lifelikeness of expression, which, at first startling, finally confounded, subdued and appalled me. With deep and reverent awe I replaced the candelabrum in its former position. The cause of my deep agitation being thus shut from view, I sought eagerly the volume which discussed the paintings and their histories. Turning to the number which designated the oval portrait, I read there the vague and quaint words which follow:

"She was a maiden of rarest beauty, and not more lovely than full of glee. And evil was the hour when she saw, and loved, and wedded the painter. He, passionate, studious, austere, and having already a bride in his Art: she a maiden of rarest beauty, and not more lovely than full of glee; all light and smiles, and frolicsome as the young fawn; loving and cherishing all things; hating only the Art which was her rival; and dreading only the palette and brushes and other untoward instruments which deprived her of the countenance of her lover. It was thus a terrible thing for this lady to hear the painter speak of his desire to portray even his young bride. But she was humble and obedient, and sat meekly for many weeks in the dark high turret-chamber where the light dripped upon the pale canvas only from overhead. But he, the painter, took glory in his work, which went on from hour to hour, and from day to day. And he was a passionate, and wild, and moody man, who became lost in reveries; so that he *would* not see that the light which fell so ghastly in that lone turret withered the health and the spirits of his bride, who pined visibly to all but him. Yet she smiled on and still on, uncomplainingly, because she saw that the painter (who had high renown) took a fervid and burning pleasure in his task, and wrought day and night to depict her who so loved him, yet who grew daily more dispirited and weak. And in sooth some who beheld the portrait spoke of its resemblance in low words, as of a mighty marvel, and a proof not less of the power of the painter than of his deep love for her whom he depicted so surpassingly well. But at length, as the labor drew nearer to its conclusion, there were admitted none into the turret; for the painter had grown wild with the ardor of his work, and turned his eyes from the canvas rarely, even to regard the countenance of his wife. And he *would* not see that the tints which he spread upon the canvas were drawn from the cheeks of her who sat beside him. And when many weeks had passed, and but little remained to do, save one brush upon the mouth and one tint upon the eye, the spirit of the lady again flickered up as the flame within the socket of the lamp. And then the brush was given, and then the tint was placed; and for one moment the painter stood entranced before the work which he had wrought; but in the next, while he yet gazed, he grew tremulous and very pallid, and aghast, and crying with a loud voice, 'This is indeed *Life* itself!' turned suddenly to regard his beloved:— *She was dead!"*

EDGAR ALLAN POE *The Oval Portrait*

The short short-story below * is almost a complete antithesis of the one above. It is direct and realistic; it emphasizes both character and atmosphere to a degree; chiefly, it emotionalizes war and soldiery. The postponed handling of the surprise element to the very last sentence and word, yields a unique quality, and clinches the impression the reader has already formed but does not expect in quite such a concrete and telling parting shot.

That Sunday afternoon we sat with the Swedish girl in the big café in Valencia. We had vermouth in thick goblets, each with a cube of honeycombed gray ice in it. The waiter was so proud of that ice he could hardly bear to leave the glasses on the table, and thus part from

---

* Used by permission of Miss Dorothy Parker and *The New Yorker.*

it forever. He went to his duty—all over the room they were clapping their hands and hissing to draw his attention—but he looked back over his shoulder.

It was dark outside, the quick, new dark that leaps down without dusk on the day; but, because there were no lights in the streets, it seemed as set and as old as midnight. So you wondered that all the babies were still up. There were babies everywhere in the café, babies serious without solemnity and interested in a tolerant way in their surroundings.

At the table next ours, there was a notably small one; maybe six months old. Its father, a little man in a big uniform that dragged his shoulders down, held it carefully on his knee. It was doing nothing whatever, yet he and his thin young wife, . . . sat watching it in a sort of ecstasy of admiration, while their coffee cooled in front of them. The baby was in Sunday white; its dress was patched so delicately that you would have thought the fabric whole had not the patches varied in their shades of whiteness. In its hair was a bow of new blue ribbon, tied with absolute balance of loops and ends. The ribbon was of no use; there was not enough hair to require restraint. The bow was sheerly an adornment, a calculated bit of dash.

"Oh, for God's sake, stop that!" I said to myself. "All right, so it's got a piece of blue ribbon on its hair. All right, so its mother went without eating so it could look pretty when its father came home on leave. All right, so it's her business, and none of yours. All right, so what have you got to cry about?"

The big, dim room was crowded and lively. That morning there had been a bombing from the air, the more horrible for broad daylight. But nobody in the café sat tense and strained, nobody desperately forced forgetfulness. They drank coffee or bottled lemonade, in the pleasant, earned ease of Sunday afternoon, chatting of small, gay matters, all talking at once, all hearing and answering.

There were many soldiers in the room, in what appeared to be the uniforms of twenty different armies until you saw that the variety lay in the differing ways the cloth had worn or faded. Only a few of them had been wounded; here and there you saw one stepping gingerly, leaning on a crutch or two canes, but so far on toward recovery that his face had color. There were many men, too, in civilian clothes—some of them soldiers home on leave, some of them governmental workers, some of them anybody's guess. There were plump, comfortable wives, active with paper fans, and old women as quiet as their grandchildren. There were many pretty girls and some beauties, of whom you did not remark,

"There's a charming Spanish type," but said, "What a beautiful girl!" The women's clothes were not new, and their material was too humble ever to have warranted skilful cutting.

"It's funny," I said to the Swedish girl, "how when nobody in a place is best dressed, you don't notice that everybody isn't."

"Please?" the Swedish girl said.

No one, save an occasional soldier, wore a hat. When we had first come to Valencia, I lived in a state of puzzled pain as to why everybody on the streets laughed at me. It was not because "West End Avenue" was writ across my face as if left there by a customs officer's chalked scrawl. They like Americans in Valencia, where they have seen good ones—the doctors who left their practices and came to help, the calm young nurses, the men of the International Brigade. But when I walked forth, men and women courteously laid their hands across their splitting faces and little children, too innocent for dissembling, doubled with glee and pointed and cried, *"Olé!"* Then, pretty late, I made my discovery, and left my hat off; and there was laughter no longer. It was not one of those comic hats, either; it was just a hat.

The café filled to overflow, and I left our table to speak to a friend across the room. When I came back to the table, six soldiers were sitting there. They were crowded in, and I scraped past them to my chair. They looked tired and dusty and little, the way that the newly dead look little, and the first things you saw about them were the tendons in their necks. I felt like a prize sow.

They were all in conversation with the Swedish girl. She has Spanish, French, German, anything in Scandinavian, Italian, and English. When she has a moment for regret, she sighs that her Dutch is so rusty she can no longer speak it, only read it, and the same is true of her Rumanian.

They had told her, she told us, that they were at the end of forty-eight hours' leave from the trenches, and, for their holiday, they had all pooled their money for cigarettes, and something had gone wrong, and the cigarettes had never come through to them. I had a pack of American cigarettes—in Spain rubies are as nothing to them—and I brought it out, and by nods and smiles and a sort of breast stroke, made it understood that I was offering it to those six men yearning for tobacco. When they saw what I meant, each one of them rose and shook my hand. Darling of me to share my cigarettes with the men on their way back to the trenches. Little Lady Bountiful. The prize sow.

Each one lit his cigarette with a contrivance of yellow rope that stank when afire and was also used, the Swedish girl translated, for igniting grenades. Each one received what he had ordered, a glass of coffee, and each one murmured appreciatively over the tiny cornucopia of coarse sugar that accompanied it. Then they talked.

They talked through the Swedish girl, but they did to us that thing we all do when we speak our own language to one who has no knowledge of it. They looked us square in the face, and spoke slowly, and pronounced their words with elaborate movements of their lips. Then, as their stories came, they poured them at us so vehemently, so emphatically that they were sure we must understand. They were so convinced we would understand that we were ashamed for not understanding.

But the Swedish girl told us. They were all farmers and farmers' sons, from a district so poor that you try not to remember there is that kind of poverty. Their village was next that one where the old men and the sick men and the women and children had gone, on a holiday, to the bullring; and the planes had come over and dropped bombs on the bullring, and the old men and the sick men and the women and the children were more than two hundred.

They had all, the six of them, been in the war for over a year, and most of that time they had been in the trenches. Four of them were married. One had one child, two had three children, one had five. They had not had word from their families since they had left for the front. There had been no communication; two of them had learned to write from men fighting next them in the trench, but they had not dared to write home. They belonged to a union, and union men, of course, are put to death if taken. The village where their families lived had been captured, and if your wife gets a letter from a union man, who knows but they'll shoot her for the connection?

They told about how they had not heard from their families for more than a year. They did not tell it gallantly or whimsically or stoically. They told it as if— Well, look. You have been in the trenches, fighting, for a year. You have heard nothing of your wife and your children. They do not know if you are dead or alive or blinded. You do not know where they are, or if they are. You must talk to somebody. That is the way they told about it.

One of them, some six months before, had heard of his wife and his three children—they had such beautiful eyes, he said—from a brother-in-law in France. They were all alive then, he was told, and had a bowl of beans a day. But his wife had not complained of the food, he heard. What had troubled her was that she had no thread to mend the children's ragged clothes. So that troubled him, too.

"She has no thread," he kept telling us. "My wife has no thread to mend with. No thread."

We sat there, and listened to what the Swedish girl told us they were saying. Suddenly one of them looked at the clock, and then there was excitement. They jumped up, as a man, and there were calls for the waiter and rapid talk with him, and each of them shook the hand of each of us. We went through more swimming motions to explain to them that they were to take the rest of the cigarettes—fourteen cigarettes for six soldiers to take to war—and then they shook our hands again. Then all of us said *"Salud!"* as many times as could be for six of them and three of us, and then they filed out of the café, the six of them, tired and dusty and little, as men of a mighty horde are little.

Only the Swedish girl talked, after they had gone. The Swedish girl had been in Spain since the start of the war. She has nursed splintered men, and she has carried stretchers into the trenches and, heavier laden, back to the hospital. She has seen and heard too much to be knocked into silence.

Presently it was time to go, and the Swedish girl raised her hands above her head and clapped them twice together to summon the waiter. He came, but he only shook his head and his hand, and moved away.

The soldiers had paid for our drinks.

DOROTHY PARKER *Soldiers of the Republic*

The short short-story has been facetiously called "the while-you're-waiting storyette." The following is a perfect example of the tense, compact, absorbing method in story telling that will make the reader miss his train if he has less than five minutes to wait. The reading time is four minutes for the rapid reader; twice as much for the slow reader. But the entertainment value cannot be measured by any clock, for in its short space it runs a whole gamut of emotions and yields a wealth of commentary on human conduct.*

Judge Henry heard the front door bell and opened a door on the second floor. He stepped into the hall quickly, pulled the door after him, and went down the stairs.

He walked ponderously but with his usual dignity. He crossed the hall, opened the front door, and stared into the leering face of Simon Oldholt.

"Oh!" he said. "What brings you here, Simon?"

"A lot," Oldholt said. "Ben, I'm going to tell you something that's going to take the starch out of you."

* Used by permission of Mr. Neil Moran and the *New York Herald Tribune.*

Judge Henry knew what he meant. Simon Oldholt had never liked him, and for years had taken exception to his judicial manner. "Always the Judge," Simon would say. "Have you ever seen him any different? Always the Judge. Big and pompous, walking along without blinking an eye. Never nettled. No, sir, never saw him nettled, not once."

Now, however, Simon had something of the greatest import to tell the Judge, which he believed would flatten him against that wall. "It's about Robert," he said. "Has he come home?"

"Robert? No." The Judge looked up. "No one is in the house but myself, Simon."

"Well, he'll be along. Any minute. Can we go into that room?"

"Yes, come along." The Judge entered. Simon followed and sat down. He was a wizened man, cashier for Towney and Company, local manufacturers, Robert's employers.

"Now, what I got to tell you," said Simon, "is going to take something out of your sails. You might think I'm a vindictive man talking like that, but I don't like you, Ben, and you know it."

The Judge nodded. He looked to Simon, sitting there, as if he might have been on the bench, with his robe on him. Always the Judge. Even now, in the face of this crude opening, he hadn't batted an eye. His face was set, his large hands folded.

"Once," said Simon, "you decided a case against me."

"Yes. I went by the law."

"Well, this is another case, Ben, and you can go by the law. It's the law that's brought me here. You're a judge, ain't you?"

"I've always been given reason to believe I am." Always the Judge. There he was. Weighing his answers, not the least nettled, disquieting and making smaller the ruthless man.

"Well, as a judge, then, you can tell me what's going to happen." Simon laughed.

The Judge folded his arms as if he might have been listening to a character witness.

"Before you do," he said, "I must remind you, Simon, that your attitude is very offensive. But accustomed as I am to dealing with all kinds of people, I long ago learned that to lose patience is a foolish thing. Rather would I admonish a person as I am doing you. Now, proceed."

Simon gaped at him. For a moment that speech had taken the wind out of Simon's sails, but he rallied.

"Well, then," he said, "for twenty years, Ben, ever since I've known you, I've wanted to see you nettled. I've wanted to see you come down off your high horse. I've wanted to see you stop being the Judge."

"Your prattling, Simon, is taking you off the main theme. In a court, a judge would have the right to reprove you for not keeping to the facts. Now, proceed."

Again Simon gaped at him.

"Well," he said, standing up to deliver better his bombshell, "I've come here to tell you that your son is a thief!"

The Judge never batted an eye. His brows contracted, then raised.

"I'm waiting, Simon," he said, very patiently. "The charge? The proof?"

"Proof, eh? Well, I guess they have all the proof in the world! A half hour ago old man Towney quizzed him and he confessed. Towney said that he wanted to see you first. I told him I'd come up and tell you."

"So kind of you, Simon."

"Oh, you needn't go on that way with me! Haven't you anything to say about it? Are you going to sit there and take this as if you were a piece of wood? Good Lord, man, are you human, or are you a machine?"

"A judge," said Ben Henry, looking at him.

"Yes, a judge. And the father of a son who embezzled ten thousand dollars. That's what he took. Lost it gambling. He's afraid to come home. But this afternoon, Ben Henry, there'll be a warrant for his arrest. And you can sit here just as if—"

"I can sit here, Simon, and what you say doesn't mean a thing. You thought you could shock me. You thought you could bring me to my knees. You thought you could see me for once, not always the Judge, as you said. Well, Simon, I've disappointed you."

"You ain't human," Simon roared. "Or else you're acting. No, you ain't acting. You sit there as if you grew in that chair. Yes, nothing could shock you."

"Is that all, Simon? I'll see you to the door."

After Simon had gone, Judge Ben Henry went ponderously up the stairs, with his usual dignity. When he reached the top, he turned and faltered for a moment, as his hand clasped the bannister. Then he went down the hall.

He had defeated Simon Oldholt at his own game. A thousand Simons couldn't nettle him.

He opened the door of the room he had left. He looked at the body on the bed. "So that was the reason."

He turned, and with set face went out of the room. Ponderously and with dignity, he descended the stairs. At the bottom he sank to his knees and bowed his head. . . .

"Yep, the man ain't human," said Simon, as he crossed the street. "Ain't human. But you've got to say for him, he's always the Judge!"

NEIL MORAN *Not Human*

The high-sounding term *architectonics* is sometimes applied to literature by critics and professors to denote construction or plan or organization or systematization of composition. The term connotes on sight that it has something to do with architecture. Well, applied to a piece of literature, it may just exactly be called by the better-known term. But *plan* will do as well. Note in the following realistic story * how the author's plan is made to drive incisively, without the slightest waste or "padding," toward effective conclusion. This is a story of character, a story of incident, a story of a good deal of local color. And while it is all of these it is, in addition, a masterpiece in construction, a fine example of the application of architectonics, or plan, in composition.

The boys in the stock room sent Bud and me over to order a bouquet. They said we could go up to fifteen dollars, if necessary, and this certainly is a case where a skimpy floral tribute would look worse than none at all. So give us the best in the greenhouse, something more showy and bigger, but along the same lines as that basket the dye crew bought for their old boss, when he passed away.

Russ Braley had a dirty deal, right from the start, but there's no reason why we can't show our respect for him now.

It was only two weeks ago last Monday morning that he came to the mill. We were all standing there in the main aisle, chinning and waiting for the whistle to blow, when we noticed this stranger on the front stairs.

He was about twenty-four, medium-sized and wiry, sandy-haired, freckled as a rainbow trout, with a heavy tan from wind and sunburn. He wore a black shop shirt, a leather bow tie and, although his pants were mended, they looked awful clean and neat.

What struck you most was the fellow's manner—eager as a spaniel pup who has scented a covey of partridges. He smiled at us as if wanting to say "good morning," but waiting from politeness, so that we could say it first.

"Is this the stock room?" he asked.

"No, you dumb bobbin. It's the laundry," said Charley Laughlin. "Don't you see all the tubs?"

Of course, the joke was that there weren't any tubs. The way the second floor in the main building is fixtured, it couldn't possibly be anything except storage space for finished stock. There are eleven rows of hanger racks, under individual dust covers, on one side of the center aisle. On the other side are all the shelf racks for cartons.

Even the newcomer had to laugh at himself for asking such a silly question. Then he said, "I'm looking for the foreman, Mr. Laughlin."

"That's me," Charley answered.

"Mr. Laughlin, I'm glad to meet you. My name's Russ Braley." He set down his dinner pail, ready to be introduced to the gang.

"Yeah? What of it?" Laughlin's hands stayed in his pockets.

"Why, I'm your new man. I'm here to go to work."

"Who said so?"

"The young lady at the window by the gate. She stamped my time card and—"

Charley scowled. "Them fools in the front office have bulled things up again." He clattered downstairs, two steps at a time. The smile on Russ Braley's face disappeared slowly. All of Laughlin's pals took their cue from the boss and glared.

"Ever worked in a mill before?" someone asked.

"Sure."

"How long?"

"All my life."

"Where?"

"Careyville."

"That's not the same. Careyville is a cotton town."

Braley shook his head.

"Are they going into wool?"

"No. They're not doing anything. The mill's closed."

"Why?"

"They weren't making expenses. They had to move the machinery away to some place where labor could be hired cheaper."

"Didn't the town do something about it?"

"It went on relief, mostly," said Russ Braley. "Except a few of us who left there."

Before we found out any more about Careyville, Charley Laughlin came back, puffing from the stairs. He was red-faced and ugly-tempered, as he always was when he hadn't had his own way.

"God knows what this mill is coming to," he growled. "They will always make a place on the pay roll for some half-baked stranger. But a good man, one who was born and raised right here in Union Falls, can walk the streets idle. It's a hell of a note."

We all drifted away from the trouble zone and left the new man there with the foreman.

"Mr. Laughlin," he spoke up, very businesslike, "what do you want me to do?"

"I don't care. Do anything you can."

"Then, perhaps I'd better brush the floor. It needs it. Where do you keep your tools?"

Charley looked surprised and pointed to the closet at the top of the ramp. It was the first time anyone in his gang had ever volunteered to sweep.

That morning, Bud and I were busy over in the far corner. We were closing out some fourteen-sixty-eights, which is a discontinued line of winter sports wear, and making up a shipment for the Woolen Goods Manufacturers Association annual sale of mill ends and jobbers' lots. As he worked toward us, we began noticing the new fellow. Bud agreed with me that Russ Braley was the best man with a push broom we had ever seen. He scattered the compound very even, without wasting a spoonful of it. He brushed with short strokes, so that he wouldn't raise a dust. He was fast, and when he had been through an aisle, it was clean as a finishing-room deck.

When he came where we were, he moved our dolly truck, swept and moved it back again. Not one man in a hundred is gentleman enough to do that.

"Thanks," said Bud.

Braley looked at us inquiringly and decided that Bud and I weren't against him. "Mind if I ask something?"

"Don't ask it too loud," said Bud. "This department is full of ears."

"Was it anything I did that made Mr. Laughlin sore at me?"

Bud peered around to make sure the next aisle was empty. "The boss has a nephew. This kid wanted the job you got."

"They take the applications in turn," Braley replied. "That's what they told me."

"Other people do, but the boss' relations are different," Bud explained. "Charley has been pulling wires to have the kid moved ahead, to the top of the list. He even made his brag that two weeks was the longest any Laughlin was ever out of work."

"Oh!" Braley shrugged. "That's just foreman's politics."

He went on with his job. There wasn't a lazy hair on that fellow's head. When his sweeping was finished, he made himself useful any way he could. As soon as a dolly truck was filled, he changed it for an empty and rolled the full truck down the ramp to the shipping room. All the time he was watching and learning our system of picking orders. In spite of himself, Charley warmed to him a little.

"Hey, you," he called to the new man at twelve o'clock. "It's time for spaghetti. You can come over to the diner with the rest of us."

"Thank you." Russ had gone to the coat room for his dinner pail. He held it up so Charley could see it. "I don't believe I will today. I have my lunch with me."

"Nuts to that cold stuff. A man needs a hot poultice in him, in the middle of the day."

"I don't mind sandwiches."

"It only costs you thirty cents for a square meal."

"No, it's out of the question."

"Look here. I'll lend you the money until you are paid. I won't charge you any interest," Charley offered.

"Mr. Laughlin," said Russ, "I've been out of work for eight months. Until some of my debts are paid, I can't afford to spend thirty cents a day just humoring my stomach."

"I always heard you cotton-mill fellows were cheap," sneered the boss.

The gang started over to the diner. But Bud sneaked away from the rest and went back. He felt guilty that he hadn't warned the new fellow.

"Listen, Braley," he told him. "The chow is no good, but we all eat there, even if going home would be handier. Laughlin's son-in-law runs the dump and Charley has an interest, besides his chattel mortgage on the fixtures. Wise up and come along."

Braley shook his head. "My wife put up a nice lunch. I mustn't waste it."

"Well, if you're sorry afterwards, don't blame me," Bud said.

When the mill let out at five, the new man I happened to walk out together.

"Where you living?" I asked.

"At Sawyer's farm. That's two miles outside the village. He's my wife's brother. Mr. and Mrs. Sawyer have been mighty good to us, letting us stay there and work for our board. There's still hay out and the harvesting to do, so I guess we'll stay on for a while. I can help him nights and mornings."

"Don't tell me that you're figuring on doing any more tonight."

"Oh, I'll accomplish a whole lot before dark. There are the cows, of course, and the horses to feed and bed down and the milk to cool before we eat our supper. And in the morning, by getting up at four o'clock instead of half-past, I can milk, do the other chores and still have plenty of time to change my clothes, eat breakfast and be in the mill at eight."

For a minute, I thought he was kidding me. "That's impossible," I said.

"I did it this morning."

"You can't stand it to work like that, Braley. You'll kill yourself. You'd better move to town."

"I must square up, first. I'll have plenty of time to take life easy, later on. They say this mill runs fifty-two weeks a year."

The fellow was just as interested in his job as most of us would be in a camping trip. In fact, the next noon he ate his hard-boiled eggs, sandwiches and cake, drank his tea and brushed up the crumbs as fast as he could. Then Russ took a sheet of white cardboard, thirty inches square, borrowed a straight-edge and pencil from the order desk and walked around the outside of the stock room.

Over on the north side, he found a man sitting on a window ledge. He was a big man, about forty years old, and no one Russ had seen around there before. Braley guessed he was front-office help because his pants were pressed and his shoes shined. He was in his shirt sleeves and eating his lunch. Nothing very hearty, just a couple of sandwiches wrapped in waxed paper and a half-pint bottle of certified milk with a straw stuck in it, from the dairy store.

"Hello," he said, pleasanter than most bookkeepers. "This seems to be the coolest spot in the mill. I hope you don't mind if I eat here."

"I don't care," said Russ. "Only clear up after yourself, or it will be blamed on me."

"Don't any others bring their lunches?"

"Not on the second floor. Mr. Laughlin makes everyone else who works for him go over to the diner."

"You mean he takes them to that old shack on the corner?"

"Yes," Russ nodded.

"I didn't even know that Laughlin owned it."

"I couldn't prove that he does," said Russ. "The others warned me that I'd better eat there, even if I had to borrow the money to pay for my meals. They claimed that Mr. Laughlin was behind it, but let his son-in-law run the place. But don't quote me. I'm in bad as it is."

"For not eating there?"

"Yes, for not eating there, and because Mr. Laughlin had made arrangements to give this job to his nephew. But something slipped and I got it instead."

"Oh. I see."

"Don't repeat that," Russ begged him. "I shouldn't have said anything about it."

"I won't let it go any further," the other promised. "Don't worry."

"Thanks."

Russ started on. He was counting aisles, across the end.

"What are you doing?" The man pointed to the cardboard.

"Well," Russ was embarrassed, "it's just an idea of mine. Being new here, I don't know where to find the stock. So I thought if I could make a map of all the racks in the room, it would help me find the items when Mr. Laughlin lets me start picking orders."

The other jumped up. "You mean a floor plan. And you're right. There ought to have been a blueprint of the stock locations made long ago. Have you laid out your drawing?"

"That's the part I can't figure."

"There's nothing to it. Here. Let me take the cardboard. What's your scale?"

"I guess I don't understand."

"Sure you do. One inch here is the same as three feet in the building. This line represents this wall. Pace it off, over to the door, and we'll locate the openings."

The fellow roughed in an outline sketch, showing the aisles, ramp and stairways.

"It's crude." He handed it over. "But perhaps it will serve your purpose until you get a chance to make a better one for yourself. All you have to do now is draw in the lines to represent the aisles, and crosslines, double, like this, for each rack."

"It's swell looking," said Braley. "It's beautiful. Thanks a million."

"Good luck to you." He shook hands with Russ, picked up his milk bottle and went away.

That cardboard floor plan was Braley's Bible. There was a tiny square on it to represent every rack in the room. And as fast as he learned them, Russ penciled the stock numbers in the squares where they belonged.

The result was that, after he had located a garment once, he could be sure of finding it again. He wasn't a nuisance to the old hands, the way new men usually are, while they are learning the floor. For instance, Old Gill has been in the department for five years. And if he picks a requisition for twelve-twelves, the kiddies snow suits, from the hook, he always has to ask someone where the twelve-twelves are.

Things went smoothly until Thursday, when Charley Laughlin was late coming back from his nooning. It must have been about two when he finally turned up, cursing and swearing at everything and everybody. He went over to his desk and stopped short as he noticed a blue sheet. "When did this come?" he roared, waving it around.

"During the noon hour, Mr. Laughlin," Russ Braley answered.

"Why ain't it been picked?"

"Because yesterday you told us never to touch an order sheet until after you had put it on the hook."

"Pick it, smart guy," said Charley, handing it to him.

Blue sheets are always TODAY-MUSTS and come up to the stock department only after they have received a telegraph or extra urgent order downstairs. This one called for a few dozen of our standard sixteen-oh-three B's.

The garment is a pure worsted, light-weight, pull-over sweater, regularly stocked in eleven colors: Navy, Yale and Confederate blue, light and Oxford gray, Lincoln and Hanover green, tan, russet brown, smoke and white. We also carry it special, for our Hollywood jobber, in canary, vermilion and ivory black.

It wouldn't have taken Russ twenty minutes to pick the order, if he hadn't been stopped on a size. "Mr. Laughlin," he said, "we're broken in Confederate."

"What size are we broke in?"

"Forty-two."

"Cut the size tabs of some fortys and forty-fours. Sew forty-two tabs in them. You'll find needle, thread and extra tabs in my desk."

"Is it all right to do that?" asked Russ.

"Certainly. When you buy a forty-two garment in a store, you expect that they'll run a little large or a little small."

Had anyone but Russ been picking that "immediate" the boss would have had two or three helping him. But he had to do it alone. All the afternoon he hurried like a girl whose fellow is waiting while she sews up a split seam in her party dress. Finally, he called again, "Mr. Laughlin."

"What-ch want now?"

"I've borrowed so many fortys and forty-fours to fill out the forty-twos, that now I'm broken in all three sizes."

"Mark some forty-sixes down to forty-four. Mark some thirty-eights up to forty and so on. Use your head."

It was only a few minutes short of five o'clock when Russ finished, signed "Braley" beneath the words "Filled by" on the order slip, grabbed his dolly truck and shot down to the shipping room with it.

He acted fagged out, as he came back up the ramp. He stopped at the fountain for a drink.

"Done?" asked Charley.

"Yes, Mr. Laughlin."

"You took it downstairs all right?"

"Yes. What shall I start now?"

We all had to stay a few minutes overtime, that afternoon, to catch up. A lot of new production had come in.

"Forget it, Braley," the foreman said. "You've got a long walk ahead of you. You needn't wait. You done such a nice job, I appreciate it. Take your dinner bucket and go along as soon as the whistle blows."

It was the first pleasant thing Charley had ever said to him. Russ fell for it. "Thank you, Mr. Laughlin. I hope I got it off in time. It was stamped for air-mail parcel post."

"That's not your worry."

"I did the best I could."

"Nobody can do more than that. So long, Braley." Charley watched him as the poor cuss went down the stairs.

Bud and I were sizing a rack of thirty-seven-fifty-ones for inventory. About ten after five, the phone began ringing. We saw Charley lounge over to answer it. "Stock room. Laughlin speaking."

Someone on the other end was mad. We could hear the receiver crackle.

"What order? . . . What order are you talking about? . . . What missed the night train?"

He waited.

"Yes, I know blue sheets are timed in and timed out. But I'm asking you what blue sheet this is. Who filled it? Whose name is signed? . . . Braley, eh? . . ." Charley grinned. "Go on. You'll be doing me a favor, if you kick to the front office about it. Maybe if you kick and I kick, too, the front office will let me have something to say about who is hired up here. I know the type of man I need. . . . Yes, fire him. He's just a tramp anyhow. And I'll have someone here, that I can guarantee, day after t'morrow."

The next morning, as we came through the gate, Russ was trying to explain it all to the paymaster's girl. "But I only did just exactly what I was told," he said. "They can't put the blame on me."

She didn't know what it was all about. Everyone who is fired has an alibi. She had her orders and she couldn't be bothered with some poor dub's troubles. So she shut her window in Braley's face.

He counted his money—it was only four days' pay—brushed the back of his hand across his eyes, picked up his dinner pail and left.

Russ didn't look at us. We tried not to look at him, for fear it would make him feel worse. There was nothing we could do about it.

The stock room went on as usual, and, Saturday, Charley's nephew came in, replacing Braley.

That is all that I remember until Wednesday noon, when we went over to the diner for our chow. Murph was ahead and he was the one who found the door locked. He rattled the catch, but no one came.

Laughlin blustered up. "What's the trouble here? Go on in and eat."

"The joint's closed."

"Closed? You must be crazy. I guess I'd have something to say about that."

"I wouldn't say too much. This notice on the screen reads that it's been condemned and closed as unsanitary, by order of the state board of health."

Charley hesitated. Then he put on his reading spectacles and looked at the paper. "Well," he said, "it's too bad on the boy's account. But it's nothing to me, one way or the other. It was my son-in-law's."

"The rat," said Bud to me, while we were getting our snack at the Greek's. "He took his share of the profits, but he wasn't man enough to admit it, when the time came."

Later Charley was threatening to find out who his enemies were and claimed he knew it was someone on the second floor who had reported the diner. But before he had had time to do anything about it, the production manager called for a copy of the perpetual stock inventory. Charley had to work all one afternoon and most of the night faking it, because his daily sheets had not been entered for months.

Then, yesterday, while Bud and I were doubling up two discontinued numbers in polo shirts to make room for the new product, we heard a voice shout, "Laughlin."

"Who is it?" Bud whispered to me.

I peered around the corner. "Great Peter! It's his nibs, himself."

"Wilson Hunt?"

I nodded.

"Let's hear this. Move over a couple of aisles and make believe we're dusting stock. Maybe he has found out that Charley's inventory sheets don't check with the count." Bud nudged me. "Boy! Would that be good!"

"Laughlin," the big boss shouted again.

It isn't once a week that Mr. Hunt comes around the mill. He has other interests and spends his time in Boston and New York. While he is the head of the business, he is not a part of it, the way his father was.

"Laughlin!"

That brought Charley out of his hideaway, on the pile of tarpaulins, where he sneaks to nap.

"Yes, sir."

"If you have any explanation of that error you made when you filled a telegraph order up here, perhaps ten days ago, let me have it."

"Mr. Hunt, I'm sorry to say that an air-mail parcel-post package was delayed."

"That isn't what I mean. Wrong sizes were shipped in that order. Size tabs had been changed. Fortys and forty-fours were tabbed forty-twos. We had four dozen returns from a twelve-dozen order."

Charley shook his head mournfully. "Well, I never suspected anything as bad as that. But it won't happen again, because the fellow who picked that order has been discovered and discharged."

"Go on."

"Well, that's all. Except that I told the timekeeper to make a notation against his name, so that he never will be rehired again."

"Replaced him yet?"

"Yes, Mr. Hunt. At once. We had to. We were shorthanded."

"Go on."

"I happened to know a fine young fellow, right here in the village, a high-school graduate—"

"Name?"

"William Laughlin."

"Oh. Perhaps he's a relative."

Something in Mr. Hunt's tone made Charley nervous. "Well, when you've watched a boy grow up, practically in your own family, you know more about him—"

"He's related to you. What other qualification has he for this job?"

"He's bright."

"Did he ever work in a stock department before?"

"Well, no."

"In a mill?"

"No."

"I want to talk to him."

"Certainly, sir. Billy!" Laughlin called. "Come here. Bring your diagram." The foreman turned to Mr. Hunt. "He made a pretty fine drawing to help him learn the stock room quicker."

Bud and I just gasped. The nerve of that louse, who was taking credit for Russ Braley's idea and Russ Braley's work.

Mr. Hunt looked at the pasteboard sheet. "Where did you get your training in mechanical drawing?"

"Well—uh—I—uh—that is—"

"Billy's smart as a new dollar," Charley interrupted. "He picks things up."

"I see." Mr. Hunt pointed to something on the diagram. "What's this?"

"Just part of the drawing, sir."

"Funny. I thought it indicated a steel pillar. What's this?"

"It's—oh, it's a kind of curlycue I put in there."

"What a coincidence. An engineer would have used that symbol to indicate a floor drain under a sprinkler head."

The boy gulped. "Sure. That's it. That's what I meant."

"And you drew this?"

"Yes, sir."

"Mr. Hunt," said Charley, "I saw him drawing it."

"That settles it, if you saw him," said Wilson Hunt. "This has been going on long enough."

Laughlin looked scared to death. "What do you mean?"

"Your lying and your crookedness. I had to send for the state board of health to stop your restaurant racket and get rid of your son-in-law. I'll have to pay hundreds of dollars in overtime, to correct that inventory you turned over to the production manager. But I still failed to realize what a miserable creature you are, until you two stood there and told me how he drew this while you watched."

Wilson Hunt shook the pasteboard in the Laughlins' faces. "I ate my lunch up here, one noon. I met an intelligent, hard-working young fellow. I broke an appointment to stay here and help him make this very floor plan that you swear is your work. Get out and stay out."

So that's why we're buying this floral tribute. . . . We want a ribbon on it, with gold lettering, To Russ Braley From Your True Pals in the Stock Room, Welcome Back. You ought to deliver it early, so it will be on his order desk when he comes in Monday morning.

GEORGE S. BROOKS *Floral Tribute*

The news short-story is very often the most direct and impressive of the type. An absorbing story of detection,* utterly without embroidery, is told in an engaging conversational manner.

HAS HECTIC TIME WAITING FOR WIFE

Londoner Parked Outside Store Is Persuaded to Take Stranger Into Car

THEN TO START LONG RIDE

But Adventure Complicated by Gas Shortage and a £1 Note Ends Unexpectedly for Passenger

A man in a ready-made suit of blue serge drifted over to the roadster in which James Hatton of Brighton was waiting for his wife in front of a London department store and said:

"Open the door and let me in."

"But why?" inquired James. "I am waiting for my wife, and"—then he saw why. The man held concealed from passersby by his arms as he leaned against the open window a blue automatic. So James opened the door; the man entered and told James to take the road for Southampton. James complied.

Something familiar about the face of his passenger haunted James during the first part of the drive. Then he smiled and inquired:

"Are you not Mr. Albert Reed, late of Dartmoor [penitentiary], in Devonshire, whose picture is now being printed in all the papers, together with the offer of a reward of £500 for any one who is so fortunate as to take you into custody?"

"The same," replied the passenger, "but you will never collect the 500 quid, for this side of Winchester I shall

truss you up at the wayside where you will not be found for several hours."

"Dear me," sighed James, and then, a few moments later:

"I'm very sorry, but this car is almost out of petrol. What do you suggest?"

"Pull up at that one-man station over yonder, and look sharp. No tricks."

After the car had received five gallons, the passenger turned to James and said:

"You pay."

"I am sorry, but my wife took all my change. This man wants five and a tanner, and I have only a pound note." And to the oil man: "Change it?" The oil man shook his head.

The passenger laughed. " 'Fraid you'll lose your quid," he observed.

Then James said to the oil man:

"Here, you take the note and I'll write my name on it, and collect the change when I come back."

"Right for me," said the oil man.

James wrote on the pound note, folded it twice, handed it through the window, and started the car.

Just before Winchester, there is a curve in the road.

"Beyond," said the passenger, "there is a wood. Drive into a side path and I'll tie you up."

It was a sharp curve and James slowed up, but around it he stopped. A line had been stretched across the road and two police cars were in waiting, and near by, armed with rifles, were half a dozen policemen, one of whom said:

"Well, Albert, we've got you, so drop that pistol and descend."

After certain formalities had been complied with at the Winchester police station, James, having easily obtained from the chief constable the loan of a few shillings on his prospective £500 reward, started back to London. On his way he stopped at the oil station to pay for the oil and redeem his pound note. The oil man, smiling in admiration, said:

"You're a keen un', and here's your quid. You hadn't been gone a minute when I telephoned the police, just as you wrote I was to do."

* Used by permission of *The New York Times.*

This didactic story is very largely conversational in method, and it is almost as much a collective-character story as it is a didactic one. It may be interesting to know that it was written for an annual convention of the American Booksellers' Association and was dedicated to the booksellers of the United States and Canada.* Its gentle irony was therefore probably not completely lost.

"Wish to look about the store? Oh, by all means, sir," he said.

Then, as he rubbed his hands together in an urbane fashion, he directed a piercing glance at me through his spectacles.

"You'll find some things that might interest you," he said, "in the back of the store on the left. We have there a series of reprints—'Universal Knowledge from Aristotle to Arthur Balfour,'—at seventeen cents. Or perhaps you might like to look over the 'Pantheon of Dead Authors,' at ten cents. Mr. Sparrow," he called, "just show this gentleman our classical reprints,—the ten-cent series."

With that he waved his hand to an assistant and dismissed me from his thought.

In other words, he had divined me in a moment. There was no use in my having bought a sage-green fedora in Broadway, and a sporting tie done up crosswise with spots as big as nickels. These little adornments can never hide the soul within. I was a professor, and he knew it, or, at least, as part of his business, he could divine it on the instant.

The sales manager of the biggest book store for ten blocks cannot be deceived in a customer. And he knew, of course, that, as a professor, I was no good. I had come to the store, as all professors go to book stores, just as a wasp comes to an open jar of marmalade. He knew that I would hang around for two hours, get in everybody's way, and finally buy a cheap reprint of the "Dialogues of Plato," or the "Prose Works of John Milton," or "Locke on the Human Understanding," or some trash of that sort.

As for real taste in literature—the ability to appreciate at its worth a dollar-fifty novel of last month, in a spring jacket with a tango frontispiece—I hadn't got it and he knew it.

He despised me, of course. But it is a maxim of the book business that a professor standing up in a corner buried in a book looks well in a store. The real customers like it.

So it was that even so up-to-date a manager as Mr. Sellyer tolerated my presence in a back corner of his store: and so it was that I had an opportunity of noting something of his methods with his real customers

* Used by permission of Mr. Stephen Leacock.

—methods so successful, I may say, that he is rightly looked upon by all the publishing business as one of the mainstays of literature in America.

I had no intention of standing in the place and listening as a spy. In fact, to tell the truth, I had become immediately interested in a new translation of the "Moral Discourses of Epictetus." The book was very neatly printed, quite well bound and was offered at eighteen cents; so that for the moment I was strongly tempted to buy it, though it seemed best to take a dip into it first.

I had hardly read more than the first three chapters, when my attention was diverted by a conversation going on in the front of the store.

"You're quite sure it's his *latest?*" a fashionably dressed lady was saying to Mr. Sellyer.

"Oh, yes, Mrs. Rasselyer," answered the manager. "I assure you this is his very latest. In fact they only came in yesterday."

As he spoke, he indicated with his hand a huge pile of books, gayly jacketed in white and blue. I could make out the title in big gilt lettering—*"Golden Dreams."*

"Oh, yes," repeated Mr. Sellyer. "This is Mr. Slush's latest book. It's having a wonderful sale."

"That's all right, then," said the lady. "You see one sometimes gets taken in so: I came in here last week and took two that seemed very nice, and I never noticed till I got home that they were both old books, published, I think, six months ago."

"Oh, dear me, Mrs. Rasselyer," said the manager, in an apologetic tone. "I'm extremely sorry. Pray, let us send for them and exchange them for you."

"Oh, it does not matter," said the lady, "of course, I didn't read them. I gave them to my maid. She probably wouldn't know the difference anyway."

"I suppose not," said Mr. Sellyer, with a condescending smile. "But, of course, madam," he went on, falling into the easy chat of the fashionable bookman, "such mistakes are bound to happen sometimes. We had a very painful case only yesterday. One of our oldest customers came in a great hurry to buy books to take on the steamer, and before we realized what he had done—selecting the books I suppose merely by the titles, as some gentlemen are apt to do—he had taken two of last year's books. We wired at once to the steamer, but I am afraid it's too late."

"But now, this book," said the lady, idly turning over the leaves. "Is it good? What is it about?"

"It's an extremely *powerful* thing," said Mr. Sellyer, "in fact, *masterly.* The critics are saying that it's perhaps *the* most powerful book of the season. It has a—" and here Mr. Sellyer paused, and somehow his manner reminded me of my own when I am explaining to a university class something that I don't know myself—"it has a—a—*power,* so to speak—a very exceptional power; in fact, one may say without exaggeration it is the most *powerful* book of the month. Indeed," he added, getting on to easier ground, "it's having a perfectly wonderful sale."

"You seem to have a great many of them," said the lady.

"Oh, we have to," answered the manager. "There's a regular rush on the book. Indeed, you know, it's a book that is bound to make a sensation. In fact, in certain quarters, they are saying that it's a book that ought not to—" and here Mr. Sellyer's voice became so low and ingratiating that I couldn't hear the rest of the sentence.

"Oh, really!" said Mrs. Rasselyer. "Well, I think I'll take it anyway. One ought to see what these talked-of things are about anyway."

She had already begun to button her gloves, and to readjust her feather boa with which she had been knocking the Easter cards off the counter. Then she suddenly remembered something.

"Oh, I was forgetting," she said. "Will you send something to the house for Mr. Rasselyer at the same time? He's going down to Virginia for the vacation. You know the kind of thing he likes, do you not?"

"Oh, perfectly, madam," said the manager. "Mr. Rasselyer generally reads works of—er—I think he buys mostly books on—er—"

"Oh, travel and that sort of thing," said the lady.

"Precisely. I think we have here," and he pointed to the counter on the left, "what Mr. Rasselyer wants."

He indicated a row of handsome books—"Seven Weeks in the Sahara," seven dollars; "Six Months in a Waggon," six-fifty net; "Afternoons in an Oxcart," two volumes, four-thirty with twenty off.

"I think he has read those," said Mrs. Rasselyer. "At least there are a good many at home that seem like that."

"Oh, very possibly—but here now 'Among the Cannibals of Corfu'— yes, that I think he has had; 'Among the—' that, too, I think—but this I am certain he would like—just in this morning—'Among the Monkeys of New Guinea,' ten dollars net."

And with this Mr. Sellyer laid his hand on a pile of new books, apparently as numerous as the huge pile of "Golden Dreams."

" 'Among the Monkeys,' " he repeated, almost caressingly.

"It seems rather expensive," said the lady.

"Oh, very much so—a most expensive book—" the manager repeated in a tone of enthusiasm—"you see, Mrs. Rasselyer, it's the illustrations, actual photographs," he ran the leaves over in his fingers, "of actual monkeys, taken with the camera—and the paper, you notice—in fact, madam, the book costs, the mere manufacture of it, nine dollars and ninety cents—of course, we make no profit on it. But it's a book we like to handle."

Everybody likes to be taken into the details of technical business; and, of course, everybody likes to know that a bookseller is losing money. These, I realized, were two axioms in the methods of Mr. Sellyer.

So, very naturally Mrs. Rasselyer bought "Among the Monkeys," and in another moment Mr. Sellyer was directing a clerk to write down an address on Fifth Avenue, and was bowing deeply as he showed the lady out of the door.

As he turned back to his counter his manner seemed much changed.

"That monkey book," I heard him murmur to his assistant, "is going to be a pretty stiff proposition."

But he had no time for further speculation.

Another lady entered.

This time even to an eye less trained than Mr. Sellyer's the deep, expensive mourning and the pensive eye proclaimed the sentimental widow.

"Something new in fiction," repeated the manager, "yes, madam— here's a charming thing—'Golden Dreams' "—he hung lovingly on the words, "a very sweet story, singularly sweet, in fact, madam, the critics are saying it is the sweetest thing that Mr. Slush has done."

"Is it good?" said the lady. I began to realize that all customers asked this.

"A charming book," said the manager. "It's a love story—very simple and sweet, yet wonderfully charming. Indeed, the reviews say it's the most charming book of the month. My wife was reading it aloud only last night. She could hardly read for tears."

"I suppose it's quite a safe book, is it?" asked the widow. "I want it for my little daughter."

"Oh, quite safe," said Mr. Sellyer, with an almost parental tone, "in fact, written quite in the old style, like the dear old books of the past— quite like—" here Mr. Sellyer paused, with a certain slight haze of doubt visible in his eye—"like Dickens and Fielding and Sterne, and so on. We sell a great many to the clergy, madam."

The lady bought "Golden Dreams," received it wrapped up in green enameled paper, and passed out.

"Have you any good light reading for vacation time?" called out the next customer in a loud, breezy voice—he had the air of a stock-broker starting on a holiday.

"Yes," said Mr. Sellyer, and his face almost broke into a laugh as he answered, "here's an excellent thing, 'Golden Dreams'—quite the most humorous book of the season—simply screaming—my wife was reading it aloud only yesterday. She could hardly read for laughing."

"What's the price, one dollar? One-fifty. All right, wrap it up." There was a clink of money on the counter, and the customer was gone. I began to see exactly where professors and college people, who want copies of Epictetus at eighteen cents, and sections of "World Reprints of Literature" at twelve cents a section, come in, in the book trade.

"Yes, judge!" said the manager to the next customer, a huge, dignified personage in a wide-awake hat, "sea stories? Certainly. Excellent reading, no doubt, when the brain is overcharged as yours must be. Here is the very latest—'Among the Monkeys of New Guinea,' ten dollars, reduced to four-fifty. The manufacture alone costs six-eighty. We're selling it out. Thank you, judge. Send it? Yes. Good morning."

After that the customers came and went in a string. I noticed that though the store was filled with books—ten thousand of them at a guess —Mr. Sellyer was apparently only selling two. Every woman who entered went away with "Golden Dreams," every man was given a copy of the "Monkeys of New Guinea." To one lady "Golden Dreams" was sold as exactly the reading for a holiday, to another as the very book to read *after* a holiday; another bought it as a book for a rainy day, and a fourth as the right sort of reading for a fine day. "The Monkeys" was sold as a sea story, a land story, a story of the jungle, and a story of the mountains, and it was put at a price corresponding to Mr. Sellyer's estimate of the purchaser.

At last, after a busy two hours, the store grew empty for a moment.

"Wilfred," said Mr. Sellyer, turning to his chief assistant, "I am going out to lunch. Keep those two books running as hard as you can. We'll try them for another day and then cut them right out. And I'll drop round to Docken and discount the publishers and make a kick about them and see what they'll do."

I felt that I had lingered long enough. I drew near with the Epictetus in my hand.

"Yes, sir," said Mr. Sellyer, professional again in a moment. "Epictetus? A charming thing. Eighteen cents. Thank you. Perhaps we have some other things that might interest you. We have a few second-hand things in the alcove there that you might care to look at. There's an Aristotle, two volumes—a very fine thing—practically illegible, that you might like, and a Cicero came in yesterday—very choice—damaged by damp—and I think we have a Machiavelli, quite exceptional—practically torn to pieces, and the covers gone—a very rare old thing, sir, if you're an expert."

"No thanks," I said. And then, from a curiosity that had been growing in me and that I couldn't resist, "That book—'Golden Dreams'," I said, "you seem to think it a very wonderful work?"

Mr. Sellyer directed one of his shrewd glances at me. He knew I didn't want to buy the book, but, perhaps, like lesser people, he had his off moments of confidence.

He shook his head.

"A bad business," he said. "The publishers have unloaded the thing on us, and we have to do what we can. They're stuck with it, I understand, and they look to us to help them. They're advertising it largely and may pull it off. Of course, there's just a chance. One can't tell. It's just possible we may get the church people down on it, and, if so, we're all right. But short of that we'll never make it. I imagine it's perfectly rotten."

"Haven't you read it?" I asked.

"Dear me, no!" said the manager. His air was that of a milkman who is offered a glass of his own milk. "A pretty time I'd have if I tried to *read* the new books. It's quite enough to keep track of them without that."

"But those people," I went on, deeply perplexed, "who bought the book. Won't they be disappointed?"

Mr. Sellyer shook his head. "Oh, no," he said, "you see, they won't *read* it. They never do."

"But, at any rate," I insisted, "your wife thought it a fine story."

Mr. Sellyer smiled widely.

"I am not married, sir," he said.

STEPHEN LEACOCK *The Methods of Mr. Sellyer*
(A Book Store Study)

After you have read the superb character story following, you will have in mind and heart a totality and an isolation of impression such as are all too rarely vouchsafed those who love good stories. The delineation of Rose is vivid, incisive, uncompromising; she is etched with an inevitable line of acid edge and depth and clarity. At the same time, the portrayal is eloquent of a certain ruthless tenderness and is charged with a poignant emotion that make it unique in the literature of its kind. It is excelled by nothing in the pages of Balzac, De Maupassant, Kipling, Poe, Irving, Harte, Hawthorne, Henry, or in the other pages of the author herself. It has been called the best character story in the language, not only for the revelations made by the lines themselves but for those that so inescapably stand out from between the lines.*

The Self-Complacent Young Cub leaned an elbow against the mantel as you've seen it done in English plays, and blew a practically perfect smoke ring. It hurtled toward me like a discus.

"Trouble with your stuff," he began at once (we had just been introduced), "is that it lacks plot. Been meaning to meet and tell you that for a long time. Your characterization's all right, and your dialogue. In fact, I think they're good. But your stuff lacks *raison d'être*—if you know what I mean."

"But"—in feeble self-defence—"people's insides are often so much more interesting than their outsides; that which they think or feel so much more thrilling than anything they actually do. Bennett—Wells—"

"Rot!" remarked the young cub, briskly. "Plot's the thing."

There is no plot to this because there is no plot to Rose. There never was. There never will be. Compared to the drab monotony of Rose's existence a desert waste is as thrilling as a five-reel film.

They had called her Rose, fatuously, as parents do their first-born girl. No doubt she had been normally pink and white and velvety. It is a risky thing to do, however. Think back hastily on the Roses you know. Don't you find a startling majority still clinging, sere and withered, to the family bush?

In Chicago, Illinois, a city of two millions (or is it three?), there are women whose lives are as remote, as grey, as unrelated to the world about them as is the life of a Georgia cracker's woman-drudge. Rose was one of these. An unwed woman, grown heavy about the hips and arms, as houseworking women do, though they eat but little, moving dully about the six-room flat on Sangamon Street, Rose was as much a slave as any black wench of plantation days.

There was the treadmill of endless dishes, dirtied as fast as cleansed; there were beds, and beds, and beds; gravies and soups and stews. And alway the querulous voice of the sick woman in the front bedroom demanding another hot water bag. Rose's day was punctuated by hot

* From *Cheerful by Request* by Edna Ferber. Published by Doubleday, Doran, and Company. Used by permission of the author.

water bags. They dotted her waking hours. She filled hot water bags automatically, like a machine—water half-way to the top, then one hand clutching the bag's slippery middle while the other, with a deft twist, ejected the air within; a quick twirl of the metal stopper, the bag released, squirming, and, finally, its plump and rufous cheeks wiped dry.

"Is that too hot for you, Ma? Where'd you want it—your head or your feet?"

A spinster nearing forty, living thus, must have her memories—one precious memory, at least—or she dies. Rose had hers. She hugged it, close. The L trains roared by, not thirty feet from her kitchen door. Alley and yard and street sent up their noises to her. The life of Chicago's millions yelped at her heels. On Rose's face was the vague, mute look of the woman whose days are spent indoors, at sordid tasks.

At six-thirty every night that look lifted, for an hour. At six-thirty they came home—Floss, and Al, and Pa—their faces stamped with the marks that come from a day spent in shop and factory. They brought with them the crumbs and husks of the day's happenings, and these they flung carelessly before the life-starved Rose and she ate them, gratefully.

They came in with a rush, hungry, fagged, grimed, imperious, smelling of the city. There was a slamming of doors, a banging of drawers, a clatter of tongues, quarrelling, laughter. A brief visit to the sick woman's room. The thin, complaining voice reciting its tale of the day's discomfort and pain. Then supper.

"Guess who I waited on to-day!" Floss might demand.

Rose, dishing up, would pause, interested. "Who?"

"Gladys Moraine! I knew her the minute she came down the aisle. I saw her last year when she was playing in 'His Wives.' She's prettier off than on, I think. I waited on her, and the other girls were wild. She bought a dozen pairs of white kids, and made me give 'em to her huge, so she could shove her hand right into 'em, like a man does. Two sizes too big. All the swells wear 'em that way. And only one ring—an emerald the size of a dime."

"What'd she wear?" Rose's dull face was almost animated.

"Ah yes!" in a dreamy falsetto from Al, "what *did* she wear?"

"Oh, shut up, Al! Just a suit, kind of plain, and yet you'd notice it. And sables! And a Gladys Moraine hat. Everything quiet, and plain, and dark; and yet she looked like a million dollars. I felt like a roach while I was waiting on her, though she was awfully sweet to me."

Or perhaps Al, the eel-like, would descend from his heights to mingle a brief moment in the family talk. Al clerked in the National Cigar Company's store at Clark and Madison. His was the wisdom of the snake, the weasel, and the sphinx. A strangely silent young man, this Al, thin-lipped, smooth-cheeked, perfumed. Slim of waist, flat of hip, narrow of shoulder, his was the figure of the born fox-trotter. He walked lightly, on the balls of his feet, like an Indian, but without the Indian's dignity.

"Some excitement ourselves, to-day, down at the store, believe me. The Old Man's son started in to learn the retail selling end of the business. Back of the showcase with the rest of us, waiting on trade, and looking like a Yale yell."

Pa would put down his paper to stare over his reading specs at Al.

"Mannheim's son! The president!"

"Yep! And I guess he loves it, huh? The Old Man wants him to learn the business from the ground up. I'll bet he'll never get higher than the first floor. To-day he went out to lunch at one and never shows up again till four. Wears English collars, and smokes a brand of cigarettes we don't carry."

Thus was the world brought to Rose. Her sallow cheek would show a faint hint of colour as she sipped her tea.

At six-thirty on a Monday morning in late April (remember, nothing's going to happen) Rose smothered her alarm clock at the first warning snarl. She was wide-awake at once, as are those whose yesterdays, to-days and to-morrows are all alike. Rose never opened her eyes to the dim, tantalizing half-consciousness of a something delightful or a something harrowing in store for her that day. For one to whom the washwoman's Tuesday visitation is the event of the week, and in whose bosom the delivery boy's hoarse "Grocrees!" as he hurls soap and cabbage on the kitchen table, arouses a wild flurry, there can be very little thrill on awakening.

Rose slept on the davenport-couch in the sitting-room. That fact in itself fixes her status in the family. This Monday morning she opened her eyes with what might be called a start if Rose were any other sort of heroine. Something had happened, or was happening. It wasn't the six o'clock steam hissing in the radiator. She was accustomed to that. The rattle of the L trains, and the milkman's artillery disturbed her as little as does the chirping of the birds the farmer's daughter. A sensation new, yet familiar; delicious, yet painful, held her. She groped to define it, lying there. Her gaze, wandering over the expanse of the grey woollen blanket, fixed upon a small black object trembling there. The knowledge that came to her then had come, many weeks before, in a hundred subtle and exquisite ways, to those who dwell in the open places. Rose's eyes narrowed craftily. Craftily, stealthily, she sat up, one hand raised. Her eyes still fixed on the quivering spot, the hand descended, lightning-quick. But not quickly enough. The black spot vanished. It sped toward the open window. Through that window there came a balmy softness made up of Lake Michigan zephyr, and stockyards smell, and distant budding things. Rose had failed to swat the first fly of the season. Spring had come.

As she got out of bed and thud-thudded across the room on her heels to shut the window she glanced out into the quiet street. Her city eyes, untrained to nature's hints, failed to notice that the scraggy, smoke-dwarfed oak that sprang, somehow, miraculously, from the mangey little dirt-plot in front of the building had developed surprising things all over its scrawny branches overnight. But she did see that the front windows of the flat building across the way were bare of the Chicago-grey lace curtains that had hung there the day before. House cleaning! Well, most decidedly spring had come.

Rose was the household's Aurora. Following the donning of her limp and obscure garments it was Rose's daily duty to tear the silent family from its slumbers. Ma was always awake, her sick eyes fixed hopefully on the door. For fourteen years it had been the same.

"Sleeping?"

"Sleeping! I haven't closed an eye all night."

Rose had learned not to dispute that statement.

"It's spring out! I'm going to clean the closets and the bureau drawers to-day. I'll have your coffee in a jiffy. Do you feel like getting up and sitting out on the back porch, toward noon, maybe?"

On her way kitchenward she stopped for a sharp tattoo at the door of the room in which Pa and Al slept. A sleepy grunt of remonstrance rewarded her. She came to Floss's door, turned the knob softly, peered in. Floss was sleeping as twenty sleeps, deeply, dreamlessly, one slim bare arm outflung, the lashes resting ever so lightly on the delicate curve of cheek. As she lay there asleep in her disordered bedroom, her clothes strewing chair, dresser, floor, Floss's tastes, mental equipment, spiritual make-up, innermost thoughts, were as plainly to be read by the observer as though she had been scientifically charted by a psychoanalyst, a meta-physician and her dearest girl friend.

"Floss! Floss, honey! Quarter to seven!" Floss stirred, moaned faintly, dropped into sleep again.

Fifteen minutes later, the table set, the coffee simmering, the morning paper brought from the back porch to Ma, Rose had heard none of the sounds that proclaimed the family astir—the banging of drawers, the rush of running water, the slap of slippered feet. A peep of enquiry into the depths of the coffee pot, the gas turned to a circle of blue beads, and she was down the hall to sound the second alarm.

"Floss, you know if Al once gets into the bathroom!" Floss sat up in bed, her eyes still closed. She made little clucking sounds with her tongue and lips, as a baby does when it wakes. Drugged with sleep, hair tousled, muscles sagging, at seven o'clock in the morning, the most trying hour in the day for a woman, Floss was still triumphantly pretty. She had on one of those absurd pink muslin nightgowns, artfully designed to look like crêpe de chine. You've seen them rosily displayed in the cheaper shop windows, marked ninety-eight cents, and you may have wondered who might buy them, forgetting that there is an imitation mind for every imitation article in the world.

Rose stooped, picked up a pair of silk stockings from the floor, and ran an investigating hand through to heel and toe. She plucked a soiled pink blouse off the back of a chair, eyed it critically, and tucked it under her arm with the stockings.

"Did you have a good time last night?"

Floss yawned elaborately, stretched her slim arms high above her head; then, with a desperate effort, flung back the bed-clothes, swung her legs over the side of the bed and slipped her toes into the shabby, pomponed slippers that lay on the floor.

"I say, did you have a g——"

"Oh Lord, I don't know! I guess so," snapped Floss. Temperamentally, Floss was not at her best at seven o'clock on Monday morning. Rose did not pursue the subject. She tried another tack.

"It's as mild as summer out. I see the Werners and the Burkes are housecleaning. I thought I'd start to-day with the closets, and the bureau drawers. You could wear your blue this morning, if it was pressed."

Floss yawned again, disinterestedly, and folded her kimono about her.

"Go as far as you like. Only don't put things back in my closet so's I can't ever find 'em again. I wish you'd press that blue skirt. And wash out the Georgette crêpe waist. I might need it."

The blouse, and skirt, and stockings under her arm, Rose went back to the kitchen to prepare her mother's breakfast tray. Wafted back to her came the acrid odour of Pa's matutinal pipe, and the accustomed bickering between Al and Floss over the possession of the bathroom.

"What do you think this is, anyway? A Turkish bath?"

"Shave in your own room!"

Between Floss and Al there existed a feud that lifted only when a third member of the family turned against either of them. Immediately they about-faced and stood united against the offender.

Pa was the first to demand breakfast, as always. Very neat, was Pa, and fussy, and strangely young looking to be the husband of the grey-haired, parchment-skinned woman who lay in the front bedroom. Pa had two manias: the movies, and a passion for purchasing new and complicated household utensils—cream-whippers, egg-beaters, window-clamps, lemon-squeezers, silver-polishers. He haunted department store basements in search of them.

He opened his paper now and glanced at the headlines and at the Monday morning ads. "I see the Fair's got a spring housecleaning sale. They advertise a new kind of extension curtain rod. And Scouro, three cakes for a dime."

"If you waste one cent more on truck like that," Rose protested, placing his breakfast before him, "when half the time I can't make the house-keeping money last through the week!"

"Your ma did it."

"Fourteen years ago liver wasn't thirty-two cents a pound," retorted Rose, "and besides——"

"Scramble 'em!" yelled Al, from the bedroom, by way of warning.

There was very little talk after that. The energies of three of them were directed toward reaching the waiting desk or counter on time. The energy of one toward making that accomplishment easy. The front door slammed once—that was Pa, on his way; slammed again—Al. Floss rushed into the dining-room fastening the waist-band of her skirt, her hat already on. Rose always had a rather special breakfast for Floss. Floss posed as being a rather special person. She always breakfasted last, and late. Floss's was a fastidiousness which shrinks at badly served food, a spotted table-cloth, or a last year's hat, while it overlooks a rent in an undergarment or the accumulated dust in a hairbrush. Her blouse was of the sheerest. Her hair shone in waves about her delicate cheeks. She ate her orange, and sipped her very special coffee, and made a little face over her egg that had been shirred in the oven or in some way highly specialized. Then the front door slammed again—a semi-slam, this time. Floss never did quite close a door. Rose followed her down the hall, shut and bolted it, Chicago fashion. The sick woman in the front bedroom had dropped into one of her fitful morning dozes. At eight o'clock the little flat was very still.

If you knew nothing about Rose; if you had not already been told that she slept on the sitting-room davenport; that she was taken for granted as the family drudge; that she was, in that household, merely an intelligent machine that made beds, fried eggs, filled hot water bags, you would get a characterization of her from this: She was the sort of person who never has a closet or bureau drawer all her own. Her few and negligible garments hung apologetically in obscure corners of closets dedicated to her sister's wardrobe or her brother's, or her spruce and fussy old father's. Vague personal belongings, such as combings, handkerchiefs, a spectacle case, a hairbrush, were found tucked away in a desk pigeon-hole, a table drawer or on the top shelf in the bathroom.

As she pulled the disfiguring blue gingham dust-cap over her hair now, and rolled her sleeves to her elbows you would never have dreamed that Rose was embarking upon her great adventure. You would never have guessed that the semi-yearly closet cleaning was to give to Rose a thrill as delicious as it was exquisitely painful. But Rose knew. And so she teased herself and tried not to think of the pasteboard box on the shelf in the hall closet, under the pile of reserve blankets and told herself that she would leave that closet until the last, when she would have to hurry over it.

When you clean closets and bureau drawers thoroughly you have to carry things out to the back porch and flap them. Rose was that sort of housekeeper. She leaned over the porch railing and flapped things, so that the dust motes spun and swirled in the sunshine. Rose's arms worked up and down energetically, then less energetically, finally ceased their motion altogether. She leaned idle elbows on the porch railing and gazed down into the yard below with a look in her eyes such as no squalid Chicago back yard, with its dusty débris, could summon, even in springtime.

The woman next door came out on her back porch that adjoined Rose's. The day seemed to have her in its spell, too, for in her hand was something woolly and wintry, and she began to flap it about as Rose had done. She had lived next door since October, had that woman, but the two had never exchanged a word, true to the traditions of their city training. Rose had her doubts of the woman next door. She kept a toy dog which she aired afternoons, and her kimonos were florid and numerous. Now, as the eyes of the two women met, Rose found herself saying, "Looks like summer."

The woman next door caught the scrap of conversation eagerly, hungrily. "It certainly does! Makes me feel like new clothes, and housecleaning."

"I started to-day!" said Rose, triumphantly.

"Not already!" gasped the woman next door, with the chagrin that only a woman knows who has let May steal upon her unawares.

From far down the alley sounded a chant, drawing nearer and nearer, until there shambled into view a decrepit horse drawing a dilapidated huckster's cart. Perched on the seat was a Greek who turned his dusky face up toward the two women leaning over the porch railings. "Rhubarb, leddy. Fresh rhubarb!"

"My folks don't care for rhubarb sauce," Rose told the woman next door.

"It makes the worst pie in the world," the woman confided to Rose.

Whereupon each bought a bunch of the succulent green and red stalks. It was their offering at the season's shrine.

Rose flung the rhubarb on the kitchen table, pulled her dust-cap more firmly about her ears, and hurried back to the disorder of Floss's dim little bedroom. After that it was dust-cloth, and soapsuds, and scrubbrush in a race against recurrent water bags, insistent doorbells, and the inevitable dinner hour. It was mid-afternoon when Rose, standing a-tiptoe on a chair, came at last to the little box on the top shelf under the bedding in the hall closet. Her hand touched the box, and closed about it. A little electric thrill vibrated through her body. She stepped down from the chair, heavily, listened until her acute ear caught the sound of the sick woman's slumbrous breathing; then, box in hand, walked down the dark hall to the kitchen. The rhubarb pie, still steaming in its pan, was cooling on the kitchen table. The dishes from the invalid's lunch-tray littered the sink. But Rose, seated on the kitchen chair, her rumpled dust-cap pushed back from her flushed, perspiring face, untied the rude bit of string that bound the old candy box, removed the lid, slowly, and by that act was wafted magically out of the world of rhubarb pies, and kitchen chairs, and dirty dishes, into that place whose air is the breath of incense and myrrh, whose paths are rose-strewn, whose dwellings are temples dedicated to but one small god. The land is known as Love, and Rose travelled back to it on the magic rug of memory.

A family of five in a six-room Chicago flat must sacrifice sentiment to necessity. There is precious little space for those pressed flowers, time-yellowed gowns, and ribbon-bound packets that figured so prominently in the days of attics. Into the garbage can with yesterday's roses! The janitor's burlap sack yawns for this morning's mail; last year's gown has long ago met its end at the hands of the ol'-clo'es man or the washwoman's daughter. That they had survived these fourteen years, and the strictures of their owner's dwelling, tells more about this boxful of letters than could be conveyed by a battalion of adjectives.

Rose began at the top of the pile, in her orderly fashion, and read straight through to the last. It took one hour. Half of that time she was not reading. She was staring straight ahead with what is mistakenly called an unseeing look, but which actually pierces the veil of years and beholds things far, far beyond the vision of the actual eye. They were the letters of a commonplace man to a commonplace woman, written when they loved each other, and so they were touched with something of the divine. They must have been, else how could they have sustained this woman through fifteen years of drudgery? They were the only tangible foundation left of the structure of dreams she had built about this man. All the rest of her house of love had tumbled about her ears fifteen years before, but with these few remaining bricks she had erected many times since castles and towers more exquisite and lofty and soaring than the original humble structure had ever been.

The story? Well, there really isn't any, as we've warned you. Rose had been pretty then in much the same delicate way that Floss was pretty now. They were to have been married. Rose's mother fell ill, Floss and Al were little more than babies. The marriage was put off. The illness lasted six months—a year—two years—became interminable. The breach into which Rose had stepped closed about her and became a prison. The man had waited, had grown impatient, finally rebelled. He had fled, probably to marry a less encumbered lady. Rose had gone dully on, caring for the household, the children, the sick woman. In the years that had gone by since then Rose had forgiven him his faithlessness. She only remembered that he had been wont to call her his Röschen, his Rose-bud, his pretty flower (being a German gentleman). She only recalled the wonder of having been first in some one's thoughts—she who now was so hopelessly, so irrevocably last.

As she sat there in her kitchen, wearing her soap-stained and faded blue gingham, and the dust-cap pushed back at a rakish angle, a simpering little smile about her lips, she was really very much like the disappointed old maids you used to see so cruelly pictured in the comic valentines. Had those letters obsessed her a little more strongly she might have become quite mad, the Freudians would tell you. Had they held less for her, or had she not been so completely the household's slave, she might have found a certain solace and satisfaction in viewing the Greek profile and marcel wave of the most-worshipped movie star. As it was, they were her ballast, her refuge, the leavening yeast in the soggy dough of her existence. This man had wanted her to be his wife. She had found favour in his eyes. She was certain that he still thought of her, some- times, and tenderly, regretfully, as she thought of him. It helped her to live. Not only that, it made living possible.

A clock struck, a window slammed, or a street-noise smote her ear sharply. Some sound started her out of her reverie. Rose jumped, stared a moment at the letters in her lap, then hastily, almost shamefacedly, sorted them (she knew each envelope by heart) tied them, placed them in their box and bore then down the hall. There, mounting her chair, she scrubbed the top shelf with her soapy rag, placed the box in its cor- ner, left the hall closet smelling of cleanliness, with never a hint of lavender to betray its secret treasure.

Were Rose to die and go to Heaven, there to spend her days thumb- ing a golden harp, her hands, by force of habit, would drop harp-strings at quarter to six, to begin laying a celestial and unspotted table-cloth for supper. Habits as deeply rooted as that must hold, even in after- life.

To-night's six-thirty stampede was noticeably subdued on the part of Pa and Al. It had been a day of sudden and enervating heat, and the city had done its worst to them. Pa's pink gills showed a hint of purple. Al's flimsy silk shirt stuck to his back, and his glittering pompadour was many degrees less submissive than was its wont. But Floss came in late, breath- less, and radiant, a large and significant paper bag in her hand. Rose, in the kitchen, was transferring the smoking supper from pot to platter. Pa, in the doorway of the sick woman's little room, had just put his fourteen-year-old question with his usual assumption of heartiness and cheer: "Well, well! And how's the old girl to-night? Feel like you could get up and punish a little supper, eh?" Al, engaged at the telephone with some one whom he addressed proprietorially as Kid, was deep in the plans for the evening's diversion. Upon this accustomed scene Floss burst with havoc.

"Rose! Rose, did you iron my Georgette crêpe? Listen! Guess what!" All this as she was rushing down the hall, paper hat-bag still in hand. "Guess who was in the store to-day!"

Rose, at the oven, turned a flushed and interested face toward Floss.

"Who? What's that? A hat?"

"Yes. But listen——"

"Let's see it."

Floss whipped it out of its bag, defiantly. "There! But wait a minute! Let me tell you——"

"How much?"

Floss hesitated just a second. Her wage was nine dollars a week. Then, "Seven-fifty, trimmed." The hat was one of those tiny, head-hugging absurdities that only the Flosses can wear.

"Trimmed is right!" jeered Al, from the doorway.

Rose, thin-lipped with disapproval, turned to her stove again.

"Well, but I had to have it. I'm going to the theatre to-night. And guess who with! Henry Selz!"

Henry Selz was the unromantic name of the commonplace man over whose fifteen-year-old letters Rose had glowed and dreamed an hour before. It was a name that had become mythical in that household—to all but one. Rose heard it spoken now with a sense of unreality. She smiled a little uncertainly, and went on stirring the flour thickening for the gravy. But she was dimly aware that something inside her had suspended action for a moment, during which moment she felt strangely light and disembodied, and that directly afterward the thing began to work madly, so that there was a choked feeling in her chest and a hot pounding in her head.

"What's the joke?" she said, stirring the gravy in the pan.

"Joke nothing! Honest to God! I was standing back of the counter at about ten. The rush hadn't really begun yet. Glove trade usually starts late. I was standing there kidding Herb, the stock boy, when down the aisle comes a man in a big hat, like you see in the western pictures, hair a little grey at the temples, and everything, just like a movie actor. I said to Herb, 'Is it real?' I hadn't got the words out of my mouth when the fellow sees me, stands stock still in the middle of the aisle with his mouth open and his eyes sticking out. 'Register surprise,' I said to Herb, and looked around for the camera. And that minute he took two jumps over to where I was standing, grabbed my hands and says, 'Rose! Rose!' kind of choky. 'Not by about twenty years,' I said. 'I'm Floss, Rose's sister. Let go my hands!' "

Rose—a transfigured Rose, glowing, trembling, radiant—repeated vibrantly, "You said, 'I'm Floss, Rose's sister. Let go my hands!' And——?"

"He looked kind of stunned, for just a minute. His face was a scream, honestly. Then he said, 'But of course. Fifteen years. But I had always thought of her as just the same.' And he kind of laughed, ashamed, like a kid. And the whitest teeth!"

"Yes, they were—white," said Rose. "Well?"

"Well, I said, 'Won't I do instead?' 'You bet you'll do!' he said. And then he told me his name, and how he was living out in Spokane, and his wife was dead, and he had made a lot of money—fruit, or real estate, or something. He talked a lot about it at lunch, but I didn't pay any attention, as long as he really has it a lot I care how——"

"At lunch?"

"Everything from grape-fruit to coffee. I didn't know it could be done in one hour. Believe me, he had those waiters jumping. It takes money. He asked all about you, and ma, and everything. And he kept looking at me and saying, 'It's wonderful!' I said, 'Isn't it!' but I meant the lunch. He wanted me to go driving this afternoon—auto and everything. Kept calling me Rose. It made me kind of mad, and I told him how you look. He said, 'I suppose so,' and asked me to go to a show to-night. Listen, did you press my Georgette? And the blue?"

"I'll iron the waist while you're eating. I'm not hungry. It only takes a minute. Did you say he was grey?"

"Grey? Oh, you mean—why, just here, and here. Interesting, but not a bit old. And he's got that money look that makes waiters and doormen and taxi drivers just hump. I don't want any supper. Just a cup of tea. I haven't got enough time to dress in, decently, as it is."

Al, draped in the doorway, removed his cigarette to give greater force to his speech. "Your story interests me strangely, little gell. But there's a couple of other people that would like to eat, even if you wouldn't. Come on with that supper, Ro. Nobody staked me to a lunch to-day."

Rose turned to her stove again. Two carmine spots had leaped suddenly to her cheeks. She served the meal in silence, and ate nothing, but that was not remarkable. For the cook there is little appeal in the meat that she has tended from its moist and bloody entrance in the butcher's paper, through the basting or broiling stage to its formal appearance on the platter. She saw that Al and her father were served. Then she went back to the kitchen, and the thud of her iron was heard as she deftly fluted the ruffles of the crêpe blouse. Floss appeared when the meal was half eaten, her hair shiningly coiffed, the pink ribbons of her corset cover showing under her thin kimono. She poured herself a cup of tea and drank it in little quick, nervous gulps. She looked deliciously young, and fragile and appealing, her delicate slenderness revealed by the flimsy garment she wore. Excitement and anticipation lent a glow to her eyes, colour to her cheeks. Al, glancing expertly at the ingenuousness of her artfully simple coiffure, the slim limpness of her body, her wide-eyed gaze, laughed a wise little laugh.

"Every move a Pickford. And so girlish withal."

Floss ignored him. "Hurry up with that waist, Rose!"

"I'm on the collar now. In a second." There was a little silence. Then: "Floss, is—is Henry going to call for you—here?"

"Well, sure! Did you think I was going to meet him on the corner? He said he wanted to see you, or something polite like that."

She finished her tea and vanished again. Al, too, had disappeared to begin that process from which he had always emerged incredibly sleek, and dapper and perfumed. His progress with shaving brush, shirt, collar and tie was marked by disjointed bars of the newest syncopation whistled with an uncanny precision and fidelity to detail. He caught the broken time, and tossed it lightly up again, and dropped it, and caught it deftly like a juggler playing with frail crystal globes that seem forever on the point of crashing to the ground.

Pa stood up, yawning. "Well," he said, his manner very casual, "guess I'll just drop around to the movie."

From the kitchen, "Don't you want to sit with ma a minute, first?"

"I will when I come back. They're showing the third installment of 'The Adventures of Aline,' and I don't want to come in in the middle of it."

He knew the selfishness of it, this furtive and sprightly old man. And because he knew it he attempted to hide his guilt under a burst of temper.

"I've been slaving all day. I guess I've got the right to a little amusement. A man works his fingers to the bone for his family, and then his own daughter nags him."

He stamped down the hall, righteously, and slammed the front door.

Rose came from the kitchen, the pink blouse, warm from the iron, in one hand. She prinked out its ruffles and pleatings as she went. Floss, burnishing her nails somewhat frantically with a dilapidated and greasy buffer, snatched the garment from her and slipped bare arms into it. The front door bell rang, three big, determined rings. Panic fell upon the household.

"It's him!" whispered Floss, as if she could be heard in the entrance three floors below. "You'll have to go."

"I can't!" Every inch of her seemed to shrink and cower away from the thought. "I can't!" Her eyes darted to and fro like a hunted thing seeking to escape. She ran to the hall. "Al! Al, go to the door, will you?"

"Can't," came back in a thick mumble. "Shaving."

The front door-bell rang again, three big, determined rings. "Rose!" hissed Floss, her tone venomous. "I can't go with my waist open. For heaven's sake! Go to the door!"

"I can't," repeated Rose, in a kind of wail. "I—can't." And went. As she went she passed one futile, work-worn hand over her hair, plucked off her apron and tossed it into a corner, first wiping her flushed face with it.

Henry Selz came up the shabby stairs springily as a man of forty should. Rose stood at the door and waited for him. He stood in the doorway a moment, uncertainly.

"How-do, Henry."

His uncertainty became incredulity. Then, "Why, how-do, Rose! Didn't know you—for a minute. Well, well! It's been a long time. Let's see—ten—fourteen—about fifteen years, isn't it?"

His tone was cheerfully conversational. He really was interested, mathematically. He was as sentimental in his reminiscence as if he had been calculating the lapse of time between the Chicago fire and the World's Fair.

"Fifteen," said Rose, "in May. Won't you come in? Floss'll be here in a minute."

Henry Selz came in and sat down on the davenport couch and dabbed at his forehead. The years had been very kind to him—those same years that had treated Rose so ruthlessly. He had the look of an outdoor man; a man who has met prosperity and walked with her, and followed her pleasant ways; a man who has learned late in life of golf and caviar and tailors, but who has adapted himself to these accessories of wealth with a minimum of friction.

"It certainly is warm, for this time of year." He leaned back and regarded Rose tolerantly. "Well, and how've you been? Did little sister tell you how flabbergasted I was when I saw her this morning? I'm darned if it didn't take fifteen years off my age, just like that! I got kind of balled up for one minute and thought it was you. She tell you?"

"Yes, she told me," said Rose.

"I hear your ma's still sick. That certainly is tough. And you've never married, eh?"

"Never married," echoed Rose.

And so they made conversation, a little uncomfortably, until there came quick, light young steps down the hallway, and Floss appeared in the door, a radiant, glowing, girlish vision. Youth was in her eyes, her cheeks, on her lips. She radiated it. She was miraculously well dressed, in her knowingly simple blue serge suit, and her tiny hat, and her neat shoes and gloves.

"Ah! And how's the little girl to-night?" said Henry Selz.

Floss dimpled, blushed, smiled, swayed. "Did I keep you waiting a terribly long time?"

"No, not a bit. Rose and I were chinning over old times, weren't we,

Rose?" A kindly, clumsy thought struck him. "Say, look here, Rose. We're going to a show. Why don't you run and put on your hat and come along. H'm? Come on!"

Rose smiled as a mother smiles at a child that has unknowingly hurt her. "No, thanks, Henry. Not to-night. You and Floss run along. Yes, I'll remember you to Ma. I'm sorry you can't see her. But she don't see anybody, poor Ma."

Then they were off, in a little flurry of words and laughter. From force of habit Rose's near-sighted eyes peered critically at the hang of Floss's blue skirt and the angle of the pert new hat. She stood a moment, uncertainly, after they had left. On her face was the queerest look, as of one thinking, re-adjusting, struggling to arrive at a conclusion in the midst of sudden bewilderment. She turned mechanically and went into her mother's room. She picked up the tray on the table by the bed.

"Who was that?" asked the sick woman, in her ghostly, devitalized voice.

"That was Henry Selz," said Rose.

The sick woman grappled a moment with memory. "Henry Selz! Henry—oh, yes. Did he go out with Rose?"

"Yes," said Rose.

"It's cold in here," whined the sick woman.

"I'll get you a hot bag in a minute, Ma." Rose carried the tray down the hall to the kitchen. At that Al emerged from his bedroom, shrugging himself into his coat. He followed Rose down the hall and watched her as she filled the bag and screwed it and wiped it dry.

"I'll take that in to Ma," he volunteered. He was up the hall and back in a flash. Rose had slumped into a chair at the dining-room table, and was pouring herself a cup of cold and bitter tea. Al came over to her and laid one white hand on her shoulder.

"Ro, lend me a couple of dollars till Saturday, will you?"

"I should say not."

Al doused his cigarette in the dregs of a convenient teacup. He bent down and laid his powdered and pale cheek against Rose's sallow one. One arm was about her, and his hand patted her shoulder.

"Oh, come on, kid," he coaxed. "Don't I always pay you back? Come on! Be a sweet ol' sis. I wouldn't ask you only I've got a date to go to the White City to-night, and dance, and I couldn't get out of it. I tried." He kissed her, and his lips were moist, and he reeked of tobacco, and though Rose shrugged impatiently away from him he knew that he had won. Rose was not an eloquent woman; she was not even an articulate one, at times. If she had been, she would have lifted up her voice to say now:

"Oh, God! I am a woman! Why have you given me all the sorrows, and the drudgery, and the bitterness and the thanklessness of motherhood, with none of its joys! Give me back my youth! I'll drink the dregs at the bottom of the cup, but first let me taste the sweet!"

But Rose did not talk or think in such terms. She could not have put into words the thing she was feeling even if she had been able to diagnose it. So what she said was, "Don't you think I ever get sick and tired of slaving for a thankless bunch like you? Well, I do! Sick and tired of it. That's what! You make me tired, coming around asking for money, as if I was a bank."

But Al waited. And presently she said, grudgingly, wearily, "There's a dollar bill and some small change in the can on the second shelf in the china closet."

Al was off like a terrier. From the pantry came the clink of metal against metal. He was up the hall in a flash, without a look at Rose. The front door slammed a third time.

Rose stirred her cold tea slowly, leaning on the table's edge and gazing down into the amber liquid that she did not mean to drink. For suddenly and comically her face puckered up like a child's. Her head came down among the supper things with a little crash that set the teacups, and the greasy plates to jingling, and she sobbed as she lay there, with great tearing, ugly sobs that would not be stilled, though she tried to stifle them as does one who lives in a paper-thin Chicago flat. She was not weeping for the Henry Selz whom she had just seen. She was not weeping for envy of her selfish little sister, or for loneliness, or weariness. She was weeping at the loss of a ghost who had become her familiar. She was weeping because a packet of soiled and yellow old letters on the top shelf in the hall closet was now only a packet of soiled and yellow old letters, food for the ash can. She was weeping because the urge of spring, that had expressed itself in her only this morning pitifully enough in terms of rhubarb, and housecleaning and a bundle of thumbed old love letters, had stirred in her for the last time.

But presently she did stop her sobbing and got up and cleared the table, and washed the dishes and even glanced at the crumpled sheets of the morning paper that she never found time to read until evening. By eight o'clock the little flat was very still.

EDNA FERBER *The Eldest*

The one-act play follows in essentials the formula explained on page 119, but it is as a rule a more intensive and more compact form than the full-length play. It has in condensed and concentrated form the first-act exposition (who, when, where, why, how), the second-act tying of the knot, and the third-act untying of the knot, all in straightaway presentation. It may be divided into definite scenes, but as a rule the demarcation is not mechanically made. Just as the consciously conceived and unified short-story cannot be converted into a novel by mere lengthening, so the one-act play is or should be by conception and workmanship incapable by mere extension of being made a three-act or longer play. Playwrights sometimes make the mistake of constructing a long play out of materials that have only one-act quality and content. Forcing them into three or more acts results in too thin a spread for interesting and challenging dramatic build. It sometimes happens, conversely, that a play of a single act may be so overcharged with meaning and significance and richness of treatment, that it "explodes," so to say, of its own momentum, and thus requires the more leisurely pace and steadier unfoldment of three or more acts. The one-act play below * is an excellent illustration of the concentrated method, the revelation of character through dialogue, the climactic achievement that, among other elements, characterize *par excellence* this department of dramatic composition.

THE OTHER GIRL

A play in one act and two scenes

CHARACTERS

MA CONNORS	SERGEANT JIM DURLAN
PA CONNORS	MARIE, a young Frenchwoman
MAISIE CONNORS	LIZETTE, her sister-in-law
JACQUES, a boy of six	

Note: *When professionally played the parts of* MAISIE CONNORS *and* MARIE *can be played by the same actress. If played by amateurs it will be easier to have the two parts separately taken.*

SCENE I. *A Kitchen in New York.*
SCENE II. *A Kitchen in France.*

Note: *For amateurs: To make quick change of scene the same set can be used. Reversible windows are advisable curtained for Scene I, bare for Scene II. Scene II is very bare and dim. By removing pictures, changing position of stove, running out small table and chairs, running in cot bed, stool, etc., sufficient change can be accomplished in a short space of time. No change need be made at end of play. Simply keep stage dark except for spot in which* JIM *and* MAISIE *are seated—and that needs only faint illumination.*

SCENE I

Scene represents the kitchen of a cheap flat in New York. White-washed walls, adorned with a framed text, a couple of sentimental lithographs and a picture from a newspaper supplement. Doors left and right, a stove at back on which dinner is cooking, a table set for four near center, a small table and easy chair to the left.

When the Curtain rises, MRS. CONNORS, *a middle-aged Irishwoman, is busy at stove. She takes bowl and spoon and goes to door left.*

MRS. CONNORS
(*Calling*)
Take a sup o' this now, Maisie, an' tell me how you be likin' it!
(MAISIE *opens the door and appears in undress, pink silk petticoat, white throw, black silk stockings, patent leather pumps. She is a pretty girl of twenty. She is just finishing her hair and with her hands to her head she puts her lips to the spoon her mother extends*)

MAISIE
Mmm, scrum! What's that for, Ma?

MRS. CONNORS
(*Waddling back*)
The puddin'. Jim always had a soft spot for my bananer puddin'.

MAISIE
Me too.
(*She goes on with her hair, her mother returns to the cooking*)
Say, do you know how I got the boss to let me off early this afternoon? "My beau's comin' home from the war," I says, "an' I got to go cook him such a dinner as never was!" That was a whopper but he didn't know you was there to cook it for me. "Beau *comin*?" he says. "Are you sure you

don't mean *goin'*? All the girls in this office got a beau *goin'* off to war every week. It's worse'n the baseball nuisance used to be in the days of office boys." He's real comickal, you know. "Mine's comin', all right," I says. "He's been over a year an' got wounded and they're sendin' him home." An' I showed him the telegram from Norfolk. "Well, you got me comin' an' goin'," he says. "Run along, little one, an' kill the fatted calf," he says. An' I run—to Macy's. But I wasn't tellin' him that.

(*Coming into room*)

How does my back hair look, Ma? This pesky mirror has such a crack in it, I can't see for beans.

(*She turns her head to display her coiffure adorned with a large rhinestone hairpin*)

MRS. CONNORS

It looks fine. But Jim ain't goin' to be lookin' at the *back* of your head, I warrant you. Where'd you get the hairpin?

MAISIE

It was a special. All the girls are wearin' 'em. Some class, eh?

MRS. CONNORS

Some price, too, I should be sayin'.

MAISIE

(*Proceeding with her dressing*)

Didn't I tell you it was a bargain? Did you iron my waist, Ma? Oh, here it is! An' my new skirt! Gee, don't they look good together!

(*She appears at door in pretty white crêpe waist and white sport satin skirt*)

MRS. CONNORS

All this grandness for Jim?

MAISIE

Well, would you have me lookin' a dowd when he comes back an' he used to all those slick French girls! Jim always had an eye for a swell dresser. Here's somethin' I got that's really worth lookin' at, Ma.

(*She takes pearl necklace off bureau in bedroom and hands it to her mother*)

This ain't no cheap piker imitation. Don't it look like the real thing? Well it *is*—almost! It cost *five dollars and ninety-eight cents,* and it's worth it. The girl showed it to me along side a string o' real and, believe me, I couldn't tell the difference!

MRS. CONNORS

Do you think Jim'll take it for real, an' you wearin' it, Maisie?

MAISIE

Oh it ain't that, Ma. It's the feelin' it gives you, the feelin' of bein'— of bein'——

MRS. CONNORS

Of bein' mighty extravagant, dearie, I should say.

MAISIE

Who's bein' extravagant? It's my own money, ain't it? Don't I earn every cent I spend?

MRS. CONNORS

(*Protesting feebly*)

Looks to me as if you wuz spendin' every cent you earn, too. That's what's troublin' me. An' here we are in war an' the government askin' us to be careful an' do our bit——

MAISIE

Who ain't doin' her bit? Ain't I workin' in a war office from nine to six every day o' the week?

MRS. CONNORS

An' makin' more money than you ever made in your life before.

MAISIE

What's that got to do with it? Dry up, Ma. I got a Liberty Bond an' a book o' thrift stamps, ain't I? An' it's most full, too. Whatcher want me to do? Go roun' lookin' like a hag? It's the rich ought to be savin'! All I got on wouldn't pay for half o' one o' them Fifth Avenue hats the swells wear into the office sometimes. This thrift dope makes me tired. Some people are makin' a pile o' money out o' this war, an' don't you forget it.

(*She goes angrily into bedroom*)

MRS. CONNORS

Oh, I ain't scoldin' you, Maisie. I'm proud o' you lookin' so fine an' I'm glad you can afford it. I only hope it will last.

(MIKE CONNORS *enters, a small self-important looking man—carrying a bag*)

MIKE

Hello, Ma. Victuals ready?

MRS. CONNORS

Have you forgot Jim Durlan's comin'? We gotta wait for him.

MIKE

(*Taking off hat and coat*)
I clean forgot. I've had a gran' day, Ma, a gran' day!
(*Re-enter* MAISIE)
Hello, pop! What time is it by your watch an' chain?

MIKE

Past six by me watch an' supper time by me stomach. Maisie, you sure look a queen, an' no mistake.
(*Goes to sink to wash, R*)

MAISIE

(*Pleased*)
Do you like me, Pop? Ma's been scoldin' me fer bein' extravagant.

MRS. CONNORS

(*Protesting*)
Now, Maisie——

MIKE

Never you mind your Ma, Maisie. We threatened to strike today an' they're goin' to raise us to 7.50—7.50 a day, an' mark my words we'll be gettin' ten before this war's over!

MAISIE

So why shouldn't I look nice with a Mr. Vanderbilt Carnegie for my father, is that it?

MIKE

(*Drying his face*)
Come here and buss me, Maisie. You're a pretty girl, all right, a darn sight too pretty to be throwin' yourself away on the first good for nothin' soldier that comes back from the war.

MAISIE

(*Kissing him*)
Don't you call Jim good for nothin', Pop. *You* never like any man that looks twice at me. Jim was making 25 dollars a week before he

enlisted, an' he's the finest lookin' feller that ever marched down Fifth
Avenue.

MIKE

How do you know what he looks like now or what he'll be able to make
after this? That telegram didn't tell you nuthin'! He may have lost an
arm or a leg or an eye, or all three, or double, for what you know.

MAISIE

It's not true. I had a letter from him this afternoon written in the hospital at Norfolk before he knew he was comin'.
   (*She takes a letter out of her belt*)
Listen. He says he can't wait to lay his two eyes on me, so there can't
be nothin' the matter with his sight, Pop—or to get his two arms tight
around me—so his arms must be workin' all right. An' he says he'll be
the proudest man on earth when we two go walkin' in the park Sunday
mornin', an' a man can't go walkin' without——

MIKE

   (*Interrupting*)
Legs? Perhaps not. But his insides may be gutted out for all that.

MAISIE

Drop it, Pop. I won't believe any of those awful things. But even if
they were all true I'm not goin' back on Jim. Jim's my boy—don't you
understand—*my boy!*
   (*Looking up, she sees* JIM *standing in the doorway, she gazes at
   him a second incredulously. Then she says wonderingly*)
Jim!
   (*Then joyously*)
Jim!

JIM

Maisie!
   (*She runs to him. They embrace*)
   (JIM *is a nice looking young man in khaki—a sergeant. He is
   brown but very thin*)

MIKE

Well, is it yourself, Jim Durlan? It's glad we are to have you back again.
   (*He detaches one of* JIM'S *hands from its hold on* MAISIE *and
   shakes it as he looks him over*)

An' particular glad to see you brought the usual number of arms and legs wid you.

JIM

Thanks, Pa Connors.
(*He frees his hand to resume the embrace*)

MRS. CONNORS

The blessin' o' God on you, Jim! Why you're lookin' fine! Where wuz it you wuz hurt?

MIKE

Sure I don't believe he's hurt at all. It's playin' hookey you are, isn't it, Jim?

JIM

(*Turning his eyes reluctantly from* MAISIE'S *face*)
Hello, Ma Connors. It was my side if that's what you want to know.
(*They show great interest in the spot*)
But it's all healed long ago.
(*They draw back disappointed*)
The trouble is I had to be out so long in the cold, an' fever set in, an' after that the rheumatism. They couldn't get me cured owin' to the cold an' the wet so they shipped me home.

MIKE

Rheumatism! Well, I'll be blowed! Is that all you got? An' here's mesilf, Mike Connors, been sufferin' tortures for twenty years wid the rheumatism an' no one ever called *me* a wounded hero. Such pains as *I* have from the back of me neck way down——
(*He begins an excruciating pantomime*)

MAISIE

(*Still in* JIM'S *arms*)
Oh we know all about your rheumatism, Pop. I reckon Jim's is different.

MRS. CONNORS

I'm glad it's not your stomach that's affected, Jim. I've the gran' dinner in the oven an' it'll all be spoiled if you don't sit down to it this minute.
(*They sit.* JIM *walks stiffly with a slight limp. He draws* MAISIE *down beside him.* MRS. CONNORS *serves the dinner, putting the corn beef in front of* MIKE, *and serving each person vegetables from the dishes which she then puts on the table*)

MIKE

(*Warming to his favorite subject as he serves the meat*)
Did you ever have the pains in the back o' your legs, Jim?

JIM

Don't let's be talkin' pains, Pa Connors. I'm fed up on the subject of
my own an' the other chaps. I came home on the boat with eight hundred wounded, one of them tellin' worse tales than the last.
(*Looking at* MAISIE *as she hands him his plate from* MIKE)
Well, Maisie, girl, who's been sportin' you to a string o' pearls an' me
away?

MAISIE

(*Coyly*)
Huh! That would be tellin'.

MRS. CONNORS

(*Serving* JIM *to vegetables*)
Come now, Maisie, don't be teasin' the poor chap an' he just back from
the war! She bought 'em herself, Jim, an' they cost a heap o' money too.
Maisie's quite a rich young lady these days.

JIM

Is she? Well her face is her fortune anyway, I'm thinking.
(*He kisses her*)

MIKE

Come on, Ma. Don't I get any of them spuds, just because that young
scallawag's got the rheumatism?

MRS. CONNORS

(*Serving him*)
Here you are—spuds, an' cabbage, an' I got some carrots on the stove.

MAISIE

Bread an' butter, Jim. An' here's some o' your favorite sweet pickle.

MRS. CONNORS

(*Sitting down*)
Well how does it taste, boy?

JIM

It tastes fine, Mrs. Connors. You're not short of rations over here, are you? There's a few thousand folk on t'other side would be glad to sit down to a feed like this.

MIKE

(*His mouth full*)

Sure, they try to limit us with their wheatless an' meatless days, an' all that, but I say those regulations is for the rich. The workin' man has to have good victuals or he can't earn good wages. An' vicy versy, if he don't earn good wages he can't have good victuals, so there you are!

(MAISIE *gets tea pot from stove—pours* JIM'S *tea, then passes it*)

MAISIE

They tell you, you can only have three pounds o' sugar a month, an' all that sort o' stuff, but it's easy to get round it. Ma goes to one shop, an' I go to another, an' sometimes we send Pop to a third. They can't keep track o' that.

JIM

(*Startled*)

Maisie, do you mean that?

MAISIE

Mean what?

JIM

That you really try to get round the government like that?

MAISIE

Say, do you think the rich folk is livin' on three pounds o' sugar a month —not on your tintype! An' if we can afford it I don't see why we shouldn't have it as well as they. More meat, Jim?

JIM

No, thanks.

MIKE

(*Continuing to eat heartily*)

It's all profiteering, that's what it is! Them fellers is pretendin' things is scarce to keep the price up. I'm makin' 7.50 a day an' Maisie's gettin' 21 a week an' owin' to the price things are we ain't savin' a cent more than we used to.

JIM

Well you're not goin' without anything, I should say.

MIKE

An' why should we, I want to know. The rich ain't goin' hungry, why should the poor? Tell me that, Jim. Will you tell me that?

(MRS. CONNORS *begins quietly to clear off some of the dishes*)

JIM

There's a great difference, Pa Connors, between goin' hungry an' going without. An' believe me, if we folks don't begin going without this year we'll be goin' hungry next, like those poor creatures in France. I've seen it, an' I suppose you can't feel it till you *do* see it. It's pretty bad over there. People—women and kids, mind you—freezin' in the winter, dyin' of disease in the summer, an' starvin' all the year round.

MRS. CONNORS

(*Bringing dish from oven*)

Oh it's terruble. I can't read the papers any more, they're so upsettin'! The stories o' them starvin' babies just makes me cry. Pudding, Jim. Your favorite banana pudding.

(*She helps him*)

MAISIE

(*Eating*)

But *you* didn't have to go hungry?

JIM

Only when the mess sergeant got plugged on the way up to our lines. I ain't complainin'. We had enough to eat but we learned somethin' too.

MAISIE

(*Her spoon suspended in mid air*)

What?

JIM

That enough ain't all you want by a long shot.

MAISIE

(*Noticing* JIM *isn't eating*)

Well, you can have all you want here, Jim. No need makin' ourselves miserable before we have to. You're worse than the movies! For Heaven's sake, forget all those horrors for a while an' just remember you're back again with us—with me.

(*She leans against him*)

JIM

(*Slipping an arm around her*)
You're right. It's great. You've no idea how much we boys think of home out there, Maisie, nor how often I used to fancy myself sitting down here with you all just like this. Havin' no family I used to think o' your folks as mine, sort of.

MRS. CONNORS

Bless your heart, boy.

JIM

I could see this room just as plain, with the clock on the shelf back of the stove, an' Ma Connors' basket on the little table, an' the picture Maisie an' I cut out o' the Times a year ago. I used to put myself to sleep thinkin' of it an' forgettin' the mud an' the rats an' how damn uncomfortable I was.

MAISIE

Well, here you are, Jim, so forget all that for good.

JIM

(*Slowly straightening and laying down his spoon*)
Ain't it funny, I can't? Here I am with everything just as I hoped an' I'm thinking of it all out there harder than ever, of the boys standin' for hours in the mud, of the way a feller flops over comical-like when he's hit, of the little kids that used to come beggin' for bits of our rations, an' the women that waved to us so gallant like from the fields as we went by.
(*He is looking ahead of him, seeing it all*)
It's got me, Maisie, I can't forget. By God, I hope they'll let me go back!

MAISIE

(*Feeling this sudden distance between them*)
Back? You want to go back when you just got home? What's the matter with you, Jim? It's a queer way to be talking an' we not having seen each other for a year. There's something happened to you, Jim. You're not loving me the way you did when you went away or you wouldn't talk so.
(*As he does not answer*)
There's some girl over there. I might have known!
(*She rises and crosses angrily. Then adds, sarcastically*)
Or it is homesick you are for the mud an' the dirt an' the hunger?

JIM

(Following her)

You've said it, Maisie. I'm just that. I want to go back to it all. Sure I don't seem to belong here at all where it's all so comfortable an' easy. There's a kind of a gulf between us. War's hell, all right, but it's the realest thing I ever came up against and I can't forget it—an' what's more I don't want to, not for a minute.

MIKE

Who's forgettin'? We couldn't if we wanted to. What with the mornin' papers an' the Liberty Loans an' the thrift stamps an' the Red Cross. Do you think we ain't doin' our bit? Why a man's hand is never out of his pocket.

MAISIE

Nor a girl's either. Pop's right. Never a day passes but what someone comes round the office collecting for one thing or another. An' we're not complainin'. We're glad to give.

JIM

I'm sure you are, Maisie, but it's not only the givin'—it's the givin' up that counts—givin' up puddin', an' pearl necklaces, an' fine dresses an' all.

MAISIE

Jim! How can you! I only got these for you—because you were coming home. It's a queer state of things we've come to when a string of beads an' a pretty dress can come between a man an' his girl!

JIM

(Earnestly)

It *is* a queer state of things we've come to, Maisie. It's war, an' you don't seem to realize it. It's not the things but the meanin' back of them. Don't you know when you buy stuff like that you're takin' labor that might go to makin' guns, an' money that might be loaned to Uncle Sam for ships. You don't need the beads the way we need ships an' guns. God, how we need 'em, Maisie!

MIKE

Sure you've no call to come home posin' as a hero an' preachin' to us about our war duty. I reckon we know our duty as well as any.

JIM

(Breaking out)

Duty! Who's talkin' o' duty! We'll never win this war on duty, an' that's just it. Do you think we're killin' Germans over there for duty? We're killin' 'em because if we don't they'll kill us, an' we're goin' to lick 'em because if we don't they're goin' to lick us an' then there'll be hell to pay. We didn't start this war but we're goin' to finish it, an' we can't finish it unless we're willin' to do a darn sight more than you people over here seem to realize. Maybe I'm crazy, but I reckon we're all crazy over there. It's that I miss here. Lord, if you could see them people in France livin' on carrots and potatoes, without coal, or clothes, or houses, some of them, an' *givin'*, all the time, an' not only givin' but *lovin'!* It's the *lovin'* to do it all that counts. I've seen a woman give her last bit of bread to a hungry soldier and laugh with the joy of it. That's the spirit that backs up an army. An' it's that sense of the people at home goin' the whole hog with us that counts more to a man at the front than all the chocolate an' cigarettes an' vaudeville shows on earth! There was one woman I know, she——

MAISIE

Huh! I knew there was a woman back of all this. I don't want to hear about her, thanks.

MRS. CONNORS

Whist, Maisie, Jim ain't been playin' fast and loose with you. I can see it in his eyes.

JIM

(Slowly, with dawning comprehension)

You're right, Maisie. There *is* a woman between us, only not the way you think. She was small, an' she had dark eyes, an' there was something like you in the way she held her head. It was the night I was wounded.

MAISIE

I don't want to hear.

JIM

(Not heeding her, absorbed in his reminiscence, sinks into big chair, left)

It was the night I was wounded. You know they had found out I was nuts on a motor cycle so they had put me on dispatch duty. It was cold, one o' those wet cold nights they specialize on over there. Fritz's artillery was givin' us an exhibition. No tellin' what they might do next. The Colonel gave me some papers an' told me to race to headquarters. That was about fourteen miles away. Of course I'd been over the roads enough, first with a Frenchy and then alone, but I tell you roads is mighty different when you're speeding at night with no lights an' shell holes likely to ditch you at any minute. Only the day before I'd met a poor chap who had struck one accidental like and landed on his head. He was done for. Well, I was trusting in my luck an' gettin' on fine when all of a sudden I heard one of them long distance whiz bangs comin' straight for me. I tried to dodge, which is no easy job on a motor cycle, but the next minute everythin' seemed to blow up in front of me an' I got a queer sharp pain in my side. I had the sense to shut off the gas an that's all I knew, till I found myself lyin' on the ground, I don't know how much later, feelin' damn sick an' uncomfortable. I tried to get up an' I fainted. Then I waited for someone to come—an' no one did. I thought I was done with this little old planet for good. Then I saw a light off somewhere in the distance an' I made up my mind to get there before I bled to death. (*Stage begins to darken*) I found my cycle but it was too heavy to push so I left it an' started on alone. That little wisp of a light was about eighty miles farther away than I thought, but at last I got up to a little tumble-down sort of a house. I found the window an' looked in.

(*By now only* JIM *is visible and* MAISIE *staring at him from a little distance*)

There was a woman inside. I felt for the door an' pushed it open. Then I must have fainted again for everythin' got black around me—an' then —an' then——

(*The stage has become completely black*)

SCENE II

Gradually the stage becomes lighter, revealing the very bare and dim interior of a French cottage. Small stove, sink, bed, table, cupboard, a small old chest and a plain wooden stool are all the furniture it contains. MARIE, *a young Frenchwoman, and* JACQUES, *a boy of six, are sitting opposite to each other at the table.* MARIE *on the stool,* JACQUES *on the little chest.* MARIE *wears a dark skirt and a shawl over her shoulders. The boy is a shabby hodgepodge of garments. He is eating from a bowl. A small pot and a kettle are on the stove. The sole light in the room comes from a candle on the table. The distant rumble of guns can be heard from time to time.*

MARIE

Slowly, *mon petit,* slowly. It will last longer.

JACQUES

(*Slowing down*)
You are not eating, *petite mère.*

MARIE

Later. I am not yet hungry.

JACQUES

You always say that. It is not so. It is because of me you do not eat.
Is there no more?

MARIE

Yes, little tyrant, there is more. See.
(*She shows him the pot and puts more in his bowl*)

JACQUES

I will watch when I am in bed to see that you eat.

MARIE

You are not to sleep here tonight, little son. You are going to Tante
Lizette.

JACQUES

Why must I go to Tante Lizette, *Maman?*

MARIE

Because she has a fire and it is warmer.

JACQUES

But *we* have a fire tonight.

MARIE

(*Looking in stove*)
It is almost gone and we have no more to give it. I could get nothing
today. Fires must be fed like little boys. Are you not happy with your
cousins, Jacques?

JACQUES

Fairly happy, *Maman.*
(*Proudly*)
I can spit farther than Paul, *Maman.*

MARIE

(*Smiling*)
You can! Think of that!

JACQUES

I can spit almost as far as a real soldier, *Maman*.

MARIE

(*Kissing the top of his head*)
Tiens, you will be a great man some day, *mon petit.*

JACQUES

I would like to show Papa. He would laugh and lift me on his shoulder, would he not, *Maman*.

MARIE

Yes, *cheri*. You shall show him when he comes home.

JACQUES

When will that be, *Maman?*

MARIE

Soon, dear, soon.

JACQUES

Oh, you always say soon, *Maman,* but he does not come.

MARIE

But things are different now, sweetheart. Anything may happen now. The Americans have come to help us.

JACQUES

I am afraid of the Americans, *Maman*. I learned about them in school —when we had school. They are fierce and brown and they wear no clothes. They must be worse than the Boches.

MARIE

Not these Americans, dear. They are soldiers like ours, and big and strong and brave. They are not savages, dear. They are more like gods for they have come to help us.

JACQUES

What will they do, *Maman*. Will they bring us things to eat?

MARIE

Yes, *cheri.*

JACQUES

And coal?

MARIE

Yes, *cheri.* And they will end the war and bring us back Papa. Only have patience, *mon petit*—only have patience.

JACQUES

We've been having patience for a very long time now, *Maman.*

MARIE

Jacques, I am ashamed of you. It is nothing what we have borne compared to the others, those poor people whom we saw go by with nothing left. You remember the little children who cried, they were so tired?

JACQUES

I remember. But I often want to cry, *Maman,* when I don't.

MARIE

(*Embracing him*)
That is my brave boy.
(*Listening to sound of guns*)
Tiens, they are growling at each other tonight. It is more than usual.

JACQUES

And there is Tante Lizette!
(*The door opens and a middle-aged woman stands there, wearing sabots, and a shawl over her head. She carries a small basket on her arm*)

LIZETTE

Nom de Dieu, it is cold. Is the child ready?

MARIE

In a moment. Come in and rest, Lizette.

LIZETTE

(*Shutting door and standing by it*)
No, I must get back. The guns are bad tonight. The children are frightened. Will you not come with us, Marie?

MARIE

(*Bundling* JACQUES *in her shawl*)
No, thank you, Lizette.

JACQUES

Why do you never come, *Maman?*

MARIE

(*Gaily*)
La la. Someone must be here in case Father comes home.

LIZETTE

You are foolish, Marie. He will not come tonight. You will hear when
he is coming.

MARIE

I did not hear before. It just happened he passed near by with a message.
And I was at mother's. I did not see him. I have not seen him since. I
take no more chances.

LIZETTE

As you will. Oh, I almost forgot.
(*She takes a bowl from the basket on her arm*)
I have brought you something. Soup—*real soup!* We killed the hen.
We *had* to. She was so old she was nearly dead of herself. You must eat
this, Marie. You need it. It is not for the child.

MARIE

Thank you, Lizette. I will eat it. You are good.

LIZETTE

Eh bien, come on, Jacques. Are you warm? Why, Marie, you have given
him your shawl. You will freeze!

MARIE

(*Pointing to the bed*)
No, there is the blanket. I will put that around me till I go to bed.
(*She kisses* LIZETTE)
A demain, Lizette. *Que Dieu te garde.*
(*She kisses* JACQUES)
Take care of Tante Lizette like a good soldier.

JACQUES

I will, *Maman.* Like an American!

(He marches out proudly, holding his aunt's hand)
*(*MARIE *watches them out, holding candle for them. Then she shuts the door, shivering. She goes to stove with soup, looks at fire, shakes her head and puts bowl on shelf. She takes* JACQUES' *little bowl and spoon and begins to wash it at sink with water from a pail. The roll of the guns becomes more audible in the silence. Suddenly she starts listening. A face is seen for a second at the window, then the door bursts open and* JIM, *wounded, dirty, exhausted, staggers in)*

JIM

Beg pardon, ma'am, but—
(He falls unconscious. She runs to his aid)

MARIE

Mon dieu! Qu'il ne soit pas mort!
(She loosens his clothes, get water, sprinkles his face and holds some to his lips)

JIM

(Coming to, weakly, and trying to raise himself)
I can't see. Say something! *Parlez! Sprechen!*

MARIE

Il vit. Dieu soit benit! Ça va mieux, maintenant, Monsieur?

JIM

French! Thank God!
(He falls back)

MARIE

Mais oui, I am French. What did you think?

JIM

(Weakly)
I forgot. I thought I might be a prisoner.

MARIE

Do not talk yet. Take some water.

JIM

(Sipping obediently)
You speak English.

MARIE

A little. I work once in Paris for an English lady.

JIM

Thank God. Where am I?

MARIE

About three kilos from Vitry le Fer.

JIM

I remember now. I was on my way to Rougeville with dispatches. Dispatches!

(*He feels for his pocket*)

Good Lord, I must be getting on.

(*He tries to rise*)

MARIE

Not yet, *Monsieur le soldat*. Lie quiet. Ze English—zey ar at Rougeville?

JIM

(*Groaning from his effort*)

Not the English. The Americans.

MARIE

Americains! You—you are an American? Oh, God is good!

(*She seizes his hand and kisses it*)

JIM

(*Protesting*)

I say—what's the matter?

MARIE

I have prayed to see one of ze Americans. My prayer is answered.

JIM

Well, you've got hold of a pretty poor specimen this time. Still, I think I might get up if you give me a hand.

MARIE

Could you get to the bed? It will be better. I will fix your wound a little.

(*She helps him to rise and manages to get him on the bed*)

How did it come?

JIM

(*Suppressing his groans*)

Shell! Hit in front of my motor cycle. Lucky it left enough of me to talk about it!

MARIE

Sh! It is bad! Oh, if only I had some warm water.

JIM

Might as well ask for diamonds in this country.

MARIE

Wait, I will get some. Lie still.

(*She puts blanket over him. Then she goes out into what should be a woodshed—comes back empty handed, looks round desperately, sees stool—takes it, breaks the legs off and puts them in the stove. She feels the kettle. As she is returning to* JIM *she sees bowl on shelf and puts that on stove*)

JIM

(*Hearing the breaking of the wood*)
What's that?

MARIE

Nossing. In a moment we will have warm water. An' some soup—some hot soup. You are cold?

JIM

You bet. But I'm getting used to that.

(*She chafes his hands a moment. Then she helps him slip off his coat. She cuts away shirt around the wound and examines it. All this of course is done in semidarkness invisible to audience, but indicates business for* MARIE)

JIM

Some little mosquito bite, ain't it?

MARIE

There may be steel in zere. I cannot tell. I can only bind it up.

JIM

That's all right. I'll keep the steel for a souvenir. It's valuable.

MARIE

(*Getting water from stove*)
You suffer an' you are gay! Zis will hurt more. I am sorry.

JIM

Fire ahead.

(*She washes out the wound*)

MARIE

An' now, what to bind it with! Something broad an' long. Ah yes, I know!

(*She goes to little chest and takes out cloth*)

JIM

What's that?

MARIE

It is a tablecloth. It is all zat is left in my marriage chest. My old mother wove it for me. Zat is why I still have it.

(*She tears it in strips*)

JIM

An' you're tearin' it up for me?

MARIE

For you an' your America. I am proud zat I have it to tear for you.

JIM

Well, you're *some class,* you French. That's all I've got to say.

MARIE

I don' understand. Can you sit up a little, *Monsieur?* There!

(*She binds up his wound*)

Zat is better! It will not bleed. It will hold till you get to ze doctor.

JIM

If it'll only hold till I get to Rougeville, that's all I care.

(*He tries to rise and clutches her. He is dizzy*)

MARIE

Wait. You are too weak.

(*She puts him down, and goes to stove*)

JIM

(*Angrily*)

But I must get on.

MARIE

(*Bringing soup*)

Drink this. It will put ze new blood into you.

(*She holds bowl while he eats*)

It is good, *hein?*

JIM

(*Looking at her*)
Good! Say, if it weren't for this itch in my side, I'd think I was in heaven. Aren't you goin' to have some o' this with me?

MARIE

(*Shaking her head*)
I have had my supper.

JIM

Say, do you live here all alone?

MARIE

Wiz my little boy. He has gone to my sister's for the night. My husband, he has been away four years now. He is dispatch rider like you.

JIM

Do you see him often?

MARIE

I have not seen him in six months. Once he ride by an' I was not here. I always hope he come again.

JIM

Not a very cheerful life this for you, is it?

MARIE

Oh *la la,* it is the same for all. What can one expect *avec ces cochons de Boches?* You, *Monsieur,* you have a wife at home?

JIM

No, but I've a girl an' she's a peach. I've her picture in my coat. Can you find it for me?
(MARIE *takes wallet from his coat pocket. He finds picture and hands it to her*)

MARIE

Ah, *elle est belle.* You have children?

JIM

Lord no, we're not married yet. But we're going to be when I get back.

MARIE

(*Comprehending at last*)
Oh, *fiancé!* I wish you joy, Monsieur.

JIM

You've done more than *wish* it. I reckon there wouldn't be any more love makin' for me if it hadn't been for you tonight. I'll tell Maisie about this, you bet!

(*He sits up*)

And don't think I don't know what you've done. I saw you break up that stool an' I know I got your one an' only tablecloth about my waist. Lord, I don't know how to thank you.

MARIE

Why you thank me? We are friends, *alliés,* are we not? It is my joy that I can help you. Your girl, she do the same for my man if he were hurt in her country, would she not?

JIM

I hope so.

MARIE

And you have come all zis way to fight for France—for France! Ah, Monsieur, all we have is not enough for you if you can save France from her enemies!

JIM

And by God, we *will* save France if it takes *all we have* to do it!

MARIE

(*Fervently*)

If you feel like zat, Monsieur, if all in your country feel like zat, you will succeed. It is the feeling zat makes success. We have not much men or much strength left but have such a feeling for our country zat she cannot lose!

JIM

Right-o. An' here I am wasting time talking about it when I've got dispatches for Rougeville.

(*He gets up with difficulty*)

MARIE

You think you can, Monsieur?

JIM

(*Staggering a little*)

I got to. That's all there is to it. My coat.

MARIE

(Taking coat from bed)
Here it is—but it is all in rags. It will not keep you warm where you are wounded.

JIM

Never mind that. I wouldn't know how to behave if I was warm for once.

MARIE

But it is cold—like ice. Wait.
(She seizes the blanket)

JIM

What are you going to do?

MARIE

I can make you a kind of coat.
(She tears blanket. See directions)

JIM

But I can't take your blanket.

MARIE

(Lying glibly)
There is more. Do not argue. You must get to Rougeville tonight.

JIM

I've a hunch my machine isn't much hurt. If I can sit on it I'll be all right—provided I don't strike too big a shell hole on the way.
(As MARIE puts blanket over his shoulders and winds broad strip around his waist)
What's that? Well that's a cute idea.—I met a Frenchy yesterday who hit one and landed on his head. Poor chap, he was done for. He gave me his dispatches an' I took them on. His watch, too. It's still there in my wallet. Lord, I mustn't forget that, must I?
(Picks up wallet from bed)
See, here it is.
(He hands her a silver watch)

MARIE

This?

JIM

(Preoccupied with his costume)
Well, this is some get up! It feels darn good, though. I reckon I can make it to Rougeville. Guess I'd better take that along.

MARIE

(Staring at watch, softly)
What are you going to do with it?

JIM

Send it to his wife.
(Referring to memorandum)
Jeanne Marie Drouot is her name. She lives at a place called Zichy.

MARIE

(Repeating expressionlessly)
Jeanne Marie Drouot. I know her, Monsieur. Leave it here and I will see it gets to her.

JIM

You know her—that's funny.

MARIE

Why is it—funny? She is just a woman of France—like me.

JIM

Poor thing. Well, you'll see it gets to her? I'll leave it, then. I'm off. Good-bye. No use trying to say thank you.

MARIE

(Recovering herself)
Wait.
(She goes to cupboard and takes out piece of bread)
Here is a piece of bread. You may need it before you can get there.

JIM

Sure you can spare it?

MARIE

Mais oui. There is more. *Au revoir, Monsieur, et bonne chance.*

JIM

(Taking her hand)
Good-bye, and how is it you say it?—*Vive la France!*

MARIE

(Gaily)
Merci! Vive l'Amérique!
(She takes candle and holds it high to light him out of the door. He goes)

MARIE

Take care of ze wall, Monsieur! It goes all right with you?

JIM'S VOICE

All right! Good-bye!

MARIE

Adieu! Bonne chance!
(*Slowly she closes the door, walks quietly to table, picks up watch, puts it to her lips and crumples to the floor*)
(*The stage becomes black. Gradually the figure of* JIM *appears sitting as he was at the end of the first scene.* MAISIE *is on her knees before him, looking up into his face*)
(*No background necessary*)

JIM

(*As if finishing his story*)
An' when I went there a week later, what do you think, Maisie? She was dead. *Dead!* Of hunger, they said—just hunger an' cold. Good God! An' all she had given me!

MAISIE

(*Weeping*)
Jim! How dreadful.
(*She puts her hand to her throat in the gesture of relaxing the tension and feels her beads. With a quick gesture she undoes them and throws them on the floor*)
God forgive me, Jim. I didn't know. I didn't understand. God forgive me!
(*She drops her head on his knees. He bends down, puts his arms round her and kisses her hair*)
(*The light fades*)

Curtain

THERESA HELBURN *The Other Girl*

The radio play and the moving-picture play are not in themselves new types of composition, but, rather, modifications or extensions of the dramatic form. They suit or adapt what is known as dramatic literature to their respective mediums. This is achieved in radio by means of placing emphasis upon auditory appeals; the spoken word is played up for every possible dramatic quality; sound effects, including music, are used with skilful realism to make up for the absence (until television arrives) of business and scenery and costuming and lighting.

The moving picture has some advantages over both radio and legitimate stage production. It lacks, of course, the direct human or personal touch with the actor; it is not yet three-dimensional; its color effects are not yet perfect (though by way of being perfected). But it may be epic and panoramic in scope while mere stage production may not be; it may by the very perfection of photographic machinery "outrealize realism"; it may by means of the montage (pronounced *mahn tahzh*) enable an audience to "see a character's thoughts." If its formula is frequently hackneyed—boy meets girl, boy loses girl, boy gets girl—the miracle of its mechanical achievements alone may safely be depended upon to hold majorities.

It should be remembered that *scenario* is used for *play* or for *screen play* in this field of writing; it means, that is, the story of plot, the scene-by-scene development of plot, together with all essential details for acting the photoplay before the camera. It is divided into numbered sequences or "shots" rather than into acts and scenes.

One of the few great scenarios ever written—if, indeed, not the greatest—is by public consensus *In Old Chicago* by Lamar Trotti and Sonya Levien, from Niven Busch's original story. The tragic Chicago fire of 1871 is so vividly realized in the writing, and the homely yet thrilling events of the catastrophe are so magnificently portrayed in the production, that human imagination and emotion would seem to have nowhere left to go after this momentous achievement. The burning of Rome—even to the tune of Nero's fickle fiddling—seems tame enough by comparison, in spite of its centuries of historical publicity. The first twenty-six shots (there are 418 in all) of this screen masterpiece are here included through the courteous permission of Twentieth Century-Fox Film Corporation, owner of the copyright and producer of the picture.*

IN OLD CHICAGO

FADE IN

1 CREDIT TITLES—SUPERIMPOSED ON A BACKGROUND
OF CURRIER AND IVES PRINTS OF OLD CHICAGO—THE

* Copyright 1937 by Twentieth Century-Fox Film Corporation.

UNION STOCKYARDS, FIELD & LEITER STORE, PALMER
HOUSE, ETC. OVER THIS SUCH MUSIC OF THE PERIOD
AS "NELLY BLY," "WAKE NICODEMUS," "BABYLON IS
FALLEN," "OLD FOLKS AT HOME," ETC.

DISSOLVE TO:

2 TITLE

AMERICA—A MID-WESTERN PRAIRIE IN 1854 . . .

DISSOLVE TO:

3 PRAIRIE—NIGHT

The moon is just rising over a vast stretch of prairie land. The stillness of the night is broken by the approaching clop-clop of horses'
hoofs and the rumbling of wagon wheels over a hard-rutted road
that is scarcely more than a trail. Out of the darkness looms an open
wagon drawn by two horses, and loaded with members of the
O'Leary family and their household belongings.

As the wagon APPROACHES CAMERA, the occupants evolve
from the darkness. In the driver's seat, clutching the reins, is
PATRICK O'LEARY. He is a man of about forty, wild, lusty,
untamed, yet with a warm Irish-peasant quality about him—a man
with poetry in his soul despite the lack of a formal education. He
has great strength in his body and a restless, tormenting urge for
pioneering—a man always in a hurry to get somewhere. Beside him
sits his wife, MOLLY, with their youngest child, ROBERT, a boy
of six, slumped against her in sleep. Her arms are around the boy
protectingly. As the wagon MOVES PAST CAMERA we see the
remaining members of the O'Leary family—JACK, twelve, and
DION, ten. The boys occupy kitchen chairs which are roped securely
to the rest of the household furniture. They are jolting along, half
asleep.

4 CLOSE SHOT—MOLLY O'LEARY AND HER HUSBAND

as she eases the position of the boy asleep in her arms. Molly O'Leary
is a woman with iron in her, face boldly molded, hands strong and
capable of doing a man's work. There is a formidable, rigid quality
about her that comes from hard work, self-denial and sound common sense. Yet she has an immense capacity for tenderness. She is
dressed in a grey cheviot, lined, boned, basqued and braided. She
glances back at the boys in the wagon, then turns to her husband.
There is Irish phrase-making in her and her husband's speech, for
they are not long out of the Old Country, not a brogue, just the

rolling music of Irish peasant-talk. The boys, in sharp contrast, are completely Americanized.

MOLLY

(sternly)

Isn't it time to stop this travellin', and it dark, and the child shiverin'?

PATRICK

(emphatically)

We will not! And us not two hours, or maybe three, from Chicago itself!

(to the horses)

Get along with you now, you lazy devils, or I'll be layin' me whip on your backs.

MOLLY

(with same emphasis)

And what's the tearin' hurry? Chicago will not be movin' —and us livin' there for the rest of our days—

(qualifying it forcefully)

God willin'!

PATRICK

Now I'll not be held back by your tongue—and a fine city waitin' just over the rim o' the land! 'I'll rest there to-night,' I said to myself—and so I will! For it's a mighty city will be built here—the hub of the country—fillin' all this prairie land—

(over his shoulder)

—and you boys livin' to see it.

MOLLY

(snorting)

Humph!

PATRICK

(snorting back)

Humph, indeed!

(to the horses)

Get along now!

As he flips the reins, and the horses respond, the wagon lurching ahead, the asthmatic whistle of an old-fashioned railroad train is heard off-scene. Startled, the older people look off in the direction from which the sound comes.

5 MED. SHOT—THE WAGON
as the two boys, Dion and Jack, are electrified into action.

JACK

(crying out)
Look, Pa! It's a train!

6 SHOT—AN OLD-FASHIONED ENGINE AND TRAIN
chuffing and puffing in the dark, as it approaches the wagon.

7 MED. CLOSE SHOT—THE WAGON

DION

Look at it go!
(wild with excitement)
Come on, Pa! Let's race her!

PATRICK

(inflamed with excitement)
By the twinklin' stars of heaven, I will!

He starts the horses faster, and Molly bounces up and down on her sitzplatz.

MOLLY

(trying to stop him)
You'll do no such—and me half jolted out of my mind!

DION

Go on, Pa! You can lick it!

Patrick begins to whip up the horses.

PATRICK

(to the horses)
Go on, you blasted devils!

MOLLY

Sure, you are the fool of men!
  (as she bounces)
Stop it, I tell you, or I'll never be able to sit down again!

DION

We're licking it! We're licking it!

Patrick whips up the horses as the engine whistle sounds again.

8 MED. CLOSE SHOT—THE ENGINE
as it puffs and blows and shrieks and lets out a wild blast of steam and sparks.

9 MED. SHOT—THE WAGON
As the horses become suddenly frightened by the noise and the live sparks falling over their heads, they suddenly bolt off the road and across the prairie—a runaway—while behind them bounces the ungainly heavy wagon.

10 CLOSE SHOT—PATRICK
bracing his weight against the footboard in an effort to stop the runaway, twisting the reins around his wrist.

11 CLOSE FLASH SHOT—MOLLY
tense, clutching Robert, who is screaming, and at the same time holding on to the wagon as best she can.

12 CLOSE SHOT—THE TWO BOYS
in the rear, clinging to the ropes.

13 CLOSEUP—BRACES
buckling horses and wagon together, as one snaps under the strain.

14 MED. SHOT—THE WAGON AND HORSES
As the horses break away from the wagon, Patrick O'Leary is flung from his seat into the air, one rein wrapped around his arm.

15 CLOSE SHOT—PATRICK
as he falls and is dragged along by the runaway horses.

16 MED. CLOSE SHOT—MOLLY

as she grabs the brake handle and prevents the wagon from turning over. She starts to get out immediately, terror in her eyes.

17 LONG SHOT—THE TRAIN

puffing away in the distance and out of scene.

18 CLOSE SHOT—PATRICK

lying on the ground, motionless. He is suffering from internal injuries, and is hurt about the head.

19 GROUP SHOT—AROUND PATRICK

as Molly rushes in, drops on her knees beside him, frees his arm from the rein, and lifts his inert form to her lap.

> MOLLY

Jack! The water!

Jack darts away toward the wagon. Dion and Bob crowd in closer. Bob is crying hysterically. Molly is frightened, excited, but she acts with precision.

> MOLLY
>
> (to Dion)
>
> Quick—my petticoat—tear it!

Dion quickly rips off strips from his mother's white cambric petticoat for bandages.

20 THE WAGON—CLOSE SHOT—JACK

as he is filling a bucket with water from a barrel strapped to the wagon. He runs back toward Molly and his father.

21 GROUP SHOT—MOLLY, PATRICK AND THE CHILDREN

Molly is mopping the blood from her husband's face. Jack runs in with the water. Molly wets a piece of cloth, gently wipes away the blood.

> JACK
>
> (anxiously)
>
> Ma—is he hurt bad?

MOLLY

(fiercely)

How should I be knowin'!

(then indicating the bucket)

Pour a little over his head.

(mopping)

You O'Learys are a strange tribe. There's no tellin' what you'll be up to next—racin' and all manner of foolishness.

(then to Dion)

Dion—get the whiskey.

As she mentions whiskey, and Dion runs toward the wagon, eager to be helpful, Patrick opens his eyes and gasps.

PATRICK

(gasping)

I'll be needin' it—and me dyin'!

Molly speaks with a confidence she doesn't feel.

MOLLY

Listen to him! A big, strong man like himself!

(then solicitously)

Where are you hurt?

PATRICK

(weakly)

Never mind me. Are the rest unharmed?

MOLLY

Not a scratch.

Heaven be praised! . . . 'Twas my own fault, and no other.

At this moment Jack runs back to his father with the jug of liquor, which he holds to the old man's lips. The latter takes a deep swig, and the liquor seems to do him good.

PATRICK

(with a long sigh)

Ain't it the devil's own doin' to be draggin' me down and bumpin' the life out of me just when the smell of Chicago is in me nose!

(he looks at his sons)

Come here, Jack—Dion—Bob—closer—the three of you, and mind what I say. It's a grand new place, this Chicago, and them that grow with it will be rich and strong like I was always mindin' to be. It's a boom—and you'll boom with it. Some day you'll be big men and a credit to my name, and everybody speakin' with respect of the O'Learys and how they grew up with the city and put their mark on it!

MOLLY
(her heart bleeding within her)
You're wastin' yourself, Patrick—you with your fine talk!

PATRICK
(still the battler)
It's my last breath I'm usin', and I'll have my say!

By now his eyes are glazing over. The end is close at hand. He slumps. The older boys show their awe and fright in their faces. Robert is clinging to his mother's skirt, whimpering.

MOLLY
(to the boys)
Help me put him in the wagon. We've got to find a doctor.

PATRICK
(weakly)
It's no use! Just bury me here—and let Chicago come to me—that couldn't come to it . . . Molly . . .

He is dead before he can utter another word. As Molly lowers his head to the ground,

DISSOLVE TO:

22 A NEW GRAVE UNDER A TREE ON A HILL OVERLOOKING CHICAGO—NIGHT
This is immediately following Patrick's death. There is a full moon in the sky now. A rough cross, made of two sticks, marks the head of the grave. Jack and Dion are standing at one side of the grave, Molly at the other, with Robert clinging to her dress. Molly is conducting the funeral services for her husband.

MOLLY

Heavenly One, help my Pat to rest in peace—him that
was so restless on earth. He was a good man—for all his
fine ambitions. If ever there was food to be got—or shelter
—or if you wanted someone to laugh with, or for a bit of
a good time, you had no need to look further than Patrick
O'Leary! But I need not be tellin' you all this, who knows
it better than I do. Amen!

She crosses herself. The boys do likewise.

MOLLY

(quietly)
Get the horses ready, boys.

Dion and Jack start toward the wagon in the b. g. both trying to
conceal their grief. Molly lingers at the grave.

23 CLOSE SHOT—MOLLY
looking down at the grave.

MOLLY

Good-bye, Pat. Some day I'll be sendin' the priest to speak
the proper words.

Then, her job done, she turns and CAMERA PANS with her as,
dry-eyed, she starts toward the wagon which is now ready to start.
Without a word, Molly starts to climb aboard. For the first time,
Jack speaks.

JACK

(with great difficulty)
Ma, I'll take care of you . . . I'll do what he said—you
know, about Chicago, and—

He breaks off, unable to continue.

24 CLOSE SHOT—DION
He, too, is trying to fight back his tears, as he picks up where Jack
left off.

DION

Sure, Ma, we'll take care of you! I'm going to make a lot
of money and get you things, and—

He breaks off, choking.

MOLLY

(almost fiercely)
Hush it, both of you!

Then she climbs into the wagon.
Jack swings Robert up to the seat beside her. Then he and Dion
climb into the rear of the wagon, into the chairs they formerly
occupied. Molly makes Robert comfortable beside her. His head
drops down sleepily against her. She clucks to the horses, and as
they start out

FADE OUT

FADE IN

25 TITLE:

CHICAGO—1854 . . . NEW, RAW, BOLD! . . . A CITY
OF EASY MONEY, EASY WAYS, UGLY, DIRTY, OPEN
NIGHT AND DAY TO NEWCOMERS FROM ALL PARTS
OF THE WORLD . . . A FIGHTING, LAUGHING AG-
GRESSIVE AMERICAN CITY CONTENT TO BE A HOG
BUTCHER RATHER THAN A KING—CHICAGO!

DISSOLVE TO:

26 CHICAGO STREET — DAY — FULL SHOT — MOLLY
O'LEARY AND HER FAMILY

as she drives her wagon through this booming, raucous city. There
has been a recent heavy shower, and the street is a mud bank, with
great puddles of rainwater here and there, through which the horses
splash. The three boys are sitting in the body of the wagon near
Molly, all gazing about them with excitement and bewilderment at
the exhilarating spectacle on every side.

This main street of Chicago is crowded with vehicles of every kind
—prairie schooners, wagons, phaetons, victorias, etc. One man is
driving several cows through the street. An Indian from the prairies
stalks along, aloof and indifferent. The sidewalks, wooden and on
different levels, are crowded with all types and classes—a few ele-

gantly dressed ladies, men with frock coats and tall hats, thugs of the lowest character, urchins—all intermingle. Shoddy wooden shacks, stores, shops, saloons, shooting galleries, stand side by side with fine trade establishments, theaters and other imposing buildings.

WORK

The following suggestions for stories may appeal to you. If so, use them as bases for stories of the various types illustrated in this section. If not, devise others for use in the same sort of practice. You may manufacture your story plot from the "whole cloth" so to say, that is, you may make it entirely an invention. Or you may base it upon some actual experience, enlarging and enriching that experience until the major part of your story is really imaginary. In the former case your story will be creative; in the latter, derivative.

1. Concealing her enemy-spy lover in her room, a girl entertains the officers who come in his quest, by plying them with drinks. Presently the spy comes downstairs dressed as a beautiful young girl, joins the party, and by mannerism and conversation throws the officers completely off guard and exits to safety.

2. The bulky packet of money demanded by a band of kidnapers is placed in a cache at the place they designate in an anonymous letter. Among the bills, however, a virile young diamondback rattler is wrapped. Next day the kidnaped child is recovered by the police, and the bodies of the two men who kept the rendezvous for the reward are found dead along the roadway.

3. Your mother bought at an auction a very beautiful rug with an unusually thick pile. One day while you were beating it for her you noticed a sparkling object drop out of it. This turned out to be a twenty-carat diamond. Investigators discovered that the rug had once belonged to an Egyptian princess who, at a time when enemies invaded her country, concealed her jewels in rugs and pieces of furniture.

4. A handsome young football player is the cause of much admiration and jealousy among the girl students of a school or college. At an unguarded moment he tells one of his "girl friends" some of the signals that are to be used in the momentous Thanksgiving game. She reveals these to certain players on the rival team. The consequences are most serious, not only for the individuals involved but also for the institutions represented.

5. The miscarriage of justice in a certain murder case is caused by some sort of slurred pronunciation on the part of a star witness, such as, *I killed him* for *Ike killed him* or *Roe shot him* for *Rose shot him* or *Joe bumped him off* for *Job bumped him off*. Among other consequences is a new trial in which much of the testimony has to be spelled out and the attorneys have to emphasize exactness of oral English.

6. Among the passengers on a cross-country airplane is a father who has been notified that his long-lost son has been located at a certain place on the coast. He is making the journey in order to identify his son and to pay the reward offered many years ago, provided his information is authentic. Midway its journey the plane is forced down near an outlaw cabin in the prairies. Some of the passengers are killed; some are injured; some, among whom is the father, are merely shocked. All are taken in hand by the outlaws, and duly robbed. But one of the outlaws turns out to be the actual son and he obliges his associates to "lay off" and aid the victims in every way.

7. You are present one day while the student in charge of your school co-operative shop is making sales to various customers. His endeavor always is to force and compel sales by concentrating upon commodity rather than by playing up or "starring" the customer. Shortly after one purchase is made and the parcel wrapped, the buyer observes that he has been obliged to pay more for his merchandise than another standing beside him buying the same article. A colloquy ensues during which the student "salesman" is required to cancel both sales and refund the money. He also has the "pleasure" of seeing the other waiting prospects walk out of the shop without buying.

8. In a lonely railway station in the western part of the United States, the ticket agent one midnight hears the message "Murder! Help!" coded on an automobile horn. He grabs two pistols and runs out to the car. In it he finds two masked men holding his father, his wife, and his child in their power. There is some rapid fire. Then the agent recognizes one of the masked men as his brother who is an escaped convict, and the other as a tramp who jumped off a freight during the afternoon. Their intention had been, after forcing the father and wife to guide them to the station, to rob the safe and get away. But after a struggle they are worsted by the agent, who himself does some real Morse coding, and by daylight has the bandits in the hands of the sheriff.

9. When the Sunset Express arrives in Chicago on a certain morning James J. Jenkinson, prominent businessman of the Middle West, is found dead in his compartment. Traveling from California on the same train were a business rival and enemy of his, one of Mr. Jenkinson's two divorced wives, and a Pullman porter who many years ago was employed by Mr. Jenkinson. Thumb prints of all three are found on the outside of the Jenkinson compartment door. They are held on the arrival of the train in Chicago, but are not found guilty.

10. Your rich uncle disinherits you, bequeathing his large estate to two other nephews, your first cousins. Two weeks after the filing of his will, an old retainer in his household finds in a book in your uncle's library a will postdating the one by which you were disinherited. In this will you are made heir to the entire fortune, and the other two nephews are disinherited. Your uncle may have changed his mind as result of events about which you know a great deal; his first will may have been a forgery devised by the other nephews; the second will may have been a forgery by the old retainer who bears a grudge against the other two nephews.

11. The huge barn on the one-thousand acre Beaverbrook Farm recently burned to the ground. In the cornerstone there was found an iron box containing many papers, among others a series of deeds showing that the farm has come down, not to the family accredited with its ownership for the past fifty years, but to the faithful serving-woman who has been an excellent though badly treated servant to the present supposed owners. After some litigation she takes charge of the show place and becomes not only lady of the old mansion but social leader of the neighborhood. Perhaps she is domineering and brutal to the family she supplants; perhaps she is not. The story reveals her character in strong lights. It also builds a startling train of incidents.

12. Comply with some of the following narrative suggestions: Tell the story of your life to date; tell the story of a friend's life; tell the story of an old desk with many initials carved on it; of a faithful family dog or horse or cat; of an old tree under which you played as a child; of an old automobile that has traveled many miles and "stood up" under very rough usage; of a typical week in school; of the events of a single week in your home community; of world events for a given month; of your own scholarship record to date in comparison with that of a student whose record closely parallels yours; of a day's outing in the woods; of a memorable trip you once took;

of a football or a baseball that has never been owned by a losing team; of a canoe that was once sunk and now stays "on top"; of a theme from the time you outlined it until it won the prize and appeared in the school paper, and so forth.

13. A fable is a didactic narrative in which truth is presented in a homely manner through the medium of characters that are animals or abstract ideas or personified objects or generalized human beings, or all four. A myth is a fanciful or conjectural story, often masquerading as history, dealing as a rule with gods or godlike human beings, and usually explaining some belief or tradition or institution or natural phenomenon. Rewrite both the fable and the myth below in strictly dialogue or play form:

The Child of a Cottager was at play in a field at the back of his Father's house, and by chance trod upon a Snake, which turned round and bit him. The Child died of the bite, and the Father, pursuing the Snake, aimed a blow at him and cut off a piece of his tail. The Snake gained his hole, and the next day the Man came and laid at the mouth of the hole some honey, meal, and salt, and made offers of peace, thinking to entice the Snake forth and kill him. "It won't do," hissed out the Snake. "As long as I miss my tail, and you, your Child, there can be no good-will between us."

The Fable of the Serpent and the Man

Thisbe, of Babylon, had a rendezvous with Pyramus whom she loved very much. While awaiting him she saw a lioness kill an ox. Terrified, she fled, dropping her mantle in her haste, which became stained with blood. Then Pyramus appeared, and, seeing her bloody mantle, he decided that Thisbe had been killed. Forthwith he killed himself in despair. Thisbe returned and, beholding the dead body of Pyramus, she killed herself.

The Myth of Pyramus and Thisbe

PORTRAIT

PORTRAIT

IT has been pointed out (page 17) that literary or artistic description is seldom employed as an end in itself, that it is, rather, an accessory to other forms, used for the purpose of "bringing out" a story, a discussion, or an essay, for enriching and impressing and clarifying. There are very few books indeed consisting of descriptive writing only. There are practically no books in which description is not used to some extent. It was once fashionable for a novelist to introduce a character by means of a detailed description of his personal appearance. Walter Scott made this so much of a rule that many readers even of his own time found the method labored and uninteresting. Today bits of description are more likely to be given or suggested here and there as flashes or snapshots—or character actions and reactions are permitted to indicate appearance—with the result that totality of personal portrait is quite as clearly and impressively conveyed as it could be by the direct pictorial method. The deliberate photograph of a person on his entrance into a story savors somewhat too much of technical and sales descriptions. In these latter forms is it usually considered desirable to list point by point systematically, from one end to another consistently, the exact appearance of an object. As a basis in design, too, this method is imperative for the sake of proportion and harmony in the finished picture. But when you see a beautiful human body or a magnificently constructed bridge, you do not care to think of counting the bones in the one or the girders in the other.

The point is, that mere orderly enumeration has small if any place in artistic description. You may usually give a much more pointed picture of person, place, or thing by means of detached strokes of the brush here and there, by signaling effects and impressions that they make upon you, by comparing them deftly and keeping the comparison alive throughout a theme. Any method of sheer item-by-item picturization is known as objective description. The method of arraying descriptive points in some sort of deliberate order for the purpose of staging effects and impressions and comparisons is called subjective description. The latter yields lasting portraits, such as Charles Dickens inimitably painted; the former presents catalogues and works of reference that may of course have great value but, as a rule, comparatively little reading challenge.

Probably in no other kind of composition are fluidity and nicety of diction of greater importance than in word portraiture. They are to the writer very much what the mixture and application of colors are to the painter. The word that *almost* describes will never do. It must fit exactly, or it will not fit at all. The old saying "A miss is as good as a mile" applies in descriptive diction as nowhere else. Put your finger to an unplaned board. What adjective is telegraphed back to your mind—*coarse, bristly, craggy, harsh, jagged, ragged, rough, rude, rugged, sawlike, sharp, splintered, uneven, unfinished, unhewn, unpolished, wedgy,* or still some other? For the child who is just learning to talk and for the word-mute adult any one of these will do. For the person who is trained in precise habits of thinking and speaking, only one or two will do. And this example refers to a single sense only—touch—and to a single one of the many experiences of touch. The senses of tasting, smelling, hearing, and seeing make similar or perhaps even greater demands upon the careful speaker and writer for accurate reporting of impressions. Enslavement to the dictionary —which some one has called the "joyfulest serfdom of letters"—will be necessary if ever you are able to pen true and precise pictures of persons and places and things. You have many times been surprised at the deceptive powers of your senses. They will all fool you if you don't watch out. You frequently hear it said that you can trust your senses—that seeing (along with hearing and smelling and tasting and touching) is believing. But this is a truism rather than the truth. Seeing, hearing, smelling, tasting, and touching are forms of thinking. No thought—no taste or smell or sound or sight or touch! And how easy it is to be mistaken in your thinking, isn't it?

Imbedded portraits are to be found in all types of literature. They aid and abet and complete and satisfy our comprehension of oral and written themes. The character sketch, as we have seen, is rarely considered a finished piece of work unless it contains some portraiture of the person characterized. It has been made clear also that character may be and very often is deduced from pictorial detail of personal appearance. The two are as a rule profitably run together.

Sometimes a single detail of appearance is permitted to imply dominant characteristic. Sometimes a dominant trait is made to convey specialty of appearance so markedly that nothing else matters. *The Hunchback of Notre Dame* portrays as well as characterizes. *The Fawning Uriah Deep* characterizes as well as portrays. The most artistic as well as the most interesting description of people is that centered in a single detail of appearance that is thus made dominant. This is a human and natural method of indicating people. You very often designate a person by some physical characteristic— a dimpled chin, grayish-white eyes, bushy eyebrows, a sword-marked cheek, and the like. So writers very often center a theme upon some such descriptive detail as is indicated in *The Girl with the Green Eyes, The Man with the Crooked Smile, Lummox, Limping Lafe, The Round-shouldered Miser, The Maid of the Thin Lips.*

The terms *profile, thumbnail, pen-portrait, kodak, vignette, snapshot,* and others like them, are sometimes used in newspaper and periodical pictures of people, places, and things. Rarely are they purely descriptive. Nearly always they combine notes of personal appearance along with characteristics, that is, nearly always they combine description and exposition. Personified animal and place and nature pictures constitute interesting reading, provided they are consistently wrought and "true to the life." The *profile* is always something more than the word indicates; very often it is a running narrative of a person's life, as well as a side-view portrait of him and a character sketch into the bargain. The *vignette* is a kind of impressionistic portraiture that procures its effects by means of gradually shaded-off borders and backgrounds. Like the particular kind of photograph known by this name, the word picture develops the salient features out of the background, making them emerge insinuatingly. Its shadowy outlines etch rather than paint in full. Sheer clarity and definiteness are not the aim of the vignette, but its subtle touches and atmospheric quality must convey accurate if haunting impression.

The following conventional portrait of a character just prior to his introduction into a story is so regularly detailed as to be almost technical. The catalogue description of an article for sale could be hardly more minutely drawn. This is comparable with the old effects in drama wherein a person was intimately described to another, the portrayer concluding with "Tush, here he is upon us this very instant," or to those in musical productions wherein the chorus sings in "descriptive flattery" of the star and then forms two lines through which that important person makes a grand entrance.

Mr. Holdenough began to walk up the aisles of the chapel, not with the slow and dignified carriage with which the old Rector was of yore wont to maintain the dignity of the surplice, but with a hasty step like one who arrives too late at an appointment, and bustles forward to make the best use of his time. He was a tall thin man, with an adust complexion, and the vivacity of his eye indicated some irascibility of temperament. His dress was brown, not black, and over his other vestments he wore, in honour of Calvin, a Geneva cloak of blue colour, which fell backwards from his shoulders as he posted on to the pulpit. His grizzled hair was cut as short as shears could perform the feat, and covered with a black silk skull-cap, which stuck so close to his head, that the two ears expanded from under it as if they had been intended as handles by which to lift the whole person. Moreover, the worthy divine wore spectacles, and a long grizzled peaked beard, and he carried in his hand a small pocket Bible with silver clasps. Upon arriving at the pulpit, he paused a moment to take breath, then began to ascend the steps by two at a time.

WALTER SCOTT *Woodstock*

The following portrait of blue jays under highly special circumstances is inimitable. Note the proportion of composition types, as well as the delightfully "humanizing" note that permeates the whole.*

When I first begun to understand jay language correctly, there was a little incident happened here. Seven years ago, the last man in this region but me moved away. There stands his house—been empty ever since; a log house, with a plank roof—just one big room, and no more; no ceiling—nothing between the rafters and the floor. Well, one Sunday morning I was sitting out here in front of my cabin, with my cat, taking the sun, and looking at the blue hills, and listening to the leaves rustling so lonely in the trees, and thinking of the home away yonder in the states, that I hadn't heard from in thirteen years, when a blue jay

* From Mark Twain's *A Tramp Abroad.* Used by permission of Harper and Brothers.

lit on that house, with an acorn in his mouth, and says, "Hello, I reckon I've struck something." When he spoke, the acorn dropped out of his mouth and rolled down the roof, of course, but he didn't care; his mind was all on the thing he had struck. It was a knot-hole in the roof. He cocked his head to one side, shut one eye and put the other one to the hole, like a 'possum looking down a jug; then he glanced up with his bright eyes, gave a wink or two with his wings—which signifies gratification, you understand—and says, "It looks like a hole, it's located like a hole—blamed if I don't believe it *is* a hole!"

Then he cocked his head down and took another look; he glances up perfectly joyful, this time; winks his wings and his tail both, and says, "Oh, no, this ain't no fat thing, I reckon! If I ain't in luck!—why it's a perfectly elegant hole!" So he flew down and got that acorn, and fetched it up and dropped it in, and was just tilting his head back, with the heavenliest smile on his face, when all of a sudden he was paralyzed into a listening attitude and that smile faded gradually out of his countenance like breath off'n a razor, and the queerest look of surprise took its place. Then he says, "Why, I didn't hear it fall!" He cocked his eye at the hole again, and took a long look; raised up and shook his head; stepped around to the other side of the hole and took another look from that side; shook his head again. He studied awhile, then he just went into the *de*tails—walked round and round the hole and spied into it from every point of the compass. No use. Now he took a thinking attitude on the comb of the roof and scratched the back of his head with his right foot a minute, and finally says, "Well, it's too many for *me,* that's certain; must be a mighty long hole; however, I ain't got no time to fool around here; I got to 'tend to business; I reckon it's all right—chance it, anyway."

So he flew off and fetched another acorn and dropped it in, and tried to flirt his eye to the hole quick enough to see what became of it, but he was too late. He held his eye there as much as a minute; then he raised up and sighed, and says, "Confound it, I don't seem to understand this thing, no way; however, I'll tackle her again." He fetched another acorn, and done his level best to see what became of it, but he couldn't. He says, "Well, *I* never struck no such a hole as this before; I'm of the opinion it's a totally new kind of a hole." Then he begun to get mad. He held in for a spell, walking up and down the comb of the roof and shaking his head and muttering to himself; but his feelings got the upper hand of him, presently, and he broke loose and cussed himself black in the face. I never see a bird take on so about a little thing. When he got through he walks to the hole and looks in again for half a minute; then he says, "Well, you're a long hole, and a deep hole, and a mighty singular hole altogether—but I've started in to fill you, and I'll fill you, if it takes a hundred years!"

And with that, away he went. You never see a bird work so since you was born. He laid into his work and the way he hove acorns into that hole for about two hours and a half was one of the most exciting and astonishing spectacles I ever struck. He never stopped to take a look any more—he just hove 'em in and went for more. Well, at last he could hardly flop his wings, he was so tuckered out. He comes a-drooping down, once more, sweating like an ice-pitcher, drops his acorn in and says, *"Now* I guess I've got the bulge on you by this time!" So he bent down for a look. If you'll believe me, when his head come up again he was just pale with rage. He says, "I've shoveled acorns enough in there to keep the family thirty years, and if I can see a sign of one of 'em I wish I may land in a museum with a bellyful of sawdust in two minutes!"

He just had strength enough to crawl up on the comb and lean his back again the chimbly, and then he collected his impressions and begun to free his mind. I see in a second that what I had mistook for profanity in the mines was only just the rudiments, as you may say.

Another jay was going by, and heard him doing his devotions, and stops to inquire what was up. The sufferer told him the whole circumstance, and says, "Now yonder's the hole, and if you don't believe me, go and look for yourself." So this fellow went and looked, and comes back and says, "How many did you say you put in there?" "Not any less than two tons," says the sufferer. The other jay went and looked again. He couldn't seem to make it out, so he raised a yell, and three more jays come. They all examined the hole, they all made the sufferer tell it over again, then they all discussed it, and got off as many leather-headed opinions about it as an average crowd of humans could have done.

They called in more jays; then more and more, till pretty soon this whole region 'peared to have a blue flush about it. There must have been five thousand of them; and such another jawing and disputing and ripping and cussing you never heard. Every jay in the whole lot put his eye to the hole and delivered a more chuckle-headed opinion about the mystery than the jay that went there before him. They examined the house all over, too. The door was standing half open, and at last one old jay happened to go and light on it and look in. Of course, that knocked the mystery galley-west in a second. There lay the acorns, scattered all over the floor. He flopped his wings and raised a whoop.

"Come here!" he says. "Come here, everybody; hanged if this fool hasn't been trying to fill up a house with acorns!" They all came a-swooping down like a blue cloud, and as each fellow lit on the door and took a glance, the whole absurdity of the contract that that first jay had tackled hit him home and he fell over backwards suffocating with laughter, and the next jay took his place and done the same.

Well, sir, they roosted around here on the housetop and the trees for an hour, and guffawed over that thing like human beings. It ain't any use to tell me a blue jay hasn't got a sense of humor, because I know better. And memory, too. They brought jays here from all over the United States to look down that hole, every summer for three years. Other birds, too. And they could all see the point, except an owl that come from Nova Scotia to visit the Yosemite, and he took this thing in on his way back. He said he couldn't see anything funny in it. But then he was a good deal disappointed about Yosemite, too.

MARK TWAIN *Blue Jays* (from *A Tramp Abroad*)

Observe in the following portrait * not only the consistent development of the picture but the graceful shifting from one position to another, in order that the entire movement of the scene may be depicted.

It seemed to me such a piece of good fortune to have been asked down to Oxford at Commemoration by a gentleman implicated in the remarkable ceremony which goes on under that name, who kindly offered me the hospitality of his college, that I scarcely waited even to thank him, I simply took the first train. I had had a glimpse of Oxford in former years, but I had never slept in a low-browed room looking out on a grassy quadrangle, opposite a mediæval clock-tower. This satisfaction was vouchsafed me on the night of my arrival; I was inducted into the rooms of an absent undergraduate. I sat in his deep arm-chairs; I burned his candles and read his books. I hereby thank him as tenderly as possible. Before going to bed I took a turn through the streets and renewed on the silent darkness that impression of the charm imparted to them by the quiet college-fronts, which I had gathered in former years. The college-fronts were now quieter than ever, the streets were empty, and the old scholastic city was sleeping in the warm starlight. The undergraduates had retired in large numbers, encouraged in this impulse by the collegiate authorities, who deprecate their presence at

* From *Portraits of Places* by Henry James. Used by permission of Houghton Mifflin Company.

Commemoration. However many young gownsmen may be sent away, there always remain enough to make a noise. There can be no better indication of the resources of Oxford in a spectacular way than this fact that the first step toward preparing an impressive ceremony is to get rid of the undergraduates.

In the morning I breakfasted with a young American who, in common with a number of his countrymen, had come hither to seek stimulus for a finer quality of study. I know not whether he would have reckoned as such stimulus the conversation of a couple of those ingenuous youths of Britain whose society I always find charming; but it added, from my own point of view, to the local colour of the entertainment. After this was over I repaired, in company with a crowd of ladies and elderly people, interspersed with gownsmen, to the hoary rotunda of the Sheldonian theatre, which every visitor to Oxford will remember, with its curious cincture of clumsily carven heads of warriors and sages perched upon stone posts. The interior of this edifice is the scene of the classic hooting, stamping, and cat-calling by which the undergraduates confer the last consecration upon the distinguished gentlemen who come up for the honorary degree of D.C.L. It is with the design of attenuating as much as possible this incongruous chorus, that the heads of colleges, on the close of the term, a few days before Commemoration, speed their too demonstrative disciples upon the homeward way. As I have already hinted, however, the contingent of irreverent lads was on this occasion quite large enough to produce a very handsome specimen of the traditional rumpus. This made the scene a very singular one. An American of course, with his fondness for antiquity, his relish for picturesqueness, his "emotional" attitude at historic shrines, takes Oxford much more seriously than its customary denizens can be expected to do. These people are not always upon the high horse; they are not always in an acutely sentient condition. Nevertheless, there is a certain maximum of disaccord with their beautiful circumstances which the ecstatic Occidental vaguely expects them not to transcend. No effort of the intellect beforehand would enable him to imagine one of those silver-gray temples of learning converted into a semblance of the Bowery Theatre when the Bowery Theatre is being trifled with.

The Sheldonian edifice, like everything at Oxford, is more or less monumental. There is a double tier of galleries, with sculptured pulpits protruding from them; there are full-length portraits of kings and worthies; there is a general air of antiquity and dignity, which, on the occasion of which I speak, was enhanced by the presence of certain ancient scholars, seated in crimson robes in high-backed chairs. Formerly, I believe, the undergraduates were placed apart—packed together in a corner of one of the galleries. But now they are scattered among the general spectators, a large number of whom are ladies. They muster in especial force, however, on the floor of the theatre, which has been cleared of its benches. Here the dense mass is at last severed in twain by the entrance of the prospective D.C.L.'s walking in single file, clad in crimson gowns, preceded by mace-bearers and accompanied by the Regius professor of Civil Law, who presents them individually to the Vice-Chancellor of the university, in a Latin speech which is of course a glowing eulogy. The five gentlemen to whom this distinction had been offered in 1877 were not among those whom fame has trumpeted most loudly, but there was something very pretty in their standing in their honourable robes, with heads modestly bent, while the orator, equally brilliant in aspect, recited their titles sonorously to the venerable dignitary in the high-backed chair. Each of them, when the little speech is ended, ascends the steps leading to the chair; the Vice-Chancellor bends forward and shakes his hand, and the new D.C.L. goes and sits in the blushing row of his fellow-doctors. The impressiveness of all this is much diminished by the boisterous conduct of the collegians, who superabound in extravagant applause, in impertinent interrogation, and in lively disparagement of the orator's Latinity. Of the scene that precedes the episode I have just described I have given no account; vivid portrayal of it is not easy. Like the return from the Derby, it is a carnival of "chaff"; and it is a singular fact that the scholastic festival should have forcibly reminded me of the great popular "lark." In each case it is the same race enjoying a certain definitely chartered license; in the young votaries of a liberal education and the London rabble on the Epsom road it is the same perfect good humour, the same muscular jocosity.

After the presentation of the doctors came a series of those collegiate exercises which have a generic resemblance all the world over: a reading of Latin verses and English essays, a spouting of prize poems and Greek paraphrases. The prize poem alone was somewhat attentively listened to; the other things were received with an infinite variety of critical ejaculation. But after all, I reflected, as the ceremony drew to a close, this discordant racket is more characteristic than it seems; it is at bottom only another expression of the venerable and historic side of Oxford. It is tolerated because it is traditional; it is possible because it is classical. Looking at it in this light, one might manage at last to find it impressive and romantic.

I was not obliged to find ingenious pretexts for thinking well of another ceremony of which I was witness after we adjourned from the Sheldonian theatre. This was a lunch-party at the particular college in which I should find it the highest privilege to reside. I may not further specify it. Perhaps, indeed, I may go so far as to say that the reason for my dreaming of this privilege is that it is deemed by persons of a reforming turn the best-appointed abuse in a nest of abuses. A commission for the expurgation of the universities has lately been appointed by Parliament to look into it—a commission armed with a gigantic broom, which is to sweep away all the fine old ivied and cobwebbed improprieties. Pending these righteous changes, one would like while one is about it—about, that is, this business of admiring Oxford—to attach one's self to the abuse, to bury one's nostrils in the rose before it is plucked. At the college in question there are no undergraduates. I found it agreeable to reflect that those gray-green cloisters had sent no delegates to the slangy congregation I had just quitted. This delightful spot exists for the satisfaction of a small society of Fellows who, having no dreary instruction to administer, no noisy hobbledehoys to govern, no obligations but toward their own culture, no care for learning as learning and truth as truth, are presumably the happiest and most charming people in the world. The party invited to lunch assembled first in the library of the college, a cool, gray hall, of very great length and height, with vast wall-spaces of rich-looking book-titles and statues of noble scholars set in the midst. Had the charming Fellows ever anything more disagreeable to do than to finger these precious volumes and then to stroll about together in the grassy courts, in learned comradeship, discussing their precious contents? Nothing, apparently, unless it were to give a lunch at Commemoration in the dining-hall of the college. When lunch was ready there was a very pretty procession to go to it. Learned gentlemen in crimson gowns, ladies in brilliant toilets, paired slowly off and marched in a stately diagonal across the fine, smooth lawn of the quadrangle, in a corner of which they passed through a hospitable door. But here we cross the threshold of privacy; I remained on the farther side of it during the rest of the day. But I brought back with me certain memories of which, if I were not at the end of my space, I should attempt a discreet adumbration: memories of a fête champêtre in the beautiful gardens of one of the other colleges —charming lawns and spreading trees, music of Grenadier Guards, ices in striped marquees, mild flirtation of youthful gownsmen and bemus-lined maidens; memories, too, of quiet dinner in common-room, a decorous, excellent repast; old portraits on the walls and great windows open upon the ancient court, where the afternoon light was fading in the stillness; superior talk upon current topics, and over all the peculiar air of Oxford—the air of liberty to care for intellectual things, assured and secured by machinery which is in itself a satisfaction to sense.

HENRY JAMES *Portraits of Places* (*Oxford at Commemoration*)

The following vignettes * illustrate a special type of portraiture, atmospheric and more or less elusive in method and effect.

On a corner of my desk there stands a china shell; its flat and oval basin is about as broad as the palm of my hand; it is a spotted brownish-yellow on the outside, and a purply-pinkish white on the inside; and on the crinkled edge of one end there sits a green frog with his china mouth wide open, thus revealing the ruddy hollow of his interior. At the opposite end of the shell there is a page of china music, purporting to be the first four bars of a song by Schubert. Time was when the frog held in his long greenish-yellow arms a still longer trombone made of bright brass wire, bent into shape, and tipped with a flaring disk of gilded porcelain. In the days when the china frog was young he pretended to be playing on the brass trombone. Despite its musical assertiveness the function of the frog that played the trombone was humble enough; the shell was designed to serve as a receiver for the ashes of cigars and cigarettes. But it is a score of years at least since the china frog has held the brass trombone to its open lips. Only a few months after he gave his first mute concert on the corner of my table the carelessness of a chance visitor toppled him over on the floor, and broke off both his arms and so bent the trombone that even the barren pretense of his solo became an impossibility. A week or two later the battered musical instrument disappeared; and ever since then the gaping mouth of the frog has seemed to suggest that he was trying to sing Schubert's song. His open countenance, I am sorry to say, has often tempted my friends to make sport of him. They have filled the red emptiness of his body with the gray ashes of their cigars; they have even gone so far as to put the stump of a half-smoked cigarette between his lips, as though he were solacing himself thus for the loss of his voice.

BRANDER MATTHEWS *Vistas of New York*

They had been standing where they had met, at the corner of the Bowery and Rivington Street. Now, under John Suydam's guidance they walked a little way up the Bowery, beneath the single track of the

* Used by permission of Charles Scribner's Sons.

elevated railroad. Then they turned into a side street, and pushed their way westward.

Whenever they came to a crossing DeRuyter remarked that three of the corners always, and four of them sometimes, were saloons. The broad gilt signs over the open doors of these barrooms bore names either German or Irish, until they came to a corner where one of the saloons called itself the Café Cristoforo Colombo. A wooden stand, down the side street, and taking up a third of the width of the walk, had a sign announcing ice-cold soda water at two cents a glass with fruit syrups; with chocolate and cream, the price was three cents. Right on the corner of the curb stood a large washtub half filled with water, in which soaked doubtful young cabbages and sprouts; its guardian was a thin slip of a girl with a red handkerchief knotted over her head.

At this corner Suydam turned out of the side street, and went down a street no wider perhaps, but extending north and south in a devious and hesitating way not common in the streets of New York. The sidewalks of this sinuous street were inconveniently narrow for its crowded population, and they were made still narrower by tolerated encroachments of one kind or another. Here, for instance, from the side of a small shop projected a stand on which unshelled peas wilted under the strong rays of the young June sun. There, for example, were steps down to the low basement, and in a corner of the hollow at the foot of the stairs there might be a pail with dingy ice packed about a can of alleged ice cream, or else a board bore a half-dozen tough brown loaves, also proffered for sale to the chance customer. Here and there, again, the dwellers in the tall tenements had brought chairs to the common door, and were seated comfortably conversing with their neighbors, regardless of the fact that they thus blocked the sidewalk, and compelled the passer-by to go out into the street itself.

BRANDER MATTHEWS Vignettes of Manhattan

WORK

Write pen portraits or pictures of some of the following. These are suggestions merely. Select others from your everyday rounds.

The old barn
The haunted house
The storm-ridden tree
The car that looks like its owner
The street on a rainy morning

The street on a clear sunny morning
The school building covered with snow
The school auditorium decorated for commencement
The dog that has come out of a fight badly
The cat that has been out all night in the rain
The police horse standing proudly with his two forefeet on the pavement
The tramp whose coat is fastened together with clothes pegs for buttons
The scarecrow in the cherry tree
The traffic officer at the busy cross section
The airplane buzzing above you
The airplane just about to land
The clothesrack with ironed articles on it
The old well with the ivy-covered pump
The frozen waterfall
The football captain after a defeat
The "unwrappings" of a parcel as Mary left them
The baseball diamond after a storm
The auctioneer just about to say, "Three times and done"
Your teacher after you have made a good recitation
Your teacher after you have made a bad recitation
Your friend just as he was caught copying from your paper
Your toe after you stubbed it on the stone pavement
The ice-cream soda just ready for you to drink
Your brother Bill just as the alarm clock wakens him
Your favorite pitcher just as he throws the ball
Your "girl friend" as she looked at the party
The old oaken bucket
A blushing bride
Your commencement bouquet
The living room after your birthday party
The house in which beauty would be born
The hovel in which crime would be planned
The night on which romance is abroad
The night on which murder is in the air
How you looked in the concave mirror
Your idea of a certain character in a drama (do not consult a drawing or a photograph)—Shylock, Caesar, Henry Fifth, Mrs. Malaprop, Sir Anthony Absolute, Lady Teazle, and so forth.

Your idea of a typical (a composite picture) statesman, teacher, pupil, truant, "grind," kidnaper, cheater, old maid, hard drinker, "grouch," artist, movie actress, preacher, chauffeur, prize fighter, hypochondriac, prima donna, saleswoman, and so forth.

Your idea of what each of the following looked like: the guest (story on page 20), the tomboy (story on page 50), Banbury (essay on page 100), Judge Henry (story on page 137), Russ Braley (story on page 140), Mrs. Rasselyer (story on page 152), Rose (story on page 158), Maisie (play on page 174), Llewelyn (poem on page 308), Lord Ronald (poem on page 314), the mountain woman (poem on page 331).

Your idea of what each of the following places looked like: the café (story on page 133), the gas station (story on page 151), the bookshop (story on page 152), the kitchen (play on page 174), the chapel (portrait on page 220), "The Loch Achray" (poem on page 312).

ORATION

ORATION

ORATORY, like argument, is a composite form. It uses all types of composition and draws upon all kinds of literature to achieve its effects. The speeches in a formal debate constitute oratory. The sermonizing from Sunday pulpits constitutes oratory. The appeals of lawyers before judge and jury constitute oratory. And all of these, as well as the numerous other forms of oratory, may run the gamut of variety, from cold factual reason-why to irresistible human-interest. An old lady of prominence was run down and killed by a speeding automobile. The story of the tragedy was emotionally told in her behalf to the jury; the picture of the scene, including the limp and pitiable form of the victim, immediately after the accident, was vividly painted; the explanation as to how a careless driver had wronged the community was irrefutably mapped and pointed as in a classroom; and all of these were welded into argumentative oratory of such force and feeling and persuasion that the driver was jailed and the old lady's family was accorded heavy damages even though she was jay-walking and had been a defiant jay-walker in the community for years.

The oration is an *occasional* form of literature, that is, it is as a rule prepared for or in connection with some occasion. Short-stories and essays and poems are likewise sometimes written for occasions, but not as a rule. Orations or speeches practically always are. There have been people who have prepared standardized speeches to have "on tap" for regular occasions, and you will find books containing speeches as well as other types of literature devised to meet occasions. But it almost invariably happens that certain changes have to be made in these in order to make them entirely appropriate for any certain occasion. The speech for a Lincoln's birthday celebration of one year may not be at all suitable for the celebration of the same date for another year.

It follows, therefore, that while the occasion may have much to do with making the speech—may place an obligation upon the orator

233

by way of adapting what he has to say to the occasion—the direct opposite may also be the case. The subject of the speech may, in other words, make the occasion. A community may, for instance, wish to hear Mr. So-and-so speak on a certain subject. It invites him to speak on this subject at the annual Lincoln's birthday celebration. His speech is not therefore about Abraham Lincoln (except in so far as the speaker may be able coherently to draw Lincoln and his policies into the subject) but primarily about the subject assigned. Only rarely and at great risk may a speaker thwart both the occasion and the subject and "go on his own" in sheer defiance of them. An orator who is invited to speak on a certain occasion and who uses the assignment for personal exploitation for office or for some other remote purpose, violates the tenets of oratory as well as those of good taste. It so happened that Marc Antony, for dramatic purposes, violated this principle in his famous oration over the body of Caesar. He was warned and rewarned to confine himself to his subject and to the occasion. But by the adroit handling of his audience and by the staging of certain effects, he was able to defy both and to turn the event to his own purposes. Admirably as he did this, the method is nevertheless not to be recommended for general use.

The oration should be drawn, then, so that it will be appropriate for the occasion or for the assignment, or for both. It must be so drawn that it will be, in the second place, suitable for the audience. If it complies with the first it will automatically comply with the second. The occasion as a rule presupposes the character of the audience. An assigned oration certainly presupposes the character of an audience. If you will study the great orations in the history of the world—those moving word-of-mouth deliveries that have actually changed history and have thus really made it—you will find that it was this very adaptation of them to the occasion and to the audience that made them influential and significant.

Speaking on the same subject before two entirely different audiences, on two entirely different occasions, an orator should not—can not—use the same speech. Speaking on the same subject to two audiences of the same character in two different places he will as a rule find it unsatisfactory to use exactly the same oration. A speech subject needs to be freshly handled every time the speaker is called upon to discuss it, no matter how similar the speaking occasions may seem to be. Joseph Jefferson, the American actor who had played the part of Rip Van Winkle hundreds of times in all parts of the country, was once asked sympathetically whether it did not pall to play the same part so often. He resented the sympathy, and said in reply that while he did have much the same kind of audience night after night, at place after place, it was nevertheless not quite the same, and the reactions of audiences as a whole and of individuals in them were always varied and thus challenging and stimulating. The orator's situation is similar. Ask any speechmaker who has made a vigorous campaign, and he will tell you interesting stories of the audience surprises that are invariably in store.

The orator must therefore take the measure of his audience. He must take the measure of the occasion of his speech. And then he must adapt his materials accordingly. He must have a definite aim within the limits of these two considerations. He must have a definite plan of attack within the limits of these two considerations, and a plan that is easily apparent and easily followed by his audience. No mere rambling meandering jottings for the speech plan will ever do. It must have formally divided parts, and the divisions and subdivisions must be followed so that the audience will have no difficulty in keeping in step with the speaker. Organization of material in a way that enables the audience to hold the parts of a speech distinctly in mind during its progress is one of the safest courses for a speaker to take in order to ingratiate himself and his theme with his audience.

The introduction of a speech is sometimes called the *exordium*. It is proper at this place to refer briefly to the occasion itself, and to indicate what phases of a given subject a speaker intends to follow. The discussion or body of a speech should be clearly marked into divisions logically related and climactically arranged. An oration needs to be cumulative; it needs to build impression at the end but also to build it all along the way. The first point under the main body of the oration may well be one of arresting emphasis—some startling fact, some emotional appeal—that will catch attention unanimously and intensively. After this comes the danger point—the let-down point. If after arresting attention, an orator fails to hold it, he may well be apprehensive about the outcome. If there is some uneasiness on the part of the audience, some coughing, some shuffling of feet, he will do well to gather unto his address another emphatic point or two, in order to bring his hearers back to him. The last point in the body should be climactic, that is, it should be the most important and striking and far-reaching fact or argument or example or authoritative evidence that the speaker has to offer. Thereafter, he should summarize point by point in unforgettable and impressive form the claims or arguments or principles he has enunciated. This summary or "running through" is called the *peroration* of his address. It isolates for final impression those parts that he considers salients and that he wants to leave with his audience to ponder or to act upon. There can be no better method of doing this than by making short-cut staccato statements that say much in little, each one periodic in form, each one dominated by a noun or a verb kept in mind by the audience. If these can be made seriatim, without too mechanical an effect—without such notation as first, second, third, or *a, b, c*—and can be made clear and definite without any labels, so much the more impressive will they probably be. All such planning of speeches and arguments is called *briefing*.

In the old days of spread-eagle oratory it was customary to use high-sounding words and phraseology that would by their very nature create a certain reverence and dignity, no matter how empty their meaning might be. Today it is far better judgment to use the simplest language possible in a speech, to inject into it certain humorous, and if need be even human-interest elements, to keep it dignified and serious without attempting to make it forbidding and awe-inspiring. Enthusiasm without prejudice, loyalty to subject without bias, pride in the oratorical occasion without posing of any kind, simplicity and directness without talking down, courage and daring without threat or intimidation—these are the general qualities of style that should dominate the sincerely written and delivered oration. Any sort of pretentiousness or bravado will very soon reveal itself in a speech, and to the undoing of the speaker. In no other form of writing and speaking will insincerity and unreality be so quickly discerned. The greatest speeches are those that have been written and delivered with conviction and deep-seated emotional and intellectual purpose. Unless you can feel strongly about the subject you discuss in your address, do not presume to ask others to listen to you.

Young people sometimes make the mistake of regarding the speech as just another form of essay. But there is only one type of essay—the polemic or controversial—that has the quality of the speech. All other kinds are separate and apart from the oration proper. The essay does not follow the rigid construction of the speech; it does not have to achieve as the speech does; it is under no obligation to touch aggressively the mind and the heart with intention to convince or persuade. There are also technical differences between the two. The increased momentum of presentation of opinion and argument in the speech is not necessarily characteristic of the essay. Such figures of speech as *alliteration, allusion, antithesis, balance, climax, epigram, epithet, exclamation, hendiadys, interrogation, inversion, irony, litotes, paradox, repetition* belong par excellence to oratory. They are peculiarly the oral figures, devised for the ear more particularly than for the eye. All figures of speech are, of course, usable in both the essay and the oration, and all may be desirable and necessary for the sake of point and variety. But those listed just above are especially important for oratorical effects. In general, the oration is an oral type; the essay a written type. And this difference carries with it implications that will become more and more clear to you as you talk to audiences and learn to adapt what you have to say to their spur-of-the-moment reactions. These reactions are quite as often evoked by a speaker's manner and voice and diction and oral style, as by the content of his speech. An ingratiating tone and a congenial attitude on the part of a speaker, seasoned with aptness of figure and precision of diction, have been known to persuade when sheer "mental maneuvers" were quite futile.

The polemic essay should be so written as to be capable of oral delivery. It then becomes a speech, and as such must follow more or less closely the rules laid down for briefing on the preceding page. After a short introduction pertaining perhaps to the occasion, there is a case to be stated, to be followed by pro and con points and by refutation of anticipated opposition. Such polemic may cover one side only—affirmative or negative—of a debate, or it may take unto itself the task of arguing both sides and thus meeting and refuting counter arguments on both sides. The result is a complete or two-sided presentation of some controversial subject, a task that is difficult to carry through fairly to the subject inasmuch as few speakers are to be found who do not feel more strongly on one side of a question than on another. The aim of such polemic usually is—or should be—a clear exposition of all that may be said on both or all sides, without prejudice on the part of the speaker. The chairman of a general-discussion meeting frequently has the difficult job of presenting the question of the meeting from both angles of consideration in order to turn it loose fairly to the "pros" and "cons" in the house.

There are almost as many different kinds of oration as there are occasions upon which to make them and audiences to deliver them to. The names in the following list both classify and define—*anniversary* or *commemorative, dedicatory, eulogistic, exhortative, forensic, funeral, impassioned, inflammatory, patriotic, polemic* or *argumentative, political, special occasion*. The classification means little or nothing as far as method of speech preparation is concerned. But as an indication of oratorical types and occasions it may be useful.

The term *forensic* was originally—and still is—applied to oratory of a disputatious character. It has been humorously called *forumtory*, inasmuch as the root of the word refers to the forum where public debate in the oratorical manner was once much more popular than it is today. Any speech that provokes discussion and disagreement and, thus, argument, is properly called forensic. A forensic thesis is still required by some colleges as a graduation qualification. As the names indicate, the impassioned and the inflammatory orations appeal more deliberately to the emotions than do the political and the dedicatory. There are speeches that aim at securing immediate action; speeches that are calculated to send people home to think; speeches that are bent upon changing people's habits; speeches that are intended to inspire to better and more conscientious conduct. The aim of the speaker, and his method and manner of enforcing it, are the elements that decide exactly what kind of oration he shall make. By the fruits of his effort shall his oration be known.

The public speech provides contact directly with people. It takes their pulse without any intervening agencies. It is therefore destined to live as a type of literature and as a means of securing persuasion and action *en masse*. To say that the radio is making oratory an archaic function—or has done so—is to pass judgment prematurely and probably falsely. When the printing-press promised to become the power that it now is, there were prophecies everywhere to the effect that the spoken word was done for. When the moving-picture became the vogue that it now continues to be, prophecy was again busy with the report that spoken drama would soon be a thing of the past, that it had been fatally supplanted. The intimacy of oratorical occasion together with its efficacy still remains in spite of modern inventions pertaining to the human voice.

Radio is, indeed, a facile new medium for oratorical expression, extending the realm of pulpit and forum and soapbox far beyond their original limits. And it has had its good effects upon forensic composition and delivery, not by way of changing the form itself but by way, rather, of broadening treatment of subject matter and awakening a keener consciousness of the importance of the spoken word itself. "Sawing the air with the hand" counts for nothing, of course, before the "mike." The platform orator depended in no small measure upon the effectiveness of gesture; he could very often make it say more than words. This, concededly, is lost to radio delivery. (Television may soon restore it.) But in its stead have certainly come a more particular diction, a greater respect for the use and the effect of voice, a more authentic attention to emphasis and climax, a more economical and coherent organization of material (money cost alone enforces this), and a stricter regard to caution and restraint in holding to the letter of the speech. The offhand, catch-as-catch-can extempore is, for the most part, ruled out by the radio. The radio speaker *ad libs* only at great risk; he "asides" and acknowledges applause in the studio perhaps, but always with some degree of unfairness to his bigger audience. If in these few ways alone radio has made for a tauter oratorical form and for a more strictly-business delivery, it has made a distinct contribution to the cause of the Mother Tongue. It will never entirely destroy the living, breathing audience assembled in a single place on a single occasion for the purpose of listening to men and women speak. For thus exercised the listening function in the human being is quite as deep-seated and permanent and insatiable as are the other sense functions.

The present generation has had outstanding proof of all this in at least one signal historical event, namely, the radio abdication speech of Edward VIII. It was a masterpiece in form and content, and it was delivered in a masterly way. The millions who listened in to it in all parts of the world were by no means of one mind as to the circumstance that evoked it, but they were unanimous in thinking it an epochal human document and in feeling it to be the most sincerely and tenderly spoken message they had ever heard. Authorities in both statesmanship and literature are agreed that it will stand through the ages alongside the sheer half-dozen greatest utterances of man. It is here reproduced because of its historical significance and its literary quality.*

At long last I am able to say a few words of my own.

I have never wanted to withhold anything, but until now it has not been constitutionally possible for me to speak.

A few hours ago I discharged my last duty as King and Emperor, and now that I have been succeeded by my brother, the Duke of York, my first words must be to declare my allegiance to him. This I do with all my heart.

You all know the reasons which have impelled me to renounce the Throne, but I want you to understand that in making up my mind I did not forget the country or the Empire, which as Prince of Wales, and lately as King, I have for twenty-five years tried to serve.

But you must believe me when I tell you that I have found it impossible to carry the heavy burden of responsibility, and to discharge my duties as King as I would wish to do, without the help and support of the woman I love.

And I want you to know that the decision I have made has been mine, and mine alone. This was a thing I had to judge entirely for myself. The other person most nearly concerned has tried up to the last to persuade me to take a different course.

I have made this, the most serious decision of my life, only upon the single thought of what would in the end be best for all.

This decision has been made less difficult to me by the sure knowledge that my brother with his long training in the public affairs of this country and with his fine qualities, will be able to take my place forthwith, without interruption or injury to the life and progress of the Empire.

And he has one matchless blessing, enjoyed by so many of you, and not bestowed on me, a happy home with his wife and children.

During these hard days I have been comforted by Her Majesty, my mother, and my family. The Ministers of the Crown, and in particular

* Used by permission of the Duke of Windsor, formerly His Majesty Edward VIII of England.

Mr. Baldwin, the Prime Minister, have always treated me with full consideration.

There have never been any constitutional differences between me and them, and between me and Parliament. Bred in the constitutional traditions of my father, I should never have allowed any such issue to arise.

Ever since I was Prince of Wales, and later on when I occupied the Throne, I have been treated with the greatest kindness by all classes of people wherever I have lived or journeyed throughout the Empire. For that I am very grateful.

I now quit altogether public affairs, and I lay down my burden. It may be some time before I return to my native land; but I shall always follow the fortunes of the British race and Empire with profound interest, and if at any time in the future I can be found of service to His Majesty in a private station, I shall not fail.

And now we all have a new King. I wish him and you, his people, happiness and prosperity with all my heart. God bless you all. God save the King!

When in August, 1938, international affairs had, to say the least, become extremely nervous, it was thought that a clarifying statement should come from the United States regarding its position. The Secretary of State—the Honorable Cordell Hull—met the occasion with one of the most lucid, most forceful, most stabilizing public addresses that have ever been made by an American statesman. It was prepared directly for radio delivery, and was listened to eagerly in all parts of the civilized world over the network of the National Broadcasting Company. Editorial opinion everywhere agreed that it was a masterpiece of irrefutable argument in the cause of peace and amity among nations. Study it particularly for its clear-cut driving power, its cumulative construction, and its rationalized persuasiveness.*

All nations have a primary interest in peace with justice, in economic well-being with stability, and in conditions of order under law. These are constant objectives of this country. Each of these objectives is today seriously jeopardized in many parts of the world. All governments and all peoples should therefore be on guard against certain dangerous developments which imperil them, and be alive to the issues involved.

Out of these menacing developments there has arisen and there confronts the nations today a clear-cut issue: Is the future of the world to

* Used by permission of the Honorable Cordell Hull.

be determined by universal reliance upon armed force and frequent resort to aggression, with resultant autarchy, impoverishment, loss of individual independence, and international anarchy? Or will practices of peace, morality, justice, and order under law, resting upon sound foundations of economic well-being, security, and progress, guide and govern in international relations?

As modern science and invention bring nations ever closer together, the time approaches when, in the very nature of things, one or the other of these alternatives must prevail. In a smaller and smaller world it will soon no longer be possible for some nations to choose and follow the way of force and for other nations at the same time to choose and follow the way of reason. All will have to go in one direction and by one way. The first of the alternative ways leads through military adventuring to international lawlessness, the result of which is chaos and loss of the precious values which, through centuries of struggle, toil, and sacrifice, civilized nations have slowly achieved. The other way leads, through exercise of moral restraint and observance of international obligations and treaties, to conditions of order based upon law, giving security and facilitating progress.

In the circumstances which prevail in the world today, no nation and no government can avoid participation in determining which course will be taken. The issue is fundamental. Consciously or unconsciously, every country is throwing the weight of its attitude and action, positive or negative, toward one course or the other. The degree to which each nation will influence the ultimate decision will depend on the earnestness with which it espouses and supports the principles on the side of which it chooses to range itself.

The World War left a legacy of deep-seated maladjustments within and among nations. But out of it also emerged a passionate desire among peoples everywhere for enduring peace, order, and progress.

For a decade following the Peace of Versailles, the peoples of the world worked earnestly toward those ends, and considerable progress was made. But unhappily the rapid growth of economic nationalism following as an aftermath of the war culminated in 1929 in world-wide economic catastrophe. Political controversies and conflict, aggravated and intensified by world-wide depression, undermined the whole structure of world economy and of law and order among the nations.

Economic stability, financial stability, social stability, and in the last analysis political stability, are all parts of an arch resting upon the foundation of trade. No modern industrial nation can maintain proper existing standards of living without international trade. Raw materials and other commodities are indispensable for the maintenance of industrial processes; and foreign markets for the sale of a nation's products are likewise indispensable for its economic life. Shut off from international trade, nations face deterioration and decline.

As trade barriers mounted on every side, as the movement toward economic nationalism gathered momentum, it became only too clear that either the excessive trade barriers between nations must be reduced or the pressures of nations to gain access to needed raw materials and to equally necessary foreign markets by conquest of additional territory and tactics of the mailed fist would become intensified.

Against this world background this country embarked upon a program for the reduction or elimination of excessive trade barriers and for the elimination of uneconomic trade discriminations and other unfair trade methods. In 1934 the Congress passed the Trade Agreements Act for the achievement of these purposes. Since then our country has vigorously engaged in trade-agreement negotiations with an increasing number of countries, and it has tirelessly urged upon other nations the imperative need of pursuing a similar course.

Concurrently with efforts to restore international commerce upon this constructive basis, we have also pursued—and have urged upon other nations—parallel and complementary policies in the field of finance, restoration of stability of foreign exchanges and of monetary conditions, and the inviolability of financial obligations and undertakings.

Unfortunately, as time has gone on, the disintegration of the structure of world order under law and the abandonment or repudiation of the principles underlying it, have proceeded with staggering rapidity. Orderly and peaceful processes and methods of international cooperation have in many regions given way to military aggression and armed force. Today, invasion of territory of sovereign states, destruction of lawfully constituted governments and forcible seizure of hitherto independent political entities, interference in the internal affairs of other nations, wholesale violation of established treaty obligations, growing disregard of universally accepted principles of international law, attempts to adjust international differences by armed force rather than by methods of pacific settlement, contemptuous brushing aside of rules of morality— all these appalling manifestations of disintegration seriously threaten the very foundations of our civilization.

Inasmuch as the processes of disintegration and deterioration in international relations are plainly spreading in many directions, the curative processes must be no less broad in scope and more effective in character. Not only has the rebuilding of a sound economic structure become absolutely essential, but the reestablishing of order under law in relations among nations has become imperatively necessary. Hence, while continuing and intensifying our effort to promote economic reconstruction, the Government of the United States has enlarged the scope of its effort and is urging upon all nations adoption of a comprehensive program embracing both economic reconstruction and revitalizing of principles which are indispensable for restoration of order under law.

There is and there can be no doubt as to the preference and desire of the people of this country. We want peace; we want security; we want progress and prosperity—for ourselves and for all nations. Our practical problem is that of finding and employing the best methods, of keeping our eyes and our feet upon the better way, of cooperating with other nations that are seeking as are we to proceed along that way. On this problem the Government of the United States has been and is constantly at work. Toward its solution, we sought at the conference at Buenos Aires in December, 1936, to broaden our combined economic and peace program by proposing and urging upon peaceful nations everywhere adoption of a program based on principles of world law and international order. This program calls for constant reaffirmation, revitalization, and stressing of fundamental principles. Its essential points cannot be too often stated.

We believe in, we support, and we recommend to all nations economic reconstruction as the foundation of national and international well-being and stability.

We believe in, we support, and we recommend adherence to the basic principles of international law as the guiding and governing rules of conduct among nations.

We believe in, we support, and we recommend respect for and observance of treaties, including, in connection therewith, modification of provisions of treaties, when and as need therefor arises, by orderly processes carried out in a spirit of mutual helpfulness and accommodation.

We believe in, we support, and we recommend voluntary self-restraint, abstention from use of force in pursuit of policy and from interference in the internal affairs of other nations, and the settlement of differences by processes of peaceful negotiation and agreement.

We believe in, we support, and we recommend to all nations that they be prepared to limit and progressively reduce their armaments.

We believe in, we support, and we recommend collaboration between and among representatives of the nations, and in the freest possible intellectual interchange between and among their peoples—to the end that thereby understanding by each country of the problems of others and of problems that are common to all may be promoted and peaceful adjustment of controversies be made more readily possible.

We believe in, we support, and we recommend international cooperation in such ways and by such methods as may be practicable for the advancement of this program.

Taken as a whole, this program envisages continuous progress over a high and open road toward long-view objectives. We are convinced that this program offers to all nations the maximum of possible advantage and the fullest possible opportunity to safeguard and promote their own welfare and with it that of the world community of which they are members. We are also convinced that no other program can in the long run check and reverse the present ominous drift toward international anarchy and armed conflict on a gigantic scale which, if it comes, will destroy not only the material achievements of past centuries but the precious cultural and spiritual attainments of our modern civilization.

The Government of the United States, with the support of an alert public opinion in this country, has earnestly sought and is seeking to make appropriate contribution to the carrying out of this program.

The people of this country are each day more accurately visualizing the conditions which prevail and more fully understanding the problems that are involved in international relations. They are becoming increasingly concerned over the spread of international lawlessness and its adverse effect upon the present and future welfare of our own country.

Each day's developments make more and more clear the fact that our own situation is profoundly affected by what happens elsewhere in the world.

Whatever may be our own wishes and hopes, we cannot when there is trouble elsewhere expect to remain unaffected. When destruction, impoverishment, and starvation afflict other areas, we cannot, no matter how hard we may try, escape impairment of our own economic well-being. When freedom is destroyed over increasing areas elsewhere, our ideals of individual liberty, our most cherished political and social institutions are jeopardized.

When the dignity of the human soul is denied in great parts of the world, and when that denial is made a slogan under which propaganda is set in motion and armies take the field, no one of us can be sure that his country or even his home is safe. We well know, of course, that a condition of wholesale chaos will not develop overnight; but it is clear that the present trend is in that direction, and the longer this drift continues the greater becomes the danger that the whole world may be sucked into a maelstrom of unregulated and savage economic, political, and military competition and conflict.

Hence it is necessary that as a nation we become increasingly resolute in our desire and increasingly effective in our efforts to contribute along with other peoples—always within the range of our traditional policies of nonentanglement—to the support of the only program which can turn the tide of lawlessness and place the world firmly upon the one and only roadway that can lead to enduring peace and security.

So far as this country is concerned, we shall continue to do everything in our power toward keeping alive and fostering and cultivating the various features of this broad and comprehensive program, a program in which we most sincerely believe, to which we give our constant support, and which we earnestly recommend to all other governments and peoples for general adoption.

As more and more nations accept this program and demonstrate their will to work together for the restoration of sound economic relations, of international morality, and of the principles of international law and justice, it will become more clear—even to the nations which now profess to place their reliance solely on a policy of armed force—that the overwhelming majority of mankind is determined to live in a world in which lawlessness will not be tolerated, in which order under law will prevail, and in which peaceful economic and cultural relationships will be inviolate.

THE HONORABLE CORDELL HULL *International Relations and the Foreign Policy of the United States*

The three orations that follow still stand as great documentary and oratorical landmarks in the history of the United States. They could not possibly have had more far-reaching influence had they been delivered by radio, had records been made of them, had the "talkies" reproduced them. They have lived through print, it is true, but they lived first as stirring, pulsating, man-to-man appeals. How vital they still are is proved by the fact that they are almost invariably quoted by orators who are called upon to speak or write on present issues of great national importance. As a matter of fact, these great pieces of forensic literature might have lost much had they been "canned" in the first place, and now and again "turned on" for audiences to listen to—or not, as their whims decide. It has well been said that every American should read these three speeches at least once every year. The first, George Washington's *Farewell Address,* is unique in that, being an epochal oration, it was really never delivered. It was published, rather, in a Philadelphia newspaper—*The Daily Adver-tiser*—on September 19, 1796—for the reason that, while the message itself was felt by Washington and his advisers to be imperative, there was nevertheless no occasion at which it could be appropriately delivered and no desire on the part of the President and his intimate circle to make an occasion. But he had written a speech, as is evident in its construction, in its dictional and sentence quality, and in its cumulative impression. Those whose advice he took in framing the great paper were Alexander Hamilton, James Madison, and John Jay, but the document is Washington's own; it grew out of his determination not to be president a third term; it successfully and gracefully disarmed the strong inclinations of the public again to make him their president at the conclusion of his second term, and this established the precedent that has happily been observed ever since.

Friends and Fellow-Citizens: The period for a new election of a citizen, to administer the executive government of the United States, being not far distant, and the time actually arrived, when your thoughts must be employed in designating the person who is to be clothed with that important trust, it appears to me proper, especially as it may conduce to a more distinct expression of the public voice, that I should now apprise you of the resolution I have formed, to decline being considered among the number of those out of whom the choice is to be made.

I beg you, at the same time, to do me the justice to be assured that this resolution has not been taken without a strict regard to all the considerations appertaining to the relation which binds a dutiful citizen to his country; and that, in withdrawing the tender of service, which silence in my situation might imply, I am influenced by no diminution of zeal for your future interest; no deficiency of grateful respect for your past kindness; but am supported by a full conviction that the step is compatible with both.

The acceptance of, and continuance hitherto in, the office to which your suffrages have twice called me, have been a uniform sacrifice of inclination to the opinion of duty and to a deference for what appeared to be your desire. I constantly hoped that it would have been much earlier in my power, consistently with motives which I was not at liberty to disregard, to return to that retirement from which I had been reluctantly drawn. The strength of my inclination to do this, previous to the last election, had even led to the preparation of an address to declare it to you; but mature reflection on the then perplexed and critical posture of our affairs with foreign nations, and the unanimous advice of persons entitled to my confidence impelled me to abandon the idea.

I rejoice that the state of your concerns, external as well as internal, no longer renders the pursuit of inclination incompatible with the sentiment of duty or propriety; and am persuaded, whatever partiality may be retained for my services, that, in the present circumstances of our country, you will not disapprove of my determination to retire.

The impressions with which I first undertook the arduous trust were explained on the proper occasion. In the discharge of this trust, I will only say that I have, with good intentions, contributed toward the organization and administration of the government the best exertions of which a very fallible judgment was capable. Not unconscious, in the outset, of the inferiority of my qualifications, experience in my own eyes, perhaps still more in the eyes of others, has strengthened the motives to diffidence of myself; and every day the increasing weight of years admonishes me more and more that the shade of retirement is as necessary to me as it will be welcome. Satisfied that, if any circumstances have given peculiar value to my services, they were temporary, I have the consolation to believe that, while choice and prudence invite me to quit the political scene, patriotism does not forbid it.

In looking forward to the moment which is to terminate the career of my political life, my feelings do not permit me to suspend the deep acknowledgment of that debt of gratitude which I owe to my beloved country for the many honors it has conferred upon me; still more for the steadfast confidence with which it has supported me; and for the opportunities I have thence enjoyed of manifesting my inviolable attachment, by services faithful and persevering, though in usefulness unequal to my zeal. If benefits have resulted to our country from these services, let it always be remembered to your praise, and as an instructive example in our annals, that, under circumstances in which the passions, agitated in every direction, were liable to mislead, amidst appearances sometimes dubious, vicissitudes of fortune often discouraging, in situations in which not unfrequently want of success has countenanced the spirit of criticism, the constancy of your support was the essential prop of the efforts, and a guaranty of the plans by which they were effected. Profoundly penetrated with this idea, I shall carry it with me to my grave, as a strong incitement to unceasing vows that Heaven may continue to you the choicest tokens of its beneficence; that your union and brotherly affection may be perpetual; that the free constitution, which is the work of your hands, may be sacredly maintained; that its administration in every department may be stamped with wisdom and virtue; that, in fine, the happiness of the people of these States, under the auspices of liberty, may be made complete, by so careful a preservation and so prudent a use of this blessing, as will acquire to them the glory of recommending it to the applause, the affection, and adoption of every nation which is yet a stranger to it.

Here, perhaps, I ought to stop. But a solicitude for your welfare, which cannot end but with my life, and the apprehension of danger, natural to that solicitude, urge me, on an occasion like the present, to offer to your solemn contemplation, and to recommend to your frequent review, some sentiments, which are the result of much reflection, of no inconsiderable observation, and which appear to me all-important to the permanency of your felicity as a people. These will be offered to you with the more freedom, as you can only see in them the disinterested warnings of a parting friend, who can possibly have no personal motive to bias his counsel. Nor can I forget, as an encouragement to it, your indulgent reception of my sentiments on a former and not dissimilar occasion.

Interwoven as is the love of liberty with every ligament of your hearts, no recommendation of mine is necessary to fortify or confirm the attachment.

The unity of government, which constitutes you one people, is also now dear to you. It is justly so; for it is a main pillar in the edifice of your real independence, the support of your tranquillity at home, your peace abroad, of your safety, of your prosperity, of that very liberty which you so highly prize. But as it is easy to foresee that, from different causes and from different quarters, much pains will be taken, many artifices employed, to weaken in your minds the conviction of this truth; as this is the point in your political fortress against which the batteries of internal and external enemies will be most constantly and actively (though often covertly and insidiously) directed, it is of infinite moment that you should properly estimate the immense value of your national union to your collective and individual happiness; that you should cherish a cordial, habitual, and immovable attachment to it; accustoming yourselves to think and speak of it as of the palladium of your political safety and prosperity; watching for its preservation with jealous anxiety; discountenancing whatever may suggest even a suspicion that it can in any event be abandoned; and indignantly frowning upon the first dawning of every attempt to alienate any portion of our country from the rest, or to enfeeble the sacred ties which now link together the various parts.

For this you have every inducement of sympathy and interest. Citizens, by birth or choice, of a common country, that country has a right to concentrate your affections. The name of AMERICAN, which belongs to you in your national capacity, must always exalt the just pride of patriotism more than any appellation derived from local discriminations. With slight shades of difference, you have the same religion, manners, habits, and political principles. You have in a common cause fought and triumphed together; the independence and liberty you possess are the work of joint counsels and joint efforts, of common dangers, sufferings, and successes.

But these considerations, however powerfully they address themselves to your sensibility, are greatly outweighed by those which apply more immediately to your interest. Here every portion of our country finds the most commanding motives for carefully guarding and preserving the union of the whole.

The North, in an unrestrained intercourse with the South, protected by the equal laws of a common government, finds in the productions of the latter great additional resources of maritime and commercial enterprise and precious materials of manufacturing industry. The South, in the same intercourse, benefiting by the agency of the North, sees its agriculture grow and its commerce expand. Turning partly into its own channels the seamen of the North, it finds its particular navigation invigorated; and, while it contributes in different ways to nourish and increase the general mass of the national navigation, it looks forward to the protection of a maritime strength to which itself is unequally adapted. The East, in a like intercourse with the West, already finds, and in the progressive improvement of interior communications, by land and water, will more and more find, a valuable vent for the commodities which it brings from abroad, or manufactures at home. The West derives from the East supplies requisite to its growth and comfort; and, what is perhaps of still greater consequence, it must of necessity owe the secure enjoyment of indispensable outlets for its own productions to the weight, influence, and the future maritime strength of the Atlantic side of the Union, directed by an indissoluble community of interest as one nation. Any other tenure by which the West can hold this essential advantage, whether derived from its own separate strength, or from an apostate and unnatural connection with any foreign power, must be intrinsically precarious.

While, then, every part of our country thus feels an immediate and particular interest in union, all the parts combined cannot fail to find in the united mass of means and efforts greater strength, greater resource, proportionably greater security from external danger, a less frequent interruption of their peace by foreign nations; and, what is of inestimable value, they must derive from union an exemption from those broils and wars between themselves which so frequently afflict neighboring countries not tied together by the same governments, which their own rivalships alone would be sufficient to produce, but which opposite foreign alliances, attachments, and intrigues would stimulate and embitter. Hence, likewise, they will avoid the necessity of those overgrown military establishments, which, under any form of government, are inauspicious to liberty, and which are to be regarded as particularly hostile to republican liberty. In this sense it is that your union ought to be considered as a main prop of your liberty, and that the love of the one ought to endear to you the preservation of the other.

These considerations speak a persuasive language to every reflecting and virtuous mind, and exhibit the continuance of the Union as a primary object of patriotic desire. Is there a doubt whether a common government can embrace so large a sphere? Let experience solve it. To listen to mere speculation in such a case were criminal. We are authorized to hope that a proper organization of the whole, with the auxiliary agency of governments for the respective subdivisions, will afford a happy issue to the experiment. It is well worth a fair and full experiment. With such powerful and obvious motives to union, affecting all parts of our country, while experience shall not have demonstrated its impracticability, there will always be reason to distrust the patriotism of those who in any quarter may endeavor to weaken its bands.

In contemplating the causes which may disturb our union, it occurs as a matter of serious concern that any ground should have been furnished for characterizing parties by geographical discriminations, Northern and Southern, Atlantic and Western, whence designing men may endeavor to excite a belief that there is a real difference of local interests and views. One of the expedients of party to acquire influence within particular districts is to misrepresent the opinions and aims of other districts. You cannot shield yourselves too much against the jealousies and heart-burnings which spring from these misrepresentations; they tend to render alien to each other those who ought to be bound together by fraternal affection. The inhabitants of our western country have lately had a useful lesson on this head; they have seen, in the negotiation by the Executive, and in the unanimous ratification by the Senate, of the treaty with Spain, and in the universal satisfaction at that event throughout the United States, a decisive proof how unfounded were the suspicions propagated among them of a policy in the general government and in the Atlantic States unfriendly to their interests in regard to the Mississippi. They have been witnesses to the formation of two treaties, that with Great Britain and that with Spain, which secure to them everything they could desire, in respect to our foreign relations, towards confirming their prosperity. Will it not be their wisdom to rely for the preservation of these advantages on the union by which they were procured? Will they not henceforth be deaf to those advisers, if such there are, who would sever them from their brethren and connect them with aliens?

To the efficacy and permanency of your union, a government for the whole is indispensable. No alliances, however strict, between the parts can be an adequate substitute; they must inevitably experience the infractions and interruptions which all alliances in all times have experienced. Sensible of this momentous truth, you have improved upon your first essay by the adoption of a constitution of government better calculated than your former for an intimate union, and for the efficacious management of your common concerns. This government, the offspring of your own choice, uninfluenced and unawed, adopted upon full investigation and mature deliberation, completely free in its principles, in the distribution of its powers, uniting security with energy, and containing within itself a provision for its own amendment, has a just claim to your confidence and your support. Respect for its authority, compliance with its laws, acquiescence in its measures, are duties enjoined by the fundamental maxims of true liberty. The basis of our political system is the right of the people to make and to alter their constitutions of government. But the constitution which at any time exists, till changed by an explicit and authentic act of the whole people, is sacredly obligatory upon all. The very idea of the power and the right of the people to establish government presupposes the duty of every individual to obey the established government.

All obstructions to the execution of the laws, all combinations and associations, under whatever plausible character, with the real design to direct, control, counteract, or awe the regular deliberations and actions of the constituted authorities, are destructive of this fundamental principle, and of fatal tendency. They serve to organize faction, to give it an artificial and extraordinary force; to put in the place of the delegated will of the nation the will of a party, often a small but artful and enterprising minority of the community; and, according to the alternate triumphs of different parties, to make the public administration the mirror of the ill-concerted and incongruous projects of faction, rather than the organs of consistent and wholesome plans, digested by common councils and modified by mutual interests.

However combinations or associations of the above description may now and then answer popular ends, they are likely, in the course of time and things, to become potent engines by which cunning, ambitious, and unprincipled men will be enabled to subvert the power of the people and to usurp for themselves the reins of government, destroying afterwards the very engines which have lifted them to unjust dominion.

Towards the preservation of your government, and the permanency of your present happy state, it is requisite, not only that you steadily discountenance irregular oppositions to its acknowledged authority, but also that you resist with care the spirit of innovation upon its principles, however specious the pretexts. One method of assault may be to effect, in the forms of the constitution, alterations which will impair the energy of the system, and thus to undermine what cannot be directly overthrown. In all the changes to which you may be invited, remember that time and habit are at least as necessary to fix the true character of governments as of other human institutions; that experience is the surest standard by which to test the real tendency of the existing constitution of a country; that facility in changes, upon the credit of mere hypothesis and opinion, exposes to perpetual change from the endless variety of hypothesis and opinion; and remember, especially, that, for the efficient management of your common interests in a country so extensive as ours, a government of as much vigor as is consistent with the perfect security of liberty is indispensable. Liberty itself will find in such a government, with powers properly distributed and adjusted, its surest guardian. It is, indeed, little else than a name, where the government is too feeble to withstand the enterprises of faction, to confine each member of the society within the limits prescribed by the laws, and to maintain all in the secure and tranquil enjoyment of the rights of person and property.

I have already intimated to you the danger of parties in the state, with particular reference to the founding of them on geographical discriminations. Let me now take a more comprehensive view, and warn you in the most solemn manner against the baneful effects of the spirit of party, generally.

This spirit, unfortunately, is inseparable from our nature, having its root in the strongest passions of the human mind. It exists under different shapes in all governments, more or less stifled, controlled, or repressed; but in those of the popular form it is seen in its greatest rankness, and is truly their worst enemy.

The alternate domination of one faction over another, sharpened by the spirit of revenge natural to party dissension, which in different ages and countries has perpetrated the most horrid enormities, is itself a frightful despotism. But this leads at length to a more formal and permanent despotism. The disorders and miseries which result gradually incline the minds of men to seek security and repose in the absolute power of an individual; and sooner or later the chief of some prevailing faction, more able or more fortunate than his competitors, turns this disposition to the purposes of his own elevation on the ruins of public liberty.

Without looking forward to an extremity of this kind (which nevertheless ought not to be entirely out of sight), the common and continued mischiefs of the spirit of party are sufficient to make it the interest and duty of a wise people to discourage and restrain it.

It serves always to distract the public councils, and enfeeble the public administration. It agitates the community with ill-founded jealousies and false alarms, kindles the animosity of one part against another, foments occasionally riot and insurrection. It opens the doors to foreign influence and corruption, which find a facilitated access to the government itself through the channels of party passions. Thus the policy and the will of one country are subjected to the policy and will of another.

There is an opinion that parties in free countries are useful checks upon the administration of the government, and serve to keep alive the spirit of liberty. This within certain limits is probably true, and in governments of a monarchical cast, patriotism may look with indulgence, if not with favor, upon the spirit of party. But in those of the popular character, in governments purely elective, it is a spirit not to be encouraged. From their natural tendency, it is certain there will always be enough of that spirit for every salutary purpose. And there being constant danger of excess, the effort ought to be by force of public opinion to mitigate and assuage it. A fire not to be quenched, it demands a uniform vigilance to prevent its bursting into a flame, lest, instead of warming, it should consume.

It is important, likewise, that the habits of thinking in a free country should inspire caution, in those intrusted with its administration, to confine themselves within their respective constitutional spheres, avoiding in the exercise of the powers of one department to encroach upon another. The spirit of encroachment tends to consolidate the powers of all the departments in one, and thus to create, whatever the form of government, a real despotism. A just estimate of that love of power and proneness to abuse it which predominates in the human heart is sufficient to satisfy us of the truth of this position. The necessity of reciprocal checks in the exercise of political power, by dividing and distributing it into different depositories, and constituting each the guardian of the public weal against invasions by the others, has been evinced by experiments ancient and modern, some of them in our country and under our own eyes. To preserve them must be as necessary as to institute them. If, in the opinion of the people, the distribution or modification of the constitutional powers be in any particular wrong, let it be corrected by an amendment in the way which the Constitution designates. But let there be no change by usurpation; for, though this, in one instance, may be the instrument of good, it is the customary weapon by which free governments are destroyed. The precedent must always greatly overbalance in permanent evil any partial or transient benefit which the use can at any time yield.

Of all the dispositions and habits which lead to political prosperity, religion and morality are indispensable supports. In vain would that man claim the tribute of patriotism, who should labor to subvert these great pillars of human happiness, these firmest props of the duties of men and citizens. The mere politician, equally with the pious man, ought to respect and to cherish them. A volume could not trace all their connections with private and public felicity. Let it simply be asked, Where is the security for property, for reputation, for life, if the sense of religious obligation desert the oaths which are the instruments of investigation in courts of justice? And let us with caution indulge the supposition that morality can be maintained without religion. Whatever may be conceded to the influence of refined education on minds of peculiar structure, reason and experience both forbid us to expect that national morality can prevail in exclusion of religious principle.

It is substantially true that virtue or morality is a necessary spring of popular government. The rule, indeed, extends with more or less force to every species of free government. Who, that is a sincere friend to it, can look with indifference upon attempts to shake the foundation of the fabric?

Promote, then, as an object of primary importance, institutions for the general diffusion of knowledge. In proportion as the structure of a government gives force to public opinion, it is essential that public opinion should be enlightened.

As a very important source of strength and security, cherish public credit. One method of preserving it is to use it as sparingly as possible; avoiding occasions of expense by cultivating peace, but remembering also that timely disbursements to prepare for danger frequently prevent much greater disbursements to repel it; avoiding likewise the accumulation of debt, not only by shunning occasions of expense, but by vigorous exertion in time of peace to discharge the debts which unavoidable wars may have occasioned, not ungenerously throwing upon posterity the burden which we ourselves ought to bear. The execution of these maxims belongs to your representatives, but it is necessary that public opinion should cooperate. To facilitate to them the performance of their duty, it is essential that you should practically bear in mind that towards the payment of debts there must be revenue; that to have revenue there must be taxes; that no taxes can be devised which are not more or less inconvenient and unpleasant; that the intrinsic embarrassment, inseparable from the selection of the proper objects (which is always a choice of difficulties), ought to be a decisive motive for a candid construction of the conduct of the government in making it, and for a spirit of acquiescence in the measures for obtaining revenue which the public exigencies may at any time dictate.

Observe good faith and justice towards all nations; cultivate peace and harmony with all. Religion and morality enjoin this conduct; and can it be that good policy does not equally enjoin it? It will be worthy of a free, enlightened, and, at no distant period, a great nation, to give to mankind the magnanimous and too novel example of a people always guided by an exalted justice and benevolence. Who can doubt that, in the course of time and things, the fruits of such a plan would richly repay any temporary advantages which might be lost by a steady adherence to it? Can it be that Providence has not connected the permanent felicity of a nation with its virtue? The experiment, at least, is recommended by every sentiment which ennobles human nature. Alas! is it rendered impossible by its vices?

In the execution of such a plan, nothing is more essential than that permanent, inveterate antipathies against particular nations, and passionate attachments for others, should be excluded; and that, in place of them, just and amicable feelings towards all should be cultivated. The nation which indulges towards another an habitual hatred, or an habitual fondness, is in some degree a slave. It is a slave to its animosity or to its affection, either of which is sufficient to lead it astray from its duty and its interest. Antipathy in one nation against another disposes each more readily to offer insult and injury, to lay hold of slight causes of umbrage, and to be haughty and intractable when accidental or trifling occasions of dispute occur. Hence, frequent collisions, obstinate, envenomed, and bloody contests. The nation, prompted by ill will and resentment, sometimes impels to war the government, contrary to the best calculations of policy. The government sometimes participates in the national propensity, and adopts through passion what reason would reject; at other times, it makes the animosity of the nation subservient to projects of hostility instigated by pride, ambition, and other sinister and pernicious motives. The peace often, sometimes perhaps the liberty, of nations has been the victim.

So, likewise, a passionate attachment of one nation for another produces a variety of evils. Sympathy for the favorite nation, facilitating the illusion of an imaginary common interest in cases where no real common interest exists, and infusing into one the enmities of the other, betrays the former into a participation in the quarrels and wars of the latter, without adequate inducement or justification. It leads also to concessions to the favorite nation of privileges denied to others, which is apt doubly to injure the nation making the concessions, by unnecessarily parting with what ought to have been retained, and by exciting jealousy, ill will, and a disposition to retaliate in the parties from whom equal privileges are withheld. And it gives to ambitious, corrupted, or deluded citizens (who devote themselves to the favorite nation), facility to betray or sacrifice the interests of their own country, without odium, sometimes even with popularity; gilding with the appearances of a virtuous sense of obligation, a commendable deference for public opinion, or a laudable zeal for public good, the base or foolish compliances of ambition, corruption, or infatuation.

As avenues to foreign influence in innumerable ways, such attachments are particularly alarming to the truly enlightened and independent patriot. How many opportunities do they afford to tamper with domestic factions, to practise the arts of seduction, to mislead public opinion, to influence or awe the public councils! Such an attachment of a small or weak towards a great and powerful nation dooms the former to be the satellite of the latter.

Against the insidious wiles of foreign influence (I conjure you to believe me, fellow-citizens), the jealousy of a free people ought to be constantly awake, since history and experience prove that foreign influence is one of the most baneful foes of republican government. But that jealousy, to be useful, must be impartial; else it becomes the instrument of the very influence to be avoided, instead of a defence against it. Excessive partiality for one foreign nation, and excessive dislike of another, cause those whom they actuate to see danger only on one side, and serve to veil and even second the arts of influence on the other. Real patriots, who may resist the intrigues of the favorite, are liable to become suspected and odious; while its tools and dupes usurp the applause and confidence of the people to surrender their interests.

The great rule of conduct for us, in regard to foreign nations, is, in extending our commercial relations, to have with them as little political connection as possible. So far as we have already formed engagements, let them be fulfilled with perfect good faith. Here let us stop.

Europe has a set of primary interests, which to us have none, or a very remote relation. Hence she must be engaged in frequent controversies, the causes of which are essentially foreign to our concerns. Hence, therefore, it must be unwise in us to implicate ourselves, by artificial ties, in the ordinary vicissitudes of her politics, or the ordinary combinations and collisions of her friendships or enmities.

Our detached and distant situation invites and enables us to pursue a different course. If we remain one people, under an efficient government, the period is not far off when we may defy material injury from external annoyance; when we may take such an attitude as will cause the neutrality we may at any time resolve upon to be scrupulously respected; when belligerent nations, under the impossibility of making acquisitions upon us, will not lightly hazard the giving us provocation; when we may choose peace or war, as our interest, guided by justice, shall counsel.

Why forego the advantages of so peculiar a situation? Why quit our own to stand upon foreign ground? Why, by interweaving our destiny with that of any part of Europe, entangle our peace and prosperity in the toils of European ambition, rivalship, interest, humor, or caprice?

It is our true policy to steer clear of permanent alliances with any portion of the foreign world, so far, I mean, as we are now at liberty to do it; for let me not be understood as capable of patronizing infidelity to existing engagements. I hold the maxim no less applicable to public than to private affairs, that honesty is always the best policy. I repeat it, therefore; let those engagements be observed in their genuine sense. But, in my opinion, it is unnecessary and would be unwise to extend them.

Taking care always to keep ourselves, by suitable establishments, on a respectable defensive posture, we may safely trust to temporary alliances for extraordinary emergencies.

Harmony, liberal intercourse with all nations, are recommended by policy, humanity, and interest. But even our commercial policy should hold an equal and impartial hand; neither seeking nor granting exclusive favors or preferences; consulting the natural course of things; diffusing and diversifying by gentle means the streams of commerce, but forcing nothing; establishing, with powers so disposed, in order to give trade a stable course, to define the rights of our merchants, and to enable the government to support them, conventional rules of intercourse, the best that present circumstances and mutual opinion will permit, but temporary, and liable to be from time to time abandoned or varied, as experience and circumstances shall dictate; constantly keeping in view that it is folly in one nation to look for disinterested favors from another; that it must pay with a portion of its independence for whatever it may accept under that character; that, by such acceptance, it may place itself in the condition of having given equivalents for nominal favors, and yet of being reproached with ingratitude for not giving more. There can be no greater error than to expect or calculate upon real favors from nation to nation. It is an illusion, which experience must cure, which a just pride ought to discard.

In offering to you, my countrymen, these counsels of an old and affectionate friend, I dare not hope they will make the strong and lasting impression I could wish; that they will control the usual current of the passions, or prevent our nation from running the course which has hitherto marked the destiny of nations. But, if I may even flatter myself that they may be productive of some partial benefit, some occasional good; that they may now and then recur to moderate the fury of party spirit, to warn against the mischiefs of foreign intrigue, to guard against the impostures of pretended patriotism; this hope will be a full recompense for the solicitude for your welfare, by which they have been dictated.

How far in the discharge of my official duties I have been guided by the principles which have been delineated, the public records and other evidences of my conduct must witness to you and to the world. To myself, the assurance of my own conscience is that I have at least believed myself to be guided by them.

In relation to the still subsisting war in Europe, my proclamation of the 22d of April, 1793, is the index of my plan. Sanctioned by your approving voice, and by that of your Representatives in both Houses of Congress, the spirit of that measure has continually governed me, uninfluenced by any attempts to deter or divert me from it.

After deliberate examination, with the aid of the best lights I could obtain, I was well satisfied that our country, under all the circumstances of the case, had a right to take, and was bound in duty and interest to take, a neutral position. Having taken it, I determined, as far as should depend on me, to maintain it, with moderation, perseverance, and firmness.

The considerations which respect the right to hold this conduct it is not necessary on this occasion to detail. I will only observe that, according to my understanding of the matter, that right, so far from being denied by any of the belligerent powers, has been virtually admitted by all.

The duty of holding a neutral conduct may be inferred, without anything more, from the obligation which justice and humanity impose on every nation, in cases in which it is free to act, to maintain inviolate the relations of peace and amity towards other nations.

The inducements of interest for observing that conduct will best be referred to your own reflections and experience. With me, a predominant motive has been to endeavor to gain time to our country to settle and mature its yet recent institutions, and to progress without interruption to that degree of strength and consistency which is necessary to give it, humanly speaking, the command of its own fortunes.

Though, in reviewing the incidents of my administration, I am unconscious of intentional error, I am nevertheless too sensible of my defects not to think it probable that I may have committed many errors. Whatever they may be, I fervently beseech the Almighty to avert or mitigate the evils to which they may tend. I shall also carry with me the hope that my country will never cease to view them with indulgence; and that, after forty-five years of my life dedicated to its service with an upright zeal, the faults of incompetent abilities will be consigned to oblivion, as myself must soon be to the mansions of rest.

Relying on its kindness in this as in other things, and actuated by that fervent love towards it which is so natural to a man who views in it the

native soil of himself and his progenitors for several generations, I antici-
pate with pleasing expectation that retreat, in which I promise myself
to realize, without alloy, the sweet enjoyment of partaking, in the midst
of my fellow citizens, the benign influence of good laws under a free
government, the ever favorite object of my heart, and the happy reward,
as I trust, of our mutual cares, labors, and dangers.

GEORGE WASHINGTON *Farewell Address*

The Bunker Hill monument was erected in commemoration of
the Battle of Bunker Hill and to the memory of General Joseph
Warren who in 1775, at about the spot where the monument stands,
led the first battle in the cause of American independence. Though
the place had been fittingly marked after the close of the war, the
Bunker Hill Monument Association, of which Daniel Webster was
president, decided in 1825, the fiftieth anniversary of the event, that
a more imposing and distinguished monument should be erected.
The movement was memorably initiated when on June 17, 1825,
Webster delivered the following oration to an audience of many
thousands of people including all the surviving veterans of the battle,
as well as the distinguished sympathizer with the American Revolution, General Marquis de Lafayette. The occasion was one of the
great events in American history, and it was greatly met by Daniel
Webster in this memorable address. His second Bunker Hill address
was delivered eighteen years later—June 17, 1843—when the new
monument was completed. Again, the occasion was made one of
imposing significance by the presence of more than one hundred
thousand people, including the President of the United States and his
cabinet, and by the memorable words of the orator of the day. The
monument was really completed on July 23, 1842, the women of
Boston and of various other parts of the country having raised the
final necessary funds by conducting fairs and bazaars.

I

This uncounted multitude before me and around me proves the feeling which the occasion has excited. These thousands of human faces,
glowing with sympathy and joy, and from the impulses of a common
gratitude turned reverently to heaven in this spacious temple of the
firmament, proclaim that the day, the place, and the purpose of our
assembling have made a deep impression on our hearts.

If, indeed, there be anything in local association fit to affect the mind of man, we need not strive to repress the emotions which agitate us here. We are among the sepulchres of our fathers. We are on ground distinguished by their valor, their constancy, and the shedding of their blood. We are here, not to fix an uncertain date in our annals, nor to draw into notice an obscure and unknown spot. If our humble purpose had never been conceived, if we ourselves had never been born, the 17th of June, 1775, would have been a day on which all subsequent history would have poured its light, and the eminence where we stand a point of attraction to the eyes of. successive generations. But we are Americans. We live in what may be called the early age of this great continent; and we know that our posterity, through all time, are here to enjoy and suffer the allotments of humanity. We see before us a probable train of great events; we know that our own fortunes have been happily cast; and it is natural, therefore, that we should be moved by the contemplation of occurrences which have guided our destiny before many of us were born, and settled the condition in which we should pass that portion of our existence which God allows to men on earth.

We do not read even of the discovery of this continent without feeling something of a personal interest in the event, without being reminded how much it has affected our own fortunes and our own existence. It would be still more unnatural for us, therefore, than for others, to contemplate with unaffected minds that interesting, I may say that most touching and pathetic scene, when the great discoverer of America stood on the deck of his shattered bark, the shades of night falling on the sea, yet no man sleeping; tossed on the billows of an unknown ocean, yet the stronger billows of alternate hope and despair tossing his own troubled thoughts; extending forward his harassed frame, straining westward his anxious and eager eyes, till Heaven at last granted him a moment of rapture and ecstasy, in blessing his vision with the sight of the unknown world.

Nearer to our times, more closely connected with our fates, and therefore still more interesting to our feelings and affections, is the settlement of our own country by colonists from England. We cherish every memorial of these worthy ancestors; we celebrate their patience and fortitude; we admire their daring enterprise; we teach our children to venerate their piety; and we are justly proud of being descended from men who have set the world an example of founding civil institutions on the great and united principles of human freedom and human knowledge. To us, their children, the story of their labors and sufferings can never be without interest. We shall not stand unmoved on the shore of Plymouth, while the sea continues to wash it; nor will our brethren in another early and ancient Colony forget the place of its first establishment, till their river shall cease to flow by it. No vigor of youth, no maturity of manhood, will lead the nation to forget the spots where its infancy was cradled and defended.

But the great event in the history of the continent, which we are now met here to commemorate, that prodigy of modern times, at once the wonder and the blessing of the world, is the American Revolution. In a day of extraordinary prosperity and happiness, of high national honor, distinction, and power, we are brought together in this place by our love of country, by our admiration of exalted character, by our gratitude for signal services and patriotic devotion.

The Society whose organ I am was formed for the purpose of rearing some honorable and durable monument to the memory of the early friends of American Independence. They have thought that for this object no time could be more propitious than the present prosperous and peaceful period; that no place could claim preference over this memorable spot; and that no day could be more auspicious to the undertaking than the anniversary of the battle which was here fought. The foundation of that monument we have now laid. With solemnities suited to the occasion, with prayers to Almighty God for his blessing, and in the midst of this cloud of witnesses, we have begun the work. We trust it will be prosecuted, and that, springing from a broad foundation, rising high in massive solidity and unadorned grandeur, it may remain as long as Heaven permits the works of man to last, a fit emblem, both of the events in memory of which it is raised, and of the gratitude of those who have reared it.

We know, indeed, that the record of illustrious actions is most safely deposited in the universal remembrance of mankind. We know that if we could cause this structure to ascend, not only till it reached the skies, but till it pierced them, its broad surfaces could still contain but part of that which, in an age of knowledge, hath already been spread over the earth, and which history charges itself with making known to all future times. We know that no inscription on entablatures less broad than the earth itself can carry information of the events we commemorate where it has not already gone; and that no structure which shall not outlive the duration of letters and knowledge among men can prolong the memorial. But our object is, by this edifice, to show our own deep sense of the value and importance of the achievements of our ancestors; and, by

presenting this work of gratitude to the eye, to keep alive similar sentiments, and to foster a constant regard for the principles of the Revolution. Human beings are composed, not of reason only, but of imagination also, and sentiment; and that is neither wasted nor misapplied
which is appropriated to the purpose of giving right direction to sentiments, and opening proper springs of feeling in the heart. Let it not be
supposed that our object is to perpetuate national hostility, or even to
cherish a mere military spirit. It is higher, purer, nobler. We consecrate
our work to the spirit of national independence, and we wish that the
light of peace may rest upon it for ever. We rear a memorial of our conviction of that unmeasured benefit which has been conferred on our own
land, and of the happy influences which have been produced, by the
same events, on the general interests of mankind. We come, as Americans, to mark a spot which must for ever be dear to us and our posterity.
We wish that whosoever, in all coming time, shall turn his eye hither
may behold that the place is not undistinguished where the first great
battle of the Revolution was fought. We wish that this structure may
proclaim the magnitude and importance of that event to every class and
every age. We wish that infancy may learn the purpose of its erection
from maternal lips, and that weary and withered age may behold it,
and be solaced by the recollections which it suggests. We wish that labor
may look up here, and be proud, in the midst of its toil. We wish that,
in those days of disaster, which, as they come upon all nations, must be
expected to come upon us also, desponding patriotism may turn its eyes
hitherward, and be assured that the foundations of our national power
are still strong. We wish that this column, rising towards heaven among
the pointed spires of so many temples dedicated to God, may contribute
also to produce, in all minds, a pious feeling of dependence and gratitude. We wish, finally, that the last object to the sight of him who leaves
his native shore, and the first to gladden him who revisits it, may be
something which shall remind him of the liberty and the glory of his
country. Let it rise! let it rise, till it meet the sun in his coming; let the
earliest light of the morning gild it, and parting day linger and play on
its summit.

We live in a most extraordinary age. Events so various and so important that they might crowd and distinguish centuries, are, in our times,
compressed within the compass of a single life. When has it happened
that history has had so much to record, in the same term of years, as
since the 17th of June, 1775? Our own Revolution, which, under other
circumstances, might itself have been expected to occasion a war of half

a century, has been achieved; twenty-four sovereign and independent States erected; and a general government established over them, so safe, so wise, so free, so practical, that we might well wonder its establishment should have been accomplished so soon, were it not for the greater wonder that it should have been established at all. Two or three millions of people have been augmented to twelve, the great forests of the West prostrated beneath the arm of successful industry, and the dwellers on the banks of the Ohio and the Mississippi become the fellow-citizens and neighbors of those who cultivate the hills of New England. We have a commerce that leaves no sea unexplored; navies which take no law from superior force; revenues adequate to all the exigencies of government, almost without taxation; and peace with all nations, founded on equal rights and mutual respect.

Europe, within the same period, has been agitated by a mighty revolution, which, while it has been felt in the individual condition and happiness of almost every man, has shaken to the center her political fabric, and dashed against one another thrones which had stood tranquil for ages. On this, our continent, our own example has been followed, and colonies have sprung up to be nations. Unaccustomed sounds of liberty and free government have reached us from beyond the track of the sun; and at this moment the dominion of European power in this continent, from the place where we stand to the south pole, is annihilated for ever.

In the meantime, both in Europe and America, such has been the general progress of knowledge, such the improvement in legislation, in commerce, in the arts, in letters, and, above all, in liberal ideas and the general spirit of the age, that the whole world seems changed.

Yet, notwithstanding that this is but a faint abstract of the things which have happened since the day of the battle of Bunker Hill, we are but fifty years removed from it; and we now stand here to enjoy all the blessings of our own condition and to look abroad on the brightened prospects of the world, while we still have among us some of those who were active agents in the scenes of 1775, and who are now here, from every quarter of New England, to visit once more, and under circumstances so affecting, I had almost said so overwhelming, this renowned theater of their courage and patriotism.

VENERABLE MEN! you have come down to us from a former generation. Heaven has bounteously lengthened out your lives, that you might behold this joyous day. You are now where you stood fifty years ago, this very hour, with your brothers and your neighbors, shoulder to shoulder, in the strife for your country. Behold, how altered! The same heavens are indeed over your heads; the same ocean rolls at your feet; but all else how changed! You hear now no roar of hostile cannon, you see no mixed volumes of smoke and flame rising from burning Charlestown. The ground strewed with the dead and the dying; the impetuous charge; the steady and successful repulse; the loud call to repeated assault; the summoning of all that is manly to repeated resistance; a thousand bosoms freely and fearlessly bared in an instant to whatever of terror there may be in war and death—all these you have witnessed, but you witness them no more. All is peace. The heights of yonder metropolis, its towers and roofs, which you then saw filled with wives and children and countrymen in distress and terror, and looking with unutterable emotions for the issue of the combat, have presented you to-day with the sight of its whole happy population, come out to welcome and greet you wtih a universal jubilee. Yonder proud ships, by a felicity of position appropriately lying at the foot of this mount, and seeming fondly to cling around it, are not means of annoyance to you, but your country's own means of distinction and defence. All is peace; and God has granted you this sight of your country's happiness, ere you slumber in the grave. He has allowed you to behold and to partake the reward of your patriotic toils; and He has allowed us, your sons and countrymen, to meet you here, and in the name of the present generation, in the name of your country, in the name of liberty, to thank you!

But, alas! you are not all here! Time and the sword have thinned your ranks. Prescott, Putnam, Stark, Brooks, Reed, Pomeroy, Bridge! our eyes seek for you in vain amid this broken band. You are gathered to your fathers, and live only to your country in her grateful remembrance and your own bright example. But let us not too much grieve that you have met the common fate of men. You lived at least long enough to know that your work had been nobly and successfully accomplished. You lived to see your country's independence established, and to sheathe your swords from war. On the light of Liberty you saw arise the light of Peace, like

> "another morn,
> Risen on mid-noon;"

and the sky on which you closed your eyes was cloudless.

But, ah! Him! the first great martyr in this great cause! Him! the premature victim of his own self-devoting heart! Him! the head of our civil councils, and the destined leader of our military bands, whom nothing brought hither but the unquenchable fire of his own spirit!

Him! cut off by Providence in the hour of overwhelming anxiety and thick gloom; falling ere he saw the star of his country rise; pouring out his generous blood like water, before he knew whether it would fertilize a land of freedom or of bondage!—how shall I struggle with the emotions that stifle the utterance of thy name! Our poor work may perish; but thine shall endure! This monument may moulder away; the solid ground it rests upon may sink down to a level with the sea; but thy memory shall not fail! Wheresoever among men a heart shall be found that beats to the transports of patriotism and liberty, its aspirations shall be to claim kindred with thy spirit.

But the scene amidst which we stand does not permit us to confine our thoughts or our sympathies to those fearless spirits who hazarded or lost their lives on this consecrated spot. We have the happiness to rejoice here in the presence of a most worthy representation of the survivors of the whole Revolutionary army.

VETERANS! you are the remnant of many a well-fought field. You bring with you marks of honor from Trenton and Monmouth, from Yorktown, Camden, Bennington, and Saratoga. VETERANS OF HALF A CENTURY! when in your youthful days you put every thing at hazard in your country's cause, good as that cause was, and sanguine as youth is, still your fondest hopes did not stretch onward to an hour like this! At a period to which you could not reasonably have expected to arrive, at a moment of national prosperity such as you could never have foreseen, you are now met here to enjoy the fellowship of old soldiers, and to receive the overflowings of a universal gratitude.

But your agitated countenances and your heaving breasts inform me that even this is not an unmixed joy. I perceive that a tumult of contending feelings rushes upon you. The images of the dead, as well as the persons of the living, present themselves before you. The scene overwhelms you, and I turn from it. May the Father of all mercies smile upon your declining years, and bless them! And when you shall here have exchanged your embraces, when you shall once more have pressed the hands which have been so often extended to give succor in adversity, or grasped in the exultation of victory, then look abroad upon this lovely land which your young valor defended, and mark the happiness with which it is filled; yea, look abroad upon the whole earth, and see what a name you have contributed to give to your country, and what a praise you have added to freedom, and then rejoice in the sympathy and gratitude which beam upon your last days from the improved condition of mankind!

The occasion does not require of me any particular account of the battle of the 17th of June, 1775, nor any detailed narrative of the events which immediately preceded it. These are familiarly known to all. In the progress of the great and interesting controversy, Massachusetts and the town of Boston had become early and marked objects of the displeasure of the British Parlaiment. This had been manifested in the act for altering the government of the Province, and in that for shutting up the port of Boston. Nothing sheds more honor on our early history, and nothing better shows how little the feelings and sentiments of the Colonies were known or regarded in England than the impression which these measures everywhere produced in America. It had been anticipated that, while the Colonies in general would be terrified by the severity of the punishment inflicted on Massachusetts, the other seaports would be governed by a mere spirit of gain; and that, as Boston was now cut off from all commerce, the unexpected advantage which this blow on her was calculated to confer on other towns would be greedily enjoyed. How miserably such reasoners deceived themselves! How little they knew of the depth, and the strength, and the intenseness of that feeling of resistance to illegal acts of power, which possessed the whole American people! Everywhere the unworthy boon was rejected with scorn. The fortunate occasion was seized, everywhere, to show to the whole world that the Colonies were swayed by no local interest, no partial interest, no selfish interest. The temptation to profit by the punishment of Boston was strongest to our neighbors of Salem. Yet Salem was precisely the place where this miserable proffer was spurned, in a tone of the most lofty self-respect and the most indignant patriotism. "We are deeply affected," said its inhabitants, "with the sense of our public calamities; but the miseries that are now rapidly hastening on our brethren in the capital of the Province greatly excite our commiseration. By shutting up the port of Boston some imagine that the course of trade might be turned hither and to our benefit; but we must be dead to every idea of justice, lost to all feelings of humanity, could we indulge a thought to seize on wealth and raise our fortunes on the ruin of our suffering neighbors." These noble sentiments were not confined to our immediate vicinity. In that day of general affection and brotherhood, the blow given to Boston smote on every patriotic heart from one end of the country to the other. Virginia and the Carolinas, as well as Connecticut and New Hampshire, felt and proclaimed the cause to be their own. The Continental Congress, then holding its first session in Philadelphia, expressed its sympathy for the suffering inhabitants of Boston, and addresses were received from all quarters, assuring them that the cause was a common one, and should be met by common efforts and common sacrifices. The Congress of Massachusetts responded to these assurances; and in an address to the Congress at Philadelphia, bearing the official signature, perhaps among the last, of the immortal Warren, notwithstanding the severity of its suffering and the magnitude of the dangers which threatened it, it was declared that this Colony "is ready, at all times, to spend and to be spent in the cause of America."

But the hour drew nigh which was to put professions to the proof, and to determine whether the authors of these mutual pledges were ready to seal them in blood. The tidings of Lexington and Concord had no sooner spread than it was universally felt that the time was at last come for action. A spirit pervaded all ranks, not transient, not boisterous, but deep, solemn, determined,

> "totamque infusa per artus
> Mens agitat molem, et magno se corpore miscet." *

War on their own soil and at their own doors was, indeed, a strange work to the yeomanry of New England; but their consciences were convinced of its necessity, their country called them to it, and they did not withhold themselves from the perilous trial. The ordinary occupations of life were abandoned; the plough was stayed in the unfinished furrow; wives gave up their husbands, and mothers gave up their sons, to the battles of the civil war. Death might come in honor, on the field; it might come in disgrace, on the scaffold. For either and for both they were prepared. The sentiment of Quincy was full in their hearts. "Blandishments," said that distinguished son of genius and patriotism, "will not fascinate us, nor will threats of a halter intimidate; for, under God, we are determined that, wheresoever, whensoever, or howsoever we shall be called to make our exit, we will die free men."

The 17th of June saw the four New England Colonies standing here, side by side, to triumph or to fall together; and there was with them from that moment to the end of the war what I hope will remain with them for ever, one cause, one country, one heart.

The battle of Bunker Hill was attended with the most important effects beyond its immediate results as a military engagement. It created at once a state of open, public war. There could now be no longer a question of proceeding against individuals as guilty of treason or rebellion. That fearful crisis was past. The appeal lay to the sword, and the only question was whether the spirit and the resources of the people would hold out till the object should be accomplished. Nor were its

---

* "And an intelligence, spread through the parts, directs the whole mass and is mingled with the vast body."—Virgil's *Aeneid*, VI, 726.

general consequences confined to our own country. The previous proceedings of the Colonies, their appeals, resolutions, and addresses, had made their cause known to Europe. Without boasting, we may say that in no age or country has the public cause been maintained with more force of argument, more power of illustration, or more of that persuasion which excited feeling and elevated principle can alone bestow, than the Revolutionary state papers exhibit. These papers will for ever deserve to be studied, not only for the spirit which they breathe, but for the ability with which they were written.

To this able vindication of their cause, the Colonies had now added a practical and severe proof of their own true devotion to it, and given evidence also of the power which they could bring to its support. All now saw that if America fell, she would not fall without a struggle. Men felt sympathy and regard, as well as surprise, when they beheld these infant states, remote, unknown, unaided, encounter the power of England, and, in the first considerable battle, leave more of their enemies dead on the field, in proportion to the number of combatants, than had been recently known to fall in the wars of Europe.

Information of these events, circulating throughout the world, at length reached the ears of one who now hears me. He has not forgotten the emotion which the fame of Bunker Hill, and the name of Warren, excited in his youthful breast.

Sir, we are assembled to commemorate the establishment of great public principles of liberty, and to do honor to the distinguished dead. The occasion is too severe for eulogy of the living. But, Sir, your interesting relation to this country, the peculiar circumstances which surround you and surround us, call on me to express the happiness which we derive from your presence and aid in this solemn commemoration.

Fortunate, fortunate man! with what measure of devotion will you not thank God for the circumstances of your extraordinary life! You are connected with both hemispheres and with two generations. Heaven saw fit to ordain that the electric spark of liberty should be conducted, through you, from the New World to the Old; and we, who are now here to perform this duty of patriotism, have all of us long ago received it in charge from our fathers to cherish your name and your virtues. You will account it an instance of your good fortune, Sir, that you crossed the seas to visit us at a time which enables you to be present at this solemnity. You now behold the field, the renown of which reached you in the heart of France, and caused a thrill in your ardent bosom. You see the lines of the little redoubt thrown up by the incredible diligence of Prescott; defended, to the last extremity, by his lion-hearted valor; and within which the cornerstone of our monument has now taken its position. You see where Warren fell, and where Parker, Gardner, McClary, Moore, and other early patriots fell with him. Those who survived that day, and whose lives have been prolonged to the present hour, are now around you. Some of them you have known in the trying scenes of the war. Behold! they now stretch forth their feeble arms to embrace you. Behold! they raise their trembling voices to invoke the blessing of God on you and yours for ever.

Sir, you have assisted us in laying the foundation of this structure. You have heard us rehearse, with our feeble commendation, the names of departed patriots. Monuments and eulogy belong to the dead. We give them this day to Warren and his associates. On other occasions they have been given to your more immediate companions in arms, to Washington, to Greene, to Gates, to Sullivan, and to Lincoln. We have become reluctant to grant these, our highest and last honors, further. We would gladly hold them yet back from the little remnant of that immortal band. *"Serus in cœlum redeas."* * Illustrious as are your merits, yet far, O, very far distant be the day when any inscription shall bear your name, or any tongue pronounce its eulogy!

The leading reflection to which this occasion seems to invite us respects the great changes which have happened in the fifty years since the battle of Bunker Hill was fought. And it peculiarly marks the character of the present age that, in looking at these changes, and in estimating their effect on our condition, we are obliged to consider, not what has been done in our country only, but in others also. In these interesting times, while nations are making separate and individual advances in improvement, they make, too, a common progress; like vessels on a common tide, propelled by the gales at different rates, according to their several structure and management, but all moved forward by one mighty current, strong enough to bear onward whatever does not sink beneath it.

A chief distinction of the present day is a community of opinions and knowledge amongst men in different nations, existing in a degree heretofore unknown. Knowledge has, in our time, triumphed, and is triumphing, over distance, over difference of languages, over diversity of habits, over prejudice, and over bigotry. The civilized and Christian world is fast learning the great lesson, that difference of nation does not imply necessary hostility, and that all contact need not be war. The whole world is becoming a common field for intellect to act in. Energy of mind, genius, power, wheresoever it exists, may speak out in any tongue, and the world will hear it. A great chord of sentiment and feel-

* "Late may you return into heaven."—Horace, *Odes,* I, 2, 45.

ing runs through two continents and vibrates over both. Every breeze wafts intelligence from country to country; every wave rolls it; all give it forth, and all in turn receive it. There is a vast commerce of ideas; there are marts and exchanges for intellectual discoveries, and a wonderful fellowship of those individual intelligences which make up the mind and opinion of the age. Mind is the great lever of all things; human thought is the process by which human ends are ultimately answered; and the diffusion of knowledge, so astonishing in the last half-century, has rendered innumerable minds, variously gifted by nature, competent to be competitors or fellow workers on the theatre of intellectual operation.

From these causes important improvements have taken place in the personal condition of individuals. Generally speaking, mankind are not only better fed and better clothed, but they are able also to enjoy more leisure; they possess more refinement and more self-respect. A superior tone of education, manners, and habits prevails. This remark, most true in its application to our own country, is also partly true when applied elsewhere. It is proved by the vastly augmented consumption of those articles of manufacture and of commerce which contribute to the comforts and the decencies of life; an augmentation which has far outrun the progress of population. And while the unexampled and almost incredible use of machinery would seem to supply the place of labor, labor still finds its occupation and its reward; so wisely has Providence adjusted men's wants and desires to their condition and their capacity.

Any adequate survey, however, of the progress made during the last half century in the polite and the mechanic arts, in machinery and manufactures, in commerce and agriculture, in letters and in science, would require volumes. I must abstain wholly from these subjects, and turn for a moment to the contemplation of what has been done on the great question of politics and government. This is the master topic of the age; and during the whole fifty years it has intensely occupied the thoughts of men. The nature of civil government, its end and uses, have been canvassed and investigated; ancient opinions attacked and defended; new ideas recommended and resisted, by whatever power the mind of man could bring to the controversy. From the closet and the public halls the debate has been transferred to the field; and the world has been shaken by wars of unexampled magnitude, and the greatest variety of fortune. A day of peace has at length succeeded; and now that the strife has subsided, and the smoke cleared away, we may begin to see what has actually been done, permanently changing the state and condition of human society. And, without dwelling on particular circumstances, it is most apparent that, from the before-mentioned causes of augmented knowledge and improved individual condition, a real, substantial, and important change has taken place, and is taking place, highly favorable, on the whole, to human liberty and human happiness.

The great wheel of political revolution began to move in America. Here its rotation was guarded, regular, and safe. Transferred to the other continent, from unfortunate but natural causes, it received an irregular and violent impulse; it whirled along with a fearful celerity; till at length, like the chariot wheels in the races of antiquity, it took fire from the rapidity of its own motion, and blazed onward, spreading conflagration and terror around.

We learn from the result of this experiment how fortunate was our own condition, and how admirably the character of our people was calculated for setting the great example of popular governments. The possession of power did not turn the heads of the American people, for they had long been in the habit of exercising a great degree of self-control. Although the paramount authority of the parent state existed over them, yet a large field of legislation had always been open to our Colonial assemblies. They were accustomed to representative bodies and the forms of free government; they understood the doctrine of the division of power among different branches, and the necessity of checks on each. The character of our countrymen, moreover, was sober, moral, and religious; and there was little in the change to shock their feelings of justice and humanity, or even to disturb an honest prejudice. We had no domestic throne to overturn, no privileged orders to cast down, no violent changes of property to encounter. In the American Revolution, no man sought or wished for more than to defend and enjoy his own. None hoped for plunder or for spoil. Rapacity was unknown to it; the axe was not among the instruments of its accomplishment; and we all know that it could not have lived a single day under any well-founded imputation of possessing a tendency adverse to the Christian religion.

It need not surprise us, that, under circumstances less auspicious, political revolutions elsewhere, even when well intended, have terminated differently. It is, indeed, a great achievement, it is the masterwork of the world, to establish governments entirely popular on lasting foundations; nor is it easy, indeed, to introduce the popular principle at all into governments to which it has been altogether a stranger. It cannot be doubted, however, that Europe has come out of the contest in which she has been so long engaged with greatly superior knowledge, and, in many respects, in a highly improved condition. Whatever benefit has been acquired is likely to be retained, for it consists mainly in the acquisition of more enlightened ideas. And although kingdoms and provinces may be wrested from the hands that hold them, in the same manner they were obtained, although ordinary and vulgar power may, in human affairs, be lost as it has been won; yet it is the glorious prerogative of the empire of knowledge that what it gains it never loses. On the contrary, it increases by the multiple of its own power; all its ends become means; all its attainments, helps to new conquests. Its whole abundant harvest is but so much seed wheat, and nothing has limited, and nothing can limit, the amount of ultimate product.

Under the influence of this rapidly increasing knowledge, the people have begun, in all forms of government, to think, and to reason, on affairs of state. Regarding government as an institution for the public good, they demand a knowledge of its operations, and a participation in its exercise. A call for the representative system, wherever it is not enjoyed, and where there is already intelligence enough to estimate its value, is perseveringly made. Where men may speak out, they demand it; where the bayonet is at their throats, they pray for it.

When Louis the Fourteenth said, "I am the state," he expressed the essence of the doctrine of unlimited power. By the rules of that system, the people are disconnected from the state; they are its subjects, it is their lord. These ideas, founded in the love of power, and long supported by the excess and the abuse of it, are yielding, in our age, to other opinions; and the civilized world seems at last to be proceeding to the conviction of that fundamental and manifest truth, that the powers of government are but a trust, and that they cannot be lawfully exercised but for the good of the community. As knowledge is more and more extended, this conviction becomes more and more general. Knowledge, in truth, is the great sun in the firmament. Life and power are scattered with all its beams. The prayer of the Grecian champion, when enveloped in unnatural clouds and darkness, is the appropriate political supplication for the people of every country not yet blessed with free institutions: —

"Dispel this cloud, the light of heaven restore,
Give me to SEE, —and Ajax asks no more."

We may hope that the growing influence of enlightened sentiment will promote the permanent peace of the world. Wars to maintain family alliances, to uphold or to cast down dynasties, and to regulate successions to thrones, which have occupied so much room in the history of modern times, if not less likely to happen at all, will be less likely to become general and involve many nations, as the great principle shall be more and more established that the interest of the world peace, and its first great statute that every nation possesses the power of establishing a government for itself. But public opinion has attained also an influence over governments which do not admit the popular principle into their organization. A necessary respect for the judgment of the world operates, in some measure, as a control over the most unlimited forms of authority. It is owing, perhaps, to this truth that the interesting struggle of the Greeks has been suffered to go on so long, without a direct interference, either to wrest that country from its present masters, or to execute the system of pacification by force, and, with united strength, lay the neck of Christian and civilized Greek at the foot of the barbarian Turk. Let us thank God that we live in an age when something has influence besides the bayonet, and when the sternest authority does not venture to encounter the scorching power of public reproach. Any attempt of the kind I have mentioned should be met by one universal burst of indignation; the air of the civilized world ought to be made too warm to be comfortably breathed by any one who would hazard it.

It is, indeed, a touching reflection, that, while, in the fulness of our country's happiness, we rear this monument to her honor, we look for instruction in our undertaking to a country which is now in fearful contest, not for works of art or memorials of glory, but for her own existence. Let her be assured that she is not forgotten in the world; that her efforts are applauded, and that constant prayers ascend for her success. And let us cherish a confident hope for her final triumph. If the true spark of religious and civil liberty be kindled, it will burn. Human agency cannot extinguish it. Like the earth's central fire, it may be smothered for a time; the ocean may overwhelm it; mountains may press it down; but its inherent and unconquerable force will heave both the ocean and the land, and at some time or other, in some place or other, the volcano will break out and flame up to heaven.

Among the great events of the half century, we must reckon, certainly, the revolution of South America; and we are not likely to overrate the importance of that revolution, either to the people of the country itself or to the rest of the world. The late Spanish colonies, now independent states, under circumstances less favorable, doubtless, than attended our own revolution, have yet successfully commenced their national existence. They have accomplished the great object of establishing their independence; they are known and acknowledged in the world; and although in regard to their systems of government, their sentiments on religious toleration, and their provision for public instruction, they may have yet much to learn, it must be admitted that they have risen to the condition of settled and established states more rapidly than could have been reasonably anticipated. They already furnish an exhilarating example of the difference between free governments and despotic misrule. Their commerce, at this moment, creates a new activity in all the great marts of the world. They show themselves able, by an exchange of commodities, to bear a useful part in the intercourse of nations.

A new spirit of enterprise and industry begins to prevail; all the great interests of society receive a salutary impulse; and the progress of information not only testifies to an improved condition, but itself constitutes the highest and most essential improvement.

When the battle of Bunker Hill was fought, the existence of South America was scarcely felt in the civilized world. The thirteen little colonies of North America habitually called themselves the "continent." Borne down by colonial subjugation, monopoly, and bigotry, these vast regions of the South were hardly visible above the horizon. But in our day there has been, as it were, a new creation. The southern hemisphere emerges from the sea. Its lofty mountains begin to lift themselves into the light of heaven; its broad and fertile plains stretch out, in beauty, to the eye of civilized man, and at the mighty bidding of the voice of political liberty the waters of darkness retire.

And now, let us indulge an honest exultation in the conviction of the benefit which the example of our country has produced, and is likely to produce, on human freedom and human happiness. Let us endeavor to comprehend in all its magnitude, and to feel in all its importance, the part assigned to us in the great drama of human affairs. We are placed at the head of the system of representative and popular governments. Thus far our example shows that such governments are compatible, not only with respectability and power, but with repose, with peace, with security of personal rights, with good laws, and a just administration.

We are not propagandists. Wherever other systems are preferred, either as being thought better in themselves, or as better suited to existing conditions, we leave the preference to be enjoyed. Our history hitherto proves, however, that the popular form is practicable, and that with wisdom and knowledge men may govern themselves; and the duty incumbent on us is to preserve the consistency of this cheering example, and take care that nothing may weaken its authority with the world. If, in our case, the representative system ultimately fail, popular governments must be pronounced impossible. No combination of circumstances more favorable to the experiment can ever be expected to occur. The last hopes of mankind, therefore, rest with us; and if it should be proclaimed that our example had become an argument against the experiment, the knell of popular liberty would be sounded throughout the earth.

These are excitements to duty; but they are not suggestions of doubt. Our history and our condition, all that is gone before us, and all that surrounds us, authorize the belief that popular governments, though subject to occasional variations, in form perhaps not always for the better, may yet, in their general character, be as durable and permanent as other systems. We know, indeed, that in our country any other is impossible. The principle of free governments adheres to the American soil. It is bedded in it, immovable as its mountains.

And let the sacred obligations which have devolved on this generation, and on us, sink deep into our hearts. Those who established our liberty and our government are daily dropping from among us. The great trust now descends to new hands. Let us apply ourselves to that which is presented to us, as our appropriate object. We can win no laurels in a war for independence. Earlier and worthier hands have gathered them all. Nor are there places for us by the side of Solon, and Alfred, and other founders of states. Our fathers have filled them. But there remains to us a great duty of defence and preservation; and there is opened to us, also, a noble pursuit, to which the spirit of the times strongly invites us. Our proper business is improvement. Let our age be the age of improvement. In a day of peace, let us advance the arts of peace and the works of peace. Let us develop the resources of our land, call forth its powers, build up its institutions, promote all its great interests, and see whether we also, in our day and generation, may not perform something worthy to be remembered. Let us cultivate a true spirit of union and harmony. In pursuing the great objects which our condition points out to us, let us act under a settled conviction, and an habitual feeling, that these twenty-four States are one country. Let our conceptions be enlarged to the circle of our duties. Let us extend our ideas over the whole of the vast field in which we are called to act. Let our object be, OUR COUNTRY, OUR WHOLE COUNTRY, AND NOTHING BUT OUR COUNTRY. And, by the blessing of God, may that country itself become a vast and splendid monument, not of oppression and terror, but of Wisdom, of Peace, and of Liberty, upon which the world may gaze with admiration for ever!

DANIEL WEBSTER *First Bunker Hill Monument Address*

The second—and climactic—Bunker Hill address by Daniel Webster here follows (see page 261) :

II

A duty has been performed. A work of gratitude and patriotism is completed. This structure, having its foundations in soil which drank deep of early Revolutionary blood, has at length reached its destined height, and now lifts its summit to the skies.

We have assembled to celebrate the accomplishment of this undertaking, and to indulge afresh in the recollection of the great event which it is designed to commemorate. Eighteen years, more than half the ordinary duration of a generation of mankind, have elapsed since the corner-stone of this monument was laid. The hopes of its projectors rested on voluntary contributions, private munificence, and the general favor of the public. These hopes have not been disappointed. Donations have been made by individuals, in some cases of large amount, and smaller sums have been contributed by thousands. All who regard the object itself as important, and its accomplishment, therefore, as a good attained, will entertain sincere respect and gratitude for the unwearied efforts of the successive presidents, boards of directors, and committees of the Association which has had the general control of the work. The architect, equally entitled to our thanks and commendation, will find other reward, also, for his labor and skill, in the beauty and elegance of the obelisk itself, and the distinction which, as a work of art, it confers upon him.

At a period when the prospects of further progress in the undertaking were gloomy and discouraging, the Mechanic Association, by a most praiseworthy and vigorous effort, raised new funds for carrying it forward, and saw them applied with fidelity, economy, and skill. It is a grateful duty to make public acknowledgments of such timely and efficient aid.

The last effort and the last contribution were from a different source. Garlands of grace and elegance were destined to crown a work which had its commencement in manly patriotism. The winning power of the sex addressed itself to the public, and all that was needed to carry the monument to its proposed height, and to give to it its finish, was promptly supplied. The mothers and the daughters of the land contributed thus, most successfully, to whatever there is of beauty in the monument itself, or whatever of utility and public benefit and gratification there is in its completion.

Of those with whom the plan originated, of erecting on this spot a monument worthy of the event to be commemorated, many are now present; but others, alas! have themselves become subjects of monumental inscription. William Tudor, an accomplished scholar, a distinguished writer, a most amiable man, allied both by birth and sentiment to the patriots of the Revolution, died while on public service abroad, and now lies buried in a foreign land. William Sullivan, a name fragrant of Revolutionary merit, and of public service and public virtue, who himself partook in a high degree of the respect and confidence of the community, and yet was always most loved where best known, has also been gathered to his fathers. And last, George Blake, a lawyer of learning and eloquence, a man of wit and of talent, of social qualities the most agreeable and fascinating, and of gifts which enabled him to exercise large sway over public assemblies, has closed his human career. I know that in the crowds before me there are those from whose eyes tears will flow at the mention of these names. But such mention is due to their general character, their public and private virtues, and especially, on this occasion, to the spirit and zeal with which they entered into the undertaking which is now completed.

I have spoken only of those who are no longer numbered with the living. But a long life, now drawing towards its close, always distinguished by acts of public spirit, humanity, and charity, forming a character which has already become historical, and sanctified by public regard and the affection of friends, may confer even on the living the proper immunity of the dead, and be the fit subject of honorable mention and warm commendation. Of the early projectors of the design of this monument, one of the most prominent, the most zealous, and the most efficient, is Thomas H. Perkins. It was beneath his ever-hospitable roof that those whom I have mentioned, and others yet living and now present, having assembled for the purpose, adopted the first step towards erecting a monument on Bunker Hill. Long may he remain, with unimpaired faculties, in the wide field of his usefulness! His charities have distilled like the dews of heaven; he has fed the hungry, and clothed the naked; he has given sight to the blind; and for such virtues there is a reward on high of which all human memorials, all language of brass and stone, are but humble types and attempted imitations.

Time and nature have had their course, in diminishing the number of those whom we met here on the 17th of June, 1825. Most of the Revolutionary characters then present have since deceased; and Lafayette sleeps in his native land. Yet the name and blood of Warren are with us; the kindred of Putnam are also here; and near me, universally beloved for his character and his virtues, and now venerable for his years, sits the son of the noble-hearted and daring Prescott. Gideon Foster of Danvers, Enos Reynolds of Boxford, Phineas Johnson, Robert

Andrews, Elijah Dresser, Josiah Cleaveland, Jesse Smith, Philip Bagley, Needham Maynard, Roger Plaisted, Joseph Stephens, Nehemiah Porter, and James Harvey, who bore arms for their country, either at Concord and Lexington, on the 19th of April, or on Bunker Hill, all now far advanced in age, have come here today to look once more on the field where their valor was proved, and to receive a hearty outpouring of our respect.

They have long outlived the troubles and dangers of the Revolution; they have outlived the evils arising from the want of a united and efficient government; they have outlived the menace of imminent dangers to the public liberty; they have outlived nearly all their contemporaries; but they have not outlived, they cannot outlive, the affectionate gratitude of their country. Heaven has not allotted to this generation an opportunity of rendering high services, and manifesting strong personal devotion, such as they rendered and manifested, and in such a cause as that which roused the patriotic fires of their youthful breasts, and nerved the strength of their arms. But we may praise what we cannot equal, and celebrate actions which we were not born to perform. *Pulchrum est benefacere reipublicæ; etiam benedicere haud absurdum est.**

The Bunker Hill Monument is finished. Here it stands. Fortunate in the high natural eminence on which it is placed, higher, infinitely higher in its objects and purpose, it rises over the land and over the sea; and, visible, at their homes, to three hundred thousand of the people of Massachusetts, it stands a memorial of the last, and a monitor to the present, and to all succeeding generations. I have spoken of the loftiness of its purpose. If it had been without any other design than the creation of a work of art, the granite of which it is composed would have slept in its native bed. It has a purpose, and that purpose gives it its character. That purpose enrobes it with dignity and moral grandeur. That well-known purpose it is which causes us to look up to it with a feeling of awe. It is itself the orator of this occasion. It is not from my lips, it could not be from any human lips, that that strain of eloquence is this day to flow most competent to move and excite the vast multitudes around me. The powerful speaker stands motionless before us. It is a plain shaft. It bears no inscriptions, fronting to the rising sun, from which the future antiquary shall wipe the dust. Nor does the rising sun cause tones of music to issue from its summit. But at the rising of the sun, and at the setting of the sun; in the blaze of noonday, and beneath the milder effulgence of lunar light; it looks, it speaks, it acts, to the full

---

* "It is a good thing to serve the state; it is not a bad thing to speak well of it."—Sallust's *Catiline,* Chapter III.

comprehension of every American mind, and the awakening of glowing enthusiasm in every American heart. Its silent but awful utterance; its deep pathos, as it brings to our contemplation the 17th of June, 1775, and the consequences which have resulted to us, to our country, and to the world, from the events of that day, and which we know must continue to rain influence on the destinies of mankind to the end of time; the elevation with which it raises us high above the ordinary feelings of life, surpass all that the study of the closet, or even the inspiration of genius, can produce. Today it speaks to us. Its future auditories will be the successive generations of men, as they rise up before it and gather around it. Its speech will be of patriotism and courage; of civil and religious liberty; of free government; of the moral improvement and elevation of mankind; and of the immortal memory of those who, with heroic devotion, have sacrificed their lives for their country.

In the older world, numerous fabrics still exist, reared by human hands, but whose object has been lost in the darkness of ages. They are now monuments of nothing but the labor and skill which constructed them.

The mighty pyramid itself, half buried in the sands of Africa, has nothing to bring down and report to us, but the power of kings and the servitude of the people. If it had any purpose beyond that of a mausoleum, such purpose has perished from history and from tradition. If asked for its moral object, its admonition, its sentiment, its instruction to mankind, or any high end in its erection, it is silent; silent as the millions which lie in the dust at its base and in the catacombs which surround it. Without a just moral object, therefore, made known to man, though raised against the skies, it excites only conviction of power, mixed with strange wonder. But if the civilization of the present race of men, founded, as it is, in solid science, the true knowledge of nature, and vast discoveries in art, and which is elevated and purified by moral sentiment and by the truths of Christianity, be not destined to destruction before the final termination of human existence on earth, the object and purpose of this edifice will be known till that hour shall come. And even if civilization should be subverted, and the truths of the Christian religion obscured by a new deluge of barbarism, the memory of Bunker Hill and the American Revolution will still be elements and parts of the knowledge which shall be possessed by the last man to whom the light of civilization and Christianity shall be extended.

This celebration is honored by the presence of the chief executive magistrate of the Union. An occasion so national in its object and character, and so much connected with that Revolution from which the government sprang at the head of which he is placed, may well receive from him this mark of attention and respect. Well acquainted with Yorktown, the scene of the last great military struggle of the Revolution, his eye now surveys the field of Bunker Hill, the theatre of the first of those important conflicts. He sees where Warren fell, where Putnam, and Prescott, and Stark, and Knowlton, and Brooks fought. He beholds the spot where a thousand trained soldiers of England were smitten to the earth, in the first effort of revolutionary war, by the arm of a bold and determined yeomanry, contending for liberty and their country. And while all assembled here entertain towards him sincere personal good wishes and the high respect due to his elevated office and station, it is not to be doubted that he enters, with true American feeling, into the patriotic enthusiasm kindled by the occasion which animates the multitudes that surround him.

His Excellency, the Governor of the Commonwealth, the Governor of Rhode Island, and the other distinguished public men whom we have the honor to receive as visitors and guests today, will cordially unite in a celebration connected with the great event of the Revolutionary War.

No name in the history of 1775 and 1776 is more distinguished than that borne by an ex-president of the United States whom we expected to see here, but whose ill health prevents his attendance. Whenever popular rights were to be asserted, an Adams was present; and when the time came for the formal Declaration of Independence, it was the voice of an Adams that shook the halls of Congress. We wish we could have welcomed to us this day the inheritor of Revolutionary blood, and the just and worthy representative of high Revolutionary names, merit, and services.

Banners and badges, processions and flags, announce to us that amidst this uncounted throng are thousands of natives of New England now residents in other states. Welcome, ye kindred names, with kindred blood! From the broad savannas of the South, from the newer regions of the West, from amidst the hundreds of thousands of men of Eastern origin who cultivate the rich valley of the Genesee, or live along the chain of the Lakes, from the mountains of Pennsylvania, and from the thronged cities of the coast, welcome, welcome! Wherever else you may be strangers, here you are all at home. You assemble at this shrine of liberty, near the family altars at which your earliest devotions were paid to Heaven, near to the temples of worship first entered by you, and near to the schools and colleges in which your education was received. You come hither with a glorious ancestry of liberty. You bring names which are on the rolls of Lexington, Concord, and Bunker Hill. You come, some of you, once more to be embraced by an aged Revolutionary father, or to receive another, perhaps a last, blessing, bestowed in love and tears, by a mother, yet surviving to witness and to enjoy your prosperity and happiness.

But if family associations and the recollections of the past bring you hither with greater alacrity, and mingle with your greeting much of local attachment and private affection, greeting also be given, free and hearty greeting, to every American citizen who treads this sacred soil with patriotic feeling, and respires with pleasure in an atmosphere perfumed with the recollections of 1775! This occasion is respectable; nay, it is grand, it is sublime, by the nationality of its sentiment. Among the seventeen millions of happy people who form the American community, there is not one who has not an interest in this monument, as there is not one that has not a deep and abiding interest in that which it commemorates.

Woe betide the man who brings to this day's worship feeling less than wholly American! Woe betide the man who can stand here with the fires of local resentments burning, or the purpose of fomenting local jealousies and the strifes of local interests festering and rankling in his heart! Union, established in justice, in patriotism, and the most plain and obvious common interest—union, founded on the same love of liberty, cemented by blood shed in the same common cause—union has been the source of all our glory and greatness thus far, and is the ground of all our highest hopes. This column stands on union. I know not that it might not keep its position, if the American Union, in the mad conflict of human passions, and in the strife of parties and factions, should be broken up and destroyed. I know not that it would totter and fall to the earth, and mingle its fragments with the fragments of Liberty and the Constitution, when state should be separated from state, and faction and dismemberment obliterate for ever all the hopes of the founders of our republic and the great inheritance of their children. It might stand. But who, from beneath the weight of mortification and shame that would oppress him, could look up to behold it? Whose eyeballs would not be seared by such a spectacle? For my part, should I live to such a time, I shall avert my eyes from it for ever.

It is not as a mere military encounter of hostile armies that the battle of Bunker Hill presents its principal claim to attention. Yet, even as a mere battle, there were circumstances attending it extraordinary in character, and entitling it to peculiar distinction. It was fought on this eminence; in the neighborhood of yonder city; in the presence of many more spectators than there were combatants in the conflict. Men, women, and children, from every commanding position, were gazing at the battle, and looking for its results with all the eagerness natural to those who knew that the issue was fraught with the deepest consequences to themselves, personally, as well as to their country. Yet, on the 16th of June, 1775, there was nothing around this hill but verdure and culture. There was, indeed, the note of awful preparation in Boston. There was the Provincial army at Cambridge, with its right flank resting on Dorchester, and its left on Chelsea. But here all was peace. Tranquillity reigned around. On the 17th, everything was changed. On this eminence had arisen, in the night, a redoubt, built by Prescott, and in which he held command. Perceived by the enemy at dawn, it was immediately cannonaded from the floating batteries in the river and from the opposite shore. And then ensued the hurried movement in Boston, and soon the troops of Britain embarked in the attempt to dislodge the Colonists. In an hour everything indicated an immediate and bloody conflict. Love of liberty on one side, proud defiance of rebellion on the other, hopes and fears, and courage and daring, on both sides, animated the hearts of the combatants as they hung on the edge of battle.

I suppose it would be difficult, in a military point of view, to ascribe to the leaders on either side any just motive for the engagement which followed. On the other hand, it could not have been very important to the Americans to attempt to hem the British within the town, by advancing one single post a quarter of a mile; while, on the other hand, if the British found it essential to dislodge the American troops, they had it in their power at no expense of life. By moving up their ships and batteries, they could have completely cut off all communications with the mainland over the Neck, and the forces in the redoubt would have been reduced to a state of famine in forty-eight hours.

But that was not the day for any such consideration on either side! Both parties were anxious to try the strength of their arms. The pride of England would not permit the rebels, as she termed them, to defy her to the teeth; and, without for a moment calculating the cost, the British general determined to destroy the fort immediately. On the other side, Prescott and his gallant followers longed and thirsted for a decisive trial of strength and of courage. They wished a battle, and wished it at once. And this is the true secret of the movements on this hill.

I will not attempt to describe that battle. The cannonading; the landing of the British; their advance; the coolness with which the charge was met; the repulse; the second attack; the second repulse; the burning of Charlestown; and, finally, the closing assault and the slow retreat of the Americans—the history of all these is familiar.

But the consequences of the battle of Bunker Hill were greater than those of any ordinary conflict, although between armies of far greater force, and terminating with more immediate advantage on the one side or the other. It was the first great battle of the Revolution; and not only the first blow, but the blow which determined the contest. It did not, indeed, put an end to the war, but, in the then existing hostile state of feeling, the difficulties could only be referred to the arbitration of the sword. And one thing is certain; that, after the New England troops had shown themselves able to face and repulse the regulars, it was decided that peace never could be established but upon the basis of the independence of the Colonies. When the sun of that day went down, the event of independence was no longer doubtful. In a few days Washington heard of the battle, and he inquired if the militia had stood the fire of the regulars. When told that they had not only stood that fire, but reserved their own till the enemy was within eight rods, and then poured it in with tremendous effect, "Then," exclaimed he, "the liberties of the country are safe!"

The consequences of this battle were just of the same importance as the Revolution itself.

If there was nothing of value in the principles of the American Revolution, then there is nothing valuable in the battle of Bunker Hill and its consequences. But if the Revolution was an era in the history of man favorable to human happiness, if it was an event which marked the progress of man all over the world from despotism to liberty, then this monument is not raised without cause. Then the battle of Bunker Hill is not an event undeserving celebrations, commemorations, and rejoicings, now and in all coming times.

What, then, is the true and peculiar principle of the American Revolution, and of the systems of government which it has confirmed and established? The truth is that the American Revolution was not caused by the instantaneous discovery of principles of government before unheard of, or the practical adoption of political ideas such as had never before entered into the minds of men. It was but the full development of principles of government, forms of society, and political sentiments, the origin of all which lay back two centuries in English and American history.

The discovery of America, its colonization by the nations of Europe, the history and progress of the colonies, from their establishment to the time when the principal of them threw off their allegiance to the respec-

tive states by which they had been planted, and founded governments
of their own, constitute one of the most interesting portions of the annals
of man. These events occupied three hundred years; during which
period civilization and knowledge made steady progress in the Old
World; so that Europe, at the commencement of the nineteenth century,
had become greatly changed from that Europe which began the colonization of America at the close of the fifteenth, or the commencement
of the sixteenth. And what is most material to my present purpose is
that in the progress of the first of these centuries, that is to say, from the
discovery of America to the settlements of Virginia and Massachusetts,
political and religious events took place which most materially affected
the state of society and the sentiments of mankind, especially in England and in parts of Continental Europe. After a few feeble and unsuc-
cessful efforts by England, under Henry the Seventh, to plant colonies in America, no designs of that kind were prosecuted for a long
period, either by the English Government or any of its subjects. Without
inquiring into the causes of this delay, its consequences are sufficiently
clear and striking. England, in this lapse of a century, unknown to herself, but under the providence of God and the influence of events, was
fitting herself for the work of colonizing North America, on such principles and by such men, as should spread the English name and English
blood, in time, over a great portion of the Western hemisphere. The
commercial spirit was greatly fostered by several laws passed in the reign
of Henry the Seventh; and in the same reign encouragement was given
to arts and manufactures in the eastern counties, and some not unimportant modifications of the feudal system took place by allowing the
breaking of entails. These and other measures, and other occurrences,
were making way for a new class of society to emerge, and show itself,
in a military and feudal age: a middle class, between the barons or great
landholders and the retainers of the crown on the one side, and the
tenants of the crown and barons, and agricultural and other laborers, on
the other side. With the rise and growth of this new class of society,
not only did commerce and the arts increase, but better education, a
greater degree of knowledge, juster notions of the true ends of government, and sentiments favorable to civil liberty, began to spread abroad,
and become more and more common. But the plants springing from
these seeds were of slow growth. The character of English society had
indeed begun to undergo a change; but changes of national character
are ordinarily the work of time. Operative causes were, however, evi-
dently in existence, and sure to produce, ultimately, their proper effect.
From the accession of Henry the Seventh to the breaking out of the civil

wars, England enjoyed much greater exemption from war, foreign and domestic, than for a long period before, and during the controversy between the houses of York and Lancaster. These years of peace were favorable to commerce and the arts. Commerce and the arts augmented general and individual knowledge; and knowledge is the only fountain, both of the love and the principles of human liberty.

Other powerful causes soon came into active play. The Reformation of Luther broke out, kindling up the minds of men afresh, leading to new habits of thought, and awakening in individuals energies before unknown even to themselves. The religious controversies of this period changed society as well as religion; indeed, it would be easy to prove, if this occasion were proper for it, that they changed society to a considerable extent, where they did not change the religion of the state. They changed man himself, in his modes of thought, his consciousness of his own powers, and his desire of intellectual attainment. The spirit of commercial and foreign adventure, therefore, on the one hand, which had gained so much strength and influence since the time of the discovery of America, and, on the other, the assertion and maintenance of religious liberty, having their source indeed in the Reformation, but continued, diversified, and constantly strengthened by the subsequent divisions of sentiment and opinion among the Reformers themselves, and this love of religious liberty, drawing after it or bringing along with it, as it always does, an ardent devotion to the principle of civil liberty also, were the powerful influences under which character was formed, and men trained, for the great work of introducing English civilization, English law, and what is more than all, Anglo-Saxon blood, into the wilderness of North America. Raleigh and his companions may be considered as the creatures, principally, of the first of these causes. High-spirited, full of the love of personal adventure, excited, too, in some degree, by the hopes of sudden riches from the discovery of mines of the precious metals, and not unwilling to diversify the labors of settling a colony with occasional cruising against the Spaniards in the West Indian seas, they crossed and recrossed the ocean, with a frequency which surprises us when we consider the state of navigation, and which evinces a most daring spirit.

The other cause peopled New England. The Mayflower sought our shores under no high-wrought spirit of commercial adventure, no love of gold, no mixture of purpose warlike or hostile to any human being. Like the dove from the ark, she had put forth only to find rest. Solemn supplications on the shore of the sea, in Holland, had invoked for her, at her departure, the blessings of Providence. The stars which guided her were the unobscured constellations of civil and religious liberty. Her deck was the altar of the living God. Fervent prayers on bended knees, mingled, morning and evening, with the voices of ocean and the sighing of the wind in her shrouds. Every prosperous breeze, which, gently swelling her sails, helped the Pilgrims onward in their course, awoke new anthems of praise; and when the elements were wrought into fury, neither the tempest, tossing their fragile bark like a feather, nor the darkness and howling of the midnight storm, ever disturbed, in man or woman, the firm and settled purpose of their souls, to undergo all, and to do all, that the meekest patience, the boldest resolution, and the highest trust in God could enable human beings to suffer or to perform.

Some differences may, doubtless, be traced at this day between the descendants of the early colonists of Virginia and those of New England, owing to the different influences and different circumstances under which the respective settlements were made, but only enough to create a pleasing variety in the midst of a general family resemblance.

> "Facies non omnibus una,
> Nec diversa tamen; qualem decet esse sororum." *

But the habits, sentiments, and objects of both soon became modified by local causes, growing out of their condition in the New World, and as this condition was essentially alike in both, and as both at once adopted the same general rules and principles of English jurisprudence, and became accustomed to the authority of representative bodies, these differences gradually diminished. They disappeared by the progress of time and the influence of intercourse. The necessity of some degree of union and cooperation to defend themselves against the savage tribes tended to excite in them mutual respect and regard. They fought together in the wars against France. The great and common couse of the Revolution bound them to one another by new links of brotherhood; and at length the present constitution of government united them happily and gloriously, to form the great republic of the world, and bound up their interests and fortunes, till the whole earth sees that there is now for them, in present possession as well as in future hope, but "One Country, One Constitution, and One Destiny."

The colonization of the tropical region, and the whole of the southern parts of the continent, by Spain and Portugal, was conducted on other principles, under the influence of other motives, and followed by far different consequences. From the time of its discovery, the Spanish

* "They have not at all the same appearance, and yet not altogether different, as it should be with sisters."—Ovid's *Metamorphoses*, Book II, line 13.

Government pushed forward its settlements in America, not only with vigor, but with eagerness; so that, long before the first permanent English settlement had been accomplished in what is now the United States, Spain had conquered Mexico, Peru, and Chile, and stretched her power over nearly all the territory she ever acquired on this continent. The rapidity of these conquests is to be ascribed in a great degree to the eagerness, not to say the rapacity, of those numerous bands of adventurers who were stimulated by individual interests and private hopes to subdue immense regions, and take possession of them in the name of the Crown of Spain. The mines of gold and silver were the incitements to these efforts, and accordingly settlements were generally made, and Spanish authority established immediately on the subjugation of territory, that the native population might be set to work by their new Spanish masters in the mines. From these facts, the love of gold—gold not produced by industry, nor accumulated by commerce, but gold dug from its native bed in the bowels of the earth, and that earth ravished from its rightful possessors by every possible degree of enormity, cruelty, and crime—was long the governing passion in Spanish wars and Spanish settlements in America. Even Columbus himself did not wholly escape the influence of this base motive. In his early voyages we find him passing from island to island, inquiring everywhere for gold; as if God had opened the New World to the knowledge of the Old only to gratify a passion equally senseless and sordid, and to offer up millions of an unoffending race of men to the destruction of the sword, sharpened both by cruelty and rapacity. And yet Columbus was far above his age and country. Enthusiastic, indeed, but sober, religious, and magnanimous; born to great things, and capable of high sentiments, as his noble discourse before Ferdinand and Isabella, as well as the whole history of his life, shows. Probably he sacrificed much to the known sentiments of others, and addressed to his followers motives likely to influence them. At the same time, it is evident that he himself looked upon the world which he discovered as a world of wealth, all ready to be seized and enjoyed.

The conquerors and the European settlers of Spanish America were mainly military commanders and common soldiers. The monarchy of Spain was not transferred to this hemisphere, but it acted in it, as it acted at home, through its ordinary means, and its true representative, military force. The robbery and destruction of the native race was the achievement of standing armies, in the right of the King, and by his authority, fighting in his name, for the aggrandizement of his power and the extension of his prerogatives, with military ideas under arbitrary maxims—a portion of that dreadful instrumentality by which a perfect despotism governs a people. As there was no liberty in Spain, how could liberty be transmitted to Spanish colonies?

The colonists of English America were of the people, and a people already free. They were of the middle, industrious, and already prosperous class, the inhabitants of commercial and manufacturing cities, among whom liberty first revived and respired, after a sleep of a thousand years in the bosom of the Dark Ages. Spain descended on the New World in the armed and terrible image of her monarchy and her soldiery; England approached it in the winning and popular garb of personal rights, public protection, and civil freedom. England transplanted liberty to America; Spain transplanted power. England, through the agency of private companies and the efforts of individuals, colonized this part of North America by industrious individuals, making their own way in the wilderness, defending themselves against the savages, recognizing their right to the soil, and with a general honest purpose of introducing knowledge as well as Christianity among them. Spain swooped on South America like a vulture on its prey. Everything was force. Territories were acquired by fire and sword. Cities were destroyed by fire and sword. Hundreds of thousands of human beings fell by fire and sword. Even conversion to Christianity was attempted by fire and sword.

Behold, then, fellow citizens, the difference resulting from the operation of the two principles! Here, today, on the summit of Bunker Hill, and at the foot of this monument, behold the difference! I would that the fifty thousand voices present could proclaim it with a shout which should be heard over the globe. Our inheritance was of liberty, secured and regulated by law, and enlightened by religion and knowledge; that of South America was of power, stern, unrelenting, tyrannical, military power. And now look to the consequences of the two principles on the general and aggregate happiness of the human race. Behold the results, in all the regions conquered by Cortes and Pizarro, and the contrasted results here. I suppose the territory of the United States may amount to one-eighth, or one-tenth, of that colonized by Spain on this continent; and yet in all that vast region there are but between one and two millions of people of European color and European blood, while in the United States there are fourteen millions who rejoice in their descent from the people of the more northern part of Europe.

But we may follow the difference in the original principle of colonization, and in its character and objects, still further. We must look to moral and intellectual results; we must consider consequences, not only as they show themselves in hastening or retarding the increase of population and the supply of physical wants, but in their civilization, improvement, and happiness. We must inquire what progress has been made in the true science of liberty, in the knowledge of the great principles of self-government, and in the progress of man, as a social, moral, and religious being.

I would not willingly say anything on this occasion discourteous to the new governments founded on the demolition of the power of the Spanish monarchy. They are yet on their trial, and I hope for a favorable result. But truth, sacred truth, and fidelity to the cause of civil liberty compel me to say that hitherto they have discovered quite too much of the spirit of that monarchy from which they separated themselves. Quite too frequent resort is made to military force; and quite too much of the substance of the people is consumed in maintaining armies, not for defence against foreign aggression, but for enforcing obedience to domestic authority. Standing armies are the oppressive instruments for governing the people in the hands of hereditary and arbitrary monarchs. A military republic, a government founded on mock elections and supported only by the sword, is a movement indeed, but a retrograde and disastrous movement, from the regular and old-fashioned monarchial systems. If men would enjoy the blessings of republican government, they must govern themselves by reason, by mutual counsel and consultation, by a sense and feeling of general interest, and by the acquiescence of the minority in the will of the majority, properly expressed; and, above all, the military must be kept, according to the language of our Bill of Rights, in strict subordination to the civil authority. Wherever this lesson is not both learned and practised, there can be no political freedom. Absurd, preposterous is it, a scoff and a satire on free forms of constitutional liberty, for frames of government to be prescribed by military leaders, and the right of suffrage to be exercised at the point of the sword.

Making all allowance for situation and climate, it cannot be doubted by intelligent minds that the difference now existing between North and South America is justly attributable, in a great degree, to political institutions in the Old World and in the New. And how broad that difference is! Suppose an assembly, in one of the valleys or on the side of one of the mountains of the southern half of the hemisphere, to be held this day in the neighborhood of a large city;—what would be the scene presented? Yonder is a volcano, flaming and smoking, but shedding no light, moral or intellectual. At its foot is the mine, sometimes yielding, perhaps, large gains to capital, but in which labor is destined to eternal and unrequited toil, and followed only by penury and beggary. The city is filled with armed men; not a free people, armed and coming forth voluntarily to rejoice in a public festivity, but hireling troops, supported by forced loans, excessive impositions on commerce, or taxes wrung from a half-fed and a half-clothed population. For the great there are palaces covered with gold; for the poor there are hovels of the meanest sort. There is an ecclesiastical hierarchy, enjoying the wealth of princes; but there are no means of education for the people. Do public improvements favor intercourse between place and place? So far from this, the traveller cannot pass from town to town without danger, every mile, of robbery and assassination. I would not overcharge or exaggerate this picture; but its principal features are all too truly sketched.

And how does it contrast with the scene now actually before us? Look round upon these fields; they are verdant and beautiful, well cultivated, and at this moment loaded with the riches of the early harvest. The hands which till them are those of the free owners of the soil, enjoying equal rights, and protected by law from oppression and tyranny. Look to the thousand vessels in our sight, filling the harbor, or covering the neighboring sea. They are the vehicles of a profitable commerce, carried on by men who know that the profits of their hardy enterprise, when they make them, are their own; and this commerce is encouraged and regulated by wise laws, and defended, when need be, by the valor and patriotism of the country. Look to that fair city, the abode of so much diffused wealth, so much general happiness and comfort, so much personal independence, and so much general knowledge, and not undistinguished, I may be permitted to add, for hospitality and social refinement. She fears no forced contributions, no siege or sacking from military leaders of rival factions. The hundred temples in which her citizens worship God are in no danger of sacrilege. The regular administration of the laws encounters no obstacle. The long processions of children and youth, which you see this day, issuing by thousands from her free schools, prove the care and anxiety with which a popular government provides for the education and morals of the people. Everywhere there is order; everywhere there is security. Everywhere the law reaches to the highest and reaches to the lowest, to protect all in their rights, and to restrain all from wrong; and over all hovers Liberty; that Liberty for which our fathers fought and fell on this very spot, with her eye ever watchful and her eagle wing ever wide outspread.

The colonies of Spain, from their origin to their end, were subject to the sovereign authority of the mother country. Their government, as well as their commerce, was a strict home monopoly. If we add to this the established usage of filling important posts in the administration of the colonies exclusively by natives of Old Spain, thus cutting off for ever all hopes of honorable preferment from every man born in the Western hemisphere, causes enough rise up before us at once to account fully for the subsequent history and character of these provinces. The vice-roys and provincial governors of Spain were never at home in their governments in America. They did not feel that they were of the people whom they governed. Their official character and employment have a good deal of resemblance to those of the pro-consuls of Rome, in Asia, Sicily, and Gaul; but obviously no resemblance to those of Carver and Winthrop, and very little to those of the governors of Virginia after that Colony had established a popular House of Burgesses.

The English colonists in America, generally speaking, were men who were seeking new homes in a new world. They brought with them their families and all that was most dear to them. This was especially the case with the colonists of Plymouth and Massachusetts. Many of them were educated men, and all possessed their full share, according to their social condition, of the knowledge and attainments of that age. The distinctive characteristic of their settlement is the introduction of the civilization of Europe into a wilderness, without bringing with it the political institutions of Europe. The arts, sciences, and literature of England came over with the settlers. That great portion of the common law which regulates the social and personal relations and conduct of men came also. The jury came; the *habeas corpus* came; the testamentary power came; and the law of inheritance and descent came also, except that part of it which recognizes the rights of primogeniture, which either did not come at all, or soon gave way to the rule of equal partition of estates among children. But the monarchy did not come, nor the aristocracy, nor the church, as an estate of the realm. Political institutions were to be framed anew, such as should be adapted to the state of things. But it could not be doubtful what should be the nature and character of these institutions. A general social equality prevailed among the settlers, and an equality of political rights seemed the natural, if not the necessary consequence. After forty years of revolution, violence, and war, the people of France have placed at the head of the fundamental instrument of their government, as the great boon obtained by all their sufferings and sacrifices, the declaration that all Frenchmen are equal before the law. What France has reached only by the expenditure of so much blood and treasure, and the perpetration of so much crime, the English colonists obtained by simply changing their place, carrying with them the intellectual and moral culture of Europe, and the personal and social relations to which they were accustomed, but leaving behind their political institutions. It has been said with much vivacity that the felicity of the American colonists consisted in their escape from the past. This is true so far as respects political establishments, but no farther. They brought with them a full portion of all the riches of the past, in science, in art, in morals, religion, and literature. The Bible came with them. And it is not to be doubted, that to the free and universal reading of the Bible, in that age, men were much indebted for right views of civil liberty. The Bible is a book of faith, and a book of doctrine, and a book of morals, and a book of religion, of especial revelation from God; but it is also a book which teaches man his own individual responsibility, his own dignity, and his equality with his fellow man.

Bacon and Locke, and Shakespeare and Milton, also came with the colonists. It was the object of the first settlers to form new political systems, but all that belonged to cultivated man, to family, to neighborhood, to social relations, accompanied them. In the Doric phrase of one of our own historians, "they came to settle on bare creation"; but their settlement in the wilderness, nevertheless, was not a lodgment of nomadic tribes, a mere resting place of roaming savages. It was the beginning of a permanent community, the fixed residence of cultivated men. Not only was English literature read, but English, good English, was spoken and written, before the axe had made way to let in the sun upon the habitations and fields of Plymouth and Massachusetts. And whatever may be said to the contrary, a correct use of the English language is, at this day, more general throughout the United States than it is throughout England herself.

But another grand characteristic is that, in the English Colonies, political affairs were left to be managed by the colonists themselves. This is another fact wholly distinguishing them in character, as it has distinguished them in fortune, from the colonists of Spain. Here lies the foundation of that experience in self-government, which has preserved order, and security, and regularity amidst the play of popular institutions. Home government was the secret of the prosperity of the North American settlements. The more distinguished of the New England colonists, with a most remarkable sagacity and a long-sighted reach into futurity, refused to come to America unless they could bring with them charters providing for the administration of their affairs in this country. They saw from the first the evils of being governed in the New World by a power fixed in the Old. Acknowledging the general superiority of the crown, they still insisted on the right of passing local laws, and of local administration. And history teaches us the justice and the value of this determination in the example of Virginia. The early attempts to settle that colony failed, sometimes with the most melancholy and fatal consequences, from want of knowledge, care, and attention on the part of those who had the charge of their affairs in England; and it was only after the issuing of the third charter that its prosperity fairly commenced. The cause was that by that third charter the people of Virginia, for by this time they deserved to be so called, were allowed to constitute and establish the first popular representative assembly which ever convened on this continent, the Virginia House of Burgesses.

The great elements, then, of the American system of government, originally introduced by the colonists, and which were early in operation, and ready to be developed, more and more, as the progress of events should justify or demand, were—

Escape from the existing political systems of Europe, including its religious hierarchies, but the continued possession and enjoyment of its science and arts, its literature, and its manners;

Home government, or the power of making in the colony the municipal laws which were to govern it;

Equality of rights;

Representative assemblies, or forms of government founded on popular elections.

Few topics are more inviting, or more fit for philosophical discussion, than the effect on the happiness of mankind of institutions founded upon these principles; or, in other words, the influence of the New World upon the Old.

Her obligations to Europe for science and art, laws, literature, and manners, America acknowledges as she ought, with respect and gratitude. The people of the United States, descendants of the English stock, grateful for the treasures of knowledge derived from their English ancestors, admit also, with thanks and filial regard, that among those ancestors, under the culture of Hampden and Sidney and other assiduous friends, that seed of popular liberty first germinated, which on our soil has shot up to its full height, until its branches overshadow all the land.

But America has not failed to make returns. If she has not wholly cancelled the obligation, or equalled it by others of like weight, she has, at least, made respectable advances towards repaying the debt. And she admits that, standing in the midst of civilized nations and in a civilized age, a nation among nations, there is a high part which she is expected to act, for the general advancement of human interests and human welfare.

American mines have filled the mints of Europe with the precious metals. The productions of the American soil and climate have poured out their abundance of luxuries for the tables of the rich, and of necessaries for the sustenance of the poor. Birds and animals of beauty and value have been added to the European stocks; and transplantations from the unequalled riches of our forests have mingled themselves profusely with the elms, and ashes, and druidical oaks of England.

America has made contributions to Europe far more important. Who can estimate the amount, or the value, of the augmentation of the commerce of the world that has resulted from America? Who can imagine to himself what would now be the shock to the Eastern Continent, if the Atlantic were no longer traversable, or if there were no longer American productions, or American markets?

But America exercises influences, or holds out examples, for the consideration of the Old World, of a much higher, because they are of a moral and political character.

America has furnished to Europe proof of the fact that popular institutions, founded on equality and the principle of representation, are capable of maintaining governments able to secure the rights of person, property, and reputation.

America has proved that it is practicable to elevate the mass of mankind—that portion which in Europe is called the laboring, or lower class —to raise them to self-respect, to make them competent to act a part in the great right and great duty of self-government; and she has proved that this may be done by education and the diffusion of knowledge. She holds out an example, a thousand times more encouraging than ever was presented before, to those nine-tenths of the human race who are born without hereditary fortune or hereditary rank.

America has furnished to the world the character of Washington. And, if our American institutions had done nothing else, that alone would have entitled them to the respect of mankind.

Washington! "First in war, first in peace, and first in the hearts of his countrymen!" Washington is all our own! The enthusiastic veneration and regard in which the people of the United States hold him prove them to be worthy of such a countryman; while his reputation abroad reflects the highest honor on his country. I would cheerfully put the question today to the intelligence of Europe and the world, What character of the century, upon the whole, stands out in the relief of history, most pure, most respectable, most sublime? and I doubt not that, by a suffrage approaching to unanimity, the answer would be Washington!

The structure now standing before us, by its uprightness, its solidity, its durability, is no unfit emblem of his character. His public virtues and public principles were as firm as the earth on which it stands; his personal motives as pure as the serene heaven in which its summit is lost. But, indeed, though a fit, it is an inadequate emblem. Towering high above the column which our hands have builded, beheld, not by the inhabitants of a single city or a single state, but by all the families of man, ascends the colossal grandeur of the character and life of Washington. In all the constituents of the one, in all the acts of the other, in all its titles to immortal love, admiration, and renown, it is an American production. It is the embodiment and vindication of our Transatlantic liberty. Born upon our soil, of parents also born upon it; never for a moment having had sight of the Old World; instructed, according to the modes of his time, only in the spare, plain, but wholesome elementary knowledge which our institutions provide for the children of the people; growing up beneath and penetrated by the genuine influences of American society; living from infancy to manhood and age amidst our expanding, but not luxurious civilization; partaking in our great destiny of labor, our long contest with unreclaimed nature and uncivilized man, our agony of glory, the war of Independence, our great victory of peace, the formation of the Union, and the establishment of the Constitution; he is all, all our own! Washington is ours. That crowded and glorious life,

> "Where multitudes of virtues passed along,
> Each pressing foremost, in the mighty throng
> Ambitious to be seen, then making room
> For greater multitudes that were to come,"—

that life was the life of an American citizen.

I claim him for America. In all the perils, in every darkened moment of the state, in the midst of the reproaches of enemies and the misgivings of friends, I turn to that transcendant name for courage and for consolation. To him who denies or doubts whether our fervid liberty can be combined with law, with order, with the security of property, with the pursuits and advancement of happiness; to him who denies that our forms of government are capable of producing exultation of soul and the passion of true glory; to him who denies that we have contributed anything to the stock of great lessons and great examples;—to all these I reply by pointing to Washington!

And now, friends and fellow-citizens, it is time to bring this discourse to a close.

We have indulged in gratifying recollections of the past, in the prosperity and pleasures of the present, and in high hopes for the future.

But let us remember that we have duties and obligations to perform, corresponding to the blessings which we enjoy. Let us remember the trust, the sacred trust, attaching to the rich inheritance which we have received from our fathers. Let us feel our personal responsibility, to the full extent of our power and influence, for the preservation of the principles of civil and religious liberty. And let us remember that it is only religion, and morals, and knowledge, that can make men respectable and happy under any form of government. Let us hold fast the great truth that communities are responsible, as well as individuals; that no government is respectable which is not just; that without unspotted purity of public faith, without sacred public principle, fidelity, and honor, no mere forms of government, no machinery of laws, can give dignity to political society. In our day and generation let us seek to raise and improve the moral sentiment, so that we may look, not for a degraded, but for an elevated and improved future. And when both we and our children shall have been consigned to the house appointed for all living, may love of country and pride of country glow with equal fervor among those to whom our names and our blood shall have descended! And then, when honored and decrepit age shall lean against the base of this monument, and troops of ingenuous youth shall be gathered round it, and when the one shall speak to the other of its objects, the purposes of its construction, and the great and glorious events with which it is connected, there shall rise from every youthful breast the ejaculation, "Thank God, I—I also—AM AN AMERICAN!"

DANIEL WEBSTER *Second Bunker Hill Monument Address*

It is the merest half-truth to say that the statesman achieves his ends through oratory; the politician, through intrigue. But it is whole truth to say that eloquence—the complete fusion of thought and feeling in impassioned utterance—is part and parcel of true oratory and that such oratory has shaped the course of history more than events themselves have done. For eloquence initiates and sustains the spirit that begets event, and it curbs and halts that spirit once the event is proved. The names of those who have inspired greatly— Beaconsfield, Burke, Canning, Chatham, Cobden, Eliot, Erskine, Fox, Gladstone, Macaulay, Mackintosh, Pitt, Pym, of Britain, and Beecher, Brooks, Cochran, Douglas, Everett, Hale, Hay, Henry, Jefferson, Lincoln, Phillips, Washington, Webster, Wilson, of America—endure in memory far beyond the names of those who discharged the event in response to eloquence. The lists pretend nothing by way of completeness. Additions, which could easily be made, would but emphasize the point, namely, that the pen is not only mightier than the sword but that it is also more memorable.

The dear old lady who loved her Shakspere because she found him so full of familiar quotations, would have loved her orator, too, if she had given him the same chance. The literature of oratory stands second to no other in its yield of "familiar quotation," as witness Patrick Henry's "Give me liberty or give me death," Charles Cotesworth Pinckney's "Millions for defense but not one cent for tribute," Ulysses S. Grant's "I propose to fight it out on this line if it takes all summer," Nathan Hale's "I only regret that I have but one life to lose for my country," Wendell Phillips' "War and Niagara thunder to a music of their own," Arthur Wellesley Wellington's "Nothing except a battle lost can be half so melancholy as a battle won," Thomas Jefferson's "We mutually pledge to each other our lives, our fortunes, and our sacred honor," Stephen Decatur's "Our country! In her intercourse with foreign nations may she always be right; but our country, right or wrong," to mention sufficient only for corroboration. The Lincoln, Washington, and Webster speeches reproduced in this book are a never-failing source of quotable inspiration for those in the daily walks of life, and especially for those required to prepare and deliver public speeches.

WORK

Following are a hundred or more suggestions for speeches. Use such as appeal to you. But, better, use subjects of your own—subjects upon which you have a strong desire to convert others to certain points of view. Be sure to state your speech title in a challenging form, that is, in a way to encourage others to take a stand for or against you immediately they hear what you are going to talk about. Your speech title, in other words, should in and of itself, stir and agitate.

Luck isn't everything
The right to be honest
Cowardice should be punishable
Drudgery versus work
The punishment of the kidnaper
Too many columnists

Make movies safe for youth
The radio is a time waster
The radio is an educator
Unfit mankind
Try it again
Make schools of our prisons
There is no such word as *guilty*
Limit the use of the auto
Limit the use of the telephone
Equality of suffrage a hindrance
Weakness of human character, the source of all ills
American dominance of the Western Hemisphere
War is contagious
The discipline of repression
The discipline of liberty
Cremation as a public service
Tariffs, and bad international feeling
The necessity for world free trade
Standing up for the crook
The real crux of character
Crime prevention or substitution—which?
Tax the churches
The honesty of impulses
Wanted: a twentieth-century Napoleon
Slavery still exists
Misplaced loyalties
Misguided loyalists
Treachery among the mighty
The politician versus the statesman
Public office as a trust
The public official as a pirate
Too much luxury
Unlegalized prohibition
Modern youth a failure
Modern youth a divine promise
Grandfather's old-fashioned theories
Too little faith
Outlook—and our boys and girls
Do it—not now—but a little later
The incomparable example of Jefferson
Leadership impossible without character

Is democracy the best form of government?
Those good old maxims!
The decadent age of chicle
Achievement is the only test
Money means everything
Treason to the soul
Commencements are ironic
The trial-and-error fiction
Too much baggage imperils progress
Hobbies for relief
Work with your hands
Hitting the line hard
Regulation of air traffic
Return to the simple life our only salvation
The power of the ballot is nonsense
Permanent peace a fanciful hope
Too much money for roads
Too little money for education
The balance of peace—and war
The veterans as unmatchable inspiration
Holding our own in foreign trade
The disadvantages of coeducation
Sports are overdone in high schools
The justice of the sales tax
The federal regulation of crops
Government control of banks
"Passing up" school opportunities
Making the most of a textbook
The losses of leisure
Capitalizing school activities
Are there any individual rights?
"Shirts" and their policies
Democracy—or what?
The folly of relief contributions
"What's thine is mine"
Unemployment as a sickness
Our present inequitable taxation
The impotence of the press
The power of the press
Railway traffic is antiquated
Who wants to work?

Monopoly, and the price of gasoline
Inventive progress balked by capitalization
The two-house system of government retards progress
More power to the right president
Gettysburg and Chateau-Thierry
The annual scandal of the wheat-corner
The public doesn't care, really
What women have not done at the polls
Reclaiming the western deserts a political disgrace
Too many schools and colleges
The threat of our movie-audience infantilism
Back to the farm at once
The cowardice of city civilization
Studying to pass or to know?
The economic value of the high-school diploma
The automobile as an inducement to waywardness in youth
The university of hard knocks
Is there useless knowledge?
Is poverty necessary?

THE KINDS OF POETRY

THE KINDS OF POETRY

I^T is customary to classify poetry into three kinds—epic, lyric, and dramatic. As a matter of fact there are but two general divisions —narrative and lyric. Epic poetry, like dramatic poetry, is narrative, for they are both story forms. Lyric poetry does not tell a story, but rather analyzes, speculates, broods, hopes, worships, celebrates, and gives expression to still other subjective and introspective moods. There are, therefore, just two main divisions of poetry—poetry that tells story and poetry that does not tell story.

The *epic* gathers up the traditions that have been loosely handed down, and welds them together into a kind of legendary and mythological whole. The Greek word *epos* means word, narrative, song. Epic poetry is sometimes called *heroic poetry*. This is because the epic is a type of poetry in which an almost superhuman hero leads in some great and unified action. He is, at least figuratively, of more than "human size," and is usually himself present in the story, telling the story, achieving the deeds of glory. Every minor episode in the story of an epic must arise from the main or central theme, and all characters besides the hero must be moved by and concerned in the deeds of the hero. Epic poetry is therefore narrative poetry plus. For the epic, if it have any characteristics that distinguish it from simple narrative poetry, must be longer, must be grander in scale and sweep and scope of treatment, and must have impressive singleness and concentration of action.

The epic tells a story for the sake of the story; it makes no moral applications. It contains much dialogue, many songs, numerous episodes, and withal remains simple and direct in construction and keeps the central paramount action well within a comparatively small margin of space and time. The meter of the main story is uniform. It draws upon folk and tribe tradition and mythology, that is, upon the conventions and superstitions that man in the mass has set up for himself in fear and explanation of natural phenomena. It depends upon legend, that is, the hearsay of the past and the fictitious history before the days of civilization. And it is composite, that is, it is an accumulation of lore welded together into a continuous and varied narrative usually by more than one hand. Homer's *Iliad* (the happenings of which take but a few days) and Homer's *Odyssey* (the happenings of which take about six weeks) are the two most famous epics of world literature. Virgil's *Æneid* and John Milton's *Paradise Lost* follow closely upon these for breadth of scope and workmanship. The one great Anglo-Saxon epic is *Beowulf*. It is impossible to reproduce in this book an epic in its entirety. But this very brief précis of *Beowulf* will help to convey something of the spirit and "size" of epic composition:

A Danish King, Hrothgar, erects a great banquet hall. The monster Grendel lives in a nearby fen, and hearing much merrymaking in the new hall, decides to investigate. He enters at midnight and devours thirty of the king's guests and relatives. The hall is useless and desolate until the superhuman hero Beowulf comes from overseas with his men to render succor to Hrothgar in his plight. On his arrival another grand banquet is held, and he and his men are left to guard the hall after the festivities are over. Grendel appears; Beowulf gives battle, and tears out Grendel's mighty arm. The monster disappears and dies in the sea, his disappearance accompanied with an uncanny death dirge. There is much rejoicing among the Danes, and Beowulf takes his leave. But when night comes again the mother of Grendel appears to avenge her son's cruel death, and she kills one of the most loyal of the king's vassals. Beowulf returns, dives into the waters, and slaughters the hideous creature and all her kind. Hrothgar showers him with gifts as he returns to his native Briton to rule over it to the end of his days. Toward the end of his life a dragon comes to ravage his beloved land. His henchmen fail him when they see the dragon belching flame and poison. Only one vassal remains to accompany the old warrior beneath the sea to fight the monster which they kill. But Beowulf, mortally wounded in the battle, dies with a message of exultant courage on his lips. His memorial is a huge mound by the sea where he is buried with song and ceremony.

The *ballad* was originally a folksong derived from the primitive choral dance. It concerns itself, as epic does, with tradition, but with the local tradition of home and village. It therefore lacks the breadth and comprehensiveness of the epic. It is the simple and forward moving narration of homely or adventurous experiences. It is characterized by a frankness and directness and naïveté of delineation that establishes it distinctly as a type. Its metrical form is explained on page 368. Samuel Taylor Coleridge's *The Rime of the Ancient Mariner* is a superstitious ballad of adventure; John Greenleaf Whittier's *Maud Muller* is a Puritan love ballad; certain of Thomas Babington Macaulay's *The Lays of Ancient Rome* are historical ballads. These are all imitations of the old anonymous ballads, such as *Chevy Chase, Sir Patrick Spens, The Twa Sisters,* and the *Robin Hood* cycle. The ballad—especially in its original form—usually has a refrain, and in some instances consists principally of song quality. For this reason, ballads are sometimes classifiable under both epic and lyric.

Like the epic, the ballad is a collection, a poem-story constructed by a people or a folk group. The minstrel formerly sang in the hall of lord and baron, but as he gradually disappeared from this congenial environment and descended among the people, he gathered unto himself their homely tales and songs, and put them together for their entertainment and amusement. The ballad is thus an objective form, living by its story and its wholesome popular tone and spirit. It differs also from the bigger and more powerful epic from which it descends, in the absence of the heroic quality and in its form. Though it may tell of heroic deeds, of romance, of tragic love, of the legends and superstitions of folk and fairy, it does so always for the sake of the deed, never for the exploitation of the hero. One of its most noteworthy qualities is the immediacy with which the story is begun. There is neither introduction nor explanation. Coleridge caught this quality, too, in his admirable ballad imitation *The Rime of the Ancient Mariner* when he began "It is an Ancient Mariner, and he stoppeth one of three." While early ballads are characterized by old and archaic spelling and by quaint phraseology, these are by no means to be regarded as essentials to ballad making. The quality of remoteness is inherent in the simplicity of unfolding the story, in the naïve repetition for emphasis, and in the recurrence of the primitive refrain that reminds of the spontaneous folk movements of simple-minded people. The delight that minstrels took in mere rhetoric is evidenced not only in these refrains but also frequently in mere repetitions to please the ear. Both folk myth and folk legend are likewise imprinted indelibly upon the authentic ballad as marks of identification, many old ballads having spontaneously followed closely upon an event of patriotic grandeur just as war songs are composed today in celebration of a battle or other military event. The confusion of person—first, second, third—and of tenses—present and imperfect— that exists in many early ballads adds testimony to their composite origin as well as to the quality of childlike simplicity and innocence. But these violations of sequence may sometimes make the ballad story difficult to understand.

The following ballad is representative though written as late as the eighteenth century. The story itself exists in Persia, in India, and in China. This Welsh version locates the action near Snowdon in North Wales. *Beth* (Welsh *Bedd*), in the title *Beth Gelêrt,* means grave. Llewelyn was one of the last princes of Wales.

> The spearmen heard the bugle sound,
> 　And cheerily smiled the morn;
> And many a brach, and many a hound,
> 　Obeyed Llewelyn's horn.
>
> And still he blew a louder blast,
> 　And gave a lustier cheer:
> "Come, Gêlert, come, wert never last
> 　Llewelyn's horn to hear.
>
> "Oh, where doth faithful Gêlert roam,
> 　The flower of all his race;
> So true, so brave—a lamb at home,
> 　A lion in the chase?"
>
> 'Twas only at Llewelyn's board
> 　The faithful Gêlert fed;
> He watched, he served, he cheered his lord,
> 　And sentineled his bed.
>
> In sooth he was a peerless hound,
> 　The gift of royal John;
> But now no Gêlert could be found,
> 　And all the chase rode on.

And now, as o'er the rocks and dells
  The gallant chidings rise,
All Snowdon's craggy chaos yells
  The many-mingled cries!

That day Llewelyn little loved
  The chase of hart and hare;
And scant and small the booty proved,
  For Gêlert was not there.

Unpleased, Llewelyn homeward hied,
  When, near the portal seat,
His truant Gêlert he espied,
  Bounding his lord to greet.

But, when he gained his castle-door,
  Aghast the chieftain stood;
The hound all o'er was smeared with gore;
  His lips, his fangs, ran blood.

Llewelyn gazed with fierce surprise;
  Unused such looks to meet,
His favorite checked his joyful guise,
  And crouched and licked his feet.

Onward, in haste, Llewelyn passed,
  And on went Gêlert too;
And still, where'er his eyes he cast,
  Fresh blood-gouts shocked his view.

O'erturned his infant's bed he found,
  With blood-stained covert rent;
And all around, the walls and ground
  With recent blood besprent.

He called his child—no voice replied,—
  He searched with terror wild;
Blood, blood he found on every side,
  But nowhere found his child.

"Hell-hound! my child's by thee devoured,"
  The frantic father cried;
And to the hilt his vengeful sword
  He plunged in Gêlert's side.

His suppliant looks as prone he fell,
  No pity could impart;
But still his Gêlert's dying yell
  Passed heavy o'er his heart.

Aroused by Gêlert's dying yell,
  Some slumberer wakened nigh:
What words the parent's joy could tell
  To hear his infant's cry!

Concealed beneath a tumbled heap
  His hurried search had missed,
All glowing from his rosy sleep,
  The cherub boy he kissed.

Nor scathe had he, nor harm, nor dread,
  But, the same couch beneath,
Lay a gaunt wolf, all torn and dead,
  Tremendous still in death.

Ah, what was then Llewelyn's pain!
  For now the truth was clear;
His gallant hound the wolf had slain,
  To save Llewelyn's heir.

Vain, vain was all Llewelyn's woe:
  "Best of thy kind, adieu!
The frantic blow, which laid thee low,
  This heart shall ever rue."

And now a gallant tomb they raise,
  With costly sculpture deckt;
And marbles, storied with his praise,
  Poor Gêlert's bones protect.

There never could the spearman pass,
    Or forester, unmoved;
There oft the tear-besprinkled grass
    Llewelyn's sorrow proved.

And there he hung his sword and spear,
    And there as evening fell,
In Fancy's ear he oft would hear
    Poor Gêlert's dying yell.

And till great Snowdon's rocks grow old,
    And cease the storm to brave,
The consecrated spot shall hold
    The name of "Gêlert's Grave."

WILLIAM ROBERT SPENCER *Beth Gêlert*

When the style of either epic or ballad is applied to a trivial or petty subject, *mock* or *parody* forms result. Humorous literature abounds in such forms. Alexander Pope's *The Rape of the Lock* and Samuel Butler's *Hudibras* are mock epics; Oliver Goldsmith's *Elegy on the Death of a Mad Dog* and Thomas Gray's *On the Death of a Favorite Cat Drowned in a Tub of Gold Fishes* are mock ballads. The term *mock heroic* is sometimes applied to parodies of these kinds.

Narrative or story poetry exclusive of the epic and the ballad covers a large field and includes many types. One of these is the *metrical romance* in which the glamor and the adventurous spirit of chivalrous love play a large part. It is written in easy and familiar style, less grandly and nobly than the epic, and it plays up the love interest which is almost entirely absent from the epic. Its episodic elements are less closely knitted to the main theme than are similar elements in the epic. Walter Scott's *Marmion* and *The Lady of the Lake* are metrical romances.

The *poetic tale* is a simpler, less pretentious narrative poem than the epic. It takes love or adventure, or both, as its theme, and embodies a complete story. Geoffrey Chaucer's *The Canterbury Tales,* Alfred Tennyson's *Enoch Arden,* Henry Wadsworth Longfellow's *Tales of a Wayside Inn,* and Robert Burns' *Tam O'Shanter* are excellent poetic tales.

The *following* narrative tale or yarn * has much of the ring of the old ballad in it, some of which the refrain is responsible for. The satiric note at the end is conspicuous for the reason that it injects the tragic or unhappy ending—the ending that decidedly does not indicate that "they lived happily ever after." This is by no means the usual outcome of the narrative tale.

> The "Loch Achray" was a clipper tall
> With seven-and-twenty hands in all.
> Twenty to hand and reef and haul,
> A skipper to sail and mates to bawl
> "Tally on to the tackle-fall,
> Heave now 'n' start her, heave 'n' pawl!"
> > Hear the yarn of a sailor,
> > An old yarn learned at sea.
>
> Her crew were shipped and they said "Farewell,
> So-long, my Tottie, my lovely gell;
> We sail to-day if we fetch to hell,
> It's time we tackled the wheel a spell."
> > Hear the yarn of a sailor,
> > An old yarn learned at sea.
>
> The dockside loafers talked on the quay
> The day that she towed down to sea:
> "Lord, what a handsome ship she be!
> Cheer her, sonny boys, three times three!"
> And the dockside loafers gave her a shout
> As the red-funnelled tugboat towed her out;
> They gave her a cheer as the custom is,
> And the crew yelled "Take our loves to Liz—
> Three cheers, bullies, for old Pier Head
> 'N' the bloody stay-at-homes!" they said.
> > Hear the yarn of a sailor,
> > An old yarn learned at sea.
>
> In the grey of the coming on of night
> She dropped the tug at the Tuskar Light,
> 'N' the topsails went to the topmast head
> To a chorus that fairly awoke the dead.

* *The Yarn of the "Loch Achray"* from John Masefield's *Poems*. Used by permission of The Macmillan Company.

She trimmed her yards and slanted South
With her royals set and a bone in her mouth.
> Hear the yarn of a sailor,
> An old yarn learned at sea.

She crossed the Line, and all went well,
They ate, they slept, and they struck the bell
And I give you a gospel truth when I state
The crowd didn't find any fault with the Mate
But one night off the River Plate.
> Hear the yarn of a sailor,
> An old yarn learned at sea.

It freshened up till it blew like thunder
And burrowed her deep lee-scuppers under.
The old man said, "I mean to hang on
Till her canvas busts or her sticks are gone"—
Which the blushing looney did, till at last
Overboard went her mizzen-mast.
> Hear the yarn of a sailor,
> An old yarn learned at sea.

Then a fierce squall struck the "Loch Achray"
And bowed her down to her water-way;
Her main-shrouds gave and her forestay,
And a green sea carried her wheel away;
Ere the watch below had time to dress
She was cluttered up in a blushing mess.
> Hear the yarn of a sailor,
> An old yarn learned at sea.

She couldn't lay-to nor yet pay-off,
And she got swept clean in the bloody trough;
Her masts were gone, and afore you knowed
She filled by the head and down she goed.
Her crew made seven-and-twenty dishes
For the big jack-sharks and the little fishes,
And over their bones the water swishes.
> Hear the yarn of a sailor,
> An old yarn learned at sea.

The wives and girls they watch in the rain
For a ship as won't come home again.
"I reckon it's them head-winds," they say,
"She'll be home to-morrow, if not to-day.
I'll just nip home 'n' I'll air the sheets
'N' buy the fixins 'n' cook the meats
As my man likes 'n' as my man eats."

So home they goes by the windy streets,
Thinking their men are homeward bound
With anchors hungry for English ground,
And the bloody fun of it is, they're drowned!
  Hear the yarn of a sailor,
  An old yarn learned at sea.
   JOHN MASEFIELD *The Yarn of the "Loch Achray"*

  The following metrical romance likewise follows the ballad in both form and spirit. The style is easy and conversational, and the conclusion is true to the standards of chivalry. When all things come out happily and satisfactorily, as in this poem, the work is said to have the "Sunday-school" stop or the "full-dress" ending.

It was the time when lilies blow,
 And clouds are highest up in air,
Lord Ronald brought a lily-white doe
 To give his cousin, Lady Clare.

I trow they did not part in scorn:
 Lovers long-betrothed were they:
They two shall wed the morrow morn;
 God's blessing on the day.

"He does not love me for my birth,
 Nor for my lands, so broad and fair;
He loves me for my own true worth,
 And that is well," said Lady Clare.

In there came old Alice, the nurse,
 Said, "Who was this that went from thee?"
"It was my cousin," said Lady Clare;
 "Tomorrow he weds with me."

"Oh God be thanked!" said Alice, the nurse,
   "That all comes round so just and fair:
Lord Ronald is heir of all your lands,
   And you are not the Lady Clare."

"Are ye out of your mind, my nurse, my nurse?"
   Said Lady Clare, "that ye speak so wild?"
"As God's above," said Alice, the nurse,
   "I speak the truth; you are my child.

"The old earl's daughter died at my breast:
   I speak the truth as I live by bread!
I buried her like my own sweet child,
   And put my child in her stead."

"Falsely, falsely have ye done,
   O mother," she said, "if this be true,
To keep the best man under the sun
   So many years from his due."

"Nay now, my child," said Alice the nurse,
   "But keep the secret for your life,
And all you have will be Lord Ronald's
   When you are man and wife."

"If I'm a beggar born," she said,
   "I will speak out, for I dare not lie:
Pull off, pull off the brooch of gold,
   And fling the diamond necklace by."

"Nay now, my child," said Alice the nurse,
   "But keep the secret all ye can."
She said, "Not so: but I will know,
   If there be any faith in man."

"Nay now, what faith?" said Alice the nurse,
   "The man will cleave unto his right."
"And he shall have it," the lady replied,
   "Though I should die tonight."

"Yet give one kiss to your mother dear!
    Alas, my child, I sinned for thee."
"O mother, mother, mother!" she said,
    "So strange it seems to me.

"Yet here's a kiss for my mother dear,
    My mother dear, if this be so;
And lay your hand upon my head,
    And bless me, mother, ere I go."

She clad herself in a russet gown—
    She was no longer Lady Clare:
She went by dale, and she went by down,
    With a single rose in her hair.

The lily-white doe Lord Ronald had brought
    Leapt up from where she lay,
Dropt her head in the maiden's hand,
    And followed her all the way.

Down stept Lord Ronald from his tower:
    "O Lady Clare, you shame your worth!
Why come you drest like a village maid,
    That are the flower of the earth?"

"If I come drest like a village maid,
    I am but as my fortunes are:
I am a beggar born," she said,
    "And not the Lady Clare."

"Play me no tricks," said Lord Ronald,
    "For I am yours in word and deed.
Play me no tricks," said Lord Ronald,
    "Your riddle is hard to read."

Oh, and proudly stood she up!
    Her heart within her did not fail:
She looked into Lord Ronald's eyes,
    And told him all her nurse's tale.

> He laughed a laugh of merry scorn:
>   He turned and kissed her where she stood:
> "If you are not the heiress born,
>   And I," said he, "the next of blood—
>
> "If you are not the heiress born,
>   And I," said he, "the lawful heir,
> We two will wed tomorrow morn,
>   And you shall still be Lady Clare."
>
> ALFRED TENNYSON Lady Clare

Allegory or allegorical narrative is a didactic type. The word *allegory* comes from two Greek words *allos,* other; *agoreus,* speak; that is, an "other speaking." It means the telling of something under guise of something else in parallel terms. The story in this kind of composition, either prose or poetry, is not based upon legend or mythology, but upon imagination. It is an applied invention. The events are devised for the purpose of exposing or teaching. A few of the greatest allegories in English are Edmund Spenser's *The Faerie Queene,* William Wordsworth's *The Excursion,* Alexander Pope's *Essay on Man* and *Moral Essays* (poetical essays), and John Bunyan's *The Pilgrim's Progress.*

The allegory makes moral appeals through the intellect as a rule, and very often by means of satire. The satirical allegory has in the past been the means whereby social and political reforms were attempted and sometimes effected. It holds up to scorn; it reproves; it inferiorizes. Some authorities contend that satire can never be real poetry—that the true poet cannot descend to the level of the mere reformer. But Samuel Johnson's *London,* George Gordon Noel Byron's *English Bards and Scotch Reviewers,* James Russell Lowell's *The Biglow Papers,* and John Dryden's *Absalom and Achitophel* (to mention but a few of this type), are not only to be classed as poetry but at the time when they were written they were likewise effective poetical weapons in the cause of right and justice.

In *Absalom and Achitophel* Dryden pretended to be telling a Bible story, but he was in fact flaying British politicians and their policies, Charles the Second being disguised as David and Oliver Cromwell as Saul. Done in briefer scope and on less pretentious canvas, the parallel being worked out through the personification of animals, this form of didactic composition is called *fable*. Used for strictly moral or religious purposes, without the use of animals in the parallel, this kind of symbolic composition in prose or poetry is called *parable*. Prose fables and parables are more frequent in literature than poetical ones.

Hidden allegorical meanings are not to be forced into the reading of literature. Most literary prose and poetry must be taken at face value, for pure pleasure and enjoyment. It is easy to build allegory into a poem or a story which the author himself probably never thought of conveying. And there can be no particular harm in a reader's doing this; neither can there be any particular point in his belaboring a piece of literature with an enforced interpretation that may not really be in it. It is sometimes contended that all great literature is allegorical. And this may be so. But allegory in the strict sense of the term applies to literature that is written definitely and consciously in parallel, not to a story or a poem that is written for the sake of enjoyment purely and which may mean one thing to one person and another to another.

Two other kinds of poetry, sometimes classed as narrative and sometimes as lyric, according to the amount of action involved, are *pastoral* and *idyll*. They are at best mixed types. Their mood is one of calm and quiet, growing much more out of setting and situation than out of movement or event, and appealing always to the gentler emotions.

Pastoral is a special mood rather than a special form. Pastoral poetry (as well as prose) deals with the simple life and pursuits of rustics, and accordingly with rustic settings. It is chiefly descriptive and introspective. It has come to include any kind of descriptive poetry that attributes rustic qualities to scenes and to characters that may not in themselves be really rustic. John Keats' *Endymion*, Oliver Goldsmith's *The Deserted Village*, James Thomson's *The Seasons* are pastoral poems. Prose may likewise be pastoral in mood and quality, such for instance as Thomas More's *Utopia*, Philip Sidney's *Arcadia*, Izaak Walton's *The Compleat Angler*. Such works as these are sometimes called prose pastorals; sometimes prose idylls. The term *bucolic* (Greek *boukolos*, cowherd or herdsman; hence, rustic shepherd) is applied to the works of the early pastoral writers—Virgil's *Bucolics*.

The word *idyll* means a little portrait. It was formerly a short descriptive poem of rustic or pastoral setting and event. Now, however, it may be, in addition, any highly wrought description or representation whether in prose or poetry. There are also idylls in music and painting, their mood deciding the classification. The chief characteristic of the idyll may be said to be picturesqueness, and it may have a more pronounced narrative quality than the pastoral. But the two are much the same. Contemplation of the simpler elements of life and their revivification may likewise characterize this form. Henry Wadsworth Longfellow's *Evangeline,* John Greenleaf Whittier's *Snowbound,* Robert Burns' *The Cotter's Saturday Night,* with their mildly narrative and vividly picturesque qualities, are idylls. Alfred Tennyson's *The Idylls of the King* are not ideally titled. They are really legendary epic, and they are too frequently dramatic and emotional and spectacular (rather than merely picturesque) to be regarded as idylls in the strict sense of the term. Like the terms *ode, ballad, sonnet, rondeau,* pastoral and idyll are frequently used in a generic sense for songs and short poems, regardless of their specific type.

The following poem is a pastoral. Note the implied and restrained narrative as well as the picturesque emotional quality:

> On a hill there grows a flower,
>   Fair befall the dainty sweet!
> By that flower there is a bower,
>   Where the heavenly Muses meet.
>
> In that bower there is a chair,
>   Fringèd all about with gold;
> Where doth sit the fairest fair,
>   That did ever eye behold.
>
> It is Phyllis fair and bright,
>   She that is the shepherds' joy;
> She that Venus did despite,
>   And did blind her little boy.
>
> This is she, the wise, the rich,
>   And the world desires to see;
> This is *ipsa quae* the which
>   There is none but only she.

Who would not this face admire?
 Who would not this saint adore?
Who would not this sight desire,
 Though he thought to see no more?

O, fair eyes! yet let me see,
 One good look, and I am gone;
Look on me, for I am he,
 Thy poor silly Corydon.

Thou that art the shepherd's queen,
 Look upon thy silly swain;
By thy comfort have been seen
 Dead men brought to life again.

NICHOLAS BRETON *A Pastoral of Phyllis and Corydon*

In epic poetry, while the poet himself tells the story as if he were actually present at the events recounted, he is nevertheless an eyewitness only, not a participant. The epic poem is therefore objective. Most narrative poetry is objective. But when the narrator of the action is himself an actor—perhaps chief actor—in the happenings, and when he tells not only what occurs but also explains the effect of what occurs, upon himself and others, the story is subjective. Lyric poetry is consistently subjective poetry, that is, it almost invariably expresses the emotion and the passion of the writer; it is personal to the experience of the one expressing himself or to the one through whom the poem is expressed. The lyric is somewhat more fluid in its technique than narrative poetry. Its meters are more varied; its rhymes more deliberate and pliable; its subject matter of more comprehensive range. A few forms, such as the sonnet, once one of the most frequently used of lyric vehicles, are fixed within certain mechanical limitations (see page 375), but in the main the author of a lyric has wide choice among a variety of molds into which he may pour his thoughts and emotions. The true lyric is always short and is frequently impressionistic in tone; and it may be applied therefore to almost any subject that comes within the realm of human experience. The term *long lyric* is self-contradictory as well as suggestive of befuddled emotions.

The simple song lyric is the most common of this type. It may be an interpolated song in some novel or play, or it may be written as an independent composition. Roughly there are two groups of song lyrics—sacred or religious, such as hymns, anthems, cantatas (interpolated), psalms, musical collects and responses; secular or nonsacred, such as martial lyrics (those dealing with war), love (madrigal or sentimental lyrics), drink (convivial lyrics), death (dirge), marriage (epithalamium), home (domestic), nature (philosophic or reflective), and so on, the subject, be it casual or otherwise, deciding the classification.

The *madrigal* originally consisted of two or three tercets followed by one or two couplets or a quatrain, but it has come to be applied to any lyric that deals with the subject of love and has an epigrammatic quality of style. It usually has not fewer than eight verses and not more than eleven or twelve. It is commonly imbedded in other forms —novel, play, opera, cantata, oratorio, epic itself. It was formerly sung to an accompaniment on the lyre. The following lyrics will illustrate something of the variety of lyrical subject matter and its treatment:

> My heart has grown rich with the passing of years,
>   I have less need now than when I was young
> To share myself with every comer
>   Or shape my thoughts into words with my tongue.
>
> It is one to me that they come or go
>   If I have myself and the drive of my will,
> And strength to climb on a summer night
>   And watch the stars swarm over the hill.
>
> Let them think I love them more than I do,
>   Let them think I care, though I go alone;
> If it lifts their pride, what is it to me
>   Who am self-complete as a flower or a stone.
>
> <div align="right">Sara Teasdale <i>The Solitary</i> *</div>

> The shutters of my soul are closed
>   And yet within it is not night;
> The fire flames upon the hearth
>   And all the candles are alight.

---

* Used by permission of The Macmillan Company.

So many times you pass my door
    And never pause! Does not one ray
Of urgent brightness filter through
    To bid you stay?

The shutters of my soul are closed;
    In vain I try to fling them wide.
How should you know—who scarcely look—
    The bars are fastened from outside?

How should you guess I sit alone
    Where it is neither night nor day,
Watching the candles burning low,
    Hearing your footsteps die away?

SUSAN TEVIS *To You* *

You see youth dancing down green budding aisles,
You glimpse her dancing limbs, her hair of gold,
The carefree sweet defiance of her smiles,
For you are old.

But I can see her eyes, grey with alarm,
Misty with longings that can find no tongue,
The hooded future clutching at her arm,
For I am young.

THERESA HELBURN *Youth* †

Ye bubbling springs that gentle music makes
    To lovers' plaints with heart-sore throbs immixed,
Whenas my dear this way her pleasure takes,
    Tell her with tears how firm my love is fixed;
And, Philomel, report my timorous fears,
And, Echo, sound my heigh-ho's in her ears:
But if she asks if I for love will die,
Tell her, "Good faith, good faith, good faith,—not I."

THOMAS GREAVES *Madrigal*

---

* Used by permission of *The Poetry Journal.*
† Used by permission of Harper and Brothers.

I heard an old farm-wife,
Selling some barley,
Mingle her life with life
And the name "Charley."

Saying: "The crop's all in,
We're about through now;
Long nights will soon begin,
We're just us two now.

"Twelve bushels at sixty cents,
It's all I carried—
He sickened making fence;
He was to be married—

"It feels like frost was near—
His hair was curly.
The spring was late that year,
But the harvest early."

RIDGELY TORRENCE *The Son* *
(Southern Ohio Market Town)

Serene the silver fishes glide,
Stern-lipped, and pale, and wonder-eyed!
As, through the aged deeps of ocean,
They glide with wan and wavy motion.
They have no pathway where they go,
They flow like water to and fro,
They watch with never-winking eyes,
They watch with staring, cold surprise,
The level people in the air,
The people peering, peering there:
Who wander also to and fro,
And know not why or where they go,
Yet have a wonder in their eyes,
Sometimes a pale and cold surprise.

MAX EASTMAN *At the Aquarium* †

They are all gone away,
The house is shut and still,
There is nothing more to say.

Through broken walls and gray
The winds blow bleak and shrill;
They are all gone away.

Nor is there one today
To speak them good or ill:
There is nothing more to say.

Why is it then we stray
Around that sunken sill?
They are all gone away.

And our poor fancy-play
For them is wasted skill:
There is nothing more to say.

There is ruin and decay
In the House on the Hill:
They are all gone away;
There is nothing more to say.

EDWIN ARLINGTON ROBINSON
The House on the Hill *

I do not pity the old men, fumbling after
The golden bird of love, the purple grapes of laughter;
They drank honey once, they fingered the falcon's hood.
I do not pity the old, with ash in their veins for blood.
It is the young whom I pity, the young who are lovely and cruel,
The young whose lips and limbs are time's quick-colored fuel.
Death can comfort the old; pain, age understands—
Not the tossed bright head of folly, the soft impatient hands.
I do not pity the old men's forgetful tears and mirth.
But the young must eat pomegrante seeds in the darkness under
the earth.

BABETTE DEUTSCH *Pity* †

* Used by permission of Charles Scribner's Sons.
† From Babette Deutsch, *Honey Out of the Rocks*. Used by permission of D. Appleton-Century Company, Inc.

A star looks down at me,
And says: "Here I and you
Stand, each in our degree:
What do you mean to do—
    Mean to do?"

I say: "For all I know,
Wait, and let Time go by,
Till my change come."—"Just so,"
The star says: "So mean I—
    So mean I."
                THOMAS HARDY *Waiting Both* *

Its edges foamed with amethyst and rose,
Withers once more the old blue flower of day:
There where the ether like a diamond glows,
    Its petals fade away.

A shadowy tumult stirs the dusky air;
Sparkle the delicate dews, the distant snows;
The great deep thrills—for through it everywhere
    The breath of Beauty blows.

I saw how all the trembling ages past,
Moulded to her by deep and deeper breath,
Near'd to the hour when Beauty breathes her last
    And knows herself in death.
      "Æ" (GEORGE WILLIAM RUSSELL) *The Great Breath* *

The lyric may be allegorical also. The parallelism by way of didactic "life lesson" is apparent in each of the following. The hymn quality is not lacking in them, and, indeed, the hymn is itself very likely to be an allegorical lyric. Brief allegorical lyrics such as these are sometimes called poetic parables:

    The time you won your town the race
    We chaired you through the market-place;
    Man and boy stood cheering by,
    And home we brought you shoulder-high.

* Used by permission of The Macmillan Company.

Today, the road all runners come,
Shoulder-high we bring you home,
And set you at your threshold down,
Townsman of a stiller town.

Smart lad, to slip betimes away
From fields where glory does not stay
And early though the laurel grows,
It withers quicker than the rose.

Eyes the shady night has shut
Cannot see the record cut,
And silence sounds no worse than cheers
After earth has stopped the ears:

Now you will not swell the rout
Of lads that wore their honours out,
Runners whom renown outran
And the name died before the man.

So set, before its echoes fade,
The fleet foot on the sill of shade,
And hold to the low lintel up
The still-defended challenge-cup.

And round that early-laurelled head
Will flock to gaze the strengthless dead,
And find unwithered on its curls
The garland briefer than a girl's.

A. E. HOUSMAN *To an Athlete Dying Young* *

My life is like a stroll upon the beach,
    As near the ocean's edge as I can go;
My tardy steps its waves sometimes o'er-reach,
    Sometimes I stay to let them overflow.

My sole employment is, and scrupulous care,
    To place my gains beyond the reach of tides,—
Each smoother pebble, and each shell more rare,
    Which Ocean kindly to my hand confides.

* From *A Shropshire Lad.* Used by permission of Dodd, Mead, and Company.

I have but few companions on the shore:
They scorn the strand who sail upon the sea;
Yet oft I think the ocean they've sailed o'er
Is deeper known upon the strand to me.

The middle sea contains no crimson dulse,
Its deeper waves cast up no pearls to view;
Along the shore my hand is on its pulse,
And I converse with many a shipwrecked crew.

HENRY DAVID THOREAU *The Fisher's Boy* *

He entered; but the mask he wore
Concealed his face from me.
Still, something I had seen before
He brought to memory.

"Who art thou? What thy rank, thy name?"
I questioned, with surprise;
"*Thyself*," the laughing answer came,
"*As seen of others' eyes.*"

JOHN BANNISTER TABB *The Stranger* †

How many an acorn falls to die
For one that makes a tree!
How many a heart must pass me by
For one that cleaves to me!

How many a suppliant wave of sound
Must still unheeded roll,
For one low utterance that found
An echo in my soul!

JOHN BANNISTER TABB *Compensation* ‡

By *descriptive lyric* is usually meant a short poem that deals with some scene in nature. The following descriptive lyric is a sonnet of such distinction as to be unique. Study well the pictorial diction of this beautiful poem:

* Used by permission of Houghton Mifflin Company.
† Used by permission of Hale, Cushman, Flint, Inc.
‡ Used by permission of Hale, Cushman, Flint, Inc.

Poets make pets of pretty, docile words:
I love smooth words, like gold-enameled fish
Which circle slowly with a silken swish,
And tender ones, like downy-feathered birds:
Words shy and dappled, deep-eyed deer in herds,
Come to my hand, and playful if I wish,
Or purring softly at a silver dish,
Blue Persian kittens, fed on cream and curds.

I love bright words, words up and singing early;
Words that are luminous in the dark, and sing;
Warm lazy words, white cattle under trees;
I love words opalescent, cool, pearly,
Like midsummer moths, and honied words like bees,
Gilded and sticky, with a little sting.

Elinor Wylie Pretty Words *

The *elegy* is an expression of grief or mourning or melancholy evoked by the contemplation of death. It philosophizes on the uncertainty of life and the problem of immortality. Properly speaking, the elegy is a collective or general form; that is, it treats of death not individually but in the mass, so to say. Thomas Gray's *An Elegy Written in a Country Churchyard* is a true elegy, for it pertains to all those who lie buried in the churchyard at Stoke Poges. But John Milton's *Lycidas* (inspired by the death of Edward King), Percy Bysshe Shelley's *Adonais* (inspired by the death of John Keats), Alfred Tennyson's *In Memoriam* (inspired by the death of Arthur Hallam), Matthew Arnold's *Thyrsis* (inspired by the death of Arthur Hugh Clough) are all individual expressions of mourning, and as such are not elegies in the strict sense of the word, but monodies or threnodies. The *monody* or *threnody* may generalize about death from its special subject of inspiration but it may never forget that special subject. Note the quality and spirit of the first four stanzas of Shelley's *Adonais* given below. The poem is too long for complete reproduction here—there are fifty-five similarly constructed stanzas in all—but you will do well to take it from the library and study it from beginning to end.

* Used by permission of Alfred A. Knopf, Inc.

I.

I weep for Adonais—he is dead!
Oh, weep for Adonais! though our tears
Thaw not the frost which binds so dear a head!
And thou, sad Hour, selected from all years
To mourn our loss, rouse thy obscure compeers,
And teach them thine own sorrow; Say: "With me
Died Adonais; Till the Future dares
Forget the Past, his fate and fame shall be
An echo and a light unto eternity!"

II.

Where wert thou, mighty Mother, when he lay,
When thy Son lay, pierced by the shaft which flies
In darkness? where was lorn Urania
When Adonais died? With veilèd eyes,
'Mid listening Echoes, in her Paradise
She sate, while one, with soft enamoured breath,
Rekindled all the fading melodies,
With which, like flowers that mock the corse beneath,
He had adorned and hid the coming bulk of death.

III.

Oh, weep for Adonais—he is dead!
Wake, melancholy Mother, wake and weep!
Yet wherefore? Quench within their burning bed
Thy fiery tears, and let thy loud heart keep
Like his a mute and uncomplaining sleep;
For he is gone where all things wise and fair
Descend. Oh, dream not that the amorous Deep
Will yet restore him to the vital air;
Death feeds on his mute voice, and laughs at our despair.

IV.

Most musical of mourners, weep again!
Lament anew, Urania!—He died,
Who was the sire of an immortal strain,
Blind, old, and lonely, when his country's pride
The priest, the slave, and the liberticide

Trampled and mocked with many a loathèd rite
Of lust and blood; he went, unterrified,
Into the gulf of death; but his clear Sprite
Yet reigns o'er earth, the third among the sons of light.

The *ode* is a lyric characterized by nobility of sentiment and dignity of style. It was, as originally written, capable of being set to music and chanted by a chorus in strophe and antistrophe movement. The true or *Pindaric ode* (named for the Latin poet Pindar) followed such partitioning and was, thus, regular in form. But Abraham Cowley, in his popularization of the Pindaric ode in his *Pindarics,* broke away from type and established the irregular or pseudo ode. He ignored the ebb-and-flow balance of parts, established irregular and unsystematized lines and meters and rhymes, and used three changes in form to reflect a more impassioned and enraptured subject matter. In these respects the ode is direct ancestor of *vers libre*. Thomas Gray's *Bard* is a Pindaric ode. John Keats' *Ode to a Nightingale* and William Wordsworth's *Ode on the Intimations of Immortality* and Alfred Tennyson's *Ode on the Death of the Duke of Wellington* belong to the second type here explained, the type that is now usually meant when the ode is discussed (see page 378).

All is over and done:
Render thanks to the Giver,
England, for thy son.
Let the bell be toll'd.
Render thanks to the Giver,
And render him to the mould.
Under the cross of gold
That shines over city and river,
There he shall rest forever
Among the wise and the bold.
Let the bell be toll'd:
And a reverent people behold
The towering car, the sable steeds:
Bright let it be with his blazon'd deeds,
Dark in its funeral fold.
Let the bell be toll'd:
And a deeper knell in the heart be knoll'd;
And the sound of sorrowing anthem roll'd

Thro' the dome of the golden cross;
And the volleying cannon thunder his loss;
He knew their voices of old,
For many a time in many a clime
His captain's ear has heard them boom,
Bellowing victory, bellowing doom:
When he with those deep voices wrought,
Guarding realms and kings from shame;
With those deep voices our dead captain taught
The tyrant, and asserts his claim
In that dread sound to the great name,
Which he has worn so pure of blame,
In praise and in dispraise the same,
A man of well-attemper'd frame,
O civic muse, to such a name,
To such a name for ages long,
To such a name,
Preserve a broad approach of fame,
And ever-echoing avenues of song.

ALFRED TENNYSON *Ode on the Death of the
Duke of Wellington*

The so-called *dramatic lyric* is one that suggests or implies action
without openly narrating it. It may be conveyed by means of a group
of pictures or pastels, each marking a definite step forward in the
indirect story. The following * illustrates:

Among the sullen peaks she stood at bay
And paid life's hard account from her small store.
Knowing the code of mountain wives, she bore
The burden of the days without a sigh;
And, sharp against the somber winter sky,
I saw her drive her steers afield each day.

Hers was the hand that sunk the furrows deep
Across the rocky, grudging southern slope.
At first youth left her face, and later hope;
Yet through each mocking spring and barren fall,
She reared her lusty brood, and gave them all
That gladder wives and mothers love to keep.

* From *Skyline and Horizons* by DuBose Heyward, copyright 1924, and reprinted by permission of Farrar & Rinehart.

And when the sheriff shot her eldest son
Beside his still, so well she knew her part,
She gave no healing tears to ease her heart;
But took the blow upstanding, with her eyes
As drear and bitter as the winter skies.
Seeing her then, I thought that she had won.

But yesterday her man returned too soon
And found her tending, with a reverent touch,
One scarlet bloom; and having drunk too much,
He snatched its flame and quenched it in the dirt.
Then, like a creature with a mortal hurt,
She fell, and wept away the afternoon.

DuBose Heyward *The Mountain Woman*

In the epic and the ballad the action is paramount, the characters being dependent upon it, victimized or glorified by it. In many types of drama the opposite is more likely to be the case—the characters may be paramount, may give source to the action, may sustain and direct it. The epic and the ballad tell of the past, though they may do so by the historical present tense. The lyric confines itself principally to the present. The drama unites past with present in setting forth some *typical* action through *typical* characters.

The various forms of the drama and its general characteristics have been explained on pages 119 to 121. Poetic drama, which is in the main tragic, is written principally in blank verse, but this may be relieved by the interpolation of lyrics of different kinds. It reached its height of perfection during the Elizabethan era, and the development of the iambic pentameter verse became a powerful and moving vehicle of poetic expression during that time. It has never since been used so majestically, with such sweep of meaning and emotion, with such beauty of sound and movement. Present-day tragedy is written chiefly in prose, as comedy has for the most part always been.

There are, of course, passages in novels, short-stories, narrative poetry, and in much lyric poetry that are dramatic in quality. But the term *drama* applies to form as well as to content—to the direct dialogue form whereby characters are made to speak directly to and about one another, the author being apparently completely effaced.

The pure form and the pure quality of dramatic expression are naturally found only in the best drama.

Dialogue that alternates line by line equally, rhymed or unrhymed, as below, is called *stichomythia*. It is common to Greek drama; it occurs only occasionally in English drama. Carried to any great extent this kind of dialogue becomes stilted and overbalanced, and thus monotonous. The following illustrates:

Hermia: I frown upon him, yet he loves me still.
Helena: O, that your frowns would teach my smiles such skill!
Hermia: I give him curses, yet he gives me love.
Helena: O, that my prayers could such affection move!
Hermia: The more I hate, the more he follows me.
Helena: The more I love, the more he hateth me.
Hermia: His folly, Helen, is no fault of mine.
Helena: None but your beauty's: Would that fault were mine!

WILLIAM SHAKSPERE *A Midsummer Night's Dream*

Sometimes even a mildly argumentative descriptive lyric may be given reality and vividness through the use of the dialogue form, as the following poem * illustrates; but this must not, of course, be mistaken for drama:

NELLIE.

If I were you, when ladies at the play, sir,
    Beckon and nod, a melodrama through,
I would not turn abstractedly away, sir,
    If I were you!

FRANK.

If I were you, when persons I affected,
    Wait for three hours to take me down to Kew,
I would, at least, pretend I recollected,
    If I were you!

NELLIE.

If I were you, when ladies are so lavish,
    Sir, as to keep me every waltz but two,
I would not dance with *odious* Miss M'Tavish,
    If I were you!

* Used by permission of The Oxford University Press.

FRANK.

If I were you, who vow you cannot suffer
   Whiff of the best,—the mildest "honey-dew,"
I would not dance with smoke-consuming Puffer,
   If I were you!

NELLIE.

If I were you, I would not, sir, be bitter,
   Even to write the "Cynical Review"—

FRANK.

No, I should doubtless find flirtation fitter,
   If I were you!

NELLIE.

Really! You would? Why, Frank, you're quite delightful—
   Hot as Othello, and as black of hue;
Borrow my fan. I would not look so *frightful,*
   If I were you!

FRANK.

"It is the cause." I mean your chaperon is
   Bringing some well-curled juvenile. Adieu!
I shall retire. I'd spare that poor Adonis,
   If I were you!

NELLIE.

Go, if you will. At once! And by express, sir!
   Where shall it be? To China—or Peru?
Go.   I should leave inquirers my address, sir,
   If I were you!

FRANK.

No,—I remain. To stay and fight a duel
   Seems, on the whole, the proper thing to do—
Ah, you are strong—I would not then be cruel,
   If I were you!

NELLIE.

One does not like one's feelings to be doubted—

FRANK.

One does not like one's friends to misconstrue—

NELLIE.

If I confess that I a wee-bit pouted?

FRANK.

I should admit that I was *piqué,* too.

NELLIE.

Ask me to dance! I'd say no more about it,
If I were you!

[Waltz—*Exeunt.*]

AUSTIN DOBSON *Tu Quoque*
(An Idyll in the Conservatory)

Soliloquy is found in all types of dramatic composition, and especially in tragedy which invariably calls for a character's inner searching and meditation. A soliloquy is thinking aloud—talking to oneself. It is spoken with the feeling that no one is hearing what is being said, whereas monologue always presupposes others present to hear what is said and perhaps to act upon it. Marc Antony's speech to the mob in Act IV, scene ii, of *Julius Caesar,* is really a monologue.

Neither soliloquy nor monologue is to be confused with so-called dramatic monologue. This is a lyric or a narrative, or a poem having elements of both in it, that suggests human action with all the vividness of reality. A character speaks to the reader or to a supposed audience or interlocutor, and recounts a happening (narrative) as it takes place or a mood or emotion (lyric) as it is felt. The scene and atmosphere and characterization are dramatically built in by the narrator, that is to say, he stages scenes and actions as he goes along, as a rule using the historical present to give life to the composition, and always presupposes a listener. Robert Browning was a master in this type of poetry, as witness his *Confessions, The Patriot, An Incident of the French Camp, The Bishop Orders his Tomb at Saint Praxed's* (a title suggesting dramatic treatment), and the following, among many other of his poems:

What a pretty tale you told me
  Once upon a time
—Said you found it somewhere (scold me!)
  Was it prose or was it rhyme,
Greek or Latin? Greek, you said,
While your shoulder propped my head.

Anyhow, there's no forgetting
  This much if no more,
That a poet (pray, no petting!)
  Yes, a bard, sir, famed of yore,
Went where suchlike used to go,
Singing for a prize, you know.

Well, he had to sing, nor merely
  Sing but play the lyre;
Playing was important clearly
  Quite as singing: I desire,
Sir, you keep the fact in mind
For a purpose that's behind.

There stood he, while deep attention
  Held the judges round,
—Judges able, I should mention,
  To detect the slightest sound
Sung or played amiss: such ears
Had old judges, it appears!

None the less he sang out boldly,
  Played in time and tune,
Till the judges, weighing coldly
  Each note's worth, seemed, late or soon,
Sure to smile "In vain one tries
Picking faults out: take the prize!"

When, a mischief! Were they seven
  Strings the lyre possessed?
Oh, and afterwards eleven,
  Thank you! Well, sir—who had guessed
Such ill luck in store?—it happed
One of those same seven strings snapped.

All was lost, then! No! a cricket
  (What "cicada"? Pooh)
—Some mad thing that left its thicket
  For mere love of music—flew
With its little heart on fire,
Lighted on the crippled lyre.

So that when (Ah joy!) our singer
  For his truant string
Feels with disconcerted finger,
  What does cricket else but fling
Fiery heart forth, sound the note
Wanted by the throbbing throat?

Ay and, ever to the ending,
  Cricket chirps at need,
Executes the hand's intending,
  Promptly, perfectly,—indeed
Saves the singer from defeat
With her chirrup low and sweet.

Till, at ending, all the judges
  Cry with one assent
"Take the prize—a prize who grudges
  Such a voice and instrument?
Why, we took your lyre for harp,
So it shrilled us forth F sharp!"

Did the conqueror spurn the creature,
  Once its service done?
That's no such uncommon feature
  In the case when Music's son
Finds his Lotte's power too spent
For aiding soul-development.

No! This other, on returning
  Homeward, prize in hand,
Satisfied his bosom's yearning:
  (Sir, I hope you understand!)
—Said "Some record there must be
Of this cricket's help to me!"

So, he made himself a statue:
  Marble stood, life-size;
On the lyre, he pointed at you,
  Perched his partner in the prize;
Never more apart you found
Her, he throned, from him, she crowned.

That's the tale: its application?
  Somebody I know
Hopes one day for reputation
  Thro' his poetry that's—Oh,
All so learned and so wise
And deserving of a prize!

If he gains one, will some ticket,
  When his statue's built,
Tell the gazer " 'T was a cricket
  Helped my crippled lyre, whose lilt
Sweet and low, when strength usurped
Softness' place i' the scale, she chirped?

"For as victory was nighest,
  While I sang and played,—
With my lyre at lowest, highest,
  Right alike,—one string that made
'Love' sound soft was snapt in twain,
Never to be heard again,—

"Had not a kind cricket fluttered,
  Perched upon the place
Vacant left, and duly uttered
  'Love, Love, Love,' whene'er the bass
Asked the treble to atone
For its somewhat sombre drone."

But you don't know music! Wherefore
  Keep on casting pearls
To a—poet? All I care for
  Is—to tell him that a girl's
"Love" comes aptly in when gruff
Grows his singing. (There, enough!)

ROBERT BROWNING *A Tale*

WORK

I. Justify the title of each of the following poems by its mood or form, or both:

> Golden slumber kiss your eyes,
> Smiles awake you when you rise.
> Sleep, pretty wantons, do not cry,
> And I will sing a lullaby:
> Rock them, rock them, lullaby.
>
> Care is heavy, therefore sleep you;
> You are care, and care must keep you.
> Sleep, pretty wantons, do not cry,
> And I will sing a lullaby:
> Rock them, rock them, lullaby.
>
> <div align="right">THOMAS DEKKER <i>Lullaby</i></div>

> Underneath this sable hearse
> Lies the subject of all verse,
> Sidney's sister, Pembroke's mother:
> Death, ere thou hast slain another,
> Fair, and learned, and good as she,
> Time shall throw a dart at thee.
>
> Marble piles let no man raise
> To her name: in after days,
> Some kind woman born as she,
> Reading this, like Niobe
> Shall turn marble, and become
> Both her mourner and her tomb.
>
> <div align="right">WILLIAM BROWNE <i>Epitaph—
On the Countess of Pembroke</i></div>

> Love, if a god thou art,
>   Then evermore thou must
>   Be merciful and just.
> If thou be just, O wherefore doth thy dart
> Wound mine alone, and not my Lady's heart?

If merciful, then why
Am I to pain reserved,
Who have thee truly served;
While she, that by thy power sets not a fly,
Laughs thee to scorn and lives in liberty?

Then, if a god thou wouldst accounted be,
Heal me like her, or else wound her like me.

FRANCIS DAVISON *Madrigal—To Cupid*

Lay me on an anvil, O God!
Beat me and hammer me into a crowbar.
Let me pry loose old walls;
Let me lift and loosen old foundations.
Lay me on an anvil, O God!
Beat me and hammer me into a steel spike.

Drive me into the girders that hold a skyscraper together.
Take red-hot rivets and fasten me into the central girders.
Let me be the great nail holding a skyscraper through blue
      nights into white stars.

CARL SANDBURG *Prayers of Steel* *

If ever age
Remembers youth,
Is it something sharp—
Time's tooth—

Or does it arrive
With sudden might,
Like all of the West
On a windy night—

Out of nothing,
Into the heart,
That leaps and follows
And roars apart;

* From *The Cornhuskers*. Used by permission of Henry Holt and Company.

Till the wind dies
And the world is still. . . .
And teeth begin
To drill, drill?

MARK VAN DOREN *Bitten* *

Through the shrubs as I can crack
  For my lambs, little ones,
    'Mongst many pretty ones,—
Nymphs I mean, whose hair was black
    As the crow:
    Like the snow
Her face and browès shined I ween!—
  I saw a little one,
  A bonny pretty one,
As bright, buxom, and as sheen
    As was she
    On her knee
That lulled the god, whose arrow warms
  Such merry little ones,
  Such fair-faced pretty ones
As dally in love's chiefest harms:
    Such was mine,
    Whose grey eyne
Made me love. I gan to woo
  This sweet little one,
  This bonny pretty one.
I wooed hard a day or two,
    Till she bade
    'Be not sad,
Woo no more, I am thine own,
  Thy dearest little one,
  Thy truest pretty one.'
Thus was faith and firm love shown,
    As behoves
    Shepherd's loves.

ROBERT GREENE *Doran's Jig*

* From *7 P.M. and Other Poems.* Used by permission of Albert and Charles Boni, Inc.

Fear no more the heat o' the sun
    Nor the furious winters' rages;
Thou thy worldly task hast done,
    Home art gone, and ta'en thy wages:
Golden lads and girls all must,
As chimney-sweepers, come to dust.

Fear no more the frown o' the great,
    Thou art past the tyrant's stroke;
Care no more to clothe and eat;
    To thee the reed is as the oak:
The sceptre, learning, physic, must
All follow this, and come to dust.

Fear no more the lightning-flash,
    Nor the all-dreaded thunder-stone;
Fear not slander, censure rash;
    Thou hast finished joy and moan:
All lovers young, all lovers must
Consign to thee, and come to dust.

No exorciser harm thee!
Nor no witchcraft harm thee!
Ghost unlaid forbear thee!
Nothing ill come near thee!
Quiet consummation have,
And renownèd be thy grave.

                WILLIAM SHAKSPERE *Dirge*

II. In your reading of poetry you should aim to get the *feel* or the *touch* of its spirit. Following are some special meters and movements. Explain them. A reviewer once called this a "zephyr lyric." Why?

        Airy, fairy Lilian,
        Flitting, fairy, Lilian,
    When I ask her if she love me,
    Claps her tiny hands above me,
        Laughing all she can;
    She'll not tell me if she love me,
        Cruel little Lilian.

                ALFRED TENNYSON *Lilian*

What is the effect of the initial repetition—*anaphora*—in this poem?

> Who gave me the goods that went since?
> Who raised me the house that sank once?
> Who helped me to gold I spent since?
> Who found me in wine you drank once?

(Chorus, answering) —
> King Charles, and who'll do him right now?
> King Charles, and who's ripe for fight now?
> Give a rouse: here's, in hell's despite now,
> > King Charles!

> > > ROBERT BROWNING *Give a Rouse*

Do you feel an ominous staccato in the following that shocks or frightens? What is the effect of the short final verse of each stanza?

> The waters are flashing,
> The white hail is dashing,
> The lightnings are glancing,
> The hoar-spray is dancing—
> Away!

> The whirlwind is rolling,
> The thunder is tolling,
> The forest is swinging,
> The minster bells ringing—
> Come away!

> The earth is like Ocean,
> Wreck-strewn and in motion;
> Bird, beast, man, and worm,
> Have crept out of the storm—
> Come away!

> > > PERCY BYSSHE SHELLEY *A Ballad*

Can you feel the sheer beauty of this poem? Explain its poetic "points."

> Hush!
> With a sudden gush
> As from a fountain, sings in yonder bush
> The hermit thrush.

Hark!
Did ever lark
With swifter scintillations fling the spark
That fires the dark?

Again,
Like April rain
Of mist and sunshine mingled, moves the strain
O'er hill and plain.

Strong
As love, O Song,
In flame or torrent sweep through life along
O'er grief and wrong.

JOHN BANNISTER TABB *Overflow* *

Can you sense an unpoetic and labored quality in these verses? Can you explain why certain reviewers called these lines the "merest doggerel"?

As Sir Launfal made morn through the darksome gate
He was 'ware of a leper crouched by the same;
Who begged with his hands and moaned as he sate,
And a loathing over Sir Launfal came.

JAMES RUSSELL LOWELL *The Vision of Sir Launfal*

Do you gather the close human touch and the universal sympathy expressed in these verses? Point out words and phrases that contribute to these effects:

I hear America singing, the varied carols I hear,
Those of mechanics, each one singing his as it should be blithe and
    strong,
The carpenter singing his as he measures his plank or beam,
The mason singing his as he makes ready for work, or leaves off work,
The boatman singing what belongs to him in his boat, the deckhand
    singing on the steamboat deck,
The shoemaker singing as he sits on his bench, the hatter singing as he
    stands,

* Used by permission of Hale, Cushman, and Flint, Inc.

The wood-cutter's song, the ploughboy's on his way in the morning, or
    at noon intermission or at sundown,
The delicious singing of the mother, or of the young wife at work, or of
    the girl sewing or washing,
Each singing what belongs to him or her and to none else,
The day what belongs to the day—at night the party of young fellows,
    robust, friendly,
Singing with open mouths their strong melodious songs.

Walt Whitman *I Hear America Singing*
(From *Leaves of Grass*)

Is there anything in the form and movement of the following war
lyrics that stirs and challenges? Is the form well suited to the theme
in each?

There's a tremor in the trenches, there's a tension in the air;
There's a hurry and a scurry and a worry everywhere;
There's a nervousness apparent, there's a sort of last despair,
As the Huns observe the Yankees lining up just over there!

There's a tumult at headquarters, there's a terror 'long the Rhine;
There's a hunting and a shunting and a grunting of the swine;
There's a hounded look upon them, there's a sort of baffled whine,
As the Huns observe the Yankees stretching out their battle-line!

There's a twitching tokens trouble, there's a trembling omens ill;
There's a shaking and a quaking and a breaking of the will;
There's a panic of the spirit, there's a sort of deadening chill,
As the Huns observe the Yankees coming over, dressed to kill!

There's a hand-to-hand encounter, there's a storm of shot and shell;
There's a grabbing and a jabbing and a stabbing with a yell;
There's a poniard in the in'ards, there's a slaughter, grim and fell,
As the Huns are yanked by Yankees into Hun-Deserving hell!

Oliver Opdyke *There's a Reason* *

    Over the top to battle the Hun
      With all of your vigor and verve!
    Thrust your bayonet, aim your gun,
      Steady your hand and nerve.

* Used by permission of *The New York Times*.

Tatter 'em, scatter 'em,
Shatter 'em, batter 'em—
Hand 'em the hell they deserve.

Over the top to slaughter the swine;
O flourish your trusty blade!
Never mind signal or step or line;
Break in a riotous raid.
Jam 'em, ram 'em,
Slam 'em, damn 'em—
Give 'em the hell they have made.

Over the top to finish Fritz
With all of the strafe you know!
Shiver his timbers, blow him to bits;
Don't give the brute a show.
Lash 'em, slash 'em,
Crash 'em, smash 'em—
Pay 'em the hell that you owe!

Over the top to butcher the Boche!
Oh, charge him with skill and speed!
Put an end to their Kultur tosh;
Teach 'em that brigands must bleed.
Tame 'em, shame 'em,
Lame 'em, maim 'em—
Deal 'em the hell that they need!

Over the top for justice and right,
With victory all but won!
Finish the fight, strike with your might,
Every American son.
Mill 'em, grill 'em,
Kill 'em, still 'em—
Send 'em to hell and have done!

OLIVER OPDYKE *Charge* *

* Used by permission of *New York Herald Tribune, Inc.*

VERSE AND STANZA FORMS

VERSE AND STANZA FORMS

WHEN the accents in a line fall at regular intervals or at such intervals as to make reading smooth and musical, it is said to have rhythm. In poetry, word accent and verse or swing accent must fall on the same syllable; otherwise one or the other will be strained or wrenched and will produce an unmusical effect. It is true that the swing of the line in much Shaksperian poetry requires the accenting of a word on a syllable that is not accented today in the prose use of that word. But the pronunciation has changed in the course of centuries and the accent was not wrenched in Shakspere's time. In the following lines the accent is wrenched if the rhythm in the one requires stress upon the last syllable of *sitting,* and in the other upon the last syllable of *player:*

> Thŏu sing'st ālone, sĭtting bў nīght
> Ăs rāimĕnt, ăs songs, ŏf thĕ harp-plāyer

Regular movement in reading matter of any kind anticipates harmonious sounds or euphony, and euphony anticipates rhythmic movement. A pleasant and agreeable sound or note came first in the evolution of music. Then followed another, that blended with it, and melody was born. And then came a number of corresponding and agreeably sounding notes all placed in pleasant and accordant and natural relationship, and harmony resulted. Rhyme is melody and rhythm is harmony. There is melody in every tune. There is also a harmonious arrangement of melodic parts to enrich the tune and give it fully rounded accordance.

Rhythm is measured or metered by the regularity of the rise and fall of its movement. The units of measure or meter are called poetic feet. The act of measuring these units and marking them off into feet is called scanning or scansion. The young student frequently makes the mistake of thinking that scansion means merely the measuring or counting off syllables into equal partitions of accented and unaccented units. Nothing could be more damaging to the composition

349

of verse or to the appreciation of poetry. The mere mechanical count is minor, though it should be made. But the important thing is to determine the stresses in a given verse by the sense of it and by the rules of pronunciation as laid down in the dictionary. Sometimes liberties may be taken with the latter by way of running two syllables together, or slurring. Read the verse aloud, however, with these two considerations in mind and see whether you are conscious of a rhythm—a rhythm that is varied perhaps but nevertheless a rhythm that in no way destroys the sense and the logical way of speaking and pronouncing words, and above all a rhythm that does no violence by way of slighting words important to the meaning. Only after you have done these things—made these investigations— should you attempt to mark the scansion mechanically, and then only as a test of your study of the line.

For our present purposes the unaccented syllables in a verse or line are marked with a curve ‿ and the accented ones with a dash ‾ Words that would be unimportant monosyllabics and syllables that would be unaccented in prose should as a rule have the curve placed over them. The syllables that are left, with the dash above them to indicate major tone values of the line, will almost invariably be found to convey the central idea of the line. Note that in these words, for instance, resides the full meaning of the line:

$$\overline{\text{what}} \qquad \overline{\text{rare}} \qquad \overline{\text{day}} \qquad \overline{\text{June}} \;\; ?$$

If there were no other words to be built into this line, it would nevertheless convey a meaning. Supply the six comparatively unimportant words to complete the line, and you add to the mechanics of rhythm without adding very much if anything to the idea:

$$\overline{\text{And}} \; \overline{\text{what}} \mid \breve{\text{is}} \; \breve{\text{so}} \; \overline{\text{rare}} \mid \breve{\text{as}} \; \breve{\text{a}} \; \overline{\text{day}} \mid \breve{\text{in}} \; \overline{\text{June?}} \mid$$

The vertical lines are used to separate the rhythmic units or feet (see table on page 352).

This is merely one way of arriving at the number of stressed syllables in a verse, and therefore of finding the number of poetic feet. It is valuable for those who are without musical ear. It is by no means the best method for those who have an ear for music. These should read the verse aloud, lilting or singing it, and counting the accents. This audible swing or cadence will be easily countable. The most musical verse gets itself thus automatically measured, and very often by large audiences, even those least musically inclined being "carried along" by the movement. Proportionately as verse is difficult to feel in this way is it said to be labored or studied or pedestrian or prosaic, judged by the highest poetical standards (see page 5). But it must not, on the other hand, be so pat and glib as to sound "machine-made." The most commonly used poetic feet in English versification are named, defined, and illustrated in the table on page 352.

Pyrrhic is a two-syllable foot, both syllables being unaccented. Some authorities do not admit this foot, their contention being that there can be no metrical foot without an accent, or that, by merging, it may be absorbed by the commoner forms. Note:

But fooled | with hope | men fav|or the | deceit

As a rule there is a spondee adjacent to every pyrrhic in English poetry to balance the two unaccented syllables.

Tribrach is a foot of three light or unaccented syllables, as in de ci|pher a ble. But it does not commonly occur, and some authorities declare that it cannot, that is, that it may always be merged with another foot or slurred into a shorter one.

Monometer is verse of one accented syllable. In the first of the examples below the feet are trochaic, and the verse is therefore called *trochaic monometer;* the verse of the second example is *iambic monometer.*

Take me	Here end
Leave me	As just
Shake me	A friend
Grieve me	I must

Monometer is sometimes imbedded in a stanza, that is, placed among other longer verses. When it is left hanging at the end of a stanza it is called "bob-wheel," as:

> Love is a torment of the mind,
> A tempest everlasting;
> And Jove hath made it of a kind
> Not well, nor full, nor fasting.

Table of Poetic Feet

Noun Name	Adjective Form	Number of Syllables	Illustrations	Comment
iambus	iambic	dissyllabic	decéive	This foot blends with anapest.
trochee	trochaic	dissyllabic	hámmer	This foot blends with dactyl.
spondee	spondaic	dissyllabic	chóo-chóo	This foot appears but little in English verse. Few English dissyllabic words are now evenly accented.
anapest	anapestic	trisyllabic	introdúce	This foot blends with iambus.
dactyl	dactylic	trisyllabic	éuphony	This foot blends with trochee.
amphibrach	amphibrachic	trisyllabic	recéption	This foot can usually be merged into iambic, trochaic, anapestic, or dactylic rhythm.
amphimacer	amphimacic	trisyllabic	vís-a-vís	This foot is rare in English verse. English trisyllabic words do not, as a rule, have two syllables evenly accented.

                    Why so?
          More we enjoy it, more it dies;
          If not enjoyed, it sighing cries,
                    Heigh-ho!

                                        THOMAS CAMPION

Dimeter is verse of two accented syllables. The first illustration below is *trochaic dimeter;* the second, *iambic dimeter:*

Tell the | story | Away, | away |
Wave old | Glory | 'Tis break | of day |

Trimeter is verse of three accented syllables. The first illustration below is *iambic trimeter;* the second, *trochaic trimeter:*

          Ŏ Po|et, then, | forbear |
          The loose|lў-san|dalled verse,|
          Choose rath|er thou | to wear |
          The bus|kin-strait | and terse.|

                                        AUSTIN DOBSON

          Every | drop we | sprinkle |
          Smooths a|way a | wrinkle |

Verses in which there is one kind of foot only are said to be written in *pure meter;* those in which two or more kinds of feet occur, in *mixed meter.* The two are blended to a degree in the best poetry. The former continued to great length becomes monotonous and mechanical, and it may induce a person unconsciously to swing his body or tap his foot in time with it. The latter, if it goes to the extreme of mixing three or more different kinds of feet in successive lines, becomes confused and unmusical, and may fall into sheer prose.

Tetrameter is verse of four accented syllables. The first illustration below is mixed *anapestic tetrameter,* sometimes called *galloping meter* because of its short syllables and consequent rapid forward movement; the second is pure *iambic tetrameter:*

I sprang | to the stir|rup, and Jor|is, and he,|
I gal|loped, Dirck gal|loped, we gal|loped all three.|

                                        ROBERT BROWNING

Lŏve gīlds | thē rōs|ĕs ōf | thў līps |
  Ănd flīes | ăbōut | thĕm līke | ă bēe;
Ĭf Ī | ăpprōach | hĕ fōr|wărd skīps,|
    | Ĭ kīss | hĕ stīng|ĕth mē.|

Thomas Lodge

Pentameter is verse of five accented syllables. This form and tetrameter are the two most commonly used meters in English poetry.
Pentameter is adapted to the more stately and heroic themes; tetrameter is the more versatile, and lends itself to the more popular
themes. The first illustration below is *blank verse—unrhymed iambic
pentameter*. The second is an *iambic pentameter couplet;* each may
be called a *distich* (see page 366) :

Ĭn sōoth | Ĭ knōw | nŏt whȳ | Ĭ ām | sŏ sād.|
Ĭt wēa|rĭes mē, | yŏu sāy | ĭt wēa|rĭes yōu.|

William Shakspere

Thĕ glāss | ĭs fūll, | ănd nōw | mў glāss | ĭs rūn,|
Ănd nōw | Ĭ līve,| ănd nōw | mў līfe | ĭs dōne.|

Chidick Tychborne

Hexameter is verse of six accented syllables. These are *iambic
hexameter:*

Fŏr īf | thŏu dīest, | mў Lōve, | Ĭ knōw | nŏt whēre | tŏ gō.|

John Keats

Sŏ dīes | ănd sō | dĭssōlves | ĭn sū|pĕrnăt | ŭral līght.|

John Dryden

Diest in the first example is slurred from dissyllabic into monosyllabic,
and *supernatural* in the second from polysyllabic to quadrisyllabic.

In the longer meters—verse of more than four feet—there is sometimes a break or a pause called *caesura,* in the rhythmic flow of a
verse. This may fall at any point in a line and may even break a
foot, its varied placement in successive lines making for relief in the
monotony of regular movement. It corresponds somewhat to the
rest in music and very often to the emphatic pause in oratory. In
the two examples following it is indicated by the vertical line.
When the caesura occurs after a light or unaccented syllable, as in the

first example below, it is called *feminine caesura;* after an accented syllable, as in the second example, it is called *masculine caesura.*

This is the forest primeval | the murmuring pines and the hemlocks,
HENRY WADSWORTH LONGFELLOW

Through all restraint broke loose | he wings his way,
JOHN MILTON

A half verse occurring here and there among regular ones of equal length is called a *hemistich.* One part of an entire verse divided by the *caesura* is also sometimes called *hemistich.* Note the following:

Tell me where is fancy bred,
Or in the heart or in the head?
How begot, how nourishèd?
Reply, reply.
WILLIAM SHAKSPERE

Heptameter is verse of seven accented syllables. This is mixed *iambic heptameter:*

Oh, East | is East, | and West | is West, | and nev | er the twain | shall meet.
RUDYARD KIPLING

Octameter is verse of eight accented syllables. This is mixed *iambic anapestic octameter* with an initial trochaic:

Inno | cence seethed | in her moth|er's milk | and char|ity set|ting the mar|tyr aflame |
ALFRED TENNYSON

These longer meters—hexameter, heptameter, octameter—occur less commonly in English poetry than the shorter ones. Moreover, they are capable of doubling—hexameter into two trimeters; octameter into two tetrameters; heptameter into one tetrameter and one trimeter. Note the examples above written as double in each case (see also *ballad* on page 368):

So dies and so dissolves
In supernatural light

Oh, East is East, and West is West,
And never the twain shall meet

Innocence seethed in her mother's milk
And charity setting the martyr aflame

It is possible, of course, to construct verses of nine, ten, eleven, and still more poetic feet. Sometimes the longer lines are desirable to indicate suspended thought and extension of connotation. Long syllables and long sounds usually presuppose the longer measures and the consequent slower movement of the line.

It will be noted that the iambus and the anapest predominate in the above examples. So do they also in the field of English poetry generally. They are the popular accents. They are used for the expression of rhymes and rhythms and reasonings that are close and intimate to the hearts of the people. They are the inductive or rising movements leading on to periodic and climactic conclusion. They have a rapid, dramatic, forward swing, and seem to leap from lower to higher place with a dynamic thud. They are, therefore, the narrative accents. Most of the everyday two- and three-syllable verbs are iambic or anapestic: *control, demand, arrive, depart, ascend, remain, reply, assault, introduce, understand, intercede.*

The trochee and the dactyl have the opposite effects. They begin with a dynamic thud, with an arresting note. They are best adapted to martial airs and to themes that emphasize dignity and seriousness. They make a striking and immediate first impression, but are loose and anticlimactic in construction. They are frank, simple, straightforward, impulsive, and primitive in their connotations. They are, perhaps, less the human-interest accents than iambic and anapest, but more the descriptive and reason-why accents. Sentimental songs and children's rhymes are better written in iambic or anapestic rhythms; marching tunes and airs, in trochaic and dactylic. The former are also adapted to humor, to sentiment, and to the lighter vein; the latter, to sedate and more exalted themes. But this is to be taken as tendency, rather than as hard and fast rule. There is much good poetry in which just the opposite applications are made. At the ends of poetic lines, the trochee and the dactyl leave a haunting echoing effect upon the reader's feelings that may better help to fix the theme in memory than the sharp, conclusive note of the iambic and the anapest. The following poetical summary by Coleridge is clarifying:

> Trochee trips from long to short;
> From long to long in solemn sort
> Slow Spondee stalks; strong foot! yet ill able
> Ever to come up with Dactyl trisyllable.
> Iambics march from short to long;
> With a leap and a bound the swift Anapests throng;
> One syllable long, with one short at each side,
> Amphibrachys hastes with a stately stride;—
> First and last being long, middle short, Amphimacer
> Strikes his thundering hoofs like a proud highbred racer.
>
> SAMUEL TAYLOR COLERIDGE Metrical Feet—
Lesson for a Boy

A verse that wants a syllable at the end is called *weak* or *truncated* or *catalectic;* if it lacks a whole foot it is called *brachycatalectic.* Such omissions are sometimes deliberately made for the purpose of a lingering or haunting or echoing effect. Sometimes a catalectic verse is merged with the succeeding verse to form a complete run-on or run-over foot. The thought, too, is preferably run over in such case. A verse that is complete or metrically perfect is called *acatalectic.* The end-stopped quality of such verse signals finality of movement and also very often partition or conclusion of thought. A *hypercatalectic* or *redundant* verse is one that has a superfluous syllable or foot; it may have much the same effects upon the ear as a catalectic foot. Note in the following that the odd unaccented syllable left at the end of the first verse merges with the next to form an anapestic foot, and that the thought is continuous:

> The snow | had begun | in the gloam|ing
> And bus|ily all | the night |

But the light syllable is not always merged in this way. Sometimes the foot is left incomplete to suggest easy and natural pause, just as pause is made in prose, as

> Bright and | yellow, | hard and | cold |

> Listen, my | children, and | you shall | hear |

or

> Listen, | my chil|dren, and you | shall hear |

In Tennyson's *Gareth and Lynette,* when Gareth's mother, Bellicent, urges him to remain home with her instead of going out to the adventurous and uncertain life of knighthood, she uses among other arguments the appealing ones of the safety and protection and *comfort* of home. She promises to find out for him a suitable bride, but her actual words are:

> And seek you out some comfortable bride

The conclusiveness of the iambic meter is notable. It has end-stopped finality. But even more artistic, if possible, is the snug fitting of the word *comfortable* into the metrical swing. Scan the line and you will see that the quadrisyllable is tucked cozily in, without slurring or hovering or wrenching of any kind. This rhythmic echoism characterizes all the best poetry. Combined with dictional echoism—onomatopoeia —it doubles emotional appeal. Marlowe's "Shallow rivers by whose falls Melodious birds sing madrigals" registers the light, clear touch of rippling streams and clear-voiced birds. Shakspere's "Multitudinous sea" feeds the imagination at once with the fullness of the tides and the *busyness* of the waves. Note by way of contrast this harsh, "consonanted" line from Milton's *Lycidas:*

> Grate on their scrannel pipes of wretched straw

This takes the fingers automatically to the ears to stop the discordant sounds. One of Tennyson's most noteworthy devices for getting startling effects is, in the midst of smoothly and rapidly running iambic and anapestic verses, to hammer suddenly and dynamically with a trochee or a dactyl at the beginning of a verse. This is done, of course, when the idea conveyed justifies the sharp hold-up. And observe in the following excerpt how in the fourth line the action of the cataract is reflected in the broken meter of the line, how the rush and tumble of accent is contrasted with the quiet and peaceful movement of the lines preceding the fourth:

> The splendor falls on castle walls,
> And snowy summits old in story
> The long lights shake across the lake
> And the wild cataract leaps in glory.

But it will be noted that the last line contains four accents, as do the others, in spite of its rhythmical onslaught. The adaptation of meter to meaning must not be allowed to break the movement entirely away from the regulation measure. Just as the notes in a bar of music may be of different value and yet follow the same count, so, too, the notes in a verse of poetry may vary in tone and accentual value and still follow the count to which the whole section is written. And this rule applies in a similar way to word accent. The poet does not strain or misplace the correct accent of a word in order to make it fit into his metrical scheme. His problem is to make words as customarily and correctly accented fit easily and naturally into his measure. "Just the words for the meter, just the meter for the words" must be the rule, if the reader's mind and emotion are to be spared jolts. This is one reason why poets are usually better "wordologists" than prose writers, and another reason why prose writers would do well to practice versification.

The rhythmic swing through a poetic work should be kept true to the scale or standard established at the outset. There may be interpolated songs of varied meters, to be sure, but these should be permitted to interrupt only temporarily the set time. *The Merchant of Venice* is written in blank verse. Unrhymed iambic pentameter predominates. But it is not monotonously pure. Besides, short lyrics are introduced; there are some rhymed couplets; even prose occurs. If the poet starts with an iambic tetrameter verse, he thus establishes the time of his selection. If he changes the time abruptly in the middle of it—say, from 2/4 to 3/4—he may throw his dancers out of rhythm, from two-step to waltz. It has been pointed out above in connection with the quotation from Tennyson that the poet started with a four-accented line, and that he thereby not only "set his pace" but that he kept to it even in the passage where he made the metrical form characteristic of the thought pictured. And this applies to some extent to the style of foot as well as to the pace of the line. In general, iambic and anapestic feet keep good company, and trochaic and dactylic. But this is an observation rather than a rule. Lowell's echoing line

The but|tercup catch|es the sun | in its chal|ice

would measure perfectly as amphibrachic tetrameter:

The butter|cup catches | the sun in | its chalice |

but the poem is written in iambic-anapestic-tetrameter time and quantity, and the verse should therefore be measured as hypercatalectic tetrameter.

Rhyme means a correspondence of sounds between two or more syllables or words. The ear decides it; the eye does not do so by any means always. By sight alone, *break* ought to sound like *streak,* but it does not. Rhyme, therefore, is not always to be deduced from spelling. If it could be, we should have fewer bad versifiers. The ear must be nicely attuned to distinctions in sound. *Bees* rhymes perfectly with *fleas* and *frees,* but these words do not rhyme perfectly with *grieves, leaves,* and *sieves. Break* rhymes with *rake, bake,* and *take,* but these words do not rhyme perfectly with *streak, leak,* and *freak.* To make *fab* rhyme with *fad,* or *home* with *cone,* is to evince inaccurate ear. To such an ear occasional discords in music would cause no shock whatever, for it is not sensitively constituted. Now, poetic licence does allow of the rhyming of certain words that are spelled alike but pronounced differently, like *home* and *come* above, just as it allows of the abbreviation of words (*e'er* for *ever*), and of inversion or transposition of grammatical order, and of archaism and word invention, and so on. But the fastidious poetizer—and every beginner should strive to be fastidious—does not avail himself of special privilege in these matters. The less license he takes the better poet he will be. For him, merely assonantal rhyme will not do. Assonance requires that the last accented vowels, along with succeeding vowels, be identical in sound, such as, *fate, take; story, holy.* Genuine rhyme requires, in addition, the identity of sound in succeeding consonants, and it is therefore both assonantal and consonantal—*fate, pate, rate.* W. S. Gilbert deplored the paucity of rhymes in the English language.* While there is a wealth of harmonious sounds among English words, the tongue is nevertheless not rich in rhyming facility. This is the reason for so much hackneyed or monotonous rhyme, as *love, dove; June, tune; boy, joy;* for so much visual or echo or identical rhyme, as *dual, duel; meat, meet; leak, steak;* for so much false or crippled rhyme, as *die, sincerity; praise, lace; smooth, youth.* The identical rhyme that "sounds" a word with itself, as *hold* (noun) and *hold* (verb) is no longer to be tolerated even in doggerel.

* See *Rime* in *Don't Say it,* published by Funk and Wagnalls Company.

Rhymed monosyllabic words, such as *good—wood, might—right, flow—low, run—pun,* are sometimes called *masculine* or *single rhyme;* rhymed dissyllabic words, such as *deceive—receive, happy—snappy, telling—selling,* are called *feminine* or *double rhyme;* rhymed trisyllabic words, such as *attitude—gratitude, vanity—sanity, scornfully—mournfully,* are called *triple rhyme.* Rhymed polysyllabic words, such as *preparation—separation, preferential—deferential, platitudinous—latitudinous,* are called *quadruple* and *quintuple rhyme,* as the case may be. It is not essential that the rhymed syllables all belong to the same words. Some very clever and engaging rhyming devices can be worked out by such combinations as the following: *winsome—within some, down the bay—roundelay, surrender never —pretender ever, recreation—wreck the nation, having struck a hitch in betting—they're reduced to kitchenetting.*

Vowels and the liquid consonants are the most melodious letters for blending into word harmonies. Words and combinations of words that are difficult to pronounce should be avoided for the sake of euphony. And the same word should not be repeated, even in different form, in a sentence except for conscious emphasis. In *Golden glow will make you grow,* we hear principally the agreeable sounds *l, m, n, ow.* But in *Golden glow will make you glow with glowing health* there is surfeit of the *ow* sound. It ceases to be euphonious, like the note on the pianoforte that is monotonously struck by a child.

Rhyme is a most valuable element of poetry, or has been so for many centuries, inasmuch as it sets up through the ear a bond of harmony and understanding—a rapport—between poet and audience. It prevents the poet's becoming too isolated, too apart, from his reader —or, better, his listener—for poetry and especially rhymed poetry must always be regarded as an oral or spoken form. The expectation of concluding rhymes on the part of an audience, moreover, holds suspense and seals satisfaction when the rhyme is suitably and climactically consummated. There are both anticipation and cooperation, then, on the part of the audience, begotten of the stimulus of rhyme. Moreover, rhyme aids memory, leaves lasting impression, and, as above indicated, presupposes agreeable and ingratiating rhythm.

Unrhymed iambic pentameter is called *blank verse.* The most perfect blank verse consists of consecutive lines of iambic pentameter or of iambic slightly mixed with other feet, especially with trochaic at the beginnings of lines. Straightaway iambic pentameter to the extent of several hundred lines would be extremely monotonous and artificial. Blank verse is paragraphed as prose is, by means of indention or extension or blocking, usually by the first. These thought partitions are called verse paragraphs. Both rhymed and unrhymed free verse are also usually paragraphed in this way.

It has been indicated above that poets are sometimes obliged to take liberty not only with the language itself but with the prescribed forms of their poetic vehicle. Such liberty is called *poetic license* (it were better called *poetic liberty*). Both prose writers and poets make deviations from the customary uses of language, consisting mainly of contractions and transpositions. The better the writer, the fewer such deviations found in his work. The true poet never exercises this privilege except for something more important than mere compliance with dictional and grammatical and metrical requirements, such as euphony, impact, variation, emphasis, smoothness, memorableness of epithet, significance of verse movement, preservation of thought in the most economical mold. For these, and for still other effects, he is justified in taking liberty with expression, and he may be forgiven much for doing so provided worthiness of thought compensates. Authorities are agreed that false and imperfect rhymes (see above) are the least forgivable of licenses, and that the use of such misshapen terms as *mayn't* and *sha'n't* and *won't* run close second in defection. Moreover, no poet must abuse his privilege of license. If he thinks that, just because he sits him down to write in rhyme and rhythm, he must invariably write *e'er* for *ever, com' plete* for *com plete', th'* for *the,* and the like, in every instance of their use, or if he feels that he must warp or contract or invert his expression when it may easily be made to conform with grammatical and metrical rule, then he badly mistakes liberty for license. To some extent the poet is a law unto himself, but he may not forget that this is special rather than general law. Following are a few of the poetic liberties that may be taken, all of which may be run down in the excerpts in this chapter and the preceding one.

The following licenses pertain to the individual word:

Archaism is a word or term belonging to old or ancient usage, revived in poetry very often for the sake of bringing the past to life or recreating bygone atmosphere, as *stomake* for *stomach* and *stoppe* for *stop.*

Diaeresis or *dieresis* is the separation into two pronounced syllables, two vowels standing together as a diphthong, as *aëronaut* rather than *æronaut* and *coöperate* rather than *cooperate.* The two dots indicating breakage into syllables are also called dieresis. The breakage caused by the coincidence of the end of a word with the end of a poetic foot is known as poetic dieresis.

Elision is the omission of a letter or a syllable for the sake of euphony or meter. If it is made at the beginning of a word, as *'gan* for *began* and *'neath* for *beneath,* it is called *aphaeresis;* if in the middle of a word, as *e'en* for *even* and *o'er* for *over,* it is called *syncope;* if at the end of a word, as *tho'* for *though* and *th' eternal* for *the eternal,* it is called *apocope.* Where such elision does not take place as in the last illustration, *hiatus* results; that is, if the four full syllables—*the e ter nal*—are required for pronunciation rather than the slurred first two—*th' ter nal.*

Epenthesis is an insertion made in a word to extend it or to secure to it some dialectic quality of pronunciation, as *b-a-a-a-d* for *bad* and *b-a-a-a-h* for *bah.*

Metathesis is the transposition of letters or syllables in a word, or the substitution of one syllable for another, as *Bedlam* for *Bethlehem.*

Mimesis is the attempt to produce a mimicking effect by means of spelling a word in such manner as to suggest actual dialect or other speech characteristic, as *rawther* for *rather* and *te-he* for a giggle.

Paragogue is the addition of a sound or a syllable to a word, as *beholden* for *behold* and *withouten* for *without.* Archaic words are frequently paragogic words, as are those to which diminutive endings are given, as *dearie, Jimmie, sweetie.* The requirement of metrical accent on the last syllable of such words, like *me lo dee'* for *melody* in the old ballads, is a frequently revived license.

Prosthesis is the prefixing of an extra syllable, as *adown* for *down* and *beloved* for *loved.*

Synaeresis or *syneresis* is the merging of two or more syllables into one, as *alyen* for *alien* and *disobedyence* for *disobedience* and *infectshal* for *ineffectual.*

Tmesis is the insertion of a word between members of a fixed compound expression, as *what place soever* for *whatsoever place* and *to God ward* for *toward God.*

The following licenses pertain to words in relationship:

Asyndeton is the omission of connecting words for the purpose of giving pace and vigor to an expression, as *Let us our lives, our souls, our debts, our careful wives, our children, our sins lay on the king.*

Anacoluthon is a change of construction in the midst of an expression, as

> Both turned, and under open sky adored
> The God that made both sky, earth, air, heaven,
> And starry pole. Thou also madest the night,
> Maker Omnipotent, and Thou the day.

Note the change to second person in the third verse. This is less frequently a deliberate license than an evidence of carelessness. But anacoluthon sometimes vivifies one passage in contrast with another.

Ellipsis is the omission of a word or words that may be clearly and easily understood, and thus not be imperative to a construction, as

> In Heaven, yclept Euphrosyne,
> But by men, heart-easing mirth,

that is, by men *called* heart-easing mirth. In ordinary speech and writing ellipsis is of common occurrence, and is more or less expected. In poetry it is a convenience of workmanship as well as a device for emphasis and dramatic effect. The ellipsis in Macbeth's "What! all my pretty chickens and their dam at one fell swoop!" yields a poignancy that would be almost completely lacking in a full-worded expression of the tragic exclamation. In such expression as "Nay, tell me true—but stop, I must not hear!" the ellipsis indicates sudden change of mind or feeling, and is in such use sometimes called *aposiopesis,* from a Greek word meaning quite silent.

Pleonasm is "overfullness" or superfluity of words. As a rule, it is regarded as a fault, especially when it is the result of carelessness, as it usually is. But it may be both impressive and elegant if used skilfully to strengthen discourse by means of repetition or to animate it by keeping certain elements of expression before the mind of a reader or hearer. *Anaphora* is pleonasm at the beginning of successive lines, as

And do you now put on your best attire?
And do you now cull out a holiday?
And do you now strew flowers in his way?

The opposite of anaphora—pleonasm at the end of successive lines or expressions—is called *epistrophe,* as

. . . rapping at my chamber door
. . . tapping at my chamber door

The repetition of "If any, speak; for him have I offended" in Brutus' speech to the citizens is an excellent example of oratorical epistrophe. If a word or a sound is repeated successively for the sake of begetting a mood, the pleonasm is called *epizeuxis,* as

Alone, alone, all, all alone,
Alone on a wide, wide sea.

Polysyndeton is the opposite of *asyndeton,* that is, it is the unnecessary repetition of a conjunction in close succession and in the same construction, as, *Here's health and wealth and luck and pluck.* This makes for emphasis by "placing" or staging every item individually. It is a very accommodating device, too, in making metrical adjustments and compensations.

Enallage is the use of one part of speech for another, as *They fall successive and successive rise* and *Sure some disaster has befell.*

Hyperbation is the transposition of words, usually adjectives and nouns, as *His coward lips did from their color fly* and *He wandered through the forest fell.*

Syllepsis is the use of the same word with different senses in a single expression, usually a verb or a preposition, as *He is the captor of our enemy and our lady's heart.*

A *stanza* is a division of a poem marked off as a rule by some rhyming scheme or system. It is not a thought division necessarily, though in much poetry the stanza-rhyming unit happily parallels the thought units. Sometimes, however, unrhymed verse is partitioned by line groups that may be called stanzas. Technically it is a mistake to call a stanza or a group of lines a verse. A verse is really a single line, and a stanza is a group of interrhymed verses.

A series of stanzas constituting one grand division of a long poem is called a *canto*. Walter Scott partitioned *The Lady of the Lake* into six cantos. Some poets prefer to call such divisions merely parts.

When rhyme occurs in the middle of a verse it is called *middle* or *medial* or *internal* or *leonine rhyme*. When it occurs at the ends of verses it is called *end* or *final* or *external rhyme*. Note that

<blockquote>The feast is *set,* the guests are *met*</blockquote>

becomes a *couplet,* a stanza of two consecutive rhyming verses, or as two such verses rhymed or unrhymed may be called, a *distich.*

<blockquote>
The feast is set,   *a*
The guests are met   *a*
</blockquote>

(Henceforth rhyming plans or systems will be indicated by italicized letters at the ends of verses.)

Below are further examples. The first is called the *heroic couplet* because of its popular use for epic or heroic stories in poetry. It is always written in iambic pentameter. The second and the third are *octosyllabic couplets,* the one in pure meter and the other in mixed:

<blockquote>
Be not the first by whom the new is tried,   *a*
Nor yet the last to lay the old aside.   *a*
ALEXANDER POPE
</blockquote>

<blockquote>
Faustina hath the fairer face,   *a*
And Phyllida the feater grace.   *a*
JOSHUA SYLVESTER
</blockquote>

<blockquote>
Now in her green mantle blythe nature arrays,   *a*
And listens the lambkins that bleat o'er the braes. *a*
ROBERT BURNS
</blockquote>

All of the foregoing are *closed* or *end-stopped* couplets, that is, the second verse completes a thought division and ends with a period or a semicolon. In the *run-on* verses in the following excerpt, the rhymes are completed couplet by couplet but the thought is not:

<blockquote>
Women! who shall one day bear   *a*
Sons to breathe New England air,   *a*
If ye hear, without a blush,   *b*
Deeds to make the roused blood rush   *b*
</blockquote>

Like red lava through your veins,   c
For your sisters now in chains,   c
Answer! are ye fit to be   d
Mothers of the brave and free?   d

JAMES RUSSELL LOWELL

A run-on couplet is said to have *enjambement,* that is, the putting over into a following line of a word or words necessary to complete the sense.

A *tercet* or *triplet* or *tristich* is a stanza of three consecutive rhyming verses. Or it may be three grouped verses, two of which or none of which rhyme, as

Father! The little girl we see   a
Is not, I fancy, so like me;   a
You never hold her on your knee.   a

WALTER SAVAGE LANDOR

A *quatrain* is a stanza of four consecutive verses interrhymed in different ways. It may consist of two consecutive couplets or it may be like any of the following. The example just below is called the *heroic quatrain* or the *elegiac stanza.* It consists of alternately rhymed iambic pentameters, as

Full many a gem of purest ray serene   a
The dark unfathom'd caves of ocean bear,   b
Full many a flower is born to blush unseen,   a
And waste its sweetness on the desert air.   b

THOMAS GRAY

This is called the *In-Memoriam stanza* for the reason that it was the stanza popularized by Alfred Tennyson in his monody *In Memoriam.* The verse is iambic tetrameter, as follows:

Strong Son of God, immortal Love,   a
Whom we, that have not seen thy face,   b
By faith and faith alone embrace,   b
Believing where we cannot prove.   a

ALFRED TENNYSON

This is called the *Omar quatrain.* This stanza came into vogue with Edward Fitz Gerald's use of it in his translation of *The Rubáiyát of Omar Khayyám.* The verse is iambic pentameter, as

Some for the glories of this World; and some   *a*
Sigh for the Prophets' Paradise to come,   *a*
   Ah, take the Cash, and let the Credit go,   *b*
Nor heed the rumble of a distant Drum!   *a*

EDWARD FITZ GERALD

Note that, with the beginning of alternating rhymes in stanza structure, indention may be made in accordance with end-rhymes, or all lines may, as in the couplet and in blank verse, begin on the same margin. The former style is the earlier and the clearer, and is regarded by many as a more beautiful printing arrangement. When the indented style is used, it is imperative that rhymed lines start on exactly the same margin; many rhymes in a stanza therefore means many margins of varying insets.

The *ballad stanza* was formerly a couplet consisting of two iambic heptameter verses. Later each was divided into two, one of iambic tetrameter and one of iambic trimeter. This is sometimes called *common meter*. Note:

The one of them was clad in green, another was clad in pall;   *a*
And then came in Lord Barnard's wife, the fairest amongst
   them all   *a*

   The one of them was clad in green,   *a*
     Another was clad in pall;   *b*
And then came in Lord Barnard's wife,   *c*
    The fairest amongst them all.   *b*

A quatrain having four iambic tetrameters alternately rhymed is called *long meter,* as in:

   Hence away, you Sirens, leave me,   *a*
    And unclasp your wanton arms;   *b*
 Sugared words shall ne'er deceive me   *a*
   Though you prove a thousand charms.   *b*

GEORGE WITHER

A quatrain having three iambic trimeters—verses one, two, and four—and one iambic tetrameter—verse three—alternately rhymed is called *short meter,* as

The world can never give a
The bliss for which we sigh: b
'Tis not the whole of life to live, a
Nor all of death to die. b

James Montgomery

A *quintet* is a stanza of five verses interrhymed according to some definite system. As stanzas increase in length, it will be noted that they are sometimes made up of combinations of shorter stanzas. The quatrain may, for instance, be composed of two couplets; a quintet may consist of a tercet and a couplet. It will be observed also that the greater the number of lines in a stanza, the greater the number of rhyme sounds may be, and the greater the variety of their arrangement. The fewer the sounds used, however, the greater the limitations the poet imposes upon himself. These illustrate:

I have been here before a
But when or how I cannot tell: b
I know the grass beyond the door, a
The sweet keen smell, b
The sighing sound, the lights around the shore. a

Dante Gabriel Rossetti

Go, lovely Rose— a
Tell her that wastes her time and me, b
That now she knows, a
When I resemble her to thee, b
How sweet and fair she seems to be. b

Edmund Waller

You're embarked on a Ship called Can-Be-Done, a
And your orders are Do-It-Now; b
There'll be Storm and Stress to obscure the Sun, a
But a Star will Pilot you, Every One, a
From the Stern of the Craft to the Bow. b

The popular *limerick* is a quintet rhymed *a a b b a,* the two *b* lines being shorter than the other three. Or these may be combined into one long line with internal rhyme:

There was a young lady of Crewe	*a*
Who wanted to make the two two;	*a*
Said the porter: "Don't hurry,	*b*
Or flurry or scurry,	*b*
It's a minute or two to two two."	*a*

or

There was a young lady of Crewe	*a*
Who wanted to make the two two;	*a*
Said the porter: "Don't hurry or flurry or scurry,	*b*
It's a minute or two to two two."	*a*

A *sestet* is a stanza of six consecutive verses interrhymed according to some definite scheme. It may consist of three couplets, of two tercets, of a quatrain and a couplet, of alternating rhymes, and so on.

I wandered lonely as a cloud	*a*
That floats on high o'er vales and hills	*b*
When all at once I saw a crowd,	*a*
A host of golden daffodils;	*b*
Beside the lake, beneath the trees,	*c*
Fluttering and dancing in the breeze.	*c*

WILLIAM WORDSWORTH

Yet what is love, I prithee, say?	*a*
It is a work on holiday,	*a*
It is December matched with May,	*a*
When lusty bloods in fresh array	*a*
Hear ten months after of the play:	*a*
And this is love, as I hear say.	*a*

WALTER RALEIGH

Sing me a story—let it be	*a*
A ballad in swinging melodee	*a*
Of warriors and derring-do;	*b*
Give it a sounding march refrain	*c*
To spread a spirit of might and main	*c*
'Mongst loyal hearts and true.	*b*

Sometimes the last two verses of a sestet constitute a *refrain*, as here:

When thou hast taken thy repast,   *a*
Repose, my babe, on me;   *b*
So may thy mother and thy nurse   *c*
Thy cradle also be.   *b*
Sing lullaby, my little boy,   *d*
Sing lullaby, mine only joy.   *d*

MARTIN PEERSON

A *heptad* or *septet* may consist of a quatrain and a tercet or of two couplets and a tercet; it may follow a specially interrhymed form; it may be written in iambic pentameter to constitute the special Chaucerian stanza known as *rhyme royal:*

Now voucheth safe this day, ere it be night,   *a*
That I of you the blissful sound may hear,   *b*
Or see your colour like the sunnë bright   *a*
That of yellowness haddë never peer.   *b*
Ye be my life! ye be mine heartës steer!   *b*
Queen of comfort and goodë company!   *c*
Beth heavy again or ellës mote I die.   *c*

GEOFFREY CHAUCER

This is the spray the bird clung to,   *a*
Making it blossom with pleasure,   *b*
Ere the high tree-top she sprung to,   *a*
Fit for her nest and her treasure: *b*
Oh, what a hope beyond measure   *b*
Was the poor spray's, which the flying feet hung to—   *a*
So to be singled out, built in, and sung to!   *a*

ROBERT BROWNING

An *octet* consists of eight interrhymed verses. These may, however, be combinations of shorter stanzas.

The four couplets on pages 366 to 367 constitute an octet. The first of the following illustrations is called *ottava rima*. It is the same as rhyme royal with the addition of an extra *a* verse. Observe:

Oh that I had the art of easy writing   *a*
What should be easy reading! could I scale   *b*
Parnassus, where the Muses sit inditing   *a*
Those pretty poems never known to fail,   *b*

How quickly would I print (the world delighting)   *a*
  A Grecian, Syrian, or Assyrian tale;   *b*
And sell you, mix'd with western sentimentalism,   *c*
Some samples of the finest Orientalism.   *c*

GEORGE GORDON NOEL BYRON

  Sweetest love, I do not go   *a*
    For weariness of thee,   *b*
  Nor in hope the world can show   *a*
    A fitter love for me;   *b*
      But since that I   *c*
  Must die at last, 'tis best   *d*
  Thus to use myself in jest,   *d*
    By feigned deaths to die.   *c*

JOHN DONNE

  Out of the dark a shadow,   *a*
    Then, a spark;   *b*
  Out of the cloud a silence,   *c*
    Then, a lark;   *b*
  Out of the heart a rapture,   *d*
    Then, a pain;   *e*
  Out of the dead cold ashes,   *f*
    Life again.   *e*

JOHN BANNISTER TABB *

The *Spenserian stanza* consists of nine verses, the first eight of which are iambic pentameter and the ninth iambic hexameter. The last line is called an *Alexandrine.* Spenser's *Faerie Queene* is written entirely in this stanza, as is also Keats' *The Eve of St. Agnes,* thus:

  Under thy mantle black there hidden lie   *a*
  Light-shunning Theft, and traitorous Intent.   *b*
  Abhorred Bloodshed, and vile Felony,   *a*
  Shameful deceit, and Danger imminent,   *b*
  Foul Horror, and eke hellish Dreariment: *b*
  All these I wot in thy protection be,   *c*
  And light do shun for fear of being shent: *b*
  For light y-like is loathed of them and thee;   *c*
  And all that lewdness love do hate the light to see.   *c*

EDMUND SPENSER

* Used by permission of Hale, Cushman, and Flint, Inc.

St. Agnes Eve—Ah, bitter chill it was!	*a*
The owl, for all his feathers, was a-cold;	*b*
The hare limped trembling through the frozen grass,	*a*
And silent was the flock in woolly fold;	*b*
Numb were the Beadsman's fingers, while he told	*b*
His rosary, and while his frosted breath,	*c*
Like pious incense from a censer old,	*b*
Seemed taking flight for heaven, without a death,	*c*
Past the sweet Virgin's picture, while his prayer he saith.	*c*

JOHN KEATS

In his exquisite *Ode to a Grecian Urn,* Keats expressed his thought in a ten-verse mold, as follows:

Thou still unravished bride of quietness,	*a*
Thou foster-child of Silence and slow Time,	*b*
Sylvan historian, who canst thus express	*a*
A flowery tale more sweetly than our rhyme:	*b*
What leaf-fringed legend haunts about thy shape	*c*
Of deities or mortals, or of both,	*d*
In Tempe or the dales of Arcady?	*e*
What men or gods are these? What maidens loth?	*d*
What mad pursuit? What struggle to escape?	*c*
What pipes and timbrels? What wild ecstasy?	*e*

But stanzas beyond this point, with the exception of the sonnet, are arbitrary arrangements, not observation of conventional rule. Thomas Gray said that the ear cannot hold a stanza of more than nine lines. It is possible, of course, for a poet to group verses into stanzas of any length, and by so doing partition stanza thoughts into short or long units. Tennyson, for instance, paragraphed both thought and rhyme in eleven-verse and twelve-verse stanzas in his *Charge of the Light Brigade* and *Sir Galahad* respectively, as:

Cannon to right of them,	*a*
Cannon to left of them,	*a*
Cannon behind them	*a*
Volleyed and thundered;	*b*
Stormed at with shot and shell,	*c*
While horse and hero fell,	*c*
They that had fought so well	*c*

Came through the jaws of Death,	*d*
Back from the mouth of Hell,	*c*
All that was left of them,	*a*
Left of six hundred.	*b*

My good blade carves the casques of men,	*a*
My tough lance thrusteth sure,	*b*
My strength is as the strength of ten,	*a*
Because my heart is pure.	*b*
The shattering trumpet shrilleth high,	*c*
The hard brands shiver on the steel,	*d*
The splintered spear-shafts crack and fly,	*c*
The horse and rider reel:	*d*
They reel, they roll in clanging lists,	*e*
And when the tide of combat stands,	*f*
Perfume and flowers fall in showers,	*g*
That lightly rain from ladies' hands.	*f*

Note in next to the last verse of the last stanza, how the medial rhyme is made to compensate for the absence of end rhyme.

And Browning, in *My Star*, wrote a verse stanza paragraph of thirteen lines as follows. Note, in addition to the form, the order of lyric progress from nature in the abstract to personal feeling and emotion:

All that I know	*a*
Of a certain star	*b*
Is, it can throw	*a*
(Like the angled spar)	*b*
Now a dart of red,	*c*
Now a dart of blue;	*d*
Till my friends have said	*c*
They would fain see, too,	*d*
My star that dartles the red and the blue!	*d*
Then it stops like a bird; like a flower hangs furled;	*e*
They must solace themselves with the Saturn above it,	*f*
What matter to me if their star is a world?	*e*
Mine has opened its soul to me; therefore I love it.	*f*

The sonnet is a lyric of fourteen verses of iambic pentameter. The thought which is usually complete in itself is partitioned so that the first part falls naturally into the first eight lines, two quatrains or octet (strophe), and the second part into the last six lines, two tercets or sestet (antistrophe). The thought must lend itself easily and gracefully to this ebb and flow. If it does not do so, then it is not a sonnet thought and should probably be expressed in some other form. In the sonnet sequence consisting of many sonnets written on a single subject, the same division is likely to be true of the individual sonnets in the sequence, though the major thought is not completed until the entire set of sonnets is finished. The rhyming systems of the principal sonnet styles are illustrated below. The sestet in the Petrarchan and the Miltonic types, it will be noted, is variable. The strophe of the Shaksperian sonnet consists of twelve verses and the antistrophe of two or a final couplet.

Petrarchan	abbaabba	cdecde
		cdcdcd
		cddece
		cdcdee
Miltonic	abbaabba	cdedce
		cdecde
Spenserian	ababbcbccdcdee	
Shaksperian	ababcdcdefefgg	
Omar	aababbcbccdcdd	

Say from what part of heaven 'twas Nature drew,
   From what idea, that no perfect mold
   To form such features, bidding us behold,
In charms below, what she above could do?
What fountain nymph, what dryad maid e'er threw
   Upon the wind such tresses of pure gold?
   What heart such numerous virtues can unfold?
Although the chiefest all my fond hopes slew.

He for celestial charms may look in vain
   Who has not seen my fair one's radiant eyes,
     And felt their glances pleasingly beguile.
How Love can heal his wounds, then wound again,
   He only knows who knows how sweet her sighs,
     How sweet her converse and how sweet her smile.

PETRARCH

Men call you fair, and you do credit it,
For that yourself ye daily such do see:
But the true fair, that is the gentle wit
And virtuous mind, is much more praised of me:
For all the rest, however fair it be,
Shall turn to naught and lose that glorious hue;
But only that is permanent and free
From frail corruption that doth flesh ensue.
That is true beauty; that doth argue you
To be divine, and born of heavenly seed;
Derived from that fair Spirit from whom all true
And perfect beauty did at first proceed:
He only fair, and what he fair hath made;
All other fair, like flowers, untimely fade.

EDMUND SPENSER

Let me not to the marriage of true minds
Admit impediments. Love is not love
Which alters when it alteration finds,
Or bends with the remover to remove:
O no; it is an ever-fixèd mark,
That looks on tempests, and is never shaken;
It is the star to every wandering bark,
Whose worth's unknown, although his height be taken.
Love's not Time's fool, though rosy lips and cheeks
Within his bending sickle's compass come;
Love alters not with his brief hours and weeks,
But bears it out even to the edge of doom.
If this be error, and upon me prov'd,
I never writ, nor no man ever lov'd.

WILLIAM SHAKSPERE

How soon hath Time, the subtle thief of youth,
Stolen on his wing my three-and-twentieth year!
My hasting days fly on with full career,
But my late spring no bud or blossom shew'th.
Perhaps my semblance might deceive the truth
That I to manhood am arrived so near;
And inward ripeness doth much less appear,
That some more timely-happy spirits endu'th.

Yet, be it less or more, or soon or slow,
It shall be still in strictest measure even
To that same lot, however mean or high,
Toward which Time leads me, and the will of Heaven:
All is, if I have grace to use it so,
As ever in my great Task-master's eye.

JOHN MILTON

When I consider how my light is spent
Ere half my days, in this dark world and wide,
And that one talent, which is death to hide,
Lodged with me useless, though my soul more bent
To serve therewith my Maker, and present
My true account, lest he, returning, chide;
Doth God exact day labor, light denied?
I fondly ask. But Patience, to prevent
That murmur, soon replies. God doth not need,
Either man's work or his own gifts. Who best
Bear his mild yoke, they serve him best. His state
Is kingly; thousands at his bidding speed,
And post o'er land and ocean without rest;
They also serve who only stand and wait.

JOHN MILTON

Day after day with patience I had sought
Deliverance from this plight with sorrow wrought,
And oft I prayed, that Thanatos might end
The ills with which my questioning soul was fraught.
All Science, all Philosophy had penned,
All that Religion from her tomes could lend,
Brought only increase of chaotic blight.
Despondent then, I found thee, Heaven-sent friend,
And scaled with thee Love's lofty mountain height.
Its topmost peak we gained, and viewed the sight
Of valleys, down the dangerous depths below,
Whose darks, all labyrinthed, now fail to fright.
Altho the mysteries neither of us know,
We care no more, for Love will have it so.

OLIVER OPDYKE

An acrostic poem or other writing is one in which certain letters—line initials or others—are so arranged as to form words and phrases.

Line initials are the most commonly used. This arrangement is called *vertical acrostic*. Edgar Allan Poe wrote a sonnet to Sarah Anna Lewis which contains *diagonal acrostic,* that is, the name, consisting of fourteen letters, is imbedded diagonally beginning with the first letter of the first line and ending with the fourteenth letter of the last line. The sonnet above contains such diagonal acrostic.

The *ode,* as generally used and understood today, is written in verses and stanzas and verse paragraphs of different lengths and rhyming schemes. In this departure from other forms it is probably capable of reflecting thought and mood more accurately than they, because less harassed by exacting mechanics. At the same time, it thus lends itself—dangerously perhaps—to digressions from the central theme, sometimes falling to the low estate of mere preachment. The term *ode* is used loosely to mean any lengthy discussion in poetic form; some poems so-called are odes in content but not in form, that is, the form adheres to some conventional lyric verse and stanza form. The latter type is sometimes called the *Lesbian* or *Horatian ode.* Shelley's *Ode to the West Wind,* for instance, is written in the Italian run-on interlocked stanza called *terza rima.* It rhymes as follows: *a b a | b c b | c d c | d e d | e e,* the last two lines constituting sometimes a refrain and sometimes a summary. The coherence and progress of the thought is thus reflected in the run-on rhyming system. The following are the first sections respectively of the poems indicated:

> There was a time when meadow, grove, and stream,
> The earth, and every common sight,
> > To me did seem
> > Apparelled in celestial light,
> The glory and the freshness of a dream.
> It is not now as it hath been of yore;—
> > Turn wheresoe'er I may,
> > > By night or day,
> The things which I have seen I now can see no more.
> > > > WILLIAM WORDSWORTH *Ode on the*
> > > > *Intimations of Immortality*

> O wild West Wind, thou breath of Autumn's being,
> > Thou from whose unseen presence the leaves dead
> Are driven, like ghosts from an enchanter fleeing,

Yellow, and black, and pale, and hectic red,
Pestilence-stricken multitudes! O thou
Who chariotest to their dark wintry bed

The wingèd seeds, where they lie cold and low,
Each like a corpse within its grave, until
Thine azure sister of the Spring shall blow

Her clarion o'er the dreaming earth, and fill
(Driving sweet buds like flocks to feed in air)
With living hues and odors plain and hill;

Wild spirit, which art moving everywhere;
Destroyer and preserver; hear, O hear!

PERCY BYSSHE SHELLEY *Ode to the West Wind*

The terms *ode, ballad, sonnet,* and those pertaining to the French forms below are frequently used in a generic sense to refer to any kind of lyric poem.

The French verse forms are sometimes regarded as the most valuable from the point of view of training in the writing of verse, because of the exacting demands they make upon form and therefore upon thought concentration and condensation. They have been called the "tighter forms," because they place still greater limitations upon the poet in the matter of sound freedom, than do the English forms. French students are trained in these verse forms, not necessarily because it is intended to make poets of them, but because such training inculcates economy in writing prose composition. In the *triolet,* for instance, there are eight verses. The first line is repeated as the fourth and the seventh, and the second line is repeated as the eighth. There are but two rhyming notes, thus:

Whatever, think you, could be worse	*a*
Than love requited—all abounding?	*b*
A wish fulfilled—a fulsome curse!	*a*
Whatever, think you, could be worse?	*a*
No poet can in numbers nurse	*a*
Such perfect state yet so confounding;	*b*
Whatever, think you, could be worse	*a*
Than love requited—all abounding?	*b*

The *rondeau* makes even more severe demands than the triolet. It consists of twelve or thirteen verses in three strophes of respectively five verses, three verses, and four or five verses. There are but two rhyming notes. The same refrain repetition or recurrence of certain verses will be noted. The opening words of line one are used after the eighth or the thirteenth line as an unrhymed refrain. This element of chorus or refrain in poetry affords emphasis by means of repetition and strikes at the hearts of people, but it has to be skilfully handled in order not to become monotonous and deadening. The following illustrates the rondeau form:

You bid me try, Blue Eyes, to write	*a*
A Rondeau. What! Forthwith?—To-night?	*a*
Reflect. Some skill I have, 'tis true;	*b*
But thirteen lines!—and rhymed on two!—	*b*
"Refrain," as well. Ah, hapless plight!	*a*
Still, there are five lines—ranged aright.	*a*
These Gallic bonds, I feared, would fright	*a*
My easy Muse. They did, till you—	*b*
You bid me try!	*c*
That makes them eight.—The port's in sight:	*a*
'Tis all because your eyes are bright!	*a*
Now just a pair to end in "oo,"—	*b*
When maids command, what can't we do!	*b*
Behold!—the Rondeau, tasteful, light,	*a*
You bid me try!	*c*

After the French of Voiture by Austin Dobson

The *rondel* is an earlier form than the rondeau, but the two names are sometimes interchangeably used. It consists of thirteen or fourteen lines arranged in two stanzas of four lines each, and one of five or six lines. Lines one and two are repeated as a refrain in lines seven and eight, and again in lines thirteen and fourteen. The rondel puts still stricter limitations upon rhyme, for but two rhyming notes are permitted. The lines of the early French rondel run from eight to ten syllables. This longer line than the English sonnet line was used, our old professor used to say, because French passion is more enduring!

Love comes back to his vacant dwelling,—	*a*
The old, old love that we knew of yore!	*b*
We see him stand by the open door,	*b*
With his great eyes sad, and his bosom swelling.	*a*
He makes as though in our arms repelling,	*a*
He fain would lie as he lay before; —	*b*
Love comes back to his vacant dwelling,—	*a*
The old, old Love that we knew of yore!	*b*
Ah, who shall keep us from over-spelling,	*a*
That sweet forgotten, forbidden lore!	*b*
E'en as we doubt in our hearts once more,	*b*
With a rush of tears to our eyelids welling,	*a*
Love comes back to his vacant dwelling.	*a*

AUSTIN DOBSON

The *rondelet* is a seven-line stanza, lines one, three, and seven constituting refrain. There are two rhyming notes, as follows:

Take what you will—	*a*
Nor leave me any little part!	*b*
Take what you will—	*a*
Be hard and unrelenting still;	*a*
But know you cannot take my heart	*b*
For that I gave you at the start—	*b*
Take what you will!	*a*

The foregoing French forms are used principally for poetry of the lighter mood; those that follow are more generally used for serious and reflective mood.

The *villanelle* runs in tercets interrhymed *aba, aba, aba,* and is thus interlocked. This continuation of sound forms a very coherent follow-on as well as a difficult condition to comply with. There is likewise a refrain element, as will be noted in the following :*

I took her dainty eyes, as well	*a*
As silken tendrils of her hair:	*b*
And so I made a Villanelle!	*a*

* Used by permission of Cassell & Company, Ltd., London.

I took her voice, a silver bell,	*a*
As clear as song, as soft as prayer;	*b*
I took her dainty eyes as well.	*a*
It may be, said I, who can tell,	*a*
These things shall be my less despair?	*b*
And so I made a Villanelle!	*a*
I took her whiteness virginal	*a*
And from her cheeks two roses rare:	*b*
I took her dainty eyes as well.	*a*
I said: "It may be possible	*a*
Her image from my heart to tear!"	*b*
And so I made a Villanelle!	*a*
I stole her laugh, most musical:	*a*
I wrought it in with artful care;	*b*
I took her dainty eyes as well,	*a*
And so I made a Villanelle.	*a*

ERNEST DOWSON *Villanelle of His Lady's Treasures*

The *chant royale* is a poem of five eleven-line stanzas of iambic tetrameter. There is a single-line refrain to each stanza, with post-script or *l'envoi* stanza at the end of the poem, and all stanzas have the same rhyming notes, the envoy echoing the last seven verses of each stanza. It is rhymed as indicated in the following poem:*

Who lives in suit of armor pent,	*a*
And hides himself behind a wall,	*b*
For him is not the great event,	*a*
The garland, nor the Capitol.	*b*
And is God's guerdon less than they?	*c*
Nay, moral man, I tell thee Nay:	*c*
Nor shall the flaming forts be won	*d*
By sneaking negatives alone,	*d*
By Lenten fast or Ramazàn,	*e*
But by the challenge proudly thrown—	*d*
Virtue is that beseems a Man!	*e*

* Used by permission of Oxford University Press.

God, in His Palace resident	*a*
Of Bliss, beheld our sinful ball,	*b*
And charged His own Son innocent	*a*
Us to redeem from Adam's fall.	*b*
—"Yet must it be that men Thee slay."	*c*
—"Yea, though it must, must I obey,"	*c*
Said Christ,—and came, His royal Son,	*d*
To die, and dying to atone	*d*
For harlot and for publican.	*e*
Read on that rood He died upon—	*d*
Virtue is that beseems a Man!	*e*

And by that rood where He was bent	*a*
I saw the world's great captains all	*b*
Go riding to the tournament—	*a*
Cyrus the Great and Hannibal,	*b*
Caesar of Rome and Attila,	*c*
Lord Charlemagne and his array,	*c*
Lord Alisaundre of Macedon—	*d*
With flaming lance and habergeon	*d*
They passed, and to the rataplan	*e*
Of drums gave salutation—	*d*
Virtue is that beseems a Man!	*e*

Had tall Achilles lounged in tent	*a*
For aye, and Xanthus neighed in stall,	*b*
The towers of Troy had ne'er been shent,	*a*
Nor stayed the dance in Priam's hall.	*b*
Bend o'er thy book till thou be gray,	*c*
Read, mark, perpend, digest, survey—	*c*
Instruct thee deep as Solomon—	*d*
One only chapter thou shalt con,	*d*
One lesson learn, one sentence scan,	*e*
One title and one colophon—	*d*
Virtue is that beseems a Man!	*e*

High Virtue's best is eloquent	*a*
With spur and not with martingall:	*b*
Sufficeth not thou'rt continent:	*a*
Be courteous, brave, and liberal.	*b*

God fashioned thee of chosen clay	*c*
For service, nor did ever say	*c*
"Deny thee this," "Abstain from yon,"	*d*
Save to inure thee, thew and bone,	*d*
To be confirmèd of the clan	*e*
That made immortal Marathon—	*d*
Virtue is that beseems a Man!	*e*

Envoy

Young Knight, the lists are set today:	*c*
Hereafter shall be long to pray	*c*
In sepulture with hands of stone,	*d*
Ride, then! outride the bugle blown!	*d*
And gaily dinging down the van	*e*
Charge with a cheer—Set on! Set on!	*d*
Virtue is that beseems a Man!	*e*

Arthur T. Quiller-Couch
Chant Royal of High Virtue

The *ballade* consists usually of three stanzas of seven or eight lines each and a postscript stanza or envoy. The last line of each stanza is a refrain, but sometimes the entire envoy *b c b c* is played after every stanza as an additional refrain. The spirit of the occasion very often decides the length and the frequency of a refrain.*

Brown's for Lalage, Jones for Lelia,	*a*
Robinson's bosom for Beatrice glows,	*b*
Smith is a Hamlet before Ophelia.	*a*
The glamor stays if the reason goes!	*b*
Every lover the years disclose	*b*
Is of a beautiful name made free.	*c*
One befriends, and all others are foes.	*b*
Anna's the name of names for me.	*c*

Sentiment hallows the vowels of Delia;	*a*
Sweet simplicity breathes from Rose;	*b*
Courtly memories glitter in Celia;	*a*
Rosalind savors of quips and hose,	*b*

* Used by permission of Charles Scribner's Sons.

Araminta of wits and beaux,   *b*
Prue of puddings, and Coralie   *c*
    All of sawdust and sprangled shows;   *b*
Anna's the name of names for me.   *c*

Fie upon Caroline, Madge, Amelia—   *a*
    These I reckon the essence of prose!—   *b*
Cavalier Katherine, cold Cornelia,   *a*
    Portia's masterful Roman nose,   *b*
    Maud's magnificence, Totty's toes,   *b*
Poll and Bet with their twang of the sea,   *c*
    Nell's impertinence, Pamela's woes!   *b*
Anna's the name of names for me.   *c*

ENVOY

Ruth like a gillyflower smells and blows,   *b*
    Sylvia prattles of Arcadee,   *c*
Sybil mystifies, Connie crows,   *b*
    Anna's the name of names for me!   *c*

WILLIAM ERNEST HENLEY *Ballade of Ladies' Names*

The *ballade royale* is a stricter form of ballade, requiring that the rhymes of all stanzas be on the same note and all the lines be decasyllabic, or ten-syllable lines.

The Italian names *terzine, sestine, canzon,* and *canzonet* are sometimes used in connection with lyric titles. The terzine has five accents to the line, rhymed *aba, bcb, cdc, ded,* and so on, a variant of the villanelle rhyme scheme (page 381).

The *sestine* consists of six stanzas each having six verses, usually concluding with a tercet envoy. The two or three terminal rhyming notes of the first stanza are repeated in the subsequent stanzas but not in the same order.

The *canzon* is a lyric of fifteen pentameter verses, rhymed as a rule in this interlocked style *abcbaccdeedefdf,* and is thus somewhat similar to the sonnet.

The *canzonet* is any short lyric of a single stanza or two or three stanzas each of which is a double quatrain or octet.

Envoy or *L'Envoi* is a separate stanza concluding a poem with a moral or an address or an application. It enforces the poetical message and climaxes it. Or it may be merely an afterthought or postscript (see pages 384 and 385).

Free verse, or *vers libre,* defies conventional verse patterns. It stresses, first, the importance of diction, the niceties of word adjustments to mental and emotional concepts. It may or may not rhyme, or it may have only such casual rhyme as is incident to perfected phraseology. It has no studied rhythm except such as derives naturally from well-considered expression. It is concerned with accuracy and simplicity and casualness of picture—an abandoned barn and a neglected weed-grown fence corner yielding more philosophic satisfaction than Ocean's bosom or Betelguese. It follows no stated form, the subject and the mood of the poet spontaneously ordering words upon the paper in inevitableness of stanza or verse-paragraph. First letters of lines may or may not be capitalized. Vividness characterizes the following free-verse compositions. They are devised by means of careful choice of diction, by pictorial sensitiveness, by the subtle music of the lines.

All day long I have been working,
Now I am tired.
I call: "Where are you?"
But there is only the oak-tree rustling in the wind.
The house is very quiet,
The sun shines in on your books,
On your scissors and thimble just put down,
But you are not there.
Suddenly I am lonely:
Where are you?
I go about searching.

Then I see you,
Standing under a spire of pale blue larkspur,
With a basket of roses on your arm.
You are cool, like silver,
And you smile.
I think the Canterbury bells are playing little tunes.

You tell me that the peonies need spraying,
That the columbines have overrun all bounds,
That the pyrus japonica should be cut back and rounded.

You tell me these things.
But I look at you, heart of silver,
White heart-flame of polished silver,
Burning beneath the blue steeples of the larkspur,
And I long to kneel instantly at your feet,
While all about us peal the loud, sweet *Te Deums* of the
    Canterbury bells.

        Amy Lowell *Madonna of the Evening Flowers* *

I am that Penelope
Who weaves the fabric of her faith
Against his coming: two stitches done and three
Undone. . . . Only the wraith
Mimicking the half-grown splendor on the cloth,
Frets my brain when I unravel at night
The diffident design that I am loth
To show my company in morning light.
The day exacts that I so brave
The inquisition of my friends:
If I be hypocrite and slave
To promise, the dark and privy hour ends
My busy lie.
There on my friendless bed
I rip the gossamer hope whose dye
Tangles my limbs with idle thread.

One day
Odysseus yet will stun this shore,
Though it be twenty years away,
And put aside his oar
And come to me.
And I shall lace the dream upon the loom
And turn the frame for men to see,
And my husband then will throng the moonwhite room
That I need fray no more
The proud accomplished plume.

        Sonia Raiziss *Parable for Weavers* †

  The foregoing explanation of verse and stanza forms is but a bird's-
eye-view survey of the broad field of versification. But it is suffi-

* Used by permission of Houghton Mifflin Company.
† Used by permission of the author.

ciently detailed to supply the young writer with the simple tools of workmanship and a general understanding of the scope and fluidity of poetic composition. It is important to remember that it is always the thought that decides form, or should be. A brief subjective theme calls for lyric treatment. A gay and lively and humorous thought is appropriately expressed in rollicking meter or perhaps in one of the French forms. If the thought is serious and stately and charged with the responsibility of lasting impression, blank-verse treatment may be evoked by it. The poet selects poetry as the vehicle of expression for his thought for personal and introspective reasons. The poetic form that it takes is dictated by that thought.

If you care to try your hand at composition in verse, decide upon a subject. Then ponder whether you would just like to talk about this subject from your mind outward to your fellows, or whether you feel about it strongly in addition. If only the former, then do not try to versify it. But, if the latter, jot down on paper in sentence form your thoughts and feelings as they come to you. Write all these sentences from the same margin instead of one after the other in paragraph style. After you have thus recorded them all, go back. Study them. Condense them. Try to re-express them in better and more precise diction and with greater harmony. Perhaps at the ends of some of these sentences you may be able to substitute words or syllables that sound alike. If you can do these things—and you can if you *feel* your subject and are willing to think about your expression —you will have made a worthy beginning in the high-purposed pursuit of versification—perhaps of poetizing.

WORK

I. In accordance with the last paragraph above write rhythmically on some of the following subjects. If you find nothing here about which you are able to *feel*, then select other subjects that will supply "inspiration" to you.

A wilted rose
Sunshine in the afternoon
A snow scene in the country
Mobs entering the subway going home from work
A stalwart athlete standing alone in the middle of a field
A mountain peak at sunrise on a summer morning

The ocean during a violent storm
The friendless, badly clad old man on a park bench
Trees swaying in a strong wind
Lillian dressed for a party
A child playing alone on the beach
The ringing of distant bells at night
A howling wind during a lonesome winter night
The singing of birds on a bright spring morning
Your mother sitting by the lamplight knitting
Your father with spectacles far down on his nose, reading the paper
Your little sister or brother caught in the act of stealing jam
A desk littered with books and papers
The school corridors the day after schools close for vacation
Children starting home from school in a heavy rain
Duty, work, loyalty, sincerity, morality, earnestness, character,
    fancy, friendship, treachery, liberty, and the like

II. Explain the rhyme, the rhythm, and the stanza form of each of
the following:

> Do but consider this small dust,
>   Here running in the glass,
>   By atoms moved;
>   Could you believe that this
>   The body was
>   Of one that loved?
> And in his mistress' flame playing like a fly
> Turned to cinders by her eye?
> Yes, and in death, as life unblest
>   To have 't expressed:
> Even ashes of lovers find no rest.
>
> Ben Jonson

> Flashed all their sabres bare,
> Flashed as they turned in air
> Sabring the gunners there,
> Charging an army, while
>   All the world wondered.
> Plunged in the battery-smoke
> Right through the line they broke;

Cossack and Russian
Reeled from the sabre-stroke
Shattered and sundered.
Then they rode back, but not,
Not the six hundred.

ALFRED TENNYSON

I sometimes think that I love strangers best,
People who catch my heart in shop or street,
At ease in anonymity. Discreet,
I praise them with my glance. No need to test
The sum of enigmatic features lest
Some lurking decadence at last defeat
Fidelity; that innocent lip, too sweet,
Must do without the pity of my breast. . . .
These chosen loves pass gently down the stream
That follows time and turns into forever
At the next corner. I bless them, for they never
Frustrate the truth of one spontaneous dream
That is no dream unless clear sight can lie:
The soul sits plain in the unguarded eye!

MARION CANBY *No Dream* *

I

No, no! go not to Lethe, neither twist
    Wolf's-bane, tight-rooted, for its poisonous wine:
Nor suffer thy pale forehead to be kiss'd
    By nightshade, ruby grape of Proserpine;
Make not your rosary of yew-berries
    Nor let the beetle nor the death-moth be
        Your mournful Psyche, nor the downy owl
A partner in your sorrow's mysteries;
    For shade to shade will come too drowsily,
        And drown the wakeful anguish of the soul.

II

But when the melancholy fit shall fall
    Sudden from heaven like a weeping cloud,
That fosters the droop-headed flowers all,
    And hides the green hill in an April shroud;

* Used by permission of *The Commonweal.*

Then glut thy sorrow on a morning rose,
  Or on the rainbow of the salt sand-wave,
    Or on the wealth of globèd peonies;
Or if thy mistress some rich anger shows,
  Imprison her soft hand and let her rave,
    And feed deep, deep upon her peerless eyes.

III

She dwells with Beauty—Beauty that must die;
  And Joy, whose hand is ever at his lips
Bidding adieu; and aching Pleasure nigh,
  Turning to poison while the bee-mouth sips;
Aye in the very Temple of Delight
  Veil'd Melancholy has her sovran shrine,
    Though seen of none save him whose strenuous tongue
Can burst Joy's grape against his palate fine;
His soul shall taste the sadness of her might,
    And be among her cloudy trophies hung.

                          JOHN KEATS *Ode on Melancholy*

        The sky may
        darken as it will
        and storms invade the world
        till every single mortal thing
        is hurled around and hurled
        against itself and all it loved
        and lived for through the ages,
        the tempest now a common war
        that every man engages;
        and there may come a passerby,
        ethereal and small,
        with nothing more than what she is
        to halt the moving wall
        and turn the world
        from what it was
        to what it ought to be:
        a little closer to the grace
        of her humanity.
        And she in her humility
        will be the least aware
        of what the fates or histories

or miracles prepare
in driving men and women through
a form that never blurs
but changes every character
to something nearer hers:
For Love that hath a woman's eyes
can conquer if it will
the blood of men,
of bloody men
who die in what they kill.

ALFRED KREYMBORG *Reconcilation* *

III. Write each of the following disarranged pieces of verse in the stanza form from which it is derived. Then name the stanza, indicate the rhyming scheme of each, and scan the verses.

Into the sunshine full of light, leaping and flashing from morn to night

---

Our very hopes belied our fears, our fears our hopes belied; we thought her dying when she slept and sleeping when she died

---

I dated Fleurette but Belle came instead; I didn't regret not meeting Fleurette, for Belle can be led (or so it is said). I cared not two pins that Belle came instead when I dated Fleurette—for you see—they are twins

---

There was a young lady of Ryde who ate some green apples and died; inside the lamented the apples fermented, and now there is cider inside her inside

---

Up in the air in a biplane—up to the moon for luck—then dodging the stars swoop over to Mars where we're to be medaled for pluck. Up in the air in a biplane—up to the Top of the Sky—to visit with Rhea and Cassiopoeia and some of the smaller fry. Up in the air in a biplane— up to the blazing Sun—and there make a pass to get some gas and tank it on the run. Up in the air in a biplane—up to the golden stair—to drink at the dipper, then off like a zipper for bearding the blinking bear. Up in the air in a biplane—up to the Brim of the Blue—to waken

* Used by permission of the author.

Aurora, celestial dumb Dora, and order a breakfast for two. Up in the air in a biplane—up to the Edge of Space—where cinders of granite are making a planet to furnish a parking place. Up in the air in a biplane—up to the Milky Way—to vamp it with Venus (the stardust will screen us) and whirl her back home distrait. Swish! Bang! Goodbye, plane! Down by the grab of our girth. It's fun to commute by a parachute provided we hit the earth

IV. By way of summarizing your study of this book, pass critical judgment upon the following excerpts. Which are genuine poetry? Which are merely doggerel? Which are poetic prose? Which are not merely prose, but prosaic? Which may be easily converted from one form to another without doing damage to content? And so forth. Remember that the forming of literary judgments demands logical explanation.

> At one stride comes the dark

> Ingratitude, more strong than traitors' arms,
> Quite vanquished him

> A cannon ball shot off his legs,
> So he laid down his arms

The man who thinks he can do without society, makes a mistake; but the man who thinks that society can do without him, makes a still greater mistake

---

Demosthenes told Phocian, "The Athenians will kill you some day when they are in a rage." "And you," replied he, "if they are once in their senses"

> Far from the madding crowd's ignoble strife,
> Their sober wishes never learned to stray;
> Along the cool sequestered vale of life
> They kept the noiseless tenor of their way

The lightless walls seem to spring from the very mud upon which the stranded barges lie; and the narrow lanes coming down to the foreshore resemble the paths of smashed bushes and crumbled earth where big game comes down to drink on the banks of tropical streams

Now blessings light on him that first invented this same sleep! It covers a man all over, thoughts and all, like a cloak; it is meat for the hungry, drink for the thirsty, heat for the cold, and cold for the hot. It is the current coin that purchases all the pleasures of the world cheap, and the balance that sets the king and the shepherd, the fool and the wise man even

Milton's poetry acts like an incantation. Its merit lies less in its obvious meaning than in its occult power, and there would seem at first sight to be no more in his words than in other words. But they are words of enchantment. No sooner are they pronounced than the past is present and the distant near. New forms of beauty start at once into existence, and all the burial-places of the memory give up their dead

His rash fierce blaze of riot cannot last,
For violent fires soon burn out themselves;
Small showers last long, but sudden storms are short;
He tires betimes that spurs too fast betimes;
With eager feeding food doth choke the feeder:
Light vanity, insatiate cormorant,
Consuming means, soon preys upon itself.
This royal throne of kings, this scepter'd isle,
This earth of majesty, this seat of Mars,
This other Eden, demi-paradise,
This fortress built by Nature for herself
Against infection and the hand of war,
This happy breed of men, this little world,
This precious stone set in the silver sea,
Which serves it in the office of a wall
Or as a moat defensive to a house,
Against the envy of less happier lands,
This blessed plot, this earth, this realm, this England,
This nurse, this teeming womb of royal kings,
Fear'd by their breed and famous by their birth,

Renowned for their deeds as far from home,
For Christian service and true chivalry,
As is the sepulchre in stubborn Jewry
Of the world's ransom, blessed Mary's Son,
This land of such dear souls, this dear dear land,
Dear for her reputation through the world,
Is now leased out, I die pronouncing it,
Like to a tenement or pelting farm

WILLIAM SHAKSPERE Richard II *

My teeth are falling one by one;
    My eyesight's very near;
Disintegration has begun
    In nose and throat and ear.

My lungs are impotent with wheeze;
    My arteries are hard;
My muscles fail me when I sneeze,
    For they have turned to lard.

My heart's not leaping when I see
    A rainbow in the sky;
I've H_2O upon the knee
    And palsy in the thigh.

I could complete the catalog,
    But it would make you weep—
This tale of nerves too much agog,
    Of blood that's fast asleep.

Who was the guy who glibly sang:
    "The cards of life are decked
To give the latter years a tang"—
    Or words to this effect?

His tongue, methinks, was in his cheek,
    Or else his glands were new.
For me, at least, he did not speak;
    I hope he did for you.

OLIVER OPDYKE Pre-Epitaph

* This passage (Act II, Scene I) is regarded by some scholars as the richest in all of Shakspere, in figurative beauty and metrical skill.

INDEX